China and Ashkenazic Jewry: Transcultural Encounters

China and Ashkenazic Jewry: Transcultural Encounters

Edited by
Kathryn Hellerstein and Song Lihong

DE GRUYTER
OLDENBOURG

ISBN 978-3-11-135345-6
e-ISBN (PDF) 978-3-11-068394-3
e-ISBN (EPUB) 978-3-11-068411-7

Library of Congress Control Number: 2021952270

Bibliographic information published by the Deutsche Nationalbibliothek
The Deutsche Nationalbibliothek lists this publication in the Deutsche Nationalbibliografie;
detailed bibliographic data are available on the Internet at http://dnb.dnb.de.

© 2023 Walter de Gruyter GmbH, Berlin/Boston
This volume is text- and page-identical with the hardback published in 2022.
Cover Image: *Mr. Nobody*, Shanghai, by David Ludwig Bloch, 1947 (Photograph courtesy of
the Leo Baeck Institute at the Center for Jewish History).
Typesetting: Integra Software Services Pvt. Ltd.
Printing and binding: CPI books GmbH, Leck

www.degruyter.com

In memory of Irene Eber
(1929–2019)

Acknowledgments

The editors would like to thank the University of Pennsylvania and Nanjing University for their generous support throughout the making of this volume. This book developed from a project sponsored by the Penn China Research and Engagement Fund and the Jewish Studies Program at the University of Pennsylvania and by the "100-Level" Research Fund in Liberal Arts for *Shuangyiliu* Construction and the Glazer Institute for Jewish and Israel Studies at Nanjing University. We express our appreciation to Ezekiel J. Emanuel, MD, PhD, Vice Provost for Global Initiatives; Amy E. Gadsden, PhD, Associate Vice Provost for Global Initiatives and Executive Director of Penn China Initiatives; and Scott Michael Moore at Penn Global International Policy, for their support of this project from its beginning through the completion of this volume. We thank Professor Zhou Xian, Dean of the Institute of Advanced Studies in Humanities and Social Sciences at Nanjing University, and the Department of Philosophy and Religious Studies for jointly hosting our first seminar and the symposium at Nanjing University. We also thank the staff at the Penn Wharton China Center in Beijing for hosting our final seminar.

We are especially grateful to Samantha Pious, PhD, for her meticulous copy editing of this book and for keeping us on track in the process of bringing it to press. We thank Professor Robert Allinson for his insightful comments on the manuscript. Julia Brauch and Carla Schmidt at De Gruyter have extended their patience and expertise to the publication of this volume. Without the attentions of Chrissy Walsh, Regina Forlano, and Jen McCart at Penn or those of Wang Jia at Nanjing, we would have missed many crucial details in the execution of this project. We thank Professors Fu Youde, Han Yi, Hu Hao, Lin Jing, Meng Zhenhua, She Gangzheng, Wang Yaqiong, Wang Yu, Zhang Shuqing, Zhou Jiaxin, Stephen Jacobs, and Jan Schwarz for their invaluable participation in the symposium and seminars. Our warmest thanks go to David Stern and Zhang Longxi for their remarks from a global perspective, which drew the symposium to a close.

With heartfelt gratitude, we dedicate this book to the memory of our friend and mentor, Irene Eber.

Kathryn HELLERSTEIN and SONG Lihong

Contents

Acknowledgments —— VII

Kathryn HELLERSTEIN
Introduction —— 1

I The Bible in China

Irene EBER
1 From Rags to Riches: Joseph and His Family —— 29

FU Xiaowei and WANG Yi
2 Why Is Having No Posterity the Worst Unfilial Thing? A Comparison of Mencius 4A:26 and Genesis 38 —— 37

CAO Jian
3 The Impact of Ancient Israelite Prophets on Modern Chinese Intellectuals —— 51

ZHONG Zhiqing
4 Reading the Song of Songs in Jewish and Chinese Tradition —— 63

LIU Yan
5 The Transcultural Characteristics of the Chinese Bible Translated by S. I. J. Schereschewsky (1831–1906): A Case Study of the Song of Songs —— 79

II Jews in Modern China

XU Xin
6 Jewish Communities and Modern China: Encounters of Modern Civilizations —— 99

AI Rengui
7 When the Muscular Jews Came to the Far East: Jewish Sports and Physical Culture in Modern China, 1912–1949 —— 109

WANG Jian
8 Tracking the Exact Number of Jewish Refugees in Shanghai —— 129

Maisie MEYER
9 The Global Reach of Shanghai's Baghdadi Jews —— 145

Nancy BERLINER
10 Jewish Refugee Artists in Shanghai: Visual Legacies of Traumatic Moments and Cultural Encounters —— 165

YANG Meng
11 Drama in Wartime Shanghai —— 185

Marc B. SHAPIRO
12 The Mir Yeshiva and Its Shanghai Sojourn —— 195

Samuel HEILMAN
13 Chabad Outreach on the Jewish Frontier: The Case of China —— 217

III Jews and Chinese

Kathryn HELLERSTEIN
14 Yiddish Translations of Chinese Poetry and Theater in 1920s New York —— 231

BAO Anruo
15 Enemy or Friend: The Image of China in Yiddish Newspapers during the Russo-Japanese War (1904–1905) —— 255

ZHANG Ping
16 To Speak or Not to Speak: Hanoch Levin's *Suitcase Packers* and Cao Yu's *Peking Man* in Light of Cross-Textual Dialogue —— 271

LI Dong
17 Teaching American Jewish Literature to Chinese College Students: Anzia Yezierska's "Children of Loneliness" as a Case Study —— 285

Rebecca KOBRIN
18 Chinese and Ashkenazic Encounters in the American Immigration Regime: Max J. Kohler, Immigration Legal Practice, and the Chinese Exclusion Act —— 297

SONG Lihong
19 A Homeless Stranger Everywhere: The Shadow of the Holocaust on an Israeli Sinologist —— 317

Contributors —— 337

Illustrations —— 343

Table —— 345

Indexes
    Personal Names —— 347
    Place Names —— 355

Kathryn HELLERSTEIN
Introduction

This volume, *China and Ashkenazic Jewry: Transcultural Encounters*, came into being as the result of a three-year project that Professor SONG Lihong and I conducted, between 2016 and 2019, funded by our home institutions (respectively, the University of Pennsylvania and Nanjing University). For this project, which bears the same name as the title of this book, we held two workshops and a conference in China – the first workshop in 2017 and the conference in 2018, both at Nanjing University, and the second workshop in 2019 at the Penn Wharton China Center in Beijing. These three events brought together American, European, Israeli, and Chinese scholars of Jewish studies to discuss exchanges and encounters between Chinese and Ashkenazic Jewish cultures.

From the start, our project has focused on the transnational and transcultural encounters specifically between Ashkenazic Jewry and China. Such encounters initially included translations, intertextuality, comparisons, and influences, both from the languages and cultures of Ashkenazic Jewry into Chinese, and from Chinese into those Jewish languages and cultures. In addition to examining the cultural ramifications of these texts and translations, the project also highlights the roles played by actual, personal contact between Jews from central and eastern Europe and Chinese people in China during the turbulent decades of the mid-twentieth century up until the present moment – that is, contact among communities as well as between individuals.

This collection of essays adds in a new way to the burgeoning studies of Jews in China. Scholarly interest in this subject dates back to the end of the nineteenth century, when the Jewish Diaspora in China began to attract the academic endeavors that have continued globally to this day. Since the turn of the twenty-first century, an outpouring of international scholarship on the Jewish presence in Shanghai and Harbin, in particular, has significantly advanced our understanding of Sino-Jewish relations, and major works outlining the history of the two communities and collecting their documents have come out. In contrast, our project aims to shift the emphasis from "Jews *in* China" to "Jews *and* China" – that is, from the presence of Jews who have lived or are living in modern China to an interdisciplinary and transcultural dialogue within the context of global thinking.

The essays gathered in this volume reflect these aims. As the table of contents indicates, we have divided the book into three sections: "The Bible in China," "Jews in Modern China," and "Jews and Chinese." The 19 essays we have selected cover a broad range of topics and disciplinary approaches, from history to literature to art history to pedagogy to classical studies to philosophy to sociology.

The first section of this book is called "The Bible in China." As its title indicates, Part I deals with the Hebrew Bible and China, but its first and last essays focus on a specific figure, S. I. J. Schereschewsky, a Jewish convert to Christianity who translated the Bible into Chinese. According to Irene Eber's study of Schereschewsky, *The Jewish Bishop and the Chinese Bible: S. I. J. Schereschewsky, 1831–1906* (Leiden: Brill, 1999), Schereschewsky was born an Ashkenazic Jew in Lithuania and received a traditional Jewish education as a child. At the Tsarist government-sponsored Jewish Rabbinic School in Zhitomir, the young boy read the New Testament in a Hebrew translation from the proselytizing London Society for Promoting Christianity amongst the Jews. During his studies in Frankfurt and at the University of Breslau, he likely met other Christian missionaries, and these encounters seem to have led him to convert to Christianity. When he emigrated to the United States, Schereschewsky undertook to train for the clergy, first at a Presbyterian and then at an Episcopal seminary. Schereschewsky was sent to Shanghai in 1859 and to Beijing (then Peking) in 1862 as a missionary for the American Episcopal Church. He served as the Anglican Bishop of Shanghai (1877–1884) and founded St. John's University in Shanghai in 1879. From 1862 to 1875, as a member of the Peking Translation Committee, he produced his first translation of the Bible into Mandarin Chinese; his second translation of the Hebrew Bible and the New Testament into Easy Wenli was published in 1902.

The first essay in this section is by the late Irene EBER, "From Rags to Riches: Joseph and His Family." Eber discusses the challenges of translating into vernacular Chinese language and culture the complex story of Joseph from the book of Genesis in the Hebrew Bible. Eber focuses on the Chinese rendition of this story by S. I. J. Schereschewsky in 1875 (revised in 1899) and on a collaborative translation, the Union Version, published in 1919, specifically because both translations attempted to reach a wide readership rather than only the highly educated. Eber emphasizes the exceptional quality of Schereschewsky's translation directly from the original Hebrew, unlike other Christian biblical translations. The later Union Version relied on Schereschewsky's translation, as well as on existing translations into English. Keeping in mind that both the Union Version and Schereschewsky's translation were produced with the goal of converting their readers to Christianity, Eber demonstrates that Schereschwesky aimed for a translation that was "faithful, idiomatic, but not literal." In other words, he was concerned at once with readability and with correct religious and cultural terminology. His translation attempted to span the distance between the ancient Near East and late nineteenth-century China, making Joseph (the favored son of Jacob) and his jealous brothers, along with his ultimate success as a political figure in Egypt who was carrying out God's plan for the Children of Israel, into a meaningful story for Chinese readers.

The second essay, by Fu Xiaowei and Wang Yi, "Why Is Having No Posterity the Worst Unfilial Thing? A Comparison of Mencius 4A:26 and Genesis 38," compares a key passage from the ancient Chinese philosopher Mencius (Mengzi, ca. 371–289 BCE) with a problematic narrative from Genesis in the Hebrew Bible in order to reevaluate the criticism of Confucian filial morality in modern China. The passage from Mencius states, "Among the three unfilial things, to have no posterity is the worst." The biblical narrative tells of Tamar, Judah's childless, widowed daughter-in-law, who deceptively seduces her father-in-law in order to perpetuate his lineage. Through close readings of the two ancient texts, Fu and Wang argue that the Chinese and Hebrew texts both reveal contrasting conceptions of the afterlife as familial posterity. Despite their vast cultural differences, these two texts illuminate a shared concern with the continuation of family lineage in both Confucian and Jewish textual traditions.

Eber's essay presented nineteenth-century Chinese translations of ancient Hebrew texts as a means of religious conversion, while Fu and Wang's essay reconsidered modern interpretations of ancient Chinese and Hebrew religious texts. In contrast, Cao Jian discusses the ways in which the Hebrew Bible influenced thinkers who conceptualized the Chinese nation in the 1920s. In "The Impact of Ancient Israelite Prophets on Modern Chinese Intellectuals," Cao argues that in the process of nation-building, during the New Culture movement of the 1910s and the May Fourth movement of 1919, Chinese intellectuals turned to the Hebrew Bible for models of "ideal men." These intellectuals encountered the prophets, especially Amos and Jeremiah, through translations of the Hebrew Bible into Chinese and associated these biblical figures with the Chinese sages, in such a way that a combination of prophet and sage would comprise the modern "ideal man." Early twentieth-century Chinese intellectuals wrote that the biblical prophets and the ancient Chinese sages shared the task of awakening or enlightening the populace to a higher truth and an ideal society, whether from the biblical God or from the Chinese *tian* ('heaven'). To this end, as Cao shows, these writers compared the Book of Deuteronomy with the *Shiji* [the Book of History] and Leviticus and Numbers with *Liji* [the Book of Rites]. Zhang Dongsun compared Amos and Jesus as idealists and, identifying them both with modern scientists (who also sought to improve the world), urged his Chinese readers to aspire toward Western achievements. Lu Xun lauded Jeremiah as a "spiritual fighter" for the common people and compared his own role as a writer in Chinese society with that of the biblical prophet in ancient Judah. Zhu Weizhi compared Amos to modern Chinese poets and Jeremiah to Confucius. Most attractive to early twentieth-century Chinese intellectuals were, in Cao's words, the "patriotism, nationalism, and universalism" of the prophets, which they expressed by comparing the Book of Lamentations with Qu Yuan's poem lamenting national catastrophe, "Lisao." In all these ways, these intellectuals developed their ideas about nationalism, patriotism, universalism, and political messianism with the aim of creating a modern China through their particular and selective understandings of the biblical prophets, of Judaism and Christianity, and of peoplehood.

Like CAO, ZHONG Zhiqing reflects on how an ancient Hebrew text has been read by modern Chinese writers and thinkers. In "Reading the Song of Songs in Jewish and Chinese Tradition," ZHONG considers this biblical text through its translations into Chinese and contrasts the Chinese tradition of reading this poem as a collection of love lyrics with the Jewish (and Christian) traditions of reading it as a theological allegory for the covenant and love between God and Israel (and the love between Jesus and the Church). ZHONG compares the placement of the Song of Songs in the 1919 Chinese Union Version Bible with its placement in the Hebrew Bible, noting the differences between the Christian textual ordering of the Chinese translation and the Jewish textual ordering of the Hebrew original. ZHONG's aim is to highlight the Jewish context of this poem for the Chinese academic reader.

ZHONG approaches this task through a close reading of the poem in Hebrew, comparing it (through an English translation) with the Chinese of the Union Version. Utilizing recent scholarship, ZHONG provides a historical perspective on textual analysis of the Song of Songs, challenging the assumptions that King Solomon was the poem's author, or that he is the male lover or speaker, and offering the possibility that the authors of the Song of Songs may have been women. Noting that Chinese scholars have ignored the question of why a poem expressing sexual love was included in the Hebrew Bible and incorporated into Jewish liturgy, ZHONG surveys the history and range of traditional Jewish interpretations of the Song of Songs, from the Talmudic sage Rabbi Akiva (Akiva ben Yosef, 50 CE–135 CE), who proclaimed the text to be "the holiest of the holy," to twentieth- and twenty-first-century scholars and translators, who have focused on the sensuality of the verse. ZHONG explains that the Chinese Union Version, which had an evangelical intent, follows the Jewish and Christian religious tradition of reading this erotic poem as a religious allegory of the love between God and Israel (as posited by Rabbi Akiva) or between Christ and the Church (as argued by Christian authorities).

When she examines the Chinese tradition of interpreting the Song of Songs, though, ZHONG demonstrates that the poem was understood to be a collection of secular love poems. It was retranslated during the May Fourth movement (which began in 1919) by a group of poets who recognized its "striking resemblance to the Chinese cultural tradition." ZHONG compares the Song of Songs to the classical

Chinese *Book of Songs*, or *Classic of Songs* (*Shijing*), focusing on the elements of sexual love, physical beauty, and natural imagery that characterize both the biblical Hebrew and the classical Chinese poems. ZHONG finds additional connections between the Song of Songs and Chinese culture: the Hebrew poem's "absence of 'female subordination' " (as read by the May Fourth movement's proponents of women's autonomy and rights) and the hopes of one Chinese literary figure, Zhou Zuoren, that the Old Testament would inspire poets to revive the Chinese national language as a model for "beautiful idylls." Some modern Chinese poets, such as Shen Congwen, included direct quotes from the Song of Songs in their poems, while others adapted metaphors from the biblical poem to describe lovers' sensations and women's beauty. Most of these Chinese poets read the Song of Songs as a collection of secular love poems. There were, however, a few Chinese writers, such as Zhu Weizhi in the 1930s, who appreciated the importance of the allegorical religious interpretation of the Song of Songs, even if they found it questionable. With one exception, most twenty-first-century scholarship in China has neglected the Jewish interpretive tradition of the Song of Songs.

The final essay in this section, LIU Yan's "The Transcultural Characteristics of the Chinese Bible Translated by S. I. J. Schereschewsky (1831–1906): A Case Study of the Song of Songs," returns to Eber's study of Schereschewsky's Bible translation and connects to ZHONG's previous study of the Song of Songs. LIU compares selections from two Chinese translations of the Song of Songs, both by Schereschewsky: the 1875 Beijing Vernacular Old Testament Version and the 1902 Easy Wenli Old and New Testaments. LIU intends this comparison to highlight the interculturality of Bible translation and how Schereschewsky's own hybrid identity affected the way he translated and then retranslated the Hebrew Bible for a broad Chinese audience. LIU begins by describing the translator's life, which we have summarized at the beginning of this section of the Introduction. Schereschewsky produced his first translation into Mandarin Chinese between 1862 and 1875. His second translation of both the Hebrew Bible and the New Testament into Easy Wenli was published in 1902.

LIU then compares Schereschewsky's two translations of the Song of Songs to some thirty other Chinese translations into various Chinese dialects, literary forms, and styles. As ZHONG does in her essay, LIU points out that the Song of Songs significantly influenced modern Chinese love poems during the 1920s and served as inspiration for a generation of young people. In this context, LIU discusses the relative importance of different levels of vernacular Chinese translations that Schereschewsky utilized: vernacular Mandarin and Easy Wenli, the "shallow vernacular," or "half-classical" Chinese, which lies "halfway between the classical and the vernacular." In his 1875 endeavor, Schereschewsky chose to translate from the Hebrew into Mandarin, which LIU describes as addressing "the general public and the lower classes" in "a popular, colloquial style." For his 1902 translation, Schereschewsky rendered the Hebrew text into Easy Wenli in an "artistic and aesthetic" style "intended for intellectual elites." Through close readings of the two Chinese versions, LIU shows how Schereschewsky codified grammatical rules for both Mandarin and Easy Wenli – rules that made his translations comprehensible to all levels of Chinese readers. LIU focuses in particular on the literary device of parallelism in biblical Hebrew and in classical Chinese poetry and explores how Schereschewsky used parallelism, couplets, and Chinese idioms in his translations. She observes how the translator conveyed the proper names of biblical people, places, and specific flora and fauna by transliterating the Hebrew or creating compound words to echo the pronunciation of the Hebrew. Most interestingly, LIU discusses how Schereschewsky combined Midrashim (rabbinic Jewish interpretations of the Bible) with traditional Chinese commentaries to create a hybrid mode of exegesis and hermeneutics. In addition, LIU describes the page design of each translation. The Mandarin translation's large-font printed page had notes in the margins and biblical passages arranged "in the traditional vertical" format of "classical Chinese texts," with pauses and periods breaking up sentences – a visual layout that appealed to an audience with a low level of literacy. In contrast, the Easy Wenli version appealed to highbrow readers, leaving out the periods and utilizing only pauses, and arranging the biblical chapters and verses according to the ancient Chinese chronological method of "Heavenly Stems and Earthly Branches," interspersing text, notes, and annotations in a complex format on each page.

LIU concludes her essay with a discussion of several ways that Schereschewsky's translation of the Song of Songs contributed to translation theory and to the intercultural dialogue between Jewish and Chinese cultures. Schereschewsky combined literal with literary translation and maintained an idiomatic register. He translated with respect for the literary traditions of China and the integrity of Chinese culture and ethnicity, while maintaining the qualities of the Hebrew source text. In this way, LIU argues, Schereschewsky created a "Chinese Christianity." In terms of his biography and his translations, in LIU's view, Schereschewsky represents a prime example of the twentieth-century scholar Itamar Even-Zohar's polysystem theory, in which various systems intersect with each other to form a dynamic yet structured whole.

Part II of this volume, "Jews in Modern China," consists of eight essays, covering a range of topics in the modern and contemporary periods. The opening essay, by XU Xin, "Jewish Communities and Modern China: Encounters of Modern Civilizations," presents an overview of the history of the Jewish Diaspora in modern China, from the mid-nineteenth century to the twenty-first century. AI Rengui's essay, "When the Muscular Jews Came to the Far East: Jewish Sports and Physical Culture in Modern China, 1912–1949," considers the establishment of athletic groups by Ashkenazic Jewish residents and refugees living in Shanghai and other cities in China. Maisie MEYER discusses the Baghdadi Jews who established trade and commerce in Shanghai starting in the mid-nineteenth century and explores their interactions with and interventions on behalf of the Ashkenazic Jews who came later. The other five essays in Part II deal with the Jewish refugees from central and eastern Europe who took shelter in Shanghai from Nazi antisemitism from 1938 through 1949. WANG Jian surveys the demographic challenges in determining the "Exact Number of the Jewish Refugees in Shanghai." Nancy BERLINER presents a study of "Jewish Refugee Artists in Shanghai." YANG Meng writes on the theater produced in "Wartime Shanghai." Marc B. SHAPIRO illuminates the survival of the students and faculty of the Mir Yeshiva in Shanghai during the war. Finally, Samuel Heilman explores the Lithuanian Hasidic Chabad movement's current efforts to establish religious outreach programs for contemporary Jews living in the People's Republic of China.

In "Jewish Communities and Modern China: Encounters of Modern Civilizations," XU Xin distinguishes between the history of Jews in modern China and that of the Jews who arrived in medieval China. The earliest Jewish communities in China arose during the Tang dynasty (618–907 CE), in approximately twelve Chinese cities, but significant material evidence of only one survives. The Kaifeng Jewish community was established in the decades following 960 CE and declined after the death of its last rabbi in the mid-nineteenth century, although its assimilated descendants still reside in Kaifeng. In contrast, the modern Jews, totaling approximately 40,000, came in three waves between 1845 and 1945: first, Sephardic Jews from Baghdad and Bombay, who established trade and commerce in the "newly opened Chinese treaty cities" of Hong Kong and Shanghai; second, Ashkenazic Jews from Russia, who traveled to Harbin in pursuit of economic opportunities offered by the antisemitic Russian government to aid the extension of the Trans-Siberian Railway across Manchuria during the early years of the twentieth century; and third, Jews who escaped from Nazi persecution in Germany, Austria, and Poland and found refuge in Shanghai from the late 1930s through the 1940s. The cumulative number of this last group allowed for more significant interaction between the Jewish immigrants and the Chinese people around them. Most of the refugee population left China at the end of World War II in 1945. Many of the Sephardic and Russian Jews, who had arrived much earlier and planned to stay in China permanently, left nonetheless after the Communists' rise to power in 1949 and the establishment of the People's Republic of China. By 1966, at the start of the Cultural Revolution, very few individual Jews remained in China.

Xu Xin goes on to discuss how the Chinese perceived these three waves of Jewish residents in China. Their sources of information about Jews and Judaism included Western missionaries, business people, and diplomats; Chinese who traveled abroad; and Chinese scholars and intellectuals who sought to modernize China. The key issues that interested these Chinese thinkers were the ways that the Jewish people survived antisemitic adversity and renewed their peoplehood, their "uniqueness," and their achievements. In particular, modern nationalist thinkers such as Doctor Sun Yat-sen and Yu Songhua found a model for a new Chinese nationalism in Zionism. Xu Xin cites the translations of modern Yiddish literary works into Chinese (by way of Russian or English) in the 1920s as an inspiration for the establishment of a modern, vernacular Chinese literature. Starting in the mid-nineteenth century, the presence of Jews themselves in China provided Chinese thinkers with models of how a tradition-bound society and people could become modern. Xu Xin discusses in detail the contributions to commerce, real estate, infrastructure, industry, international trade, and philanthropy made by foreign businessmen such as Silas Hardoon and the Kadoorie family in Shanghai and by S. Sorkin and others in Harbin. During all three periods, Jews introduced European art, medicine, engineering, and journalism to both Shanghai and Harbin. Xu Xin highlights two refugee artists in Shanghai, Friedrich Schiff and David Ludwig Bloch, as well as a number of musicians, including Alfred Wittenberg, a German-born violinist who trained many prominent Chinese musicians at the Shanghai Conservatory of Music until his death in 1952. Xu Xin concludes his historical survey with a discussion of contemporary research on "the modern Jewish Diaspora in China," including the Jewish Refugees Memorial Museum in Shanghai and the Heilongjiang Academy of Social Sciences on the Harbin Jewish community, as well as the "hundreds of books on Jewish life in China . . . published in Chinese in recent years."

In "When the Muscular Jews Came to the Far East: Jewish Sports and Physical Culture in Modern China, 1912–1949," Ai Rengui discusses how the concept and phenomenon of Muskeljudentum ('Muscular Judaism') came into play among Jews living in Shanghai. Max Nordau coined the term Muskeljudentum in a speech at the 1898 Second Zionist Conference in which he urged Jewish men to develop a new kind of masculinity through physical and mental strength in order to counteract prevalent stereotypes of Jews as scholarly, intellectual, and feminized. According to Nordau, Muscular Judaism, which drew on the philosophy of Muscular Christianity then prevalent in Great Britain, was necessary for the Zionist project of nation-building. Ai notes that in China, Muscular Judaism was a belief and practice among Ashkenazic rather than Sephardic Jews. Starting in 1912, when the Jewish Recreation Club was founded in Shanghai, sports became popular among Jews living in Shanghai and Harbin. Harbin Jews extended the Jewish Recreation Club to communities in Tientsin, Dalian, and Qingdao through the 1930s. After 1945, when the Soviet Red Army entered Northeast China, the Zionist youth organizations Betar and Maccabi were banned in Harbin; by 1949, most Jews had left China. The rise of Jewish sports in Shanghai and the attendant idea of Muscular Judaism were associated with the development of a modern nation for both Chinese nationalism and the Zionist movement.

Significantly, Shanghai was in fact where modern Chinese sports began as a way to counter the stereotype of China as the "sick man of East Asia." The perception of China's "national illness," due to the unequal treaties it had been forced to sign, led to the establishment in 1910 of the Jing Wu Athletic Association, a public martial arts and military training organization that became international and paved the way for the founding of more sports associations. In this respect, AI narrates how Jewish sports organizations were connected to politics. The Shanghai Jewish Recreation Club grew from 11 members in 1912 to over 100 as the Jewish population in Shanghai increased. After the 1917 Russian Revolution, the resulting increase in the Jewish populations of Harbin and other cities in Northeast China led to the establishment of other Jewish sports clubs such as the Harbin Maccabi Sports Association in 1921 and the Jewish Club KUNST in Tientsin in 1928. KUNST, which featured theater, billiards, chess, lectures, concerts, and dance performances alongside sports, boasted some 600 members. As the Shanghai Jewish population swelled to some 15,000 with the influx of those fleeing Nazism, Jewish sports in Shanghai grew further. The Jewish Recreation Club (JRC) was formalized into a cultural and spiritual center, including a Jewish defense league to fight antisemitism and promote "friendship between Jews of different countries." In 1935, the JRC sponsored many sports events and competitions in Shanghai, ranging from cricket, rugby, and football (soccer) to tennis, bowling, boxing, and gambling. In 1939, the JRC urged Jewish refugees to participate in athletic events, which continued even after the outbreak of the Pacific War and the Japanese occupation of Shanghai. AI discusses the specific Zionist youth organizations in China, their affiliated sports clubs and activities, and their importance for the Zionist movement and the founding of the State of Israel. What AI's essay points to is the parallel roles in both Israel and China that sports played in the ideological development of modern nationalism.

In "Tracking the Exact Number of the Jewish Refugees in Shanghai," WANG Jian demonstrates the complexity and difficulty of determining the exact number of Jewish refugees who came to Shanghai. Drawing on articles published in the Shanghai newspaper *Israel's Messenger* from 1933 through 1941 as well as on scholarly studies, WANG determines that approximately 30,000 European Jews found refuge in Shanghai between the early 1930s and 1941. According to WANG, starting in the mid-1930s, despite their own suffering under the Japanese occupation,

Chinese organizations and individuals were not only aware of the Nazi persecution of Jews in Europe – they also protested it and offered refuge to Jews escaping from Nazi Europe. WANG details the increasing numbers of Jews arriving in Shanghai. Between 1933 and the summer of 1938, the new arrivals numbered between 1,000 and 1,500; by March 1939, *Israel's Messenger* reported that close to 4,000 refugees had registered with the Jewish Refugees Committee and that hundreds of others had not registered. In June 1939, the newspaper's count was 10,506 Jewish refugees. Two months later, *Israel's Messenger* reported that from August 1938 to August 1939, over 16,000 Jewish refugees had arrived in Shanghai from Europe. This figure was almost three times the Jewish population of 6,000 Sephardic and Russian Jews who had been living in Shanghai prior to 1933.

In the first half of 1939, Shanghai Jewish community leaders recommended restrictions on immigration and appealed for help from abroad because of the growing Jewish population. At the same time, authorities in the Japanese army and government banned more Jews from arriving in Shanghai. In addition, the Shanghai Municipal Council of the International Settlement and the French consul general also denied all refugees further entry. In August 1939, the German Jewish Council in London and the American Jewish Joint Distribution Committee learned that European Jews were denied shelter in Shanghai. However, the Jewish refugees in Shanghai negotiated with the city administration to reverse these decisions, and these efforts resulted in a new agreement with the Municipal Council of the International Settlement in October 1939. Thus, from August 1939 to June 1940, approximately 1,000 refugees arrived, a process that WANG narrates in terms of the rapid developments of World War II. Around 2,000 more refugees traveled by land through Siberia and Northeast China after June 1940, until the Germans invaded the Soviet Union in 1941. WANG describes the journey of some 1,100 Polish Jews who arrived in Shanghai, among them the 400 students and teachers from the Mir and the Lublin Yeshivas, a subject discussed in detail in Marc B. Shapiro's essay later in Part II. After the bombing of Pearl Harbor on December 7, 1941, no Jewish refugees could enter Shanghai. WANG concludes his essay with three different calculations for the number of Jews who took refuge in Shanghai – either 23,310 or 25,000 or 30,000 – and asserts that, whatever the exact figures, Shanghai rescued a larger number of Jewish refugees than did any other city during World War II.

Maisie MEYER recounts the history of another part of the Shanghai Jewish community. In "The Global Reach of Shanghai's Baghdadi Jews," Meyer traces the trajectory of the Baghdadi Jewish community of Shanghai from a wealthy, insular enclave to one with international reach through its commercial successes. The essay presents the lives and influences of the key figures that Meyer has featured in her book, *Shanghai's Baghdadi Jews: A Collection of Biographical Reflections*

(Hong Kong: Blackman Books, 2015), and expands on those biographical and autobiographical accounts by arguing that these particular Jews and the community that they formed in Shanghai reached the larger world in a variety of ways. Meyer skillfully integrates the stories of families and individuals who left the centuries-old Jewish community of Baghdad, starting in the 1830s, "to escape persecution, conscription, and frequent epidemics of plague."

The lives that Meyer highlights here are of four of the best-known Baghdadi Jews of Shanghai: Eleazer ("Elly") Silas Kadoorie (1865–1944), Silas Aaron Hardoon (1851–1931), Nissim Ezra Benjamin Ezra (1881–1936), and Sir Ellice Victor Elias Sassoon (1881–1961). They and their families wandered from Bombay and Calcutta to Yangon, Singapore, Hong Kong, and Djakarta before settling in the foreign concession in Shanghai. Each of these men, in making his own fortune, helped establish Shanghai as the center of trade, real estate, and commerce in modern China. As Meyer shows, it was the global reach of their peripatetic lives that brought success to Shanghai. Although based in Shanghai, these Jews were Anglophiles, educating their children in England and keeping grand homes there as well. They socialized and did business with the British aristocracy and were also philanthropists who funded relief and educational programs for Jews and for many other peoples throughout the Middle East and Asia. They also supported the founding of the State of Israel. Some had served in the British Armed Forces during World War I. They negotiated on behalf of the Jewish and Chinese populations in Shanghai during the Japanese occupation of Shanghai during World War II. Although Meyer does not mention this fact, some members of these elite, powerful families were incarcerated in Japanese concentration camps for Allied citizens during World War II. In contrast, Sir Victor Sassoon spent significant time and funds in Hollywood's film industry in the 1940s. After 1949, the Kadoorie, Hardoon, Ezra, and Sassoon families scattered across the world – to Israel, England, the United States, Canada, Australia, Argentina, and Hong Kong, and a few to Iraq. Although Meyer's essay does not discuss the Ashkenazic Jews in Shanghai, it establishes the intercultural exchange of these Baghdadi Jews with global cultures to provide an implicit contrast with the other essays in Part II that focus on the Jews from central Europe who took refuge from the Nazis in Shanghai.

In "Jewish Refugee Artists in Shanghai: Visual Legacies of Traumatic Moments and of Cultural Encounters," Nancy BERLINER focuses on three Jewish artists, two from Vienna and one from Bavaria, who escaped Nazi Europe to Shanghai in the 1930s and 1940s. Berliner shows how the visual art that Friedrich Schiff, Paul Fischer, and David Ludwig Bloch produced during these difficult years conveyed to their contemporaries – though exhibitions, magazines and newspapers, and murals – the lived experiences of Jewish refugees in Shanghai. Berliner notes that although the legacy of these Jewish visual artists in Shanghai is acknowledged less than that of the Jewish classical musicians who trained Chinese musicians in the Shanghai Conservatory of Music, their works were well-known at the time. Friedrich Schiff, who arrived in Shanghai from Vienna in 1929 as an adventure-seeker rather than a refugee, was a portrait-painter with a modernist bent; he later became a successful book illustrator and cartoonist for local journals in Chinese and English. He was also a muralist and decorative artist, as well as the founder of the School of Applied Art. Schiff's early satirical works relied on cultural stereotypes, but during the 1940s, his drawings depicted the poverty of both European Jewish and rural Chinese refugees in Shanghai, as in his book, *Squeezing Through: Shanghai Sketches, 1941–1945*. Berliner contrasts Schiff with the refugee artists Paul Fischer and David Ludwig Bloch, whose Shanghai art evinced empathy for the poverty of the Chinese as well as for the struggles of their fellow Jews. In his booklet of postcards, "Shanghai Sketches," Fischer refused to sentimentalize or romanticize impoverished rickshaw pullers, food peddlers, a paper collector, pallbearers, and a vegetable seller performing their jobs in the Shanghai streets. Fischer's 1949 watercolor of a refugee's home (produced after he left Shanghai) portrays the crowded, makeshift interior in which he himself had lived.

Berliner devotes most of her essay to David Ludwig Bloch, whose extensive portfolio of drawings, paintings, and woodcuts demonstrates that he was the most innovative of these three artists – and the most deeply engaged with the Chinese people he encountered during his years in Shanghai. Despite arriving in 1940 as a refugee, he managed to bring with him his drawings and watercolors from his apprenticeship in a porcelain decoration workshop in Bavaria and his early woodblock prints from Munich. Orphaned as a child, rendered deaf by a disease, and having survived the Dachau concentration camp, Bloch documented his journey from Venice to Shanghai in watercolors. In Shanghai, he painted, drew, and produced some 300 woodblock prints with observations on the lives of Jewish refugees, prosperous Europeans, Chinese residents of Hongkou, and Chinese workers, especially the rickshaw pullers. His frequent exhibitions and publications received positive reviews from the Jewish and the Chinese press. The Chinese name that Bloch assumed indicates, according to Berliner, the degree to which he integrated into Chinese culture and society. In fact, Bloch married a Chinese woman, with whom he had two children. The couple eventually left Shanghai together and settled in New York.

Berliner contrasts Bloch's empathetic portrayals of rickshaw pullers with Schiff's, arguing that Schiff was "oblivious to the pullers' struggle." Regarding Bloch's series of prints centered on beggars, Berliner points to both the artist's sense of irony and the dignity he imparted to members of this other impoverished group. She also comments on Bloch's streetscapes of ordinary life in 1940s Shanghai as literally and figuratively colorful, depicting a variety of people, occupations, and activities, and describes Bloch's conventionally aesthetic works, such as images of anemones or water lilies and Chinese motifs. Most importantly, Berliner posits that Bloch's choice of the woodcut as his prime medium – he made more than 300 in Shanghai – shows the profound connection of this Jewish artist to Chinese culture. The woodcut, a traditional folk genre in China influenced by European revolutionary art, had been adapted by Lu Xun (the "founder of the modern woodcut movement in China") and his contemporaries as the primary form to promote class struggle and change. Bloch's archives at the Leo Baeck Institute include magazine pages with reproductions of contemporary Chinese woodcuts; as Berliner astutely observes, he "chose to save this magazine fold-out and carried it with him throughout his life."

Like Berliner, YANG Meng highlights the cultural life that refugee Jews created in Shanghai during World War II. In "Drama in Wartime Shanghai," YANG presents two German-language plays by Jews from Germany and Austria that were written and produced in Shanghai in 1940 and 1941, respectively: *Die Masken fallen* [The masks fall] and *Fremde Erde* [Foreign land], both by Hans Morgenstern and Mark Siegelberg. According to YANG, these two plays were the most successful of the roughly 30 new stage productions by Jews in wartime Shanghai and were also the only ones republished in Europe after 1945. Hans Morgenstern, who also wrote under the pen names of Schubert and Wiener, had been a playwright in Vienna before the war; Mark Siegelberg, born in Kiev, had studied in Switzerland and Austria and worked as a journalist. Both men were interned in the Dachau concentration camp and then fled to Shanghai.

Unlike most of the original theatrical works in Jewish Shanghai, these two plays are dramas that reflect the issues the Jews had faced in Nazi-occupied Europe. In *Die Masken fallen*, a five-act play set in Austria, an Aryan wife opposes the Nazis to protect her Jewish husband. The wife, on the verge of divorcing her Jewish husband to marry her Aryan lover, changes her mind. Instead, she acquires the papers and tickets that will enable her husband and father-in-law to flee to Shanghai and ultimately promises to accompany her husband there as well. In the four-act *Fremde Erde*, the authors depict the social, cultural, and economic problems faced by European Jewish refugees in Shanghai. The main characters are a medical doctor and his wife, who, once in Shanghai, resort to menial jobs in order to survive: the doctor becomes a soap peddler; his wife, a barmaid, earning extra money for the family's survival by providing sexual favors to a wealthy Chinese man. Discovering this situation, the husband leaves his wife, but returns when he realizes that she was acting only out of love for him.

YANG analyzes both these plays in the context of the lives led by the playwrights and their audience both in Austria and in Shanghai. She points out the shared experiences of authors and audience as persecuted Jews in Europe and as refugees struggling to survive in Shanghai. She also discusses the exceptional features of each play, such as the depiction in *Fremde Erde* of a wealthy, European-educated Chinese man, a character who at once reflects the refugees' positive image of China and yet also reveals their unexamined prejudices against the impoverished Chinese people they encountered in Hongkou. YANG also discusses the reception of these two plays, which were criticized at the time for focusing on the private lives of the characters rather than on larger political and social contexts. She counters this view by arguing that Morgenstern and Siegelberg deliberately avoided writing explicitly anti-fascist presentations in order to deflect any potential retribution from Nazi-sympathizing Germans or Japanese authorities in occupied Shanghai.

The last two essays in Part II, by Marc B. SHAPIRO and Samuel HEILMAN, discuss the religious organizational life of Jews in Shanghai. In "The Mir Yeshiva and Its Shanghai Sojourn," Shapiro tells the complicated story of how the approximately 400 students and teachers of the Mir Yeshiva in Soviet-occupied Vilna (Vilnius), Lithuania, were granted visas by the famous Japanese diplomat Chiune Sugihara and escaped to Kobe, Japan. In September 1941, the Japanese forced them to depart for Shanghai, where they stayed through December 1946. Shapiro fleshes out the historical narrative with discussions about the issues of Jewish religion and law that arose for the members of the Mir Yeshiva, such as whether, due to the time differences in Japan, the Sabbath should be observed on Saturday or Sunday.

At first in Shanghai, the Sephardic community of Baghdadi Jews permitted the Mir students and faculty to study and live in the Beth Aharon Sephardic synagogue, which had been built by Silas Aaron Hardoon in 1927. There, as Shapiro recounts, the yeshiva flourished. But in February 1943, the Japanese authorities forced all stateless Jewish refugees, including the Mir Yeshiva students and faculty, to move to Hongkou, a more crowded and impoverished section of the city. Shapiro discusses how, despite many hardships, the Mir Yeshiva did not suffer as much as the other Jewish refugees. Funds sent from the United States provided them with better food, including milk, cream, and kosher meat, while hunger and malnutrition plagued most other Hongkou residents. Throughout his narrative, Shapiro presents a twofold argument. On the one hand, the members of the Mir Yeshiva maintained their strictly Orthodox life and study, even publishing more than one hundred religious texts. Their interactions with and impact on the other Jews in Shanghai were largely positive. They allowed both Ashkenazic refugees and some Shanghai-born Sephardic boys to study in the yeshiva; they established schools for Jewish boys and girls, opened a *mikve* ('ritual bath'), and even married refugee girls. On the other hand, as Shapiro emphasizes, although some expressed empathy for the rickshaw pullers and impoverished Chinese people they observed, most had little if any contact with the surrounding culture of Shanghai. The Mir students interacted with Japanese authorities rather than with Chinese, avoided entering the Chinese sector of the city for fear of contracting disease or falling victim to crime, did not learn the language, and were encouraged by the Yeshiva rabbis not to interact with the local population. Yet, as Shapiro shows, this separation stood counter to the wishes of Shanghai Jewish community leaders, who supported some contact between Jews and their Chinese environment. For example, one school for refugee children taught the Chinese language alongside English and French and, after Pearl Harbor, added Japanese and German to the curriculum. But, as Shapiro concludes, the Mir Yeshiva sought and achieved an almost complete separation from the Chinese environment that sheltered them.

Samuel HEILMAN, in "Chabad Outreach on the Jewish Frontier: The Case of China," presents the case of Chabad Hasidic Judaism in contemporary China. As Heilman explains, the Lubavitch sect of the Hasidic Chabad dynasty (which originated in Russia in 1775, relocated to Poland in the 1930s, and, during World War II, took refuge in the United States) adheres to the belief that their actions will hasten the coming of the Messiah and the age of redemption. To this end, the Chabad movement has established a global network of *shluchim* ('messengers'): rabbis and their families, who settle wherever there are Jews in order to try "to awaken their Jewish consciousness" and facilitate their participation in Jewish practices.

Although, as Heilman argues, despite the relatively small number of Jews living in China today (estimated at only 2,600), the ten or more Chabad-Lubavitch centers (in Beijing, Chengdu, Hong Kong, Guangzhou, Kowloon, Ningbo, Shanghai, Shenzhen, and Yiwu) serve the Chabad Hasidic mission to bring on the coming of the Messiah. According to Heilman, today there are still approximately 500 Chinese Jews in Kaifeng. However, of the pre-1949 community of 10,000 to 15,000 Russian Jews in Harbin, none remain. There are no Jewish residents in Mukden, Hengdaohezi, Quiqhar, or Manchuria. The 30,000 Jews who took refuge in Shanghai during World War II left in a mass exodus in 1949. Why then do Chabad Hasidim have so many outposts in China today? Heilman's answers include several hypotheses: that the official count may actually underestimate the number of Jews in China; that Chabad may be anticipating an influx of Jews to China; or that Chabad's mission is to ensure that "no Jew should ever be lost to the Jewish people," and thus that there is "no number of Jews too few for Chabad to provide a full complement of Jewish services." Heilman sees a deeper explanation in the Chabad mission, which is that by catering to Jewish expatriates and tourists, they intend to transform the world and Jewry one Jew at a time to hasten the coming of the Messiah.

Heilman focuses the last section of his study on the Chabad community in Shanghai, its "second-generation *shaliach* Shalom Greenberg and his wife Dina," and his own encounters with the Greenbergs in 1998 and in 2018. Over those two decades, Greenberg developed the Shanghai Chabad from a mission that could barely gather a *minyan* ('quorum') of Jewish men for prayer services to a thriving endeavor with several locations in Shanghai, a nursery school, a *mikve*, and a kosher restaurant. Heilman attributes this growth to the fact that Chabad in China is now serving – along with the small number of Jews living permanently in Shanghai – a larger number of Jews who pass through China for business and tourism. He stresses that Shalom and Dina Greenberg serve *in* China, but are not *of* it. Like the members of the Mir Yeshiva during World War II, today's leaders of Chabad in Shanghai – and in Beijing, Ningbo, and Pudong – make a conscious effort to avoid any significant interaction with their Chinese neighbors. They achieve this separation by serving kosher cuisine and offering other cultural and religious activities to Jewish residents and visitors. By developing a Jewish community in China through religious, culinary, and educational outreach, Chabad continues its efforts to fulfill its fundamental purpose: to bring on the age of the messianic redemption. For both the Mir Yeshiva in the 1940s and the Chabad movement in the early twenty-first century, the sojourn in China was and is a temporary solution to their own priorities: the perpetuation of the Jewish religion and its learning, practice, and culture. With the exception of several individual Baghdadi Jews discussed by Meyer and the refugee artists discussed by Berliner, the essays in Part II show that the vast majority of Jews who lived or took shelter in modern China did not interact significantly with their environment.

In contrast, each of the six essays in Part III of this volume, "Jews and Chinese," delineates a significant cultural encounter or exchange between Jewish and Chinese people and their cultures. Communication between peoples and cultures is the key here, and it is made possible through translation, journalism, pedagogy, legal intervention, and scholarship. In "Yiddish Translations of Chinese Poetry and Theater in 1920s New York," Kathryn HELLERSTEIN discusses how modernist Jewish poets and writers in New York City during the 1920s interpreted classical Chinese texts through the act of translating them into Yiddish. She places these avant-garde works into the context of popular Yiddish song and theater, in which many other writers depicted the neighboring Chinese immigrant population in less sympathetic terms. BAO Anruo, in "Enemy or Friend: The Image of China in Yiddish Newspapers during the Russo-Japanese War (1904–1905)," explores the ways that Yiddish journalists and editors depicted China as a nation and political entity in the Yiddish press during the Russo-Japanese War. ZHANG Ping, in "To Speak or Not to Speak: Hanoch Levin's *Suitcase Packers* and Cao Yu's *Peking Man* in Light of Cross-Textual Dialogue," performs a cross-cultural analysis of two classic modern dramas: one in Chinese; the other written in Hebrew, translated into Chinese, and performed successfully in Beijing several times in the twenty-first century. LI Dong describes the pedagogical challenges of teaching Jewish American literature to college and university students in China, taking a classic immigrant short story, Anzia Yezierska's "Children of Loneliness" (1923), as his case study. In "Chinese and Ashkenazic Encounters in the American Immigration Regime: Max J. Kohler, Immigration Legal Practice, and the Chinese Exclusion Act," Rebecca KOBRIN tells the exceptional story of the Jewish American attorney Max Kohler, whose belief in freedom and equality led him in 1901 to fight against the renewal of the Chinese Exclusion Act, which severely restricted the number of Chinese people allowed to immigrate to the United States. Our volume concludes with SONG Lihong's essay, "A Homeless Stranger Everywhere: The Shadow of the Holocaust on an Israeli Sinologist," on the intriguing narrative of how the late Irene Eber, born in Germany, became a prominent scholar and professor of Chinese history and culture at the Hebrew University of Jerusalem. As will be recalled, Irene Eber was the author of the first essay in this collection, so we begin and end with our true inspiration.

In "Yiddish Translations of Chinese Poetry and Theater in 1920s New York," Kathryn HELLERSTEIN explains the central role of translation in Yiddish literary modernism in order to frame her discussion of two key renditions of classical Chinese drama and poetry into Yiddish by two New York poets. For these Yiddish writers, translating works from disparate languages was a means to expand the culture of Ashkenazic Jewry beyond its origins in Jewish eastern Europe and its adaptation to immigrant life in America. The Yiddish modernists published their translations of poetry and prose from Japanese, Egyptian, Arabic, English, and Chinese in miscellanies and journals, reaching a relatively small readership. However, contemporaneously, popular writers reached wider American audiences through formulaic subgenres of theater and song, which included narratives of various kinds of interactions between Jewish immigrants and their Chinese neighbors on the Lower East Side of New York. Of these Yiddish operettas and melodramas about Chinatown, only ephemera survive; so far none of the scripts themselves have surfaced. However, certain performances from the vaudeville stages have come down to us as jokes, songs, and musical parodies recorded by various artists from the 1920s through the 1950s. Within this context, Hellerstein focuses on the medieval Chinese classic drama by Li Qianfu, *The Story of the Circle of Chalk*, which reached the New York Yiddish Art Theater through translations and adaptations into French, German, and English and was rendered into Yiddish in 1925 by the poet Moyshe Leyb Halpern. Like those of the popular Chinatown plays, the script for *Der krayd tsirkl* [The chalk circle] has been lost, but from newspaper advertisements and a theater program, including photographs and descriptions, Hellerstein reimagines the play through an educated guess. She uses as a prooftext a Yiddish translation of another medieval Chinese classic, a set of poems by Li Bai (Li Po), which were translated into Yiddish by a younger colleague of Halpern's, Meyer Shtiker, via an English gateway translation. Shtiker compiled four poems by Li Bai into a single lyric narrative, which he called "Di froy redt" [His wife speaks]. Through her own English translations of Shtiker's Yiddish translations, Hellerstein identifies a particularly Jewish thematic phenomenon, that of the *agune* ('abandoned wife'), a legal status that spoke to the suspended cultural status of Jewish immigrants in America. Through this Jewish figure, she speculates that Shtiker's expressive manipulation of Li Bai's poems may well point to the kind of transformation that Halpern's translation might have operated on Li Qianfu's play in order to move his Jewish immigrant theater audience.

In "Enemy or Friend: The Image of China in Yiddish Newspapers during the Russo-Japanese War (1904–1905)," BAO Anruo turns to an earlier decade and focuses on how the Yiddish press in America depicted China during the Russo-Japanese War. BAO analyzes key items among the 80 clippings that mentioned China in the Yiddish press during the Russo-Japanese War and ultimately determines that these reports revealed aspects of Russian Ashkenazic Jewish self-understanding. She describes two types of clippings: news reports, which conveyed neutral or hostile attitudes toward China and Chinese people; and informational articles introducing China to Yiddish readers, which conveyed positive images of the nation and its culture. BAO explains that this difference in representation reflects a twofold perception of China and Chinese people on the part of American Jewish journalists. On the one hand, the news reports, adapted for the American Yiddish press from English or Russian sources, presented negative depictions of wartime China as an embattled region, one that could both profit Russia materially and threaten it politically, because of the Jewish immigrants' continued identification with their former homeland and its culture. On the other hand, the informational articles conveyed positive depictions of the culture and people of China. Hoping to imagine a Jewish national future, these Yiddish journalists drew parallels between the Chinese and Jewish cultures ranging from their millennia-long histories to what seemed to them to be similarities between their legendary heroic figures, religious beliefs, customs, and sacred texts, and even their nationalist idealization of territory and land. Likewise, Chinese intellectuals of the New Culture movement in the early twentieth century also articulated such "mirror images," discussing and translating literary works from Yiddish and

Hebrew, in order to overcome the isolation of a victimized people. BAO's discoveries of these exchanges between Yiddish and Chinese writers and texts echo the themes of reciprocal cultures set forth in other essays in this volume.

ZHANG Ping takes up the theme of cultural encounter and exchange in "To Speak or Not to Speak: Hanoch Levin's *Suitcase Packers* and Cao Yu's *Peking Man* in Light of Cross-Textual Dialogue." In this essay, ZHANG discusses the works of two late twentieth-century playwrights, Hanoch Levin (from Israel) and Cao Yu (from China), in order to explore the principles of cultural exchange that prompted Chinese audiences to receive these works so warmly when they were performed in China in Hebrew and in ZHANG's own Chinese translation between 2004 and 2019. ZHANG argues that these two plays, each of which is a modern classic in its own culture, share striking similarities in their subject matter: the struggle of the protagonists to escape human mortality and desperation. As ZHANG shows, Levin's play normalizes death in an absurd context; the living and the dead share the same world, even traveling together with their respective suitcases. This erasure of the boundary between life and death is caused by the desperation of the modern human condition, in which, for Levin, both life and death are characterized by triviality, boredom, hopelessness, and miscommunication. Although Levin sets his play in a familiar South Tel Aviv neighborhood, he emphasizes the universality of the characters' predicaments. In contrast, Cao Yu sets his play, *Peking Man*, in a more specific context: Beijing City in the 1930s and 1940s, a period rife with conflict between traditions and modern culture. Despite the specificity of its setting, *Peking Man* skirts realism. This intentional slippage from cultural and historical representation, ZHANG argues, places both plays firmly within the trends of modern world literature and points to the twentieth-century modernization of both traditional Jewish and Chinese civilizations.

ZHANG then turns to the differences between the two authors and their cultures. The two plays differ in their depictions of the generational struggles within Chinese and Jewish societies. *Peking Man* presents a binary between the older, tradition-bound generation, which is villainized as the cause of the desperate human condition, and the younger, revolutionary generation, which resists and offers a way out. However, *Suitcase Packers* depicts a world in which all people suffer from a shared desperation that can never change. Cao Yu's play presents the future of a nation, while Levin's play displays an inalterable world of stasis. For different reasons, both plays depict failed attempts to escape, contrasting notions of death, and diametrically opposed suggestions for how to solve the human dilemma of despair: Levin offers limited reforms and outspokenness, while Cao Yu offers a radical rejection of civilization and silence.

ZHANG explains these differences by placing the plays into the contexts of Chinese and Jewish traditional philosophies. While Chinese Confucianism values silence as the ideal aspect of Heaven, Jewish tradition (in the Bible and in rabbinic literature) presents a God who never stops talking. Confucianism posits that a person can improve the self to perfection, while in Judaism, a person's improvement is determined by his own words and deeds. Although both Hanoch Levin and Cao Yu were educated in the classical traditions of their respective cultures, each rejected his tradition's values. It seems, though, that their rebellions went only so far: Levin's choice of speech as the solution to existential despair is compatible with Judaic tradition, while the high value the Cao Yu places on silence is eminently Confucian. By showing the shared qualities of these two plays within the context of their contrasting cultural traditions, ZHANG makes the valuable argument that the universalism resulting from a modernization that rejects tradition is itself determined by its culture of origin. He contrasts two routes toward Westernization in two non-Western cultures: in Israel, Judaism has transformed itself in order to be compatible with Western values, while in China, revolution has forced the erasure of traditional Chinese culture. ZHANG attributes this difference in part to the nature of the conflicts that both nations are facing: since its beginnings, Israel has struggled against external forces, while China's clashes have been primarily internal. ZHANG concludes with a profound irony: the Chinese play presents a world that allows no compromise between the old and the new, but the new order sought by the young revolutionaries comes to resemble the stifling condition of the characters in the Israeli play, in which modernization does not lead to meaningful life. Asking how contemporary Chinese audiences, having lost all traditions, can avoid the situation of Levin's suitcase packers, ZHANG explains the attraction of Levin's play to this contemporary Chinese audience.

In "Teaching American Jewish Literature to Chinese College Students: Anzia Yezierska's 'Children of Loneliness' as a Case Study," LI Dong takes ZHANG's question – *How does a Chinese audience receive a work of Jewish literature?* – in a different direction. Instead of the Chinese theater, LI investigates the college classroom in China. LI addresses the problems encountered by an instructor when teaching a short story by an immigrant Jewish author of early twentieth-century America to undergraduate students in early twenty-first-century China. Using as his example "Children of Loneliness," a 1923 story by Anzia Yezierska, LI describes how he contextualizes a work of fiction within a religious, cultural, and historical framework. Whereas ZHANG's essay explores how the inherent commonalities of modernity, despite the cultural differences between Israel and China, can speak powerfully to the concerns of a contemporary Chinese audience, LI argues that the differences between the cultural context of a Jewish literary text and the cultural assumptions of Chinese students are so challenging that they can only be bridged by a teacher, one who can personally address the students' preconceptions and limited knowledge about American and Jewish culture. By countering stereotypes about Jews and accounting for the students' own professional priorities, the teacher will whet their curiosity through a reading of Anzia Yezierska's short story.

Yezierska's story focuses upon the process of Americanization for immigrant Jews in the early twentieth century. The protagonist, Rachel, has recently graduated from college and returns home to her parents' tenement apartment on the Lower East Side of New York City. With her newly Americanized eyes, Rachel perceives her parents, who maintain a devoutly traditional Jewish life, as backwards greenhorns. She responds to their Yiddish-inflected English, their old-world habits and mannerisms, and (in particular) her father's religiosity with impatience and embarrassment. Yet when she tries to establish herself in an American context by renting a room of her own, Rachel finds that she has only misunderstandings with her non-Jewish college beau and faces a crisis of identity. Although she has broken her ties with the traditional culture that her parents perpetuate in America, she is not wholly part of American culture. Cut off from her family and community of origin, not yet fully Americanized, she finds herself "one of the millions of immigrant children, children of loneliness, wandering between worlds that are at once too old and too new to live in."[1]

In order to help his students respond to this powerful story, Li structures his class session carefully. He asks his students to read the text, watch online videos about Jewish immigration, and pose questions about these materials before class. During the class, which he conducts as a discussion, Li provides his students with background information about the basic tenets of traditional Judaism, which becomes Orthodox Judaism in America. He also guides his students into the history of Jews in America and eastern Europe, as well as the great wave of immigration to the United States between 1881 and 1924. This cultural background allows him to explore with his students the conflicts between Yezierska's protagonist and her parents in order to understand the larger issues of culture and religion faced by Jews in the twentieth-century United States. Li's essay includes an insight that transcends the differences between Chinese and Jewish American cultures. He notes that the generational and cultural conflicts within Yezierska's short story may resemble the experiences of his students and suggests that an instructor might ask them to consider similarities and differences between intergenerational conflicts in modern-day China and those dramatized in Yezierska's work.

---

[1] Anzia Yezierska, "Children of Loneliness," in *Jewish American Literature: A Norton Anthology*, eds. Jules Chametzky, John Felstiner, Hilene Flanzbaum, and Kathryn Hellerstein (New York: W. W. Norton, 2001), 244.

Shifting from cultural interpretations to legal and political encounters, Rebecca KOBRIN, in "Chinese and Ashkenazic Encounters in the American Immigration Regime: Max J. Kohler, Immigration Legal Practice, and the Chinese Exclusion Act," recalls to our collective consciousness an important but forgotten figure in twentieth-century encounters between Jewish and Chinese people. Kobrin presents the career of Max J. Kohler, a former United States district attorney who, in 1901, challenged the Chinese Exclusion Act of 1882 and worked to have it repealed. Kohler distinguished himself from the many other American Jewish lawyers who also wanted to curtail the government's increasing restrictions on immigration in the early twentieth century. Unlike the others, Kohler deployed US trade policy with China as the basis for his legal arguments, proposing that open immigration could increase the power of the United States on the world stage. As Kobrin emphasizes, for this Jewish lawyer, exclusion was both a moral and a pragmatic issue – Congress's exclusion of Chinese immigrants could easily be applied to Jews. Kobrin brings to bear on this matter the intersection between the racial stereotypes of Chinese immigrants and antisemitic stereotypes of eastern European Jews. As a lawyer in private practice, Kohler defended detained immigrants, never charging for his services, and worked to create a perception of immigrants as contributing positively to the American economy and society. The moral aspects of these efforts were grounded in his own adherence to the tenets of American Reform Judaism. Kobrin shows how Kohler applied these principles in his work to overturn the Chinese Exclusion Act of 1882, which remains the only time that Congress has barred all members of one nationality from entering the United States. This law also prevented Chinese residents of the United States from becoming naturalized citizens. There were thus very few Chinese attorneys in the United States, and Chinese immigrants turned to Jewish lawyers for help in the courtroom. Kohler advocated for the law to be applied to immigrants of all nationalities without discrimination among them.

To counter the corrupt practices among immigration officials at entry points, Kohler himself went to Ellis Island with the HIAS (Hebrew Immigrant Aid Society) to ensure that immigrants who were about to be deported would have legal representation. He protested the inhumane and extreme treatment of Chinese immigrants – as well as of Jews and South Asians – that he witnessed there. Kobrin cites specific cases of Chinese immigrants and legal residents who were detained at the border and whom Kohler defended against the unconstitutional, prejudicial, and discriminatory application of immigration law. These cases reveal the righteous generosity and effective actions of this American Jew. His legal argument in the case of one Chinese merchant made clear that restrictive immigration policies undermined America's aims to expand its participation in international trade. Kobrin concludes that, although Kohler failed to overturn the Chinese Exclusion Act, his efforts influenced American jurisprudence for the good, securing immigrants' rights to due process and challenging the government's use of racial categories in immigration law.

Our volume concludes with the incisive, moving essay by SONG Lihong, "A Homeless Stranger Everywhere: The Shadow of the Holocaust on an Israeli Sinologist," which discusses the life and career of Irene Eber, to whom this volume is dedicated. In this essay, SONG asks why there are so many Jewish scholars among Western Sinologists, or scholars of China studies. He answers this question through a reading of Eber's scholarly work within the context of her biography. By focusing on the incongruity between Eber's 2004 memoir, *The Choice: Poland, 1939–1945*, and the rest of her extensive writings, SONG argues that Eber's memory of her own traumatic experiences during the Holocaust shaped the range, depth, and choices of subject matter in her scholarly work on China. Eber, whom SONG considers "the high priestess of China studies in Israel," deliberately shaped the narrative of her life, diminishing Germany's role. Only at the very end of her memoir does she mention the fact that she was born in Halle, Germany; instead, she emphasizes her identification with her father's hometown of Mielec, Poland, where the family found refuge for four years after they were expelled by the Nazis from Germany. SONG points out, too, that Eber worked with the translator of her memoir into Chinese to purge the names of Jews and Righteous Gentiles of all associations with Germany, despite the conventional transliteration of Jewish and German names with a Chinese character that also means "German." Yet Eber's postwar sense of not being at home anywhere in the world – in Mielec, in America, in Israel – was always fraught, as was the sense of paradox that she tried to resolve in her writings. The reason she survived the Nazis, albeit under extreme duress, as a young teenager, was because she disobeyed her father's last words to her: "Don't go." SONG sees this sense of homelessness and the emotional and psychological tension of disobedience as the key to Eber's work on China, especially her late-career focus on the Jewish refugees in Shanghai.

SONG calls Eber a "non-Jewish Jew," by which he means that she lived apart from religious belief or practice, yet expressed a complex connection to her people, one that comes into view through her scholarship on China. To this end, SONG links Eber's mid-career magnum opus, her biography of S. I. J. Schereschewsky (the Jewish-born and Jewish-educated Episcopal priest who translated the Hebrew Bible from the original directly into Chinese), to her own version of Jewish identity. SONG also calls Schereschewsky a "non-Jewish Jew," though in a different way, and suggests that Eber saw him as her own doppelganger; her biography of Schereschewsky is a veiled version of her own autobiography. SONG quotes a 2015 interview with Eber by Pei-Ying Lin, in which Eber remarks that reading Chinese philosophy as a young student finally in America "was like coming home." With this statement, SONG supports his argument that Eber's pursuit of Chinese culture and history through an intercultural perspective – as in her studies of the Chinese translations and reception of Yiddish literature and of China in the writings of Martin Buber and Franz Kafka – was a response to the trauma of the Holocaust.

Eber sought a sense of home in the most distant place and culture – China – through her scholarly works, including those reconceiving the reciprocal influence of Chinese and Jewish cultures among the Kaifeng Jews. Yet in her last years, she combined that focus with a return to the story of her own people. SONG demonstrates how, in her monumental study (2012) and her documentary history (2018) of the Jewish refugees in Shanghai before and during World War II, Eber restores with impeccable historicity the identities and experiences of individual Jews through documents of their lives before, during, and after wartime Shanghai. The home Eber found in Israel, as a professor of Sinology at the Hebrew University of Jerusalem, was itself a vexed place for her, haunted as she was by images of her father's Poland and his lost "song of Zion." Beneath the surface, SONG's essay traces a poignant, imagined dialogue between Eber and Joseph Levenson, an American Jewish Sinologist who also found links between his Jewishness and his work on ancient and modern China. In the discrepancies between Eber's life choices and her scholarship, SONG finds an "ingathering of the sparks of Yiddish culture that were scattered to the four corners of the world" as a way to mourn the losses of the Holocaust.

In the final year of her life, I had the privilege of holding weekly talks with Irene Eber on Skype. She had designated me as her literary executor; in that role, I assisted with the publication of her final (and posthumous) book, *Jews in China: Cultural Conversations, Changing Perceptions*, and with the donation of her scholarly archives to the Libraries of the University of Pennsylvania as the Irene Eber Gift of the Yedidya Geminder Memorial Archive of Sino-Judaica. In the course of these conversations, Irene told me about her own final writing project: a memoir of her time in a displaced persons camp and a study of what young Jews like herself, the remnant of a destroyed generation of children and young adolescents, had experienced in the DP camps – a subject that, she insisted, had never been fully researched or understood. Unfortunately, she was unable to bring this project to light. The point is that, as SONG intuits in his essay, Eber did intend to return full-circle to her own story of survival, the story that had led her to study China. SONG Lihong and I hope that this collection of essays on China and Ashkenazic Jewry – the first of its kind, we believe – will lead to further explorations and encounters between these cultures.

I The Bible in China

As its title indicates, Part I, "The Bible in China," deals with the Hebrew Bible and China. Its first and last essays focus on a specific figure, S. I. J. Schereschewsky, a Jewish convert to Christianity who, in the nineteenth and early twentieth centuries, translated the Hebrew Bible into Chinese. The first essay, Irene EBER's "From Rags to Riches: Joseph and His Family," discusses the challenges that Schereschewsky encountered in the process of translating into vernacular Chinese language and culture the complex story of Joseph from the book of Genesis in the Hebrew Bible. The final essay, LIU Yan's "The Transcultural Characteristics of the Chinese Bible Translated by S. I. J. Schereschewsky (1831–1906): A Case Study of the Song of Songs," compares selections from two Chinese translations of the Song of Songs, both by Schereschewsky: the 1875 Beijing Vernacular Old Testament Version and the 1902 Easy Wenli Old and New Testaments.

Between these two studies, three essays bring the Hebrew Bible into dialogue with works from the Chinese tradition. In "Why Is Having No Posterity the Worst Unfilial Thing? A Comparison of Mencius 4A:26 and Genesis 38," FU Xiaowei and WANG Yi compare a key passage from the ancient Chinese philosopher Mencius (Mengzi, ca. 371–289 BCE) with a problematic narrative from Genesis in the Hebrew Bible in order to reevaluate the criticism of Confucian filial morality in modern China. In contrast to FU and WANG's essay on two ancient classical texts, CAO Jian discusses how the Hebrew Bible influenced modern thinkers of the New Culture movement during the 1910s and the May Fourth movement of 1919 in their conceptualizations of the Chinese nation, in "The Impact of Ancient Israelite Prophets on Modern Chinese Intellectuals." Also focused on the connections between ancient texts and modern writers, ZHONG Zhiqing reflects, in "Reading the Song of Songs in Jewish and Chinese Tradition," on how this biblical text was translated and reinterpreted in modern Chinese, contrasting the Chinese reading of the Song of Songs as a collection of love lyrics with the theological and allegorical readings in Western Judaism and Christianity.

Irene EBER

1 From Rags to Riches: Joseph and His Family

Over the years, biblical scholarship has paid considerable attention to the Joseph story. Scholars have recognized it as a work of outstanding narrative art, and Robert Alter calls it a "work of consummate artistry."[1] According to Shalom Goldman, the Joseph story is "the most artfully constructed tale in the Pentateuch."[2]

Briefly, the plot relates events in the life of a tale-bearing boy, his father Jacob's favorite, who earns the jealousy of his half-brothers, especially after he tells them his dream of grandeur. The brothers want to kill him, but desist and instead sell him to itinerant merchants. These in turn sell him to a highly placed Egyptian dignitary at the Pharaoh's court. There, Joseph distinguishes himself in the management of affairs as he does similarly when imprisoned. His ascent to fame and position occurs after he correctly interprets dreams (including those of the Pharaoh) and after his responsible management of the disastrous famine that had begun to devastate the entire region. Dispatched by Jacob to buy provisions in Egypt and after several twists of the plot, the brothers are reunited with Joseph. Later Joseph resettles Jacob's entire family in Goshen – the brothers, their wives, and their children – and returns to his administrative duties at the Pharaoh's court.

The aim of this paper is to explore the ways in which a story of such complexity and artistry can be translated from one language and from one culture into another. Keeping in mind that translating the Bible in both the nineteenth and twentieth centuries was a religious as well as a literary task, missionaries engaged in translating required the assistance of Chinese scholars.[3] To these men, unfortunately for the most part not referred to by name, must go much of the credit for the translations' success.

In this paper, the Chinese versions that will be examined are that of S. I. J. Schereschewsky (1831–1906), which first appeared in 1875 and was revised in 1899, and the so-called Union Version, which was translated by committee and

---

[1] Robert Alter, "Joseph and His Brothers," *Commentary* 70, no. 5 (November 1980): 69.
[2] Shalom Goldman, *The Wiles of Women / the Wiles of Men: Joseph and Potiphar's Wife in Ancient Near Eastern Jewish and Islamic Folklore* (New York: State University of New York Press, 1995), 145.
[3] Patrick Hanan, "The Bible as Chinese Literature: Medhurst, Wang Tao and the Delegates' Version," *Harvard Journal of Asiatic Studies* 63, no. 1 (June 2003): 198.

appeared in 1919.⁴ The main reason for choosing these versions rather than earlier or classical ones is that both Bibles are translated into vernacular Chinese and are serious attempts to reach a wider public, not only the highly educated. As Schereschewsky explained to the House of Bishops in 1888, his Bible translation of 1875 was into Mandarin (*guan hua* 官話), the spoken language used by two-thirds of the Chinese population. It is the modern literary language and understood by all those who are not illiterate.⁵ Equally significant is the fact that, knowing biblical Hebrew, Schereschewsky could translate the Old Testament directly from Hebrew.⁶ The Union Version is similarly a translation into vernacular Chinese. Although it relies to a considerable extent on the earlier translation, it is often clearer than the former. Later twentieth-century Bible translators would have to consider the work of the Union Version translators.⁷ Before taking a closer look at the translation itself, some remarks about the art of translating and its implications are in order.

1 Translating and its Significance

Edith Grossman has pointed out that "world literature as a discipline fit for academic study depends on the availability of translations." As readers, we cannot conceive of a world without translations.⁸ In China, translating the Bible was part of the extensive translating activity from world literature in the modern period. But translating involves more than merely moving a text from one language into another. George Steiner reminds us that we actually always translate: "The schematic model of translation is one in which a message from a source language

---

4 The Bibles are *Jiuyue quanshu* 舊約全書 [Old Testament in the Mandarin colloquial] (Peking, 1875), *Jiuxin yue quanshu* 舊新約全書 [Old and new complete books] (British and Foreign Bible Society, 1899) rev. ed., and *Jiuxin yue quanshu* [Old and new complete books] (China Bible House, 1939).
5 S. I. J. Schereschewsky, "The Bible, Prayer Book, and Terms in Our China Mission, Addressed to the House of Bishops," pamphlet, November 5, 1888. I thank Nicolas R. Dunn for making this available to me. See also Irene Eber, "The Peking Translating Committee and S. I. J. Schereschewsky's Old Testament," *Anglican and Episcopal History* 67, no. 2 (June 1998): 212–226.
6 For a biography of Schereschewsky, see Irene Eber, *The Jewish Bishop and the Chinese Bible: S. I. J. Schereschesky (1831–1906)* (Leiden: Brill, 1999). The Chinese translation of this book is by Hu Congxian (2013).
7 For the genesis and birth of the Union Version, see the monumental work by Jost Oliver Zetzsche, *The History of the Union Version or the Culmination of Protestant Missionary Bible Translation in China* (Sankt Augustin: Monumenta Serica Institute, 1999).
8 Edith Grossman, *Why Translation Matters* (New Haven, CT: Yale University Press, 2010), 13.

passes into a receptor language via a transformative process."⁹ Where Chinese is concerned, the transformation of the text becomes especially significant because it is also a cultural transfer.¹⁰ Simon Lasair asserts that translation is not only an interlinguistic but also an intercultural phenomenon. Therefore, whereas stylistic and syntactic coherence matter, translation also concerns itself with the question of what are culturally acceptable and understandable forms of literature.¹¹ Clearly, therefore, a translation must be audience-oriented in order to succeed. Its reception in the target culture is what matters.

Still, translating the Bible was not like translating a literary work. Many if not most Bible translators believed that God had inspired the Bible's words. A translation should adhere closely to the text, since reading it would lead to conversion.¹² Yet there were also others, among them Schereschewsky, who maintained that the Bible must be read and understood by more people of the Chinese population and not only by the literati, who read the text in classical Chinese.

Numbers certainly mattered, but it was especially important, as far as Schereschewsky was concerned, not to aim for a literal translation. It should be faithful and idiomatic, but not literal. The distinction between faithfulness and literalness is significant, and it allowed Schereschewsky to emphasize the importance of stylistic refinement.¹³ Finally, the question of proper terminology must be also mentioned. To what extent could Chinese religious and philosophical concepts be utilized? Did new concepts have to be coined to introduce new ideas?

2 The Joseph Story

The story begins with Genesis 37 and ends at Genesis 50. Except for Genesis 38, which forms a kind of interlude about one of the brothers,¹⁴ the twelve chapters

---

9 George Steiner, *After Babel: Aspects of Language and Translation* (London: Oxford University Press, 1975), 28.
10 Naomi Seidman, *Faithful Renderings: Jewish-Christian Difference and the Politics of Translation* (Chicago, IL: University of Chicago Press, 2006), 202.
11 Simon G. D. A. Lasair, "Targum and Translation: A New Approach to a Classic Problem," *AJS Review* 34, no. 2 (November 2010): 271–272.
12 Hanan, "The Bible as Chinese Literature," 199.
13 Schereschewsky, "Translation of the Scripture into Chinese," in *Records of the General Conference of the Protestant Missionaries in China, 1890* (Shanghai: American Presbyterian Press, 1890), 41–42.
14 Regarding the many discussions of this chapter, see John R. Huddlestun, "Divestiture, Deception, and Demotion: The Garment Motif in Genesis 37–39," *Journal for the Study of the Old Testament* 24, no. 4 (September 1, 2002): 47–62.

are a coherent tale about a family. As a teenager, Joseph does not endear himself to his half-brothers by telling tales about them to his father, Jacob. He is, furthermore, singled out by Jacob for special favors, receiving from him a colorful garment.[15] Thus jealousy is added to dislike of this tale-bearing brat. To the reader not familiar with clothing signifying a person's station in life, this may not necessarily mean anything. Trying to convey that clothing matters without translating literally, Schereschewsky's solution is ingenious. He rendered it as 花衣 (*huayi*, 'flowery garment'), since obviously a garment consisting of flowery material would be also colorful. Both the 1899 revised edition and the Union Version retain this rendition. Thus at the very beginning of this story it is obvious that the translator had his eye on the reader and was concerned with his understanding the text.

Pharaoh has his fateful dreams about the seven lean and seven good years. The experts, when consulted, do not know how to interpret the dream. Joseph is summoned, and he knows exactly what the dream conveys about Egypt's future and, as it turns out, that of the entire region. To honor Joseph, Pharaoh gives him a special garment of fine and much valued material.[16] It is not clear exactly what kind of material this is. Schereschewsky transliterated it as 比疎衣 (*bishu yi*) from the Hebrew *bigdei shesh*, appending a note to it. In the 1899 edition, *bishu yi* is retained, but in the Union Version it is changed to 細麻衣 (*xima yi*, 'linen garment'). The Union Version translators, no doubt, had access to an English translation. In English, *bigdei shesh* is usually rendered as 'linen.'

Translating bread presented a special problem, since bread was not a customary food in the Chinese diet. A word other than "bread" had to be found. Schereschewsky thus translated bread consistently as 糧食 (*liangshi*, 'provisions') or 飯 (*fan*, 'food').

Due to the famine, Joseph institutes various reforms, including buying land for the Pharaoh and resettling the people who had lived there. But the land of the 'priests' (Hebrew: *kohanim*) he does not buy.[17] Schereschewsky translated 'priests' as 司 (*si*), which is generally used for priests but can also have secular connotations depending on context. The Union Version continued this usage. Obviously, however, the Chinese reader might be misled into thinking that it referred only to officials who did not lose their land.

Jacob is dying and is, as the idiomatic Hebrew has it, "gathered unto his people."[18] A literal translation would have made little sense to the Chinese reader. In the 1875 version, therefore, Schereschewsky opted for 祖那裏去了 (*zu nali qule*, 'Jacob going to ancestors'). In the 1899 revision, he apparently decided to

---

15 Gen. 37:3.
16 Gen. 41:42.
17 Gen. 47:22.
18 Gen. 49:33.

adhere more closely to the original so that the text approximated 他列祖那裏去了 (*ta liezu nali qule*, 'joining successive ancestors'). This reading is retained in the Union Version, but it is preceded by Jacob's dying, thus leaving no doubt about the consequences of death.

These few examples clearly demonstrate Schereschewsky's care and attention to bringing the text within the experience of readers. Schereschewsky was obviously also concerned with maintaining the distinctions in the Old Testament between the names used for God. God as *Elohim* is always 天主 (*Tianzhu*, 'Lord of Heaven'). The Tetragramaton is 主 (*zhu*, 'Lord'), and 'God Almighty' (Hebrew: *El Shadai*) is 全能的天主 (*quan neng de Tianzhu*, 'Omnipotent Heavenly Lord').

The distinction between faithful versus literal translation is also clearly demonstrated in Schereschewsky's handling of a recurrent phrase: "The Lord was with Joseph."[19] A literal translation might have been easily misunderstood.[20] Schereschewsky, therefore, opted for the verb 主保, 'protected,' as in, "The Lord protected Joseph."

3 Some General Considerations

Returning now to a question posed earlier: Can this kind of complex story be successfully conveyed in another culture? Can the nuances of a source culture be conveyed in the receptor language? The answer is affirmative, provided that certain theoretical considerations are observed by a translator. First, as Schereschewsky emphasized, a translation must be faithful and not literal. The new text in the receptor language cannot be identical with the original text, yet it must convey the meaning of the original.

To the Chinese reader, the Joseph figure was no doubt very meaningful. He was the prototype of a man who rose from humble beginnings to become important when given the opportunity to utilize his capabilities. Moreover, he did not avenge himself for the wrong he had suffered at the hands of his half-brothers, as a pettier man might have done. He was not vindictive. Nor did he blame Jacob, his father, whose favoritism was ultimately responsible for the rift between himself and his brothers. On the contrary, he was generous indeed, even magnanimous, resettling his entire family in Egypt.

Major mention was devoted to making the vernacular Bible as readable as possible. Here, much of the credit must go to the working methods of the Peking

---

19 For example, Gen. 39:2–3.
20 The Union Version returned to the literal translation.

Translating Committee and Schereschewsky's Chinese co-workers.[21] Even if the names of these men are mostly unknown, it was due to their ability to write graceful Chinese that assured the success of the translation. Scholars like Lian Yinghuang, who worked with Schereschewsky after he became paralyzed, were responsible for the stylistic elegance of the vernacular Old Testament and Bible generally. It comes as no surprise, therefore, that Bibles and especially portions of Bibles were printed in ever-increasing quantities. Among these, Genesis, which includes the Joseph story, held a dominant position.[22]

But if this is the case and if indeed these early vernacular translations are of literary excellence, did the Joseph theme find its way into Chinese literature? Was the Joseph story retold as a literary story? One could argue, for example, that the Joseph story contains structural elements also frequently found in Chinese traditional stories. There are the dreams – Joseph's, those of his fellow prisoners in Egypt, and Pharaoh's – that have a pivotal structural role in the development of the story. Furthermore, we as readers become acquainted with the characters by means of direct speech. Neither interior dialogue nor authorial descriptions are used to reveal what the characters of the story are like. And it is a known fact that although few Chinese writers used biblical themes in their literary creations, there were some who did.[23] Further research is needed to help us understand the more specific function of these early vernacular Old Testament translations and modern Chinese literature.[24]

---

21 Eber, "The Peking Translating Committee and S. I. J. Schereschewsky's Old Testament," *Anglican and Episcopal History* 67, no. 2 (June 1998): 212–226.
22 Eber, *The Jewish Bishop and the Chinese Bible*, 248–249.
23 One such theme was the Samson story as employed by Mao Dun. This was "Sansun de Fuchou" [Samson's revenge], published in 1942. I might also mention the little-known Xiang Peiliang, who recreated the Amnon and Tamar episode in the one-act drama "Annen." See Marián Gálik, *Influence, Translation and Parallels: Selected Studies on the Bible in China* (Sankt Augustin: Monumenta Serica Institute, 2004), 195–212 and 231–250.
24 A major contribution to this subject has been made by Cao Jian in *Chinese Biblical Anthropology: Persons and Ideas in the Old Testament and in Modern Chinese Literature* (Eugene, OR: Pickwick Publications, 2019).

References

Alter, Robert. "Joseph and His Brothers." *Commentary* 70, no. 5 (November 1980): 69.
Cao Jian. *Chinese Biblical Anthropology: Persons and Ideas in the Old Testament and in Modern Chinese Literature*. Eugene, OR: Pickwick Publications, 2019.
Eber, Irene. *The Jewish Bishop and the Chinese Bible: S. I. J. Schereschesky (1831–1906)*. Leiden: Brill, 1999.
Eber, Irene. "The Peking Translating Committee and S. I. J. Schereschewsky's Old Testament." *Anglican and Episcopal History* 67, no. 2 (June 1998): 212–226.
Goldman, Shalom. *The Wiles of Women / the Wiles of Men: Joseph and Potiphar's Wife in Ancient Near Eastern Jewish and Islamic Folklore*. New York: State University of New York Press, 1995.
Grossman, Edith. *Why Translation Matters*. New Haven, CT: Yale University Press, 2010.
Hanan, Patrick. "The Bible as Chinese Literature: Medhurst, Wang Tao and the Delegates' Version." *Harvard Journal of Asiatic Studies* 63, no. 1 (June 2003): 197–239.
Huddlestun, John R. "Divestiture, Deception, and Demotion: The Garment Motif in Genesis 37–39." *Journal for the Study of the Old Testament* 24, no. 4 (September 1, 2002): 47–62.
Jiuxin yue quanshu 舊新約全書 [Old and new complete books]. Revised edition. British and Foreign Bible Society, 1899.
Jiuxin yue quanshu [Old and new complete books]. China Bible House, 1939.
Jiuyue quanshu 舊約全書 [Old Testament in the Mandarin colloquial]. Peking, 1875.
Lasair, Simon G. D. A. "Targum and Translation: A New Approach to a Classic Problem." *AJS Review* 34, no. 2 (November 2010): 265–287.
Schereschewsky, S. I. J. "The Bible, Prayer Book, and Terms in Our China Mission, Addressed to the House of Bishops" (pamphlet). November 5, 1888.
Schereschewsky, S. I. J. "Translation of the Scripture into Chinese," in *Records of the General Conference of the Protestant Missionaries in China, 1890*. Shanghai: American Presbyterian Press, 1890. 41–44.
Seidman, Naomi. *Faithful Renderings: Jewish-Christian Difference and the Politics of Translation*. Chicago, IL: University of Chicago Press, 2006.
Steiner, George. *After Babel: Aspects of Language and Translation*. London: Oxford University Press, 1975.
Zetzsche, Jost Oliver. *The History of the Union Version or the Culmination of Protestant Missionary Bible Translation in China*. Sankt Augustin: Monumenta Serica Institute, 1999.

Fu Xiaowei and Wang Yi

2 Why Is Having No Posterity the Worst Unfilial Thing? A Comparison of Mencius 4A:26 and Genesis 38

Among the critiques leveled at Confucian filial morality by modern Chinese and Western scholars alike, the most convenient target is perhaps the saying in *Mencius*: "Mengzi [i.e. Mencius] said, 'Among the three unfilial things, to have no posterity is the worst.'"[1]

Modern scholars have found this Confucian value hard to accept. The most representative critique can be found in *The True Meaning of the Lord of Heaven* of Matteo Ricci, a sixteenth-century Italian missionary to China. If having a male heir is the most important thing for a filial son, Matteo Ricci said, "The son should thus put his whole heart into procreation day and night so as to have offspring. [. . .] Suppose one man claims that failing to have a son is unfilial, and having sons is filial. He marries quite a number of concubines and stays in his hometown. He does nothing good except having a good many sons. Can this be called filial?"[2] In this way, Ricci proved the absurdity of Mencius's statement.

Similarly, for modern-day theologians, the story of Judah and Tamar in Genesis 38 is perplexing, even embarrassing. No researcher has yet provided a convincing interpretation of Judah's claim that Tamar, his daughter-in-law, was more righteous than he after she cheated him into unlawful sexual intercourse.

However, a close reading of Mencius reveals that such harsh criticism is to a certain extent a misunderstanding of Mencius and of the Confucian understanding of life after death. By the same token, this essay will provide a more reasonable interpretation of Judah's obscure claim in Genesis 38, that Tamar, his daughter-in-law, "has been more righteous than I."

---

[1] *Mengzi* 4A:26.1. Mencius, a Latinate translation of Mengzi (ca. 371–ca. 289 BCE) is, after Confucius, the most famous Chinese philosopher. Unless otherwise noted, we will quote from Bryan W. Van Norden's translation, *Mengzi with Selections from Traditional Commentaries* (Indianapolis: Hackett, 2008).

[2] Matteo Ricci, *The True Meaning of the Lord of Heaven* (Taiwan: Lisi xueshe, 1985), 430. (The translation is mine.) Bertrand Russell also commented: "Filial piety, and the strength of the family generally, are perhaps the weakest point in Confucian ethics, the only point where the system departs seriously from common sense." *The Problem of China* (New York: Cosimo, 2007), 40.

1 Mencius's Intention: A Justification for Shun the Sage King

First of all, let us examine the context of this statement in order to determine Mencius's intent in saying that no posterity is the worst unfilial thing:

> Mengzi [i.e. Mencius] said, "Among the three unfilial things, to have no posterity is the worst. Shun's taking a wife without informing his parents was in order to avoid having no posterity. A gentleman regards it as if he had informed them."[3]

As there is no clear information about Mencius's interlocutor or the setting of their conversation, readers may find the above-quoted passage ambiguous. However, we can infer from the context that Mencius is trying to justify the seemingly unfilial behavior of Shun, the sage king, who has married King Yao's two daughters without first informing his parents or receiving their permission.

Mencius always takes Shun as the perfect model of filial morality, saying, "The Way of Yao and Shun is nothing other than filiality and brotherliness."[4] He quotes Shun to explain the crucial importance of filial piety to the family and even to the administration of the whole nation:

> When he [Shun] could not please his parents, he considered himself a failure as a human. When he could not get along with his parents, he considered himself a failure as a son. Shun fathomed the Way of serving one's parents, and his father, the Blind Man, became pleased. The Blind Man was pleased, and the world was transformed. The Blind Man was pleased, and in the world the roles of father and son were settled. This is what is called great filiality.[5]

Here, we see that to "please his parents" and to "get along with his parents" are essential to a filial son. Elsewhere, Mencius himself repeats the importance of getting permission from one's parents: "Those who do not wait for the command of their parents or the words of a matchmaker and instead bore holes through walls to peep at one another and jump over fences to run off together are despised by parents and everyone else in their state."[6] In fact, the marriage custom of waiting "for the command of their parents or the words of a matchmaker" existed in West Zhou (1046–771 BCE) long before Mencius's time. As the *Book of Poetry*

---

3 *Mengzi* 4A:26.1.
4 *Mengzi* 6B:2.5.
5 *Mengzi* 4A:28.1.
6 *Mengzi* 3B4.3.

(*Shijing*) says, "How should one handle taking a bride? One must inform one's father and mother."[7]

It is Shun, the man whom Mencius himself takes as the perfect model of filial morality, who violates this marriage rule – marrying Yao's two daughters without informing his parents. This is entirely at odds with Mencius's criteria of "great filiality." To date, scholarly analysis of *Mengzi* 4A:26.1 has held that Mencius is trying to justify Shun's extraordinary way of contracting marriage on the grounds that "among the three unfilial things, to have no posterity is the worst." It seems that Mencius is quoting a common saying, and one already known to his interlocutor(s). The reason "Shun did not inform his parents before marrying," Mencius says, is that he would not have received their permission and thus would not have produced an heir. And it is in this sense that Mencius considers his action equivalent to informing them, i.e., "as if he had informed them." However, Mencius does not explain the reason why Shun would not have had an offspring if he had informed his parents.

The reason is revealed in *Mengzi* 5A, in Mencius's discussion with Wan Zhang (one of his disciples). Quoting the abovementioned verses from *the Book of Poetry* – "How should one handle taking a bride? One must inform one's father and mother" – which state that before taking a wife one must first notify one's parents, Wan Zhang notes that Shun did not ask his parents for permission before he married Yao's daughters. He says pointedly: "If the rule be indeed as here expressed, no man ought to have illustrated it so well as Shun. How was it that Shun's marriage took place without his informing his parents?" Again, Mencius simply answers, "He could not have taken a bride if he had informed them."[8] He assumes that it is a known truth that Shun's parents are unusually cruel to him, and most likely would not let him marry anyone, let alone Yao's daughters. Later, Wan Zhang attests to this assumption: "Shun's parents ordered him to go up into the granary to finish building it. Then they took away the ladder, and his father set fire to the granary. They ordered him to dig a well. He had left the well, but (not knowing this) they covered the well over."[9]

With parents like these, it is almost impossible for Shun to follow the normal procedure of "waiting for the orders of their parents, and the arrangements of the go-betweens," so as to get married. But if Shun fails to take a wife, he will be in the hopeless situation of having no posterity. So when Mencius says that "a gentleman considers that his doing so was the same as if he had informed

---

[7] The *Book of Poetry* is one of the Five Confucian Classics and the oldest existing collection of Chinese poetry, dating from the eleventh to the seventh centuries BCE.
[8] *Mengzi* 5A:2.
[9] *Mengzi* 5A:2.

them," he makes an implicit distinction between two levels of 'filial piety' (*xiao*). On the one hand, if Shun had reported to his parents, he might not have received their permission, but at least he would have fulfilled a basic level of filial piety, that is, what Mencius calls "to get along with his parents." However, for Mencius, Shun's action fulfills a higher level of filial piety: marrying in order to produce offspring for his parents and his ancestors. Because Shun knows that his parents will not let him marry, the only way for him to reach that higher level of filial piety is not to ask their permission. It is in this sense that Mencius considers Shun's action equivalent to informing them, i.e., "as if he had informed them." As Zhu Xi (1130–1200 CE), a Song dynasty Confucian scholar, comments, "To inform them [Shun's parents] is ritual. Not informing them is discretion ... In general, to use discretion and hit the mean is no different from the correct standard."[10] Shun's action is thus in accordance with this higher level of filial piety.

2 Why Is Tamar More Righteous Than Judah?

After he realizes that Tamar, his daughter-in-law, has cheated him into unlawful sexual intercourse and conceived a child, Judah declares, "She has been more righteous than I, because I did not give her to Shelah my son."[11] We find it helpful to interpret Judah's obscure claim along the same lines as Mencius's.

The story of Judah and Tamar is as follows: After the death of Er, Judah's first son, Judah asks his second son, Onan, to have a son with his sister-in-law, to "raise up offspring" for his dead brother. But Onan refuses to perform his duty for Tamar and his brother, so he is killed by God. Tamar, childless, demands her right to conceive by her deceased husband's brother: in this case, Judah's youngest son, Shelah. But Judah deceives her. When Tamar realizes that Judah will never give Shelah to her, she sets a trap for Judah. Judah unwittingly has sex with her, which results in the conception of a child. When he first learns that his daughter-in-law has become pregnant, Judah calls for her execution. But when he finally comes to realize the truth, he revokes his order to "let her be burned." Instead, he acknowledges the twins Tamar will soon bear to him, saying, "She has been more righteous than I, because I did not give her to Shelah my son."[12]

Theological interpretations of Judah's comment include: 1) "once again are illustrated the effects of the covenant people forgetting the importance of marry-

---

10 Van Norden, trans., *Mengzi*, 100.
11 Gen. 38:26.
12 Gen. 38:7–26.

ing in the covenant"[13]; 2) the failure to honor one's commitments often leads to greater trouble[14]; and 3) "Judah has learned to be honest, to bear responsibility, and to be merciful."[15] But these explanations do not justify Tamar, who has also committed the crimes of adultery and licentiousness.

As this story involves an ancient custom, that of levirate marriage, we will give some explanation here. Levirate marriage, which is mandated in Deuteronomy 25 of the Hebrew Bible, obliges a man to marry the widow of his childless brother. This law demands that: 1) the brother(s) of a deceased man who has died childless must marry the widow; and 2) "the first son that she bears shall be accounted to the dead brother, that his name may not be blotted out in Israel." The duty to bear a child for the dead is extraordinarily important. If the *levir*, the 'brother-in-law,' refuses to comply with his obligation, he and his family will be humiliated.[16]

Some researchers, interpreting the story from the perspective of levirate marriage law, have concluded that the time of Judah and Tamar was long before the formal giving of the law in Deuteronomy that permits "the surviving brother to refuse to marry his brother's widow, provided he submits to the ceremony of Halizah."[17] These scholars quote examples to illustrate that "there is precedent in Assyrian law for a woman marrying her father-in-law if necessary."[18] But this does not necessarily justify Tamar's winning her right "by unorthodox and hazardous means." Otherwise, the story of Genesis would not add, "And he did not lie with her again," immediately after Judah acknowledges that Tamar "is more righteous than I."[19] Other scholars, such as Claus Westermann, interpret Tamar's story as the victory of a woman who "procures for herself her right to have a son and inheritance from husband's family."[20] Ben Spackman claims, "Tamar had

---

13 Church Educational System, "Genesis 37–50," in *Old Testament Student Manual (Religion 301)*, third edition (Salt Lake City, UT: The Church of Jesus Christ of Latter-day Saints, 2003), 93–100.
14 "Genesis–2 Samuel," in *Old Testament Student Manual*, 94.
15 Andrew Cort, "Judah and Tamar: How Judah Became a 'Tzaddik' (A Righteous Man)," Ezine Articles, December 18, 2010, accessed June 9, 2021, http://ezinearticles.com/?Judah-and-Tamar:-How-Judah-Became-a-Tzaddik-(A-Righteous-Man)&id=5577997.
16 Deut. 25:6–10.
17 Susan Niditch, "The Wronged Woman Righted: An Analysis of Genesis 38," *Harvard Theological Review* 72, no. 1 (1979): 148.
18 Claire Gottlieb, *Varieties of Marriage in the Bible: And their Analogue in the Ancient World* (New York: New York University Press, 1989), 169.
19 Gen. 38:26.
20 Claus Westermann, *Genesis 37–50: A Commentary,* trans. John J. Scullion (Minneapolis, MN: Augsburg, 1986), 52.

justifiably manipulated Judah into carrying out the responsibility he had shirked for many years, depriving her in the process of children, of inheritance, and of the opportunity to remarry."[21]

The co-authors of this essay believe that these interpretations result from the naïve assumption that the ancient Israelites adhered to the same conception of personal identity and individual rights as we do today. In ancient Israel, as Robert Di Vito accurately points out, the system "with strict subordination of individual goals to those of the extended lineal group, is designed to ensure the continuity and survival of the family."[22]

Apparently, Tamar knows the probable consequence of her actions. So she makes a careful plan: she "put[s] on a veil, wrap[s] herself up," and, pretending to be a prostitute, demands Judah's seal, cord, and staff as surety. When she is discovered to be pregnant and is brought out to be burned, she presents these tokens of Judah's identity (i.e., his staff, seal, and cord). Why does she knowingly violate the law? Because she knows that depriving the deceased of having an heir is a far graver sin than the crimes of adultery and incest. So Judah's claim that Tamar is "more righteous" follows the same logic as does Mencius's claim for Shun. Susan Niditch also takes Tamar's action as an "unusual adherence to the levirate law [that] takes precedence over an incest law."[23]

At least one other biblical story also follows this principle. Ruth has long been considered a perfect woman in Jewish and Christian traditions. She has many virtues: she is docile, kind-hearted, hard-working, and loyal to her husband's family. But one of her behaviors seems controversial. After her husband and all the other males in the family die in a famine, Ruth, with the help of her mother-in-law, Naomi, entices Boaz, a rich relative of her husband's family, in the granary. Their first child is taken by Naomi, the mother of her late husband, and becomes Naomi's son. Like Tamar, Ruth is praised by her community – her neighbors tell Naomi that Ruth "is better to you than seven sons."[24]

From the description in Genesis 38 of Tamar's death sentence for her adultery and resulting pregnancy, we can see that it was regarded as immoral and illegal for a married woman or a widow to have illicit sexual relations with a man who was not her husband. The story of Ruth was recorded in the period of Judges (1230–1030 BCE) – much later than the time of Judah and Tamar – but

---

[21] Ben Spackman, "The Story of Judah and Tamar," *Religious Educator* 11, no. 1 (2010): 65–76.
[22] Quoted in Kevin J. Madigan and Jon D. Levenson, *Resurrection: The Power of God for Christians and Jews* (New Haven, CT, and London: Yale University Press, 2008), 110.
[23] Niditch, "The Wronged Woman Righted," 148. For the text of the law concerning incest, see Leviticus 18.
[24] Ruth 4:15.

Ruth's seducing the rich old man Boaz was still a transgression of social ethics and could not be counted as a virtue. This can be inferred from the text itself. Ruth and Boaz sleep in the field and depart at dawn: "She rose before one person could distinguish another." Afterward, Boaz orders, "Let it not be known that the woman came to the threshing floor."[25] However, their behavior is not condemned. All three characters involved – Ruth, Naomi, and Boaz – receive God's blessing. Adele Reinhartz observes, "The story portrays Ruth, Naomi and Boaz as models of *hesed*, that is, of loyalty and commitment that go beyond the bounds of law or duty."[26]

The reason, we believe, is that Ruth's arguably seductive behavior is another example of choosing the lesser of the two evils. Like Tamar's seduction of her father-in-law in order to to produce an heir for her dead husband, Ruth's seduction of Boaz is also performed with the aim of continuing the afterlife of her dead husband and the life of his family line.

Now it is clear why Judah revokes his order to burn Tamar for adultery after he realizes the truth – and why he praises Tamar as "more righteous than I." The principle here is identical to that of Mencius's apology for Shun.

It is in this sense that failure to produce an offspring on behalf of the deceased or his family was the worst unfilial thing in the ancient Israelite and Chinese societies. The wise king Shun's marrying without informing his parents is a sin, and Tamar's manipulating her father-in-law into incest is also a sin. But worse is the sin of having no posterity for the deceased or his family – or not even attempting to produce an heir. The expedients by which Shun and Tamar (as well as Ruth) proceed are in service to a higher level of *xiao*, 'filial piety,' or righteousness.

3 Why Is Not Having Offspring the Gravest Unfilial Sin?

For modern readers, it is reasonable to suppose that filial piety entails respect and support for one's parents and winning honor for them rather than bringing them shame. In this sense, many would agree with Matteo Ricci when he harshly criticizes the saying, "Having no posterity is the gravest of the three unfilial things," and proves it a ridiculously absurd dogma. What does producing sons have to do with *xiao* ('filial piety')? If filial piety means serving one's parents well, one can

---

25 Ruth 3:14–15.
26 Adele Reinhartz, "Ruth," in *The Jewish Study Bible* (Oxford: Oxford University Press, 2004), 1578.

certainly do so without having sons. But as Li Chenyang points out, "People who think along this line [. . .] have overlooked the understanding of the continuation of life after death in Confucianism."[27] Similarly, we can say that those who interpret Tamar's action as justifiably procuring "for herself her right to have a son and inheritance from her husband's family" have overlooked the relationship between individual and family as well as the understanding of the continuity of life after death in ancient Israel.

But first of all, let us determine the purpose of having an heir for both the ancient Israelites and the Chinese.

3.1 Male Offspring and Ancestor Worship

Zhao Qi (d. 201 CE), a Han dynasty commentator, gives a detailed explanation of "the three actions that are said to be unfilial." "Flattering and tempting one's parents to do what is not righteous is one," he declares. "When one's household is poor and one's parents are old, to not take a job for a salary is a second one. To not take a wife and have no children, cutting off the sacrifices to one's ancestors, is a third. Among these three, to have no posterity is the worst."[28]

To be filial does not mean just taking good care of one's parents and respecting and honoring them. It also refers to the son's obligation to marry. The final purpose of marrying and begetting children is not simply to support one's own parents but to guarantee the continuation of the sacrifice to the ancestors. Examples from the earliest sources, such as the *Book of Documents* (*Shangshu*), the *Book of Poetry*, and numerous bronze inscriptions, show a close connection between *xiao* ('filial piety') and ancestor worship as early as the Western Zhou (1046–771 BCE).[29] Researchers such as Arthur Waley find that almost all passages in the *Book of Poetry* containing the word *xiao* refer in some way to ancestor worship.[30] According to Song Jinlan, the word *xiao* in the *Book of Poetry* signifies three things for a son: 1) producing offspring and passing down the family property and/or business; 2) having children to continue the family lineage; and 3) making sacrifices to one's ancestors to win their protection for numerous

---

27 Li Chenyang, "Shifting Perspectives: Filial Morality Revisited," *Philosophy East and West* 47, no. 2 (1997): 220.
28 Van Norden, trans., *Mengzi*, 100.
29 Donald Holzman, "The Place of Filial Piety in Ancient China," *Journal of the American Oriental Society* 118, no. 2 (April–June 1998): 185–199.
30 Arthur Waley, *Analects of Confucius* (London: Allen and Unwin, 1949), 38.

descendants.[31] There are more references to the relation between filial piety and ancestor worship in Confucian classics. The *Analects* quote Yao the sage king, who emphasizes the importance of ancestor worship in managing a state:

> He revived states that had been extinguished, restored families whose line of succession had been broken, and called to office those who had retired into obscurity, so that throughout the kingdom the hearts of the people turned towards him. What he attached chief importance to were the food of the people, the duties of mourning, and sacrifices.[32]

For Yao the sage king, the revival of an extinguished state and a broken family line are of equal importance. The two most important things for a ruler are "the food of the people, the duties of mourning, and sacrificing (to the dead)." Both Confucius and his disciple Zengzi explain filial piety in this way: "When parents are alive, they should be served according to propriety; when they are dead, they should be buried according to propriety; and they should be sacrificed to according to propriety – this may be called filial piety."[33] Zengzi even associates ancestor worship with the virtue of the people: "Let there be a careful attention to perform the funeral rites to parents, and let them be followed when long gone with the ceremonies of sacrifice – then the virtue of the people will resume its proper excellence."[34] The "ceremonies of sacrifice" to the ancestors, which entailed "burning incenses" in front of the tablets carved with their names, is one of the important signs of the continuation of a family line. Customarily, the host of the sacrificial rituals is the son of the dead, because, as Confucius said, "For a man to sacrifice to a spirit (ancestor) which does not belong to him is flattery."[35] That is why, in Chinese, to have male descendants is called 继香火, 'to keep the incense burning.' Without a son to worship his ancestors, the family line will be disrupted. This partly explains why King Yao considers the revival of a broken family line as important as that of an extinguished state.

However, the revival of a broken family line does not only mean the restoration of the ceremonial sacrifice to the tablets with the ancestors' names (as it is commonly understood today). It also concerns the continuation of the life after death.

---

31 Song Jinlan, "Xiao de wenhua neihan jiqi shanbian" [*Xiao* and the evolution of its connotations: A cultural interpretation of *xiao*], *Qinghai Social Sciences* 3 (1994): 72.
32 *Analects* 20:1, in *The Four Books*, trans. James Legge (Changsha: Hulan Publishing House, 1992).
33 *Analects* 2:5.
34 *Analects* 1:9.
35 *Analects* 2:24.

3.2 Posterity and the Continuation of the Dead

Researchers have noted that in Confucianism there is no Heaven to ensure an eternal life as is the case in later Judaism and Christianity. The Confucians have to look elsewhere to find the meaning of life and to satisfy the almost universal human desire for immortality.[36] One solution to this quandary is the continuation of the family line. As Wang Qingxin says, "While each individual human being is very precious as an integral part of the clan family's biological bloodline, [...] it is possible for the family bloodline to survive and live in the earthly world eternally so long as each generation of male descendants carries out their utmost filial obligations and fathers a new generation of male descendants."[37] A male heir is the assurance of the continuity of the dead and of his family bloodline. This continuity – it bears repeating – is not simply his own personal immortality but the immortality of the entire family line.

This was also true for the ancient Israelites. As Kevin Madigan and Jon Levenson observe, "There is no antipode to Sheol in the sense of a heavenly locale to which the blessed go after death – no postmortem Heaven or Garden of Eden to which those loyal to God can look forward." The happiness of the Israelites after death "had a great deal to do with the fact that their deepest identities were inextricably embedded in the continuation of their families."[38] That is to say, a happy ending for a blessed man is the continuation of his family line through later generations. It is in this way that the individual can expect the continuation of his life after death. Claire Gottlieb's study of levirate marriage arrives at a similar conclusion: "The ancients believed that a man lived on through his posterity."[39]

The reason, as Jon D. Levenson and Li Chenyang reiterate, is that individual identity and the meaning of individual life in ancient Israelite and Confucian societies are inseparable from the identity and meaning of the individual's family, clan, and nation: "The principal community in which the individual was so solidly embedded was the family. When identity continues after death, it does so in the form of descendants, not in the form of the individual." And in ancient Israelite society, Levenson and Madigan argue, "in which identity is so deeply embedded in family structures, life is, as we have seen, largely characterized by

---

[36] Li, "Shifting Perspectives: Filial Morality Revisited," 211.
[37] Qingxin K. Wang, "The Confucian Conception of Transcendence and Filial Piety," in *The Renaissance of Confucianism in Contemporary China*, ed. Fang Ruiping (New York: Springer, 2011), 80.
[38] Kevin J. Madigan and Jon D. Levenson, *Resurrection: The Power of God for Christians and Jews* (New Haven, CT, and London: Yale University Press, 2008), 80–81.
[39] Gottlieb, *Varieties of Marriage in the Bible*, 150.

the emergence of new generations who stand in continuity and deference to the old."[40] The passages about the deaths of Abraham, Jacob, Joseph, and Job in the Hebrew Bible show that "they die with lives fulfilled and seem to face no future terrors or miseries whatsoever." This is because, for the ancient Israelites, the major focus of God's blessing "is family, particularly the continuation of one's lineage through having descendants (preferably many of them) alive at one's death."[41] (See God's promise to Abram in Genesis 12, 15, and 17, as well as his promises to the other patriarchs.)

If we imagine ourselves in the position of ancient Israelites and Chinese, we may find it easier to understand why Mencius considers Shun's behavior as a higher level of filial piety and why Judah, instead of killing Tamar, claims that she is more righteous than he. It can also help us explain why those scholar-officials in the Ming dynasty (1368–1644 CE) China who wanted to convert to Christianity could not accept the bachelorhood of Jesuits like Matteo Ricci. They quoted Mencius's saying – "having no male heir is the gravest offence against filial piety" – to argue that if "the life of all our forefathers has been passed on to my generation, how can it be cut off because of me?"[42] To Confucians, the begetting of heirs is by no means a matter of personal choice – it is a matter of the life or death of all ancient ancestors and the continuity of the family line. A man cannot procure his own immortality by converting to Christianity at the cost of discontinuing his ancestors' life after death. When Matteo Ricci attacked Mencius for his teaching that the lack of a male heir was the gravest offence against filial piety, he was apparently avoiding the deeper meaning of this dogma: ancestor worship and its relation to the immortality of the dead.

3.3 Filial Piety and Concubinage

In the modern era, the teaching that the lack of a male heir is the gravest offence against filial piety has been critiqued time and time again, partly because it is often a cheap excuse for a man to procure more wives and concubines. However, modern critics frequently overlook the factor that customs like levirate marriage, sanctioned in ancient Israel and other civilizations, were forbidden in China. By requiring the brother or other male relatives of the

---

40 Madigan and Levenson, *Resurrection*, 156.
41 Madigan and Levenson, *Resurrection*, 71.
42 Ricci, *The True Meaning of the Lord of Heaven*, 430.

dead to marry the widow or father a son for the dead, levirate marriage guarantees the continuation of the life of the dead. However, Confucian culture is an exception. Early in the Western Zhou dynasty (ca. 11th century–771 BCE), Chinese law forbade marriage between members of the same family clan. It was mandated in two Confucian classics (*Guoyu*, a collection of anecdotic histories of the Spring and Autumn period, and *Zuozhuan*, a parallel tradition and commentary on the *Spring and Autumn Annals*) that marriage could not be arranged from the same surname (i.e., the same clan) and that any sexual relations between a man and his sister-in-law were to be considered as both ethically incestuous and biologically unhealthy for reproduction.

In order to ensure the ceaseless burning of incense to the ancestors, i.e. the survival of the deceased, a man was allowed to divorce his wife simply because she could not bear him a son. In Chinese traditional accounts such as the *Records of Ritual Matters by Dai the Elder*, a collection of ritual observations written from 206 BCE through 8 CE, a wife's failure to produce a male heir constitutes one of the seven compelling grounds for expelling her from the marriage. Another means of begetting sons was for a man to procure concubines. This is similar to the custom in ancient Israel. When Abraham's wife Sarah found herself unable to have children, she arranged for her maidservant Hagar to become the concubine of Abraham and to bear an heir for him. So did Rachel, Jacob's dearest wife, who gave Jacob her maid Bilhah as a concubine.

Conclusion

We have argued in this paper that a higher level of filial piety is to be found in Mencius's teaching on the lack of a male heir and in his justification of Shun's marrying without first informing his parents. We have further argued that this line of thinking may provide a more reasonable explanation for Judah's defense of Tamar as more righteous than he, insofar as she has reversed the terrible fate of her dead husband by giving him heirs.

There is one important caveat. We can by no means conclude that posterity was the only afterlife for ancient Israelites and Chinese. On contrary, we believe that there is another, more important, afterlife: the survival of one's name. But that is another topic that needs to be further discussed.

References

Church Educational System. *Old Testament: Genesis–2 Samuel: Religion 301 Student Manual*. Salt Lake City, UT: Church of Jesus Christ of Latter-day Saints, 1981.
Dai De 戴德. "Da Dai Liji" 大戴礼记 [Records of ritual matters by Dai the Elder]. Accessed October 14, 2019. http://ctext.org/da-dai-li-ji.
Di Vito, Robert. "Old Testament Anthropology and the Construction of Personal Identity." *Catholic Biblical Quarterly* 61, no. 2 (1999): 217–38.
Gottlieb, Claire. *Varieties of Marriage in the Bible and Their Analogues in the Ancient World*. New York: New York University Press, 1989.
Holzman, Donald. "The Place of Filial Piety in Ancient China." *Journal of the American Oriental Society* (April–June 1998): 185–199.
Li Chenyang. "Shifting Perspectives: Filial Morality Revisited." *Philosophy East and West* 47, no. 2 (1997): 211–232.
Madigan, Kevin J. and Jon D. Levenson. *Resurrection: The Power of God for Christians and Jews*. New Haven, CT, and London: Yale University Press, 2008.
Niditch, Susan. "The Wronged Woman Righted: An Analysis of Genesis 38." *Harvard Theological Review* 72, no. 1 (1979): 143–149.
Ricci, Matteo 利玛窦. *Tianzhu shiyi* 天主實義 [The true meaning of the Lord of Heaven]. Taiwan: Lisi xueshe, 1985.
Russell, Bertrand. *The Problem of China*. New York: Cosimo, 2007.
Song Jinlan 宋金蘭. "Xiao de wenhua neihan jiqi shanbian" "孝的文化內涵及其嬗變 —— 孝字的文化闡釋" [*Xiao* and the evolution of its connotations: A cultural interpretation of *xiao*]. *Qinghai shehui kexue* 青海社會科學 [Qinghai social sciences] 3 (1994): 70–76.
Spackman, Ben. "The Story of Judah and Tamar." *Religious Educator* 11, no. 1 (2010): 65–76.
Van Norden, Bryan W., trans. *Mengzi with Selections from Traditional Commentaries*. Indianapolis: Hackett, 2008.
Waley, Arthur. *Analects of Confucius*. London: Allen and Unwin, 1949.
Wang, Qingxin K. "The Confucian Conception of Transcendence and Filial Piety." In *The Renaissance of Confucianism in Contemporary China*, edited by Fan Ruiping, 75–90. New York: Springer, 2011.
Westermann, Claus. *Genesis 37–50: A Commentary*. Translated by John J. Scullion. Minneapolis, MN: Augsburg, 1986.

Cao Jian
3 The Impact of Ancient Israelite Prophets on Modern Chinese Intellectuals

Starting in the 1920s and for the next twenty years or more, Chinese intellectuals took certain figures from the Hebrew Bible as models for Chinese nation-building.[1] Their interpretations were in most cases receptor culture- and reader-oriented, adjusted to their own urgent concerns. In addition, they frequently modified these figures in accord with modern Euro-American ideas of the period. This essay examines writings on the Hebrew Bible by well-known as well as more obscure Chinese authors, regardless of their ideologies. Due to space constraints, my discussion relies to a large extent on several commentators only, but they are representative enough to demonstrate the growth and development of Chinese biblical commentary in this era.

Many Chinese intellectuals turned to the prophets of ancient Israel and created idealized images of them in their interpretive efforts to set ideal examples.[2] More than ever before, the period of the May Fourth movement and the New Culture movement witnessed a remarkable interest in Hebrew Bible prophets among Chinese intellectuals. To understand this interest, we must first clarify the meaning of "prophet" according to Chinese translators of the Hebrew Bible. Second, we must explore the modern outlook of Hebrew Bible prophets according to Chinese intellectuals, as well as the significance of Hebrew Bible prophets within current ideas of patriotism, nationalism, and universalism. For these writers, some prophets, such as Amos and Jeremiah, were more important than others.

---

[1] This essay is written in memory of Irene Eber (1929–2019), the late Professor Emerita of Sino-Jewish Studies at the Hebrew University of Jerusalem and the author's doctoral supervisor. Professor Eber grew up in an Ashkenazi Jewish family in Halle, Germany, survived the Holocaust, studied for degrees in the United States; and lived in Jerusalem starting in the 1970s.

This essay is a phrasal achievement of the following research projects: (1) "Historical Consciousness of Jews in the Modern Era" (18YJA730001), supported by the Research and Planning Fund for the Humanities and Social Sciences of the Ministry of Education; and (2) "Construction of a New Notion of History of the State of Israel" (19VJX057), supported by the National Social Science Fund.

[2] Almost all the interpretations of Hebrew Bible prophets were positive. Cai Yuanpei nevertheless noted that Hebrew Bible prophets were superstitious and irrational. See Guo Zhanbo, "Caiyuanpei de shidai he tade sixiang" [Cai Yuanpei's times and his thoughts], in *Caiyuanpei xiansheng quanji* [All works by Mr. Cai Yuanpei], ed. Sun Changwei (Taipei: Commercial Press, 1968), 1633.

The word "prophet" in the Hebrew Bible was usually rendered *xianzhi*, 'a person who foreknows,' but most Chinese intellectuals were more interested in its more complex meaning in the Hebrew Bible. In fact, Li Rongfang complained that the term *xianzhi* for Hebrew Bible prophets had already lost two meanings, namely 'a person who speaks in place of God' and 'a person who speaks in front of the masses.' Consequently, the prophetic spirit had not developed in Chinese society,[3] and morality and ethics had declined.[4] Since prophets were responsible to both God and man, the prophet was called "a person who demonstrates and recounts God's edict," "God's spokesman," or "an inspired preacher of foresight."[5]

For intellectuals who respected both biblical and Chinese culture, the Hebrew Bible revealed that there was no significant difference between prophets and historians. Although prophets were more interested in the present and future, while historians paid more attention to the past, both attempted to exert an impact on human life. Therefore, the prophetic and the historical writings in the Hebrew Bible were the same kind of literature, despite their different perspectives, and needed to be discussed together rather than separately.[6] Indeed, the masses did not understand the intention and meaning of history, which explained God's will and action. God had enlightened the prophets so that they would interpret the meaning of history and introduce its truths to the unenlightened masses.[7]

Some intellectuals believed that the ideal man in the modern era would combine the figures of biblical prophet and Chinese sage. Zhao Zichen, a professor of Protestant theology at Yenching University, held that the first objective of higher theological education was to train and develop prophets. But he criticized the old type of prophet in the Hebrew Bible for showing "only one side of the picture." He explained that, in antiquity, even a shepherd could be a prophet as long as he truly heard God's call – whereas in modern China, the new type of

---

3 Li Rongfang, *Amosi zhushi* [A commentary on Amos] (Shanghai: Christian Literature Society, 1933), 1.
4 Li Rongfang, "Shengjing de xiaoyong" [The usefulness of the Bible], *Zhenli yu shengming* [Truth and life] 8, no. 2 (April 1934): 86.
5 Zhu Weizhi, *Jidujiao yu wenxue* [Christianity and literature] (Shanghai: Shanghai Shudian, 1992), 196–97, first published in 1940. According to Zhu, Christianity developed the art of preaching to its climax by combining the spirit of the ancient Hebrew prophets and Greek and Latin rhetoric.
6 Li Rongfang, *Xiandai qingnian jiuyue bidu* [Hebrew Bible selections for present-day youth] (Shanghai: Zhonghua Jidujiao Nüqingnianhui Quanguo Xiehui, 1933), 48 and 89–90.
7 Ai Silan (author's original name unknown), "Xinyue yu jiuyue" [The New Testament and the Hebrew Bible], trans. Zhang Xisan, *Shengming* [Life] 3, no. 6 (March 1923): 3–5.

prophet must have perfect learning and be socially engaged.⁸ Zhao's emphasis on perfect learning and social responsibility was drawn from the Confucian ideal of the sage.

Treating *tian*, 'heaven,' as equal to God and the biblical prophets as equivalent to the Chinese sages, Liu Songyun quoted *Mencius*: "Heaven, in producing the people, has given to those who first attain understanding the duty of awakening those who are slow to understand." A merciful *tian*, or 'God,' had bestowed extraordinary spiritual enlightenment on a *xianzhi*, or 'prophet,' so that heaven might have assistance in governing the world. The aim of the prophets was to help the masses see what was right, warn them of future judgments, and save them from "the sea of retribution."⁹ Some intellectuals even wrote that the Hebrew Bible prophets, like the Chinese sages, were interested in this world and believed in rewards through one's own effort.¹⁰

Foreigners, too, joined the discussion, arguing that the Hebrew Bible prophets and the Chinese sages emphasized the same ideas. According to Lucius C. Porter, for example, the prophets and sages alike revealed the same outlook on historical philosophy, which could be easily seen by comparing the Book of Deuteronomy and *Shiji* [the Book of History]. Both sages and prophets highlighted *li*, 'rites,' which originally came from *tian*, and both took care of national, family, and personal affairs. In this aspect, the Books of Leviticus and Numbers could be compared with *Liji* [the Book of Rites]. Both emphasized morality, whether private or public. The righteousness for which the prophets advocated was identical with Mencius's ideas of *ren*, 'benevolence,' and *yi*, 'righteousness.' The Hebrews stressed personal morality, while Confucius advocated *zhong*, 'loyalty,' and *xu*, 'consideration.' Finally, both longed for an ideal society in the future.¹¹

Because the Chinese sages were highly esteemed, twentieth-century intellectuals highlighted and even exaggerated the importance of the biblical prophets to Judaism and Christianity. Yuan Ding'an declared that the prophets and the law were synonymous with Judaism, while Zhu Weizhi wrote that prophetic literature reflected the main features of Hebrew and biblical literature – that is, the intui-

---

8 Zhao Zichen, "Wo dui zhongguo gaodeng shenxue jiaoyu de mengxiang" [My dream about higher theological education in China], *Zhenli yu shengming* 8, no. 7 (December 1934): 344–45.
9 Liu Songyun, "Lun yisaiyashu shangban zhi dazhi" [The main idea of the First Isaiah], *Shenxue zhi* [Theological quarterly] 7, no. 2 (June 1921): 21. See the Chinese of the quotation in *Mengzi* [Mencius] 5B:1 and its translation in D. C. Lau, trans., *Mencius* (Hong Kong: Chinese University of Hong Kong Press, 2003), 217.
10 Yuan Dingan, *Youtaijiao gailun* [Introduction to Judaism] (Shanghai: Commercial Press, 1935), 20–21.
11 Bo Chenguang (Lucius C. Porter), "Zhongguo de jiuyue" [China's Hebrew Bible], translator unknown, *Zhenli yu shengming* 2, nos. 9–10 (May 1927): 241–43.

tive recognition of God in trials and tribulations.¹² Chinese Christian intellectuals argued that Christian ethics originated in the thoughts of the Jewish prophets, who had not only inspired Jesus's religious experience but also influenced his wisdom and virtues.¹³ Non-Christian Chinese intellectuals, like Hu Shi, also believed in an inherent relationship between the prophets of the Hebrew Bible and the messianism of Christianity.¹⁴ However, they did not consider the role of God. What excited them were the prophets themselves, whom they interpreted as ideal men. These non-Christian intellectuals, who usually displayed more freedom in advocating for their own ideas, often went beyond the limits of apologetics. Two examples of this phenomenon are Zhang Dongsun and Lu Xun.

Zhang Dongsun believed that the religious leader Amos, like Jesus, was actually an idealist. Human society improved because the ideals of such men, like sunshine, lit the way for the masses in their perpetual march toward the sun. Since the masses could never reach the sun or realize those ideals, human beings like Amos were also called "enthusiasts with fantasy" just as socialists are called utopians. However, Zhang preferred "ideal" to "fantasy" as the word for the thoughts of those enthusiasts because an ideal was always realistic insofar as it had the power to change and improve reality.

Amos and others like him were not necessarily political leaders but independent-minded individuals of action, gifted with special insights, who criticized their times and told people what society should ideally be like. That is why idealists like Amos were particularly praiseworthy. The Chinese only saw the superficial *li*, 'principle,' which implied an absolute authority, and were satisfied with retaining the status quo rather than making progress. In contrast, Westerners saw the profound and transcendental "rationality," or the so-called "natural law." They realized that no system is really perfect, hence the constant demand for correcting mistakes. As a result, Westerners had become wiser and achieved more.

Zhang further compared idealists like Amos to the scientists of modern times. By "scientists," Zhang actually meant individuals endowed with the scientific spirit of emancipation or idealists who followed the scientific method. In Zhang's view, science itself contained ideals, since its aim was to find a deeper level of

---

12 Yuan, *Youtaijiao gailun*, 72; and Zhu, *Jidujiao yu wenxue*, 52 and 55.
13 For examples of such arguments, see: Yuan Dingan, *Jidujiao gailun* [Introduction to Christianity] (Shanghai: Commercial Press, 1939), 6–8 and 20–24; Hechuan Fengyan (Kagawa Toyohiko), "Yesu de zhihui" [Wisdom of Jesus], trans. Xiao Wenan, *Zhenli yu shengming* 7, no. 6 (April 1933): 28–29; and Zhao Zichen, "Shengjing zai jinshi wenhua zhongde diwei" [The place of the Bible in modern civilization], *Shengming* 6 (January 1921): 19.
14 Hu Shi, "Shuo ru" [On Confucianism], in *Hushi wencun* [Selected works of Hu Shi] (Taipei: Yuandong Tushu Gongsi, 1953), 4:38.

rationality. Zhang highly praised individuals who, like the German philosopher and economist Karl Marx, successfully combined science and idealism. This combination, he believed, explained why Western culture had overwhelmed all others and become the world culture.[15]

In Lu Xun's eyes, Jeremiah, an unyielding "spiritual fighter" for his people's interests, was the most praiseworthy of the prophets. Jeremiah's voice was completely sincere and most powerful because he voiced the aspirations of the common people.[16] According to Kuriyagawa Hakuson, who admired Jeremiah and whose thoughts were introduced by Lu Xun to Chinese readers, the prophets had, through divine inspiration, gained knowledge of the people's unconscious desire for life. This was so because the voice of the people was also the voice of God (*Vox populi, vox Dei*).[17] In fact, this image of Jeremiah reflects Lu Xun's understanding of his own role as a writer in Chinese society. Like Jeremiah, the writer was charged with articulating feelings of discontent of which the common people were not yet consciously aware.

Lu Xun also translated an essay by Anatolij V. Lunačarskij, in which the author argued that, after the nomadic Israelites settled in Canaan, they were spoiled by their heathen agricultural neighbors, who believed in alien gods and encouraged class oppression and exploitation. As a result, the Israelite aristocrats established a monarchy and lived by exploiting the poor. It was the prophets who strongly opposed the new order of oppression and who advocated for the only life worth living: the life of truth, equality, universal love, and simplicity, which had once been ancient Israel's lifestyle and was the only kind of life that God permitted. Like the prophets, modern thinkers such as Thomas Carlyle, Leo Tolstoy, and Jean-Jacques Rousseau also turned to antiquity in order to protest the degeneracy of the modern era. Writing against capitalism and the bourgeoisie, these modern thinkers had also preferred the past, when people led godly lives, to the present, with its malevolent competition and deviation from the orig-

---

15 Zhang Dongsun, *Lixing yu minzhu* [Rationality and democracy] (Hong Kong: Longmeng Shudian, 1968), 110–12 and 114, first published in 1946. Zhang did not necessarily agree with Marxists. He wrote that ideals are often distorted in practice due to "social inertia" or "habituation in the intellectual process" or lack of "intellectual adaptation," which are neglected by Marxists; forces countering social mobility or reform remain active even after fundamental changes in the economic system have occurred. Zhang Donsun, *Sixiang yu shehui* [Thought and society] (Hong Kong: Longmeng Shudian, 1968), 187, first published in 1946.
16 Lu Xun, "Moluo shili shuo" [On the power of *mara* poetry], in *Luxun quanji* [Collected works of Lu Xun] (Beijing: Renmin Wenxue Chubanshe, 1973), 1:55–56 and 101, written in 1907.
17 Chuchuan Baicun (Kuriyagawa Hakuson), "Kumen de xiangzheng" [The symbol of depression], trans. Lu Xun, in *Luxun quanji*, 13: 96, 101, and 104.

inal perfection of human nature. Human beings, they argued, should return to a primitive social organization and a natural existence of mutual love.[18]

Since Lu Xun probably followed the idea of *tian ren heyi*, or 'the unity of heaven and man,' as Lin Yüsheng suggests, a return to the idealized, God-like human life of the past (for which the biblical prophets as well as the modern thinkers Carlyle, Tolstoy, and Rousseau had all advocated) must have sounded perfectly acceptable to him. According to Lin, the Confucian concept of the unity of heaven and man (or of the mind of the Way and the mind of man) entails that transcendental reality and human nature are both integral parts of the same cosmos.[19] If the translation of Lunz's novelette "Zai shamo shang" [In the desert] indicates Lu Xun's awareness of the destructive possibilities of a revolution and distrust of Communism in an earlier period,[20] the translation of Lunačarskij reveals Lu Xun's ideological commitment to – or at least his sympathy with – Marxism in the post-May Fourth era. The implication may be Lu Xun's rejection, or suspicion at least, of evolutionism and his development from a lover of the people to a class-conscious Marxist.[21]

Many admired the prophets because they considered them to be spokesmen for their people. Zhu Weizhi declared that the voice of the people was the voice of God. The great Book of Amos, which was written by the people, owned by the people, and read by the people in the language of the people, should also be read by the Chinese because their times were similar to those of Amos, the poet of complete sincerity.[22] Zhu compared great Chinese poets to the biblical prophets because great poets, he suggested, had prophetic consciousness.[23] His admiration for the prophets sometimes led to untenable comparisons. Zhu Weizhi freely

---

18 Anatolij V. Lunačarskij, "Tuoersitai yu Makesi" [Tolstoy and Marx], trans. Lu Xun, in *Luxun quanji*, 17:265 and 288–97. See the opposite views of Zhang Dongsun above regarding prophets and social ideals.
19 Lin Yü-sheng, "The Morality of Mind and Immorality of Politics: Reflections on Lu Xun, the Intellectual," in Leo Ou-fan Lee, ed., *Lu Xun and His Legacy* (Berkeley: University of California Press, 1985), 114–15.
20 Lev Lunz, "Zai shaomo shang" [In the desert], trans. Lu Xun, in *Luxun quanji* 19:39–49. For a detailed analysis of Lu Xun's translation of this novelette, see Cao Jian, "Moses as a Leader to Modern Chinese Intellectuals, 1920s–1940s," *Journal of Asian and African Studies* 19, no. 1 (2010): 26–47, here 27–29.
21 For Lu Xun's ideological development, see Irene Eber, "Reception of Lu Xun in Europe and America," in Lee, ed., *Lu Xun and His Legacy*, 258–65.
22 Zhu Weizhi, "Amosi – renmin de xianzhi" [Amos – the people's prophet], in Zhu Weizhi, *Wenyi zongjiao lunji* [Essays on literature and religion] (Shanghai: Qingnian Xiehui Shuju, 1951), 112–13, first published in 1949. See Amos as a poet in Zhu Weizhi, *Jidujiao yu wenxue*, 161.
23 Zhu Weizhi, "Wenyiduo lun zongjiao" [Wen Yiduo's comments on religion], in *Wenyi zongjiao lunji* 14, first published in 1949.

compared Jeremiah to Moses, Confucius, Jesus, Zhu Xi, Martin Luther, and Sun Yat-sen. Jeremiah's strong sense of mission or responsibility had made him a great preacher, teacher, hero, ruler, and literary giant, one who even deserved to be called *zhisheng xianshi*, or 'Model Teacher of Myriad Ages' – a title only Confucius himself enjoyed![24]

Finally, patriotism, nationalism, and universalism were seen as particularly attractive features of the prophets. They were passionate patriots, as was most notably expressed in the Book of Lamentations, widely believed to have been written by Jeremiah or by a prophet living at the same time as Jeremiah and influenced by him.[25] The Book of Lamentations was often compared to the poem "Lisao" [The lament] of Qu Yuan. Both works mourned national calamities, and they resembled each other in literary styles and religious morality. Also significant was Jeremiah's impact on the patriotic poet George Gordon, Lord Byron.[26]

The patriotic passion of ancient biblical prophets was often interpreted differently. Proponents of nationalism did not always distinguish it from patriotism; for them, the patriotic prophets were simply nationalists. The essential facts of life for ancient biblical prophets were national suffering as well as moral decline. National suffering gave birth to a heroic spirit among the prophets. Whenever national suffering was imminent or unbearable, the prophet played a crucial role in warning his compatriots, urging them to repent, and giving them hope of redemption.[27]

In response to those who believed Christianity and nationalism to be incompatible, the Chinese Christian scholar Wu Leichuan claimed that the best way to implement nationalism in modern China was to arm the disorganized Chinese people with the true spirit of Christianity, as exemplified by the strong national unity of the Jewish people. "Jewish prophets" through the ages had been patriots;

---

24 Zhu Weizhi, *Jidujiao yu wenxue*, 188–89 and 198–99.
25 Li Rongfang, "Xu yi" [Preface no. 1 to *Aige* (the Book of Lamentations), Li's Chinese translation of Lamentations], *Zhenli yu shengming* 5, no. 8 (June 1931): 48–9.
26 Zhu Weizhi, *Jidujiao yu wenxue*, 66 and 75.
27 Zhu Weizhi, *Jidujiao yu wenxue*, 50–52 and 55. Jian Youwen introduced Gerald B. Smith's call for a "democratic" interpretation of biblical doctrines, which focuses on the "heroic" attitude toward the "deeds as well as the sincere morality" of the biblical authors, many of whom were believed to be prophets of the Hebrew Bible. Shi Meifu (Gerald B. Smith), "Shenxue lunli de gaizao" [Reform in theological ethics], trans. Jian Youwen, *Shenming* 6, no. 1 (September 1925): 52. See the original in G. B. Smith, *Social Idealism and the Changing Theology: A Study of the Ethical Aspects of Christian Doctrine* (New York: MacMillan, 1913).

therefore, the Jews had always remained an independent people, attempting to restore their state despite many historical setbacks.[28]

For those who aimed at universalism, the patriotic prophets were not nationalists but universalists. W. H. Hudson proposed that since the function of prophets, broadly speaking, was to transform the spirit of the degenerate world, prophets were not nationalists.[29] It was the universalism expressed by such prophets as Amos, Isaiah, Micah, Jeremiah, and Jonah since the eighth century BCE that was important.[30] But for some, in spite of Amos's belief in a God of all nations,[31] universalism without Jesus was no more than imperialism. Those prophets had indeed contributed to the formation of the messianic ideal, but what they had really longed for was a Jewish empire ruled by a descendant of David. Because the monarch was to rule "from north to south" and govern *tianxia*, or 'the land under heaven,' theirs was an imperialist ideal that must be understood as political messianism.[32]

Promotion of the morality and spiritual faith of the common people would help solve social and religious problems once and for all. For this very reason, Amos and Jeremiah were the most highly praised of the prophets. Zhao Zichen proposed that Amos was the first prophet to establish ethical monotheism as the religion of Israel, even though the prophets who followed him were not completely successful in educating their people until the birth of Jesus,[33] but Li Rongfang proposed that Jeremiah was the first to preach ethical monotheism. Not only did he pronounce the idols of the nations "worthless" (Jer. 10:15 and 14:22, NIV), he also emphasized personal responsibilities and the internal experience of faith. Jeremiah was a prophet for all nations because he maintained that God was for all peoples. This commitment endowed Jeremiah with a keen sense of responsi-

---

28 Wu Zhenchun (Wu Leichuan), "Guojiazhuyi yu jidujiao shifou chongtu" [Is Christianity in conflict with nationalism?], *Shenming* 5, no. 4 (February 1925): 4–5.
29 W. H. Hudson, "Shengjing zhi wenxue de yanjiu" [A literary study of the Bible], *Xiaoshuo yuebao* [Short story monthly] 13, no. 10 (1922): 29, translated by Tang Chengbo and Ye Qifang as "The Bible as Literature," in Arthur S. Peake, ed., *A Commentary on the Bible* (London: T. C. & E. C. Jack, 1920), 18–25.
30 Li Rongfang, "Jiuyue li de guoji guannian" [International ideas in the Hebrew Bible], *Zhenli yu shengming* 2, no.16 (1927): 22.
31 Li Rongfang, *Amosi zhushi*, 3–10 and 18.
32 Li Rongfang, "Yesu yu jidu" [Jesus and Christ], *Shengming* 6, no. 3 (December 1925): 5.
33 Shi Qide (author's original name unknown), "Fazhan yu fenhua" [Development and breakup], trans. Zhao Zichen, *Zhenli yu shengming* 4, no. 12 (April 1930): 9.

bility.³⁴ Probably for that reason, Li Rongfang even felt that Jeremiah resembled Jesus, more so than any other biblical prophet.³⁵

Like Lu Xun, Li Rongfang also introduced Jeremiah as an unyielding fighter – but for a different reason. Jeremiah was a fighter for perfection. Unlike Adam and Eve, Jeremiah did not compromise his personal morality by sacrificing the less perfect for the perfect.³⁶ For this reason, Jeremiah opposed all his contemporaries. He believed that destruction would ultimately facilitate new construction and considered it his mission to destroy, thus becoming the public enemy of his people.³⁷

Even Yuan Ding'an, who was firmly committed to nationalism, admitted that if Judaism had been a tribal religion from the time of Abraham to that of Judges and a national religion during the time of the kingdom of David and Solomon, it had become a universal religion during the time of the prophets. The prophets had already transformed Judaism into an ethical religion by the end of their time. When the Judaism of the prophets spread to the entire world, there would be perpetual peace.³⁸ Interestingly, this idea of an evolution from nationalism to universalism among the Hebrews was also held by other twentieth-century Chinese intellectuals, both Christian and non-Christian. Yuan Ding'an also argued that, being stateless, Jews in the Diaspora held out hope for a national hero or Messiah who would, they believed, arise in the future and lead the conquered people to national rejuvenation. After years of failure to attain that hope, the dream of political revival was shattered, and its content was changed. The zeal for political rejuvenation was replaced by a desire for religious or cultural revival, and the Messiah was transformed from a national hero into a great sage who would deliver all humankind. It was at this very time that Jesus Christ came and was accepted by many as the Messiah.³⁹

Hu Shi pointed out that the Yin people of the Shang dynasty (ca. 1600–ca. 1046 BCE) in Chinese history also had a prophecy of a national hero who would bring about a national and political rejuvenation: "Wubainian biyou wangzhe xing" ('Every five hundred years, a true king should arise').⁴⁰ The Yin people's

---

34 Ba Eyteng (George A. Barton), "Yiselie de zongjiao – shenmingji yu yelimi" [The religion of Israel: the Books of Deuteronomy and Jeremiah], trans. Li Rongfang, *Shengming* 2, no. 3 (October 1921): 4–5; and Zhan Fumin (Fleming James), *Jiuyue renwu zhi* [Personalities of the Hebrew Bible] (Shanghai: Qingnian Xiehui Shuju, 1949), trans. Li Rongfang, 124 and 132.
35 Li Rongfang, *Xiandai qingnian jiuyue bidu*, 143–52.
36 Li Rongfang, "Zuide laiyuan yu xiaoguo" [The origin and effect of sin], *Zhenli yu shengming* 10, no. 1 (March 1936): 12–14.
37 Zhan Fumin, *Jiuyue renwu zhi*, 128–29 and 134.
38 Yuan Ding'an, *Youtaijiao gailun*, 46–47.
39 Yuan Ding'an, *Youtaijiao gailun*, 44.
40 See the Chinese quotation in *Mengzi* 2B:13 and the translation in Lau, *Mencius*, 98–99.

prophecy had partially materialized in Confucius, who, like Jesus, died while the dream of national rejuvenation was still unfulfilled. But Confucius, too, was revived after his death because "ren neng hong dao" ('it is Man who is capable of broadening the Way').[41] He broke through the limits of local cultures and laid a universal foundation for Confucian culture. Confucius thus also became "a light unto the Gentiles."[42] But Hu Shi denied that Confucius was a Messiah like Jesus.[43]

Amos and Jeremiah especially inspired Chinese Christian intellectuals, who believed that the two prophets had upheld ethics and demonstrated a harmony between patriotic passion and the universalist ideal. These major concerns of Chinese Christian intellectuals during a time of social transgression, national crisis, and imperialism clearly show their change in perspectives regarding the Hebrew Bible. Jeremiah, for example, spent much of his career prophesying doom. Yet the implication that a radical change of human nature was possible became a universal value. As a result, in the history of religion, the words of the prophet became a legacy of hope.[44] For his Chinese interpreters, a radical change of human nature did not mean repentance, as Jeremiah had advocated a message of universal moral perfection. Hence, the need to promote ethics.

However, the examples of Jeremiah and Amos do not suggest that other biblical prophets were irrelevant in the new context and not interesting to Chinese intellectuals. Other prophets inspired various interpreters in different ways. Their writings on the Hebrew Bible would seem to be an evolving Chinese exegesis, although more research is needed, to be sure, to substantiate such a bold suggestion.

References

Ai Silan (original name unknown). "Xinyue yu jiuyue" [The New Testament and the Hebrew Bible]. Translated by Zhang Xisan. *Shengming* [Life] 3, no. 6 (March 1923): 1–11. 艾思兰: "新约与旧约", 张锡三译, 《生命》

Ba Eyteng (George A. Barton). "Yiselie de zongjiao – shenmingji yu yelimi" [The religion of Israel: the Books of Deuteronomy and Jeremiah]. Translated by Li Rongfang. *Shengming* 2, no. 3 (October 1921): 1–6. 巴尔滕: "以色列的宗教-申命记与耶利米", 李荣芳译, 《生命》

---

41 See the Chinese quotation in Confucius, *Lunyu* [The Analects], Verse 29 of Book 15, and its translation in D. C. Lau, *The Analects*, 2nd edition (Hong Kong: The Chinese University Press, 1992), 157.
42 Hu Shi, "Shuo ru," 38–39 and 50–52.
43 For details, see Hu Shi, "Shuo ru," 80–81.
44 S. David Sperling, "Jeremiah," in Mircea Eliade, ed., *The Encyclopedia of Religion* (New York: Macmillan, 1987), 8:6.

Bo Chenguang (Lucius C. Porter). "Zhongguo de jiuyue" [China's Hebrew Bible]. Translator unknown. *Zhenli yu shengming* [Truth and life)] 2, nos. 9–10 (May 1927): 240–244. 博晨光: "中国的旧约",《真理与生命》

Cao Jian. "Moses as a Leader to Modern Chinese Intellectuals, 1920s–1940s." *Journal of Asian and African Studies* 19, no. 1 (2010): 26–47.

Chuchuan Baicun (Kuriyagawa Hakuson). "Kumen de xiangzheng" [The symbol of depression]. Translated by Lu Xun. In vol. 13 of *Luxun quanji* [All works by Lu Xun], 95–104. Beijing: Renmin Wenxue Chubanshe, 1973. 厨川白村: "苦闷的象征",《鲁迅全集》

Eber, Irene. "Reception of Lu Xun in Europe and America." In *Lu Xun and His Legacy*, edited by Leo Ou-fan Lee, 258–265. Berkeley: University of California Press, 1985.

Guo Zhanbo. "Caiyuanpei de shidai he tade sixiang" [Cai Yuanpei's times and thoughts]. In *Caiyuanpei xiansheng quanji* [Collected works of Cai Yuanpei], edited by Sun Changwei, 1604–1650. Taipei: Commercial Press, 1968. 郭湛波: "蔡元培的时代和他的思想",《蔡元培先生全集》

Hechuan Fengyan (Kagawa Toyohiko). "Yesu de zhihui" [Wisdom of Jesus]. Translated by Xiao Wenan. *Zhenli yu shengming* 7, no. 6 (April 1933): 23–30. 贺川丰彦: "耶稣的智慧", 萧文安译,《真理与生命》

Hu Shi. "Shuo ru" [On Confucianism]. In vol. 4 of *Hushi wencun* [Selected works of Hu Shi], edited by Hu Shi, 1–83. Taipei: Yuandong Tushu Gongsi, 1953. 胡适: "说儒",《胡适文存》, 胡适编

Hudson, W. H. "Shengjing zhi wenxue de yanjiu" [A literary study of the Bible]. *Xiaoshuo yuebao* [Short story monthly] 13, no. 10 (1922): 1–17. Translated by Tang Chengbo and Ye Qifang from Hudson's "The Bible as Literature" in *A Commentary on the Bible*, edited by Arthur S. Peake, 18–25. London: T. C. & E. C. Jack, 1920. 汤澄波和叶启芳合译: "圣经之文学的研究",《小说月报》

Lau, D. C., trans. *The Analects*. Second edition. Hong Kong: The Chinese University Press, 1992.

Lau, D. C., trans. *Mencius*. Hong Kong: Chinese University of Hong Kong Press, 2003.

Li Rongfang. "Yesu yu jidu" [Jesus and Christ]. *Shengming* 6, no. 3 (December 1925): 1–12. 李荣芳: "耶稣与基督",《生命》

Li Rongfang. "Jiuyue li de guoji guannian" [International ideas in the Hebrew Bible]. *Zhenli yu shengming* 2, no. 16 (1927): 22. 李荣芳: "旧约里的国际观念",《真理与生命》

Li Rongfang. "Xu yi" [Preface no. 1 to *Aige*, Li's Chinese translation of the Book of Lamentations]. *Zhenli yu shengming* 5, no. 8 (June 1931): 48–49. 李荣芳:《哀歌》"序一",《真理与生命》;《哀歌》, 李荣芳译

Li Rongfang. *Amosi zhushi* [A commentary on the Book of Amos]. Shanghai: Christian Literature Society, 1933. 李荣芳:《阿摩司注释》

Li Rongfang. *Xiandai qingnian jiuyue bidu* [Hebrew Bible selections for present-day youth]. Shanghai: Zhonghua Jidujiao Nüqingnianhui Quanguo Xiehui, 1933. 李荣芳:《现代青年旧约必读》

Li Rongfang. "Shengjing de xiaoyong" [The usefulness of the Bible]. *Zhenli yu shengming* 8, no. 2 (April 1934): 82–91. 李荣芳: "圣经的效用",《真理与生命》

Li Rongfang. "Zuide laiyuan yu xiaoguo" [The origin and effect of sin]. *Zhenli yu shengming* 10, no. 1 (March 1936): 7–14. 李荣芳: "罪的来源与效果",《真理与生命》

Lin Yü-sheng. "The Morality of Mind and Immorality of Politics: Reflections on Lu Xun, the Intellectual." In *Lu Xun and His Legacy*, 107–128.

Liu Songyun. "Lun yisaiyashu shangban zhi dazhi" [The main idea of the First Isaiah]. *Shenxue zhi* [Theological quarterly] 7, no. 2 (June 1921): 19–22. 刘松筠: "论以赛亚书上半之大旨", 《神学志》

Lu Xun. "Moluo shili shuo" [On the power of *mara* poetry]. In vol. 1 of *Luxun quanji*, 55–102. 鲁迅: "摩罗诗力说", 《鲁迅全集》

Lunačarskij, Anatolij V. "Tuoersitai yu makesi" [Tolstoy and Marx]. Translated by Lu Xun. In vol. 17 of *Luxun quanji*, 277–298. 卢那卡尔斯基: "托尔斯泰与马克斯", 鲁迅译, 《鲁迅全集》

Lunz, Lev. "Zai shaomo shang" [In the desert]. Translated by Lu Xun. In vol. 19 of *Luxun quanji*, 39–49. 伦支: "在沙漠上", 鲁迅译, 《鲁迅全集》

Shi Meifu (Gerald B. Smith). "Shenxue lunli de gaizao" [Reform in theological ethics]. Translated by Jian Youwen. *Shenming* 6, no. 1 (September 1925): 47–55. Original in G. B. Smith, *Social Idealism and the Changing Theology: A Study of the Ethical Aspects of Christian Doctrine*. New York: Macmillan, 1913. 史美夫: "神学伦理的改造", 简又文译, 《生命》

Shi Qide (original name unknown). "Fazhan yu fenhua" (Development and breakup). Translated by Zhao Zichen. *Zhenli yu shengming* 4, no. 12 (April 1930): 2–12. 施其德: "发展与分化", 赵紫宸译, 《真理与生命》

Sperling, S. David. "Jeremiah." In vol. 8 of *The Encyclopedia of Religion*, edited by Mircea Eliade. New York: Macmillan, 1987. 1–6.

Wu Zhenchun. "Guojiazhuyi yu jidujiao shifou chongtu" [Is Christianity in conflict with nationalism?]. *Shenming* 5, no. 4 (February 1925): 4–5. 吴震春: "国家主义与基督教是否冲突?" 《生命》

Yuan Dingan. *Youtaijiao gailun* [Introduction to Judaism]. Shanghai: Commercial Press, 1935. 袁定安: 《犹太教概论》

Yuan Dingan. *Jidujiao gailun* [Introduction to Christianity]. Shanghai: Commercial Press, 1939. 袁定安: 《基督教概论》

Zhan Fumin (Fleming James). *Jiuyue renwu zhi* [Personalities of the Hebrew Bible]. Translated by Li Rongfang. Shanghai: Qingnian Xiehui Shuju, 1949. 詹辅民: 《旧约人物志》, 李荣芳译

Zhang Dongsun. *Lixing yu minzhu* [Rationality and democracy]. Hong Kong: Longmeng Shudian, 1968. 张东荪: 《理性与民主》

Zhang Dongsun. *Sixiang yu shehui* [Thought and society]. Hong Kong: Longmeng Shudian, 1968. 张东荪: 《思想与社会》

Zhao Zichen. "Shengjing zai jinshi wenhua zhongde diwei" [The place of the Bible in modern civilization]. *Shengming* 6 (January 1921): 1–22. 赵紫宸: "圣经在近世文化中的地位", 《生命》

Zhao Zichen. "Wo dui zhongguo gaodeng shenxue jiaoyu de mengxiang" [My dream about higher theological education in China]. *Zhenli yu shengming* 8, no. 7 (December 1934): 343–353. 赵紫宸: "我对中国高等神学教育的梦想", 《真理与生命》

Zhu Weizhi. *Jidujiao yu wenxue* [Christianity and literature]. Shanghai: Shanghai Shudian, 1992. 朱维之: 《基督教与文学》

Zhu Weizhi. "Amosi – renmin de xianzhi" (Amos – the people's prophet). In *Wenyi zongjiao lunji* [Essays on literature and religion], edited by Zhu Weizhi, 112–133. Shanghai: Qingnian Xiehui Shuju, 1951. 朱维之: "阿摩司·人民的先知", 《文艺宗教论集》, 朱维之编

Zhu Weizhi. "Wenyiduo lun zongjiao" [Wen Yiduo's comments on religion]. In *Wenyi zongjiao lunji*, 12–16. 朱维之: "闻一多论宗教", 《文艺宗教论集》

ZHONG Zhiqing
4 Reading the Song of Songs in Jewish and Chinese Tradition

With a total of eight chapters and 117 verses, the Song of Songs (שִׁיר הַשִּׁירִים), also called the Song of Solomon, is one of the shortest books in the Hebrew Bible, but no other biblical book's ancient interpretations are more extensively documented.[1] A number of significant publications on the Song of Songs have recently appeared in Europe and America.[2]

In Chinese tradition, the Song of Songs has been regarded as a wondrous collection of love lyrics between a young maiden and her beloved. In the Jewish and Christian traditions, it is considered an allegorical celebration of the covenant and love between God and Israel or between Jesus and the Church.

1 Some Basic Questions on Reading the Song of Songs

The Chinese Union Version Bible (和合本圣经), which was originally published in 1919 and is commonly used in China today, follows the Christian tradition, placing the Song of Songs after the Proverbs and Ecclesiastes. The Hebrew Bible includes the Song of Songs in its third part as a collection of "writings," located between Job and Ruth. In rabbinic tradition, the Song of Songs, Ruth, Esther, Lamentations, and Ecclesiastes were together known as the Five Scrolls, or Five Megillot. Among Chinese academic circles, relatively little attention has been paid to reading the Song of Songs in a Jewish context.

---

[1] David Stern, "Ancient Jewish Interpretation of the Song of Songs in a Comparative Context," in *Jewish Biblical Interpretation and Cultural Exchange*, eds. Natalle B. Dohrmann and David Stern (Philadelphia: University of Pennsylvania Press, 2008), 82.
[2] Michael Fishbane, *The JPS Bible Commentary: Song of Songs* (Philadelphia, PA: The Jewish Publication Society, 2015); Rabbi Nosson Scherman and Rabbi Meir Zlotowitz, eds., *Shir Hashirim: A New Translation with a Commentary Anthologized From Talmudic, Midrashic and Rabbinic Sources* (New York: Mesorah, 2015); Robert Williamson Jr., *The Forgotten Books of the Bible: Recovering the Five Scrolls for Today* (Minneapolis, MN: Fortress Press, 2018); Jon D. Levenson, *The Love of God* (Princeton, NJ: Princeton University Press); and Michael V. Fox, "Rereading the Song of Songs and the Ancient Egyptian Love Songs Thirty Years Later," *Die Welt des Orients* 46, no. 1, The Song of Songs and Ancient Egyptian Love Poetry (2016): 8–21.

https://doi.org/10.1515/9783110683943-006

The original Hebrew title of the Song of Songs is שִׁיר הַשִּׁירִים (*Shir Hashirim*), which is rendered in Chinese as 歌中之歌 (*Ge zhong zhi ge*). The first verse of the Hebrew text, שִׁיר הַשִּׁירִים, אֲשֶׁר לִשְׁלֹמֹה, is translated into English as 'The song of songs, which is Solomon's.'[3] The Chinese Union Version translates it as: 所罗门的歌，是歌中的雅歌 (*suoluomen de ge, shi gezhong de yage*). The literal meaning of this sentence in Chinese is 'The song of Solomon is the Song of Songs,' which, in Chinese contexts, indicates that Solomon is the author of the Song of Songs. This Chinese interpretation is similar to Jewish tradition, which also attributed the book to King Solomon.[4] There are also other reasons for this tradition: on the one hand, Solomon is said to have spoken "three thousand proverbs, and his songs numbered a thousand and five"[5]; on the other hand, he is said to have had a sizeable harem consisting of "seven hundred wives, princesses and three hundred concubines."[6]

Although Solomon's name appears several times in the text of the Song of Songs, Michael Coogan assumes that Solomon is not the male lover who speaks in the poem but merely a character to whom the speaker refers in the third person,[7] as in the following passages: "King Solomon made himself a chariot of the wood of Lebanon. He made the pillars thereof silver, the bottom thereof gold, the covering of it of purple, the midst thereof of being with love, for the daughters of Jerusalem"; and "Solomon had a vineyard at Baalhamon; he let out the vineyard unto keepers; everyone for the fruit thereof was to bring a thousand pieces of silver."[8] Moreover, some of the vocabulary in the Song of Songs originated at a much later date than the tenth century BCE, when Solomon lived.[9] In fact, Solomon might not be the author of the Song of Songs. Israeli scholar Athalya Brenner has even proposed that some of the love lyrics – especially those which offer a woman's viewpoint – might actually have been composed by women.[10] It is difficult to date the composition of the Song of Songs with any degree of certainty.[11]

---

[3] *The Holy Scripture: A Jewish Bible According to the Masoretic Text* (Tel Aviv: SINAI, 1996). All biblical quotations in this essay are drawn from this version.
[4] Michael D. Coogan, *The Old Testament: A Historical and Literary Introduction to the Hebrew Scripture* (Oxford: Oxford University Press, 2013), 487.
[5] 1 Kings 5:12.
[6] 1 Kings 11:3.
[7] Coogan, *The Old Testament*, 271.
[8] Song of Sol. 3:9–10 and 8:11–12.
[9] Coogan, *The Old Testament*, 487.
[10] Athalya Brenner, ed., *The Song of Songs: A Feminist Companion to the Bible* (Sheffield: Academic Press, 1993), 87–88.
[11] On this point, Chinese scholars generally quote Roland E. Murphy, *The Song of Songs: A Commentary on the Book of Canticles or the Song of Songs* (Minneapolis, MN: Fortress Press, 1990), 1–5.

Through a close reading, we will see that the Song of Songs consists of poetic speeches, mainly uttered by two young lovers, though with other occasional speakers such as the woman's companions, or "daughters of Jerusalem," and her brothers.[12] The young lovers, who are apparently unmarried, refer to each other as "brother" and "sister." Their dialogue expresses the mutual love between a young woman and her lover. It is full of the pains of longing and the joy of love, which are also visible in the ancient Chinese poetry that I will present afterwards. These poems evoke lush imagery. Comparisons to nature – gardens, vineyards, birds, animals, fruits, flowers, and perfumes – pervade the sequence. Moreover, the speaker praises the loyalty of love, as in the well-known verses: "For love is as strong as death, its jealousy is cruel as the grave: the coals thereof are coals of fire, which hath a most vehement flame. Many waters cannot quench love; neither can the floods drown it: if a man would give all the substance of his house for love, it would utterly be contemned."[13] The question of why a work that expresses the love of men and women alone could be included in the Hebrew Bible and sung during important public occasions such as Passover has been ignored by many Chinese scholars.

2 Reading the Song of Songs in Jewish Tradition

Although there is a long tradition of interpreting the Song of Songs in the Jewish world, according to David Stern, it is not clear exactly when these ancient interpretations began.[14] In his *JPS Bible Commentary: Song of Songs*, Michael Fishbane summarizes two heuristics of the rabbinic tradition. The first, he maintains, takes the Song of Songs in its literal sense, filled with erotic energy, while the second is a sober reinterpretation and spiritual recasting of its contents.[15] The question is not only how these lyrics of human love first entered the Hebrew Bible but also, more significantly, how the Song of Songs was transformed from a series of love lyrics into the single song of religious love that has been so influential in Jewish and Christian traditions and has made such a great impact on modern Hebrew writers.

At this point, Fishbane argues, "We are told 'originally' some authorities decided to have the Song of Songs, Proverbs, and Ecclesiastes (Solomon's Books)

---

[12] Song of Sol. 5:8 and 8:8–9.
[13] Song of Sol. 8:6–7.
[14] David Stern, "Ancient Jewish Interpretation of the Song of Songs in a Comparative Context," in *Jewish Biblical Interpretation and Cultural Exchange*, eds. Natalie B. Dohrmann and David Stern (Philadelphia: University of Pennsylvania Press, 2008), 89.
[15] Fishbane, *The JPS Bible Commentary: Song of Songs*, xxi.

'withdrawn' from public uses because they were deemed mere 'parables' and thus not worthy to be included in the sacred 'Writings.' This action reportedly prevailed until the 'men of Hezekiah' came and 'interpreted' the parable in a way that allowed these works to return to the public domain."[16] Another source can be traced to around 100 CE, when the supreme council of rabbis in Jamnia took up the question of the canonicity of certain books of the Bible. During their discussion, Rabbi Akiva cried, "No Jew ever questioned the sanctity of the Song of Songs; for all of creation does not compare in worth to the day on which the Song of Songs was given to Israel. Indeed, all Scripture is holy, but the Song of Songs is the holiest of the holy."[17] Akiva's words, "the holiest of the holy," were later regarded as the most authoritative by succeeding generations of Jewish scholars. However, how people read the Song of Songs before Akiva was still not clear to us.[18]

Ironically, some modern scholars of biblical studies have unequivocally dismissed the theory that the Song of Songs was originally a religious work.[19] Ariel Bloch, a distinguished professor of Near Eastern studies, and Chana Bloch, an award-winning poet, wrote in the introduction to their new translation of and commentary on the Song of Songs: "The Song of Songs is a poem about the sexual awakening of a young woman and her lover."[20] Pioneering modern biblical literary scholar Robert Alter has claimed, "The POETRY of the Song of Songs is an exquisite balance of ripe sensuality and delicacy of expression and feeling."[21] From a feminist perspective, Israeli scholar Athalya Brenner maintains that the Song of Songs appears to be a completely secular collection of love lyrics, its allegorical interpretations notwithstanding.[22] The loyalty and fidelity in love of between a woman to a husband are specially manifested as: "I am my beloved's, and his desire is toward me."[23]

Although God is perhaps mentioned once, with the opaque expression of אֶשׁ שַׁלְהֶבֶתְיָה ('the blazing flame'), which is translated into 上帝的烈焰 (*shangdi de lieyan*, 'the flame of God') in Chinese, the figure of God is almost totally absent

---

16 Fishbane, *The JPS Bible Commentary: Song of Songs*, xxiii.
17 Gerson D. Cohen, "The Song of Songs and the Jewish Religious Mentality," in *The Samuel Friedland Lectures, 1960–1966* (New York: Jewish Theological Seminar of America, 1966), 1. See also Fishbane, *The JPS Bible Commentary: Song of Songs*, xxii.
18 Interview with Jon Levenson at Harvard, May 2018.
19 Cohen, "The Song of Songs and the Jewish Religious Mentality," 2.
20 Ariel Bloch and Chana Bloch, *The Song of Songs: A New Translation with an Introduction and Commentary* (New York: Random House, 1995), 3.
21 Robert Alter, "The Song of Songs," afterword to *The Song of Songs: A New Translation with an Introduction and Commentary* by Ariel Bloch and Chana Bloch, 119.
22 Brenner, *The Song of Songs*, 28–33.
23 Song of Sol. 7:11.

from the Song of Songs. Why then did a secular poem full of erotic descriptions and dominated by women enter the Hebrew Bible?

According to Gerson Cohen, the "modern" view, which dismissed the theory that the Song of Songs was originally a religious work, had its adherents even in the days of Akiva, who proclaimed anathema against those who regarded the verses of the Song of Songs as erotic. However, modern-day scholars are well aware of the importance of Akiva in the history of biblical interpretation, and all subsequent schools of traditional Judaism have accepted his opinion as fact. Today's exegetes, accordingly, indicate that the Song of Songs was originally included in the canon only because it was believed to be an allegory of the dialogue of love between God and Israel. Then, in a startling reversal, they interpret the text quite literally.[24]

Such allegorical readings of the Song of Songs certainly help guarantee its classic status. However, there is no accurate record of why anyone should have thought of treating the work as an allegory in the first place.[25] Gerson Cohen argued that the understanding of the poem as a love song between God and his chosen nation could be traced back to the time of its initial composition and might even be its original meaning. Although Cohen never said as much, his motive – that is, his desire to understand the origins of this particular allegorical interpretation – filled an important gap in the biblical corpus itself.[26] Following his methodology, we might find some evidence in Hosea 2:18–20:

> And it shall be at that day, saith the Lord,
> that thou shalt say Ishi;
> and shalt say unto me no more Baali.
> For I will take away the names of the Baalim out of her mouth,
> and they shall no more be remembered by their name.
>
> In that day, I will make a covenant for them with the beasts of the field, and with the fowls of heaven, and with the creeping things of the ground: and I will break the bow and sword and battle of the earth, and will make them to lie down in safety.
>
> And I will betroth thee unto me for ever;
> yea, I will betroth thee unto me in righteousness, and in judgment, and in loving kindness, and mercies.
>
> And I will even betroth thee onto me in faithfulness:
> And thou shalt know the Lord.

---

24 Cohen, "The Song of Songs and the Jewish Religious Mentality," 2.
25 Cohen, "The Song of Songs and the Jewish Religious Mentality," 3.
26 Stern, "Ancient Jewish Interpretation of the Song of Songs in a Comparative Context," 91.

The Chinese Union Version places these words in Chapter 16, following the Christian Bible. Most Bible translators at the turn of the century were Protestant or Catholic missionaries, but there were also some Chinese scholars who worked closely with them. The Chinese transliteration of the Hebrew word אִישִׁי (*ishi*) into 伊施 (*yish*), which does not express the meaning of "my," is problematic. In Hebrew, אִישִׁי (*ishi*) means 'my husband' or 'my man.' The Chinese transliteration of בַּעְלִי (*baali*) into 巴力 (*bali*) also lacks the sense of a first-person possessive. But the translators did add a brief explanation – "my husband, my master" – in brackets to help readers avoid misunderstanding the text. When the addresser asks the addressee to call him *ishi* ('my husband' or 'my man') rather than *baali* ('my master'), his request demonstrates that the relationship between God and Israel has been transformed from that of master and servant to one of two lovers. The verses starting from "And I will betroth you forever" emphasize this change in their relationship.

Similarly, the speaker praises Israel's loyalty to God, describing it as "love of thine espousals," or, in the JPS version, "the love as a bride."[27] The configuration of a bride following a bridegroom in the wilderness alludes to Moses leading the Israelites out of Egypt and their subsequent wanderings through the desert. Israel's loyalty to God is likened to that of a man and woman in love. It is the bond between God and Israel that made the canonization possible.[28] From this perspective, biblical hermeneutics interprets the Song of Songs as the relationship between God and Israel, or in Christian terms, between Christ and the Church.

Through the ages, this song of human love and its cultural receptions have been intricately intertwined in Jewish tradition. Even in the twentieth century, Hebrew writers often used motifs from the Song of Songs in order to articulate the relationship between God and Israel in light of modernity and atheism. A striking example is the short story "Agunot," by Shai Agnon. The title "Agunot" in Hebrew means 'the forsaken wives.' According to Halakhah, *aguna* is a special term, referring specifically to a married woman who has separated from her husband but cannot get a writ of divorce because it is unknown whether he is dead or alive. The main plot of "Agunot" revolves around the secular love and married life of several Jewish youth: Dinah, Ezekiel, Ben Uri, and Freidele. The setting is in Jerusalem. Dinah loves Ben Uri, but her marriage to Ezekiel from Poland has already been arranged. Ezekiel loves Freidele, but she has married a man in the Diaspora. Dinah and Ezekiel marry and divorce. At first glance, this is a secular love story. But from the very beginning, it follows in the tradition of midrashic writing on

---

27 Jer. 2:2.
28 Cohen, "The Song of Songs and the Jewish Religious Mentality," 4.

the Song of Songs.²⁹ Direct quotations appear frequently, such as "Behold thou art fair, my beloved, behold thou art fair,"³⁰ and "If ye find my beloved, what shall ye tell him? That I am afflicted with love."³¹ As a result, "Agunot" reads like a modern midrash on the Song of Songs. It is not only a tale of failure in love and art, but also an exploration of the tensions between God and Israel, the Diaspora and the Land of Israel, exile and redemption, life and art. In Gershon Shaked's words, it "imitates a tradition, in which the relationship between a secular story and the sacred canon having been revealed, the story itself takes on a species of sacred and sanctified significance."³²

3 Reading the Song of Songs in Chinese Tradition

Interestingly, the Song of Songs was mainly regarded as a collection of love poems by the pioneers of modern Chinese literature during the May Fourth movement (which began in 1919). During that time, the Song of Songs was retranslated by a group of literati: Xu Dishan, a famous poet; Wu Shutian, a woman writer and translator; and Chen Mengjia, a scholar, poet, and archeologist. According to a survey by Marián Gálik, the Song of Songs proved more attractive to Chinese men of letters than perhaps any other book in the Old Testament.³³ What were the sources of this fascination?

First of all, the Song of Songs bears a striking resemblance to the Chinese cultural tradition. The mutual love between men and women, the praise of the physical beauty of the hero and heroine, and the extensive use of natural images – gardens, vineyards, birds, animals, fruits, flowers, and plants – as cultural metaphors all possess clear correspondences in the Chinese lyrical tradition represented by the *Book of Songs*, sometimes referred to as the *Classic of Songs* (*Shijing* 诗经), the oldest existing collection of Chinese poetry, which comprises 305 poems dating from the eleventh to the seventh centuries BCE. Like the Song

---

29 Gershon Shaked, "Midrash and Narrative: Agnon's 'Agunot,' " in *Midrash and Theory*, eds. Geoffrey H. Hartman and Sanford Budick (New Haven and London: Yale University Press, 1986), 287.
30 Shmuel Yosef Agnon, "Agunot," in *A Book That Was Lost*, eds. Alan Mintz and Anne Golomb Hoffman (New York: Schocken Books, 1995), 35.
31 Agnon, "Agunot," 35–36.
32 For more details, see Shaked, "Midrash and Narrative: Agnon's 'Agunot,' " 285–303.
33 Marián Gálik, *Influence, Translation, and Parallels: Selected Studies on the Bible in China* (Sankt Augustin: Collectanes Serica, 2004), 66.

of Songs, the *Book of Songs* contains beautiful verses spoken from the perspective of a lover – sometimes a man, sometimes a maiden – longing for his/her beloved:

> The beautiful and good girl, waking and sleeping he wished for her; he wished for her but didn't get her, waking and sleeping he thought of her; longing, longing, he tossed and fidgeted.[34]
> 《关雎》:窈窕淑女,寤寐求之。求之不得,寤寐思服。悠哉悠哉,辗转反侧。
>
> When I have not yet seen the lord (young man) my grieved heart is agitated; but when I have seen him, when I have met him, my heart calms down.
> 《草虫》:未见君子,忧心忡忡。亦既见止,亦既觏止,我心则降。
>
> When I have not yet seen the lord my grieved heart is sad; but when I have seen him, when I have met him, my heart is pleased.
> 《草虫》:"未见君子,忧心惙惙。亦既见止,亦既觏止,我心则说。"
>
> When I have not yet seen the lord my heart is pained; but when I have seen him, when I have met him, my heart is at ease.
> 《草虫》:"未见君子,我心伤悲。亦既见止,亦既觏止,我心则夷。"[35]

As in the Song of Songs, there are numerous descriptions in praise of the beauty of the human body, most notably the following:

> Her fingers, slender as shoots of reeds. Her skin, white and soft as lard. Her neck, long and delicate as the ox-beetle's larva. Her neck, long and delicate as the ox-beetle's larva. Her teeth, even and white as ground seeds. Her forehead, full and square as that of a cicada. Her eyebrows, light as the eye marks of a moth. Sweet dimples frame her teasing smile. When she glances, behold her limpid, intimate eyes.
> 《硕人》:手如柔荑,肤如凝脂。领如蝤蛴,齿如瓠犀。螓首蛾眉,巧笑倩兮,美目盼兮。[36]

The metaphors of one culture might touch the hearts of readers from another culture. As twentieth-century Chinese essayist and translator Zhou Zuoren observed, there are many similarities between the Psalms, Lamentations, and the Song of Songs on the one hand and the *Book of Songs* on the other.[37] Recognition of this cultural relevance heightens the Chinese understanding of and interest in Hebrew literature and Jewish culture.

---

[34] Bernhard Karlgren, *The Book of Odes* (Stockholm: Musem of Far Eastern Antiquities, 1950), 2.
[35] Bernhard Karlgren, *The Book of Odes*, 7–8.
[36] *Shijing·Guofeng: Yingwen Baihua Xinyi* 诗经 ·国风:英文白话新译 [Airs of the States from *Shijing*: A New Trilingual Translation of the World's Oldest Collection of Lyric Poetry], trans. Fu-shiang Chia (Beijing: Peking University Press, 2010), 125.
[37] Zhou Zuoren 周作人, "Shengshu yu Zhongguo Wenxue" 圣书与中国文学 [The Scripture and Chinese literature], in *Yishu yu Shenghuo* 艺术与生活 [Art and life] (Beijing: Beijing October Literature and Art Publishing House, 2011), 37–49.

Secondly, the absence of "female subordination"[38] from the Song of Songs, which instead gives voice to a maiden's brave pursuit of love, met with women's new awareness of their passive role in love and marriage during the time of the May Fourth movement. In other words, Chinese women preferred to marry for love rather than submit to a marriage arranged by their parents. Further, since the early twentieth century, the writing style of the Song of Songs has inspired many Chinese writers and poets in their efforts to compose idyllic poetry. Zhou Zuoren hoped that the meeting of modern Chinese literature with the literature of the Bible (primarily the so-called Old Testament) would move Chinese poets to produce "beautiful idylls" and renew the Chinese national language.[39]

The Song of Songs had a palpable influence on the early writings of Shen Congwen, a friend of Zhou at that time and a famous writer in his own right, in the 1920s. In his preface to his own selected works, Shen Congwen wrote:

> At the beginning of my stay in Beijing (in 1922), I didn't know how to add punctuation. The only master who gave me this instruction was *The Historical Record* (*Shiji*, 《史记》). Soon afterward, I acquired a copy of the Bible, which looked worn out. I didn't have a blind faith in religion, but I liked the translation, which was close to vernacular Chinese, as well as the chapters that contained lyrical poems. By reading these two works again and again, I received useful inspiration and a basic knowledge of narrative and lyric.[40]

He sometimes made use of direct quotations from the Song of Songs in order to express an unaccomplished desire for women in his stories:

> I am dark, but lovely,
>   O daughters of Jerusalem,
>   Like the tents of Kedar,
>   Like the Curtain of Solomon,
>   Do not look upon me,
>   Because I am dark
>   Because the Sun has
>   tanned me.

This paragraph from Shen's short story "The Second Feifei" was quoted directly from the Song of Songs 1:5–6. There are two main groups of literary characters in Shen Congwen's early stories, which can be divided into two categories: the Solomon series and the Shulamite series. In the Solomon series, the descrip-

---

38 Phyllis Trible, *God and the Rhetoric of Sexuality* (Philadelphia, PA: Fortress Press, 1978), 161.
39 Zhou Zuoren, "Shengshu yu Zhongguo Wenxue," 37–49.
40 Shen Congwen 沈从文, "Shen Congwen Xiaoshuo Xuanji tiji,"《沈从文小说选集》题记 in 沈从文全集 [Collection of Shen Congwen's Works] (Taiyuan: Beiyue Literature and Art Publishing House, 2002), 16:372. My translation.

tions of some characters are very similar to those of the hero of the Song of Songs. For example, in Shen's famous short story "Lung Chu," it is written, "Lung Chu, the son of the chieftain, was seventeen years old, and the most beautiful of all the sons among the tribe. He was as strong as a lion and as tender as a lamb; the ideal of all the youths of the place, the most gifted, the most wise."[41] The appearance and characteristics of Lung Chu recall the famous verses in the Song of Songs: "Like an apple tree among the trees of the woods, so is my beloved among the sons."[42] In the Shulamite series, Shen's descriptions of female characters resemble the descriptions of women in the Song of Songs. For example, Shen wrote, "Meijin was a stunningly beautiful girl of the white-faced tribe. She and a boy from the Phoenix tribe, who was very handsome and of exemplary character, paired off while exchanging songs across mountain valleys."[43] The descriptive metaphor for the heroine's beauty here is quite similar to the description of the Song of Songs: "Like a lily among the thorns, so is my love among the daughters."[44]

Furthermore, many of the metaphors and images in Shen Congwen's early writings are derived from the Song of Songs. According to the statistics compiled by Wang Benchao, a Chinese literary critic, Shen's early works include about 21 metaphors drawn from the plants and 15 from the animals of the Song of Songs.[45] From the title of Wang's monograph, *Chinese Literature in the Twentieth Century and Christian Culture*, we can see that Chinese scholarship has long focused on Shen Congwen's relationship with Christianity, despite the fact that Shen Congwen's reading of the Bible was not motivated by religion. One reason for this oversight is the perception – widespread in China – of the Bible as part of the Christian canon. In this context, the Jewish tradition has yet to be investigated.

During the 1920s and the 1930s, Chinese writers and scholars regarded the Song of Songs as a collection of lyrical songs and paid little attention to its religious implications. Some even refused to read it from a religious perspective. Several translators, including those mentioned above, considered it idyllic or

---

41 Jin Ti and Robert Payne, trans., *The Chinese Earth: Stories by Shen Congwen* (London: George Allen and Unwin, 1947), 137.
42 Song of Sol. 2:3.
43 Caroline Mason, trans., in *Imperfect Paradise*, ed. Jeffrey Kinkley (Honolulu: University of Hawai'i Press, 1995), 83.
44 Song of Sol. 2:2.
45 Wang Benchao 王本朝, *Ershi Shiji Zhongguo Wenxueyu Jidujiao Wenhua* 20 世纪中国文学与基督教文化 [Chinese literature in the twentieth century and Christian culture] (Hefei: Anhui Educational Press, 2000), 154–164.

lyric poetry. Xu Dishan thought the Song of Songs was simply a love song between a husband and a wife; Wu Shutian regarded it as a new drama of love; in the eyes of Chen Mengjia, the Song of Songs, written by Solomon, was 最可憾人的抒情诗 ('a most shocking lyrical poem'), 又朴素，又浓密 ('simple and dense'). He translated the Song of Songs into a modern form of Chinese poetry, simply because he thought it would benefit Chinese literature.[46]

Zhou Zuoren, Lin Yutang, and Zhu Ziqing appreciated the literary value of the Song of Songs more than its religious value, though they did take note of the latter. Zhou Zuoren believed that the Song of Songs was originally a collection of love poetry – an essentially literary text – and that its religious interpretations were added later.[47] In his autobiography, Lin Yutang mentioned that he used to regard the Song of Songs as a love song. In an essay recommending ten books for the *Beijing Daily Supplement*, he pointed out that the thoughts and feelings articulated in the Song of Songs and Ecclesiastes were very close to those of many young people in modern China.[48] Zhu Ziqing simply saw the Song of the Songs as a particularly wonderful poem.[49]

Zhu Weizhi, a pioneer of biblical studies in China, regarded the Old Testament as the first part of Christian literature in the 1930s. He once said that the Psalms, the Song of Songs, the Book of Job, and the Gospel of Matthew in the Chinese Union version make people feel 'mostly beautiful' (美不胜收). In contrast to other Chinese scholars, who were mainly interested in making comparisons between the Song of Songs and the *Book of Songs*, Zhu Weizhi also compared the Song of Songs to the *Nine Songs* (*Jiuge*《九歌》) of Qu Yuan, a poet and politician of the Warring States period. In his later studies, influenced by the third-century Christian theologian Origen, he further described the Song

---

[46] See Chen Mengjia 陈梦家, "Gezhong Zhige Yixu" 《歌中之歌》译序 [A preface to the translation of the Song of Songs] (Shanghai: Liangyou Book Printing Company, 1932), 1–3. See also Ma Yuelan 马月兰, "*Yage* Chongshi de Wenxue Dongyin Fulu"《雅歌》重译的文学动因附录 [Appendix to "The literary drive to Chinese retranslation of the Song of Songs"], in *A Study of Biblical Literature*, eds. Liang Gong and Cheng Xiaojuan (Beijing: People's Literature Publishing House, 2015), 10:119.
[47] Zhou Zuoren 周作人, "Jiuyue yu Lianaishi"《旧约》与恋爱诗 [The Old Testament and love poetry], in *Tan long ji* 谈龙集 (Beijing: Beijing October Literature and Art Publishing House), 159–160.
[48] Lin Yutang 林玉堂, "Qingnian Bidushu Shibu," 青年必读书 10 部 [Ten books for young people], in *Beijing Daily Supplement*, February 24, 1925.
[49] Zhu Ziqing 朱自清, *Xinshi Zahua* 新诗杂话 [On new poetry] (Anhui: Anhui Literature and Art Publishing House, 1999), 69.

of Songs as an "elegant and purely lyrical opera" in ten acts.[50] In his *Twelve Lectures on Biblical Literature,* he proposed that this lyric poem expressing love between a man and a woman was indeed a little erotic. Touching on the question of why the Song of Songs was first canonized in the Jewish and Christian worlds, he concluded that the Song of Songs was included in the Bible for two reasons: first, because it was written by Solomon; second, because many rabbis interpreted it as a metaphor for the love between God and the people of Israel. On the other hand, however, he considered both of these reasons untenable. Quoting some examples from the Song of Songs, such as "The curves of your thighs are like jewels" and "Your navel is a rounded goblet; it lacks no blended beverage,"[51] he suggested that such descriptions of the human body were blasphemy against God.[52]

As early as the 1920s, essayist Feng Sanmei maintained that literati through the ages had considered the Song of Songs as a spiritual parable praising the love between God and Israel. Influenced by Origen, Feng Sanmei took the bridegroom as God and the bride as the Church, without mentioning the Jewish cultural tradition.[53] In the numerous Chinese essays published in recent years, scholars have explored such subjects as the atheistic value of the Song of Songs; the reception of the Song of Songs in China; comparisons between the Song of Songs and the *Book of Songs,* or between the Song of Songs and English and American literature; and women's consciousness in the Song of Songs. But seldom – with the exception of Zhang Longxi's article "The Letter or the Spirit: The Song of Songs, Allegoresis, and the Book of Poetry" have they touched on the Jewish tradition.[54] Until now, only in *Discourses and Community Identity: A Study of the Megilloth in the Hebrew Scripture*[55] by Archie Lee and You Bin, and *An Explanation of the Song of Songs*[56] by Huang Zhulun, have we seen any

---

[50] Zhu Weizhi and Han Kesheng 朱维之与韩可胜, *Gu Youtai Wenhua Shi* 古犹太文化史 [Ancient Jewish cultural history] (Beijing: Economic Daily Press, 1997), 320–321.
[51] Song of Sol. 7:1 and 7:2.
[52] Zhu Weizghi 朱维之, *Shengjing Wenxue Shi'er Jiang* 圣经文学十二讲 [Twelve lectures on Biblical literature] (Beijing: People's Literature Publishing House, 2008), 366–377.
[53] Feng Sanmei 冯三昧, "Lun Yage" 论雅歌 [On the Song of Songs], in *The Song of Songs,* trans. Wu Shutian, (Shanghai: Beixin Book Company, 1930), appendix, 26.
[54] Zhang Longxi, "The Letter or the Spirit: The Song of Songs, Allegoresis, and the Book of Poetry," *Comparative Literature* 39, no. 3 (1987), 193–217.
[55] Archie Lee, You Bin 李炽昌、游斌, *Shengming Yanshuo yu Zuqun Rentong* 生命言说与社群认同 [Discourses and community identity: A study of the Megilloth in the Hebrew Scripture] (Beijing: China Social Science Press), 166–167.
[56] Huang Zhulun 黄朱伦, *Yage Zhushi* 雅歌注释 [An explanation of the Song of Songs] (Shanghai: Sanlian Press, 2012).

exploration of the love between humans and God. Archie Lee and You Bin have argued that the Song of Songs' impact on the Hebrew cultural tradition can only be explained by paradoxical interpretations. Their approach not only finds a lawful path for the Song of Songs to enter the canon, but also alleviates theological contradictions. Zhu Tianlun has offered some significant historical context for the Song of Songs' canonization.

Conclusion

The Song of Songs, rich with symbolic and typological meanings in the Jewish and Christian traditions, has been read differently in a Chinese cultural context. Chinese writers and scholars mainly stay close to the literal sense rather than seeking to explore its figurative meanings. For the most part, they have even neglected the bond of love between God and Israel. The Song of Songs can and should be interpreted with an awareness of its different contexts and different levels of meanings, as Jon Levenson suggests. The aim of our comparison is not to substitute a modern secular interpretation for the traditional religious one, or vice versa, but rather to survey these different interpretations and to provide an example of cross-cultural reading.

References

Agnon, Shmuel Yosef. "Agunot." In *A Book That Was Lost*, edited by Alan Mintz and Anne Golomb Hoffman, 35–47. New York: Schocken Books, 1995.
Alter, Robert. Afterword to *The Song of Songs: A New Translation with an Introduction and Commentary*. Translated by Ariel Bloch and Chana Bloch. New York: Random House, 1995.
Bloch, Ariel and Chana Bloch. *The Song of Songs: A New Translation with an Introduction and Commentary*. New York: Random House, 1995.
Brenner, Athalya, ed. *The Song of Songs*. Sheffield: Academic Press, 1993.
Chen Mengjia 陈梦家. "Gezhong Zhige Yixu"《歌中之歌》译序 [Introduction to the translation of the Song of Songs]. Shanghai: Liangyou Book Printing Company, 1932.
Chia Fu-shiang 贾福相, trans. *Shijing·Guofeng: Yingwen Baihua Xinyi* 诗经·国风：英文白话新译 [Airs of the States from Shijing: A New Trilingual Translation of the World's Oldest Collection of Lyric Poetry], Beijing: Peking University Press, 2010.
Cohen, Gerson D. "The Song of Songs and the Jewish Religious Mentality." In *The Samuel Friedland Lectures, 1960–1966*, 1–21. New York: Jewish Theological Seminary of America, 1966.
Coogan, Michael D. *The Old Testament: A Historical and Literary Introduction to the Hebrew Scripture*. Oxford: Oxford University Press, 2013.

Feng Sanmei 冯三昧. "Lun Yage" 论雅歌 [On the Song of Songs]. In *The Song of Songs*, translated by Wu Shutian. Shanghai: Beixin Book Company, 1930.

Fishbane, Michael. *The JPS Bible Commentary: Song of Songs*. Philadelphia, PA: The Jewish Publication Society, 2015.

Gálik, Márian. *Influence, Translation, and Parallels: Selected Studies on the Bible in China*. Sankt Augustin: Collectanes Serica, 2004.

The Holy Scripture: A Jewish Bible According to the Masoretic Text. Tel Aviv: SINAI, 1996.

Huang Zhulun 黄朱伦. *Yage Zhushi* 雅歌注释 [An explanation of the Song of Songs]. Shanghai: Sanlian Press, 2012.

Jin Ti and Robert Payne, trans. *The Chinese Earth: Stories by Shen Congwen*. London: George Allen and Unwin, 1947.

Karlgren, Bernhard. *The Book of Odes*. Stockholm: The Musem of Far Eastern Antiquities, 1950.

Kinkley, Jeffrey. ed. *Imperfect Paradise*. Honolulu: University of Hawai'i Press, 1995.

Lee, Archie and You Bin 李炽昌、游斌. *Shengming Yanshuo yu Zuqun Rentong* 生命言说与社群认同 [Discourses and community identity: A study of the Megilloth in the Hebrew scripture]. Beijing: China Social Science Press, 2007.

Levenson, Jon D. *The Love of God*. Princeton, NJ: Princeton University Press, 2016.

Lin Yutang 林玉堂. "Qingnian Bidushu Shibu" 青年必读书 10 部 [Ten books for young people]. *Beijing Daily Supplement*, February 24, 1925.

Ma Yuelan 马月兰. "Yage Chongshi de Wenxue Dongyin Fulu"《雅歌》重译的文学动因附录 [Appendix to "The literary drive to Chinese retranslation of the Song of Songs"]. In vol. 10 of *A Study of Biblical Literature*, edited by Liang Gong and Cheng Xiaojuan, 119–121. Beijing: People's Literature Publishing House, 2015.

Murphy, Roland E. and O. Carm. *The Song of Songs: A Commentary on the Book of Canticles or the Song of Songs*. Minneapolis, MN: Fortress Press, 1990.

Shaked, Gershon. "Midrash and Narrative: Agnon's 'Agunot.'" In *Midrash and Theory*, edited by Geoffrey H. Hartman and Sanford Budick, 285–303. New Haven, CT, and London: Yale University Press, 1986.

Shen Congwen 沈从文. "*Shen Congwen Xiaoshuo Xuanji* Tiji"《沈从文小说选集》题记 [Preface to the collection of Shen Congwen's works]. In vol. 16 of *Shen Congwen Quanji* 沈从文全集 [Collection of Shen Congwen's works]. Taiyuan: Beiyue Literature and Art Publishing House, 2002.

Stern, David. "Ancient Jewish Interpretation of the Song of Songs in a Comparative Context." In *Jewish Biblical Interpretation and Cultural Exchange*, edited by Natalle B. Dohrmann and David Stern, 87–107. Philadelphia: University of Pennsylvania Press, 2008.

Trible, Phyllis. *God and the Rhetoric of Sexuality*. Philadelphia, PA: Fortress Press, 1978.

Wang Benchao 王本朝. *Ershi Shijie Zhongguo Wenxueyu Jidujiao Wenhua* 20 世纪中国文学与基督教文化 [Chinese literature in the twentieth century and Christian culture]. Hefei: Anhui Educational Press, 2000.

Zhang Longxi. "The Letter or the Spirit: The Song of Songs, Allegoresis, and the Book of Poetry." *Comparative Literature* 9 (1987): 193–217.

Zhou Zuoren 周作人. "Shengshu yu Zhongguo Wenxue" 圣书与中国文学 [The scriptures and Chinese literature]. In *Yishu yu shenghuo* 艺术与生活 [Art and life], 37–49. Beijing: Beijing October Literature and Art Publishing House, 2011.

Zhou Zuoren 周作人. "Jiuyue yu Lianaishi"《旧约》与恋爱诗 [The Old Testament and love poetry]. In *Tan long ji* 谈龙集. Beijing: Beijing October Literature and Art Publishing House, 2011.

Zhu Ziqing 朱自清. *Xinshi Zahua* 新诗杂话 [On new poetry]. Anhui: Anhui Literature and Art Publishing House, 1999.
Zhu Weizhi and Han Kesheng 朱维之与韩可胜. *Gu Youtai Wenhua Shi* 古犹太文化史 [Ancient Jewish cultural history]. Beijing: Economic Daily Press, 1997.
Zhu Weizhi 朱维之. *Shengjing Wenxue Shi'er Jiang* 圣经文学十二讲 [Twelve lectures on biblical literature]. Beijing: People's Literature Publishing House, 2008.

Liu Yan

5 The Transcultural Characteristics of the Chinese Bible Translated by S. I. J. Schereschewsky (1831–1906): A Case Study of the Song of Songs

The first nineteenth-century translator of the Old Testament from Hebrew into Mandarin Chinese was the Jewish American Samuel Isaac Joseph Schereschewsky (Joseph Shi, May 6, 1831–October 15, 1906; in Chinese, 施约瑟), who was not only a famous missionary bishop and a great Christian leader, but also a biblical scholar and a great translator who triumphed over a severe disability to complete his life's work. It is a pity that many Chinese people do not know of Schereschewsky's impressive career despite their familiarity with figures such as Matteo Ricci (利玛窦), John Marshman (马士曼), Robert Morrison (马礼逊), Calvin Wilson Mateer (狄考文), or James Legge (理雅各). This essay compares portions of two Chinese versions of the Song of Songs from Schereschewsky's Beijing Vernacular Old Testament Version (1875) and his Easy Wenli Old and New Testaments (1902), a comparison that reveals Schereschewsky's unique contribution and sheds some light on the intercultural nature of Bible translation.[1] It offers a new perspective from which to reflect on Chinese Bible translation and Jewish-Chinese cross-cultural communication in our modern, globalized world.

1 Jewish Bishop S. I. J. Schereschewsky and His Diverse Cultural Identities

Schereschewsky was born into a relatively well-to-do family of Ashkenazi Jews in Tauroggen, Russian Lithuania, in 1831. Both his parents died when he was

---

[1] I dedicate this essay to Irene Eber (1929–2019) of Hebrew University, whose groundbreaking book *The Jewish Bishop and the Chinese Bible: S. I. J. Schereschewsky (1831–1906)* has inspired much of my own scholarly work. I would like to express my deep appreciation to Kathryn Hellerstein at the University of Pennsylvania and Song Lihong at Nanjing University for their insightful comments on the revision of my paper. I am also grateful to Sharon Kim at Judson University (IL) and editor Samantha Pious for polishing this English version. My essay is supported by the Beijing Institute of Intercultural Communication / Beijing Social Science Fund, "A Study of Poet Zheng Min's Translation and Communication Overseas" (No. 17JDWXB001).

still a child. As an orphan, he lived in the house of his older half-brother, learning Hebrew prayers and studying the Bible in the family school. When he was fifteen, he left his brother's home to live on his own. He attended the government-sponsored Jewish Rabbinic School at Zhitomir, where he became familiar with the Jewish theological tradition as well as with secular subjects, including mathematics, physics, and geography. In addition to Hebrew and Russian, he mastered other languages, such as Polish, German, Yiddish, and French. At Zhitomir, he was given a copy of the New Testament in Hebrew that had been produced by the London Society for Promoting Christianity amongst the Jews. In 1852, he became "a believer in the life-giving verities of Christianity."[2] From 1852 to 1854, he studied in Frankfurt and at the University of Breslau, during which time he was probably in contact with some Christian missionaries whose focus was on converting Jews. In the summer of 1854, he immigrated to the United States, where he began training for the ministry, studying first at the Presbyterian seminary in Allegheny City and later switching to an Episcopal seminary in New York. According to Irene Eber, Schereschewsky ultimately chose the Episcopal Church's flexibility instead of the "Calvinist inflexibility" of the Presbyterian Church.[3] In December 1859, Schereschewsky was sent to Shanghai by the American Episcopal Church Mission. In the spring of 1862, he departed Shanghai for Beijing. From 1877 to 1884 he served as the Anglican Bishop in Shanghai. It was he who founded St. John's University (圣约翰大学) in 1879, the first university in modern China. Unfortunately, St. John's was demolished in 1952. Its former campus now belongs to the East China University of Political Science and Law (华东政法大学).

There was no doubt Schereschewsky had a genuine gift for language and translation. His Chinese Bible translation also provided him with an opportunity to utilize the Hebrew language and Mandarin. From 1862 to 1875, Schereschewsky devoted himself to translating the Bible into vernacular or colloquial Chinese in Peking. He joined the Peking Translation Committee (北京译经委员会) and worked as the first translator of the Old Testament from Hebrew into Beijing Mandarin. In December 1875, Schereschewsky's Mandarin Version of the Old Testament (北京官话旧约全书) was published by the American Bible Society of Shanghai (although the printing place was Kyoto Mei Hua Academy in Japan 日本京都美华书院). His other Bible translation, the Easy Wenli Old Testament and New Testament Version (施约瑟浅文理旧新约圣经), translated with the Peking Translation Committee, was published in 1902 by the American Bible

---

[2] Irene Eber, *The Jewish Bishop and the Chinese Bible: S. I. J. Schereschewsky (1831–1906)* (Leiden and Boston: Brill, 1999), 30.
[3] Eber, *The Jewish Bishop and the Chinese Bible*, 57.

Society of Shanghai. For many years, these two volumes were the only Bibles generally used in China. Schereschewsky's Mandarin Version of the Old Testament, in particular, was immediately adopted and widely used for more than forty years until the Union Mandarin Version (官话和合本) was published in 1919. Frederick R. Graves wrote, "Before the publication of the Union Version [. . .] Schereschewsky had no rival, and if it has been replaced by the Union Version, his Old Testament in Mandarin in the judgement of the best qualified critics preserves a special value which will be lasting."[4] By the time of his death in Tokyo, Japan, in 1906, Schereschewsky had translated the entire Bible into Easy Wenli. He had also written several Chinese grammars and dictionaries, sharing his vast linguistic knowledge with those who came after him.

2 Comparison of Two Versions of the Song of Songs Translated by S. I. J. Schereschewsky

The Song of Songs plays a very special and important role in the Old Testament. It has been translated into over thirty Chinese versions by various missionaries, Sinologists, Christians, scholars, and writers such as Joshua Marshman, Robert Morrison, Xu Dishan (许地山), Wu Shutian (吴曙天), Chen Mengjia (陈梦家), and Lü Zhenzhong (吕振中). Each of these translators used different dialects of Chinese (classical, easy classical, local dialects, or modern Chinese), literary forms and genres (poetry, essay, or drama), rhythm, and word choice (simple or complicated). The Song of Songs also continues to provide inspiration for modern Chinese writers and poets such as Lu Xun (鲁迅), Guo Moruo (郭沫若), Chen Mengjia (陈梦家), Bing Xin (冰心), Su Xuelin (苏雪林), Mao Dun (茅盾), Hai Zi (海子), and Xia Yu (夏宇). In particular, the Song of Songs has had an important impact on modern Chinese love poems, which have in their turn inspired young people to pursue love, personal liberation, and gender equality. By comparing the two translations of the Song of Songs in Schereschewsky's Beijing Vernacular Old Testament Version (1875) and his Easy Wenli Old and New Testaments (1902) in terms of target audience, writing style, expression in different Chinese languages (i.e. the vernacular and the shallow vernacular), syntax, grammar, punctuation, notes, and other differences, we can observe the development of his translation strategies and methodologies.

---

4 Domestic and Foreign Missionary Society, China Records, 1835–1951, FMS, RG64-29.

2.1 The Literacy Levels of the Translator's Target Readers

A successful translation should be audience-oriented, since its reception in the target culture is what matters. Early missionaries appreciated the importance of vernacular translations, which could be read aloud to illiterate audiences, in addition to translations into classical Chinese. Schereschewsky recognized that the Chinese people, more than any other, were fastidious about language. He was eventually convinced that separate Bibles were needed for readers at different literacy levels and that both the vernacular and the classical translations were equally important.[5] He translated different versions of the Song of Songs (and the entire Old Testament) into Mandarin (白话文, 'vernacular Chinese') and Easy Wenli (浅文理, 'shallow vernacular Chinese') for different kinds of readers. Mandarin, the vernacular, is essentially modern Chinese, while Easy Wenli, the shallow vernacular, is a style that lies halfway between the classical and the vernacular. The Mandarin Version, which addresses the general public and the lower classes, utilizes a popular, colloquial style. The Easy Wenli Version, intended for intellectual elites, is artistic and aesthetic.

The contrast between these different registers is particularly striking in terms of word choice: 爱慕 (*ai mu*, 'love') / 眷爱 (*juan ai*, 'preciousness'); 香味 (*xiang wei*, 'fragrance') / 馨香 (*xin xiang*, 'sweet savor'); 憩息 (*qi xi*, 'take breaks') / 歇息 (*xie xi*, 'have a rest'). Both versions use different personal pronouns: 你 (*ni*, 'you') / 尔 (*er*, 'you'); 他们 (*ta men*, 'they') / 彼众 (*bi zhong*, 'they'); 我们 (*wo men*, 'we') / 我侪 (*wo chai*, 'we'). They also use different empty words, or function words: 的 (*de*, 'of') / 之 (*zhi*, 'of'); 因此 (*yin ci*, 'so') / 故 (*gu*, 'so'). The Easy Wenli Version uses conjunctions and compound words from classical Chinese: 也 (*ye*, 'not only ... but also'), 惟 (*wei*, 'only'), 于 (*yu*, 'and'), 亦 (*yi*, 'also'), and 之 (*zhi*, 'of'). In terms of grammatical structure, the Mandarin Version emphasizes the subject "I," which is close to the daily spoken language. The Easy Wenli Version is more concise, often omitting the subject, suitable for written expression in classical Chinese. All in all, Schereschewsky codified a set of grammatical rules for Mandarin (vernacular Chinese) and Easy Wenli (half-classical Chinese) and applied them to his translation of the entire Bible. He fully considered the demands of Chinese readers.

---

5 Domestic and Foreign Missionary Society, China Records, 1835–1951, RG64-29; Schereschewsky, letter to Dr. Langford, May 18, 1895.

2.2 A Variety of Rhetorical Forms and Poetic Styles

The translation of the Bible is a cross-cultural enterprise. In translating the Song of Songs, Schereschewsky had to overcome the great differences between the Chinese and Jewish cultures. He recognized that in China the western missionaries had encountered a highly literate civilization that paid great attention to the written word. Referring to Chinese schools and the examination system, he said that "no nation on earth has such a multiplicity of histories, anthologies, encyclopedias and standard works on archeology, law, and letters, as the Chinese." In short, the Chinese are a "highly civilized and well educated people."[6] This respect for China's literary tradition made Schereschewsky increasingly aware of the importance of reproducing the Bible's literary merits in translation.

The Chinese Song of Songs is one of the most interesting and attractive religious texts, a beautiful, lyrical love poem that is sometimes compared to the first Chinese poetry collection, the *Book of Songs* (*Shijing* 诗经). Parallelism is not always repetition. It can be an intensification of the preceding line(s), a concretization, or a contrast. These techniques are all extensively used in Chinese poetry as well as in the Bible and other Western texts, often by means of the couplet form. Raoul David Findeisen points out: "The chief versification techniques in the Song of Songs are parallelisms and alliterations; no rhymes are used. The Chinese language, with its abundant tradition of parallel composition both in verse and prose, as well as a relatively restrained set of syllables, would be perfectly adapted to transpose these devices from Hebrew."[7] The close relationship between Chinese and Hebrew lyricism and rhetoric is conducive to the translation of the Old Testament, especially those poetic chapters similar to the Song of Songs, into Chinese. In order to preserve the graceful and elegant poetic style of the original text of the Song of Songs, Schereschewsky employs parallel construction and couplets in both of his versions. He translates the Song of Songs 4:1, "Behold, thou art fair, my love; Behold, thou art fair,"[8] into two Chinese styles with four words: in the Mandarin Version, 我的佳偶、你甚美丽、你甚美丽 (*wo de jia ou, ni shen mei li, ni shen mei li*); in the Easy Wenli Version, 我之佳偶、尔甚美丽、尔甚美丽 (*wo zhi jia ou, er shen mei li, er shen mei li*). When the Hebrew scriptures have implied meanings, he tends to avoid literal

---

[6] Eber, *The Jewish Bishop and the Chinese Bible*, 670 and 673.
[7] Raoul David Findeisen, "'God Was Their Souls' Love, Women Their Bodies'": Two Chinese Versions of the Song of Songs (1930/32)," in *Talking Literature: Essays on Chinese and Biblical Writings and Their Interaction*, eds. Raoul David Findeisen and Martin Slobodnik (Wiesbaden: Harrassowitz Verlag, 2013), 134.
[8] All biblical quotations in this article are from the Authorized King James Version of the Bible (KJV).

translation, adopting clear and direct expressions in accordance with the Chinese idiom. He renders Song of Songs 5:6, "My soul failed when he spake" (Hebrew: *Nafshi yatsah be'dabro*), appropriately as 神不守舍 (*shen bu shou she*, 'The Spirit has left the body'). This kind of concise and poetic four-syllable idiom is found everywhere in his translation, such as 诚诚实实 (*cheng cheng shi shi*, 'very honest').

Schereschewsky had a good sense of how to use vernacular and classical Chinese. The Mandarin version of the Song of Songs strove to allow ordinary Chinese people to understand and accept it. Likewise, in the process of translating the Song of Songs into Easy Wenli, Schereschewsky carefully chose the language form that would make it easy for readers to accept and understand. For the Easy Wenli version of the Song of Songs, Schereschewsky used a simple literary language, combining classical Chinese with the vernacular, in order to produce a richer poetic flavor of writing. He allowed the literary meaning conveyed by the Chinese characters to shape the religious ideas from his biblical source material, creating elegant literary effects. He used the 'transliteration method' (*yin yi fa* 音译法) and 'compound words' (*he cheng ci* 合成词) to translate the names of people, animals, plants, and places according to their Hebrew pronunciation. This approach allowed him not only effectively to communicate the rhythm of the original texts, but also to add numerous new words into the Chinese language, e.g. 没药 (*mo yao*, 'myrrh'), 隐基底 (*yin ji di*, 'En Gedi'), 书拉密 (*shu la mi*, 'Shulamite'), 所罗门 (*suo luo men*, 'Solomon'), 沙仑 (*sha lun*, 'Sharon'), and 香草山 (*xiang cao shan*, 'spice-laden mountain'). These transliterated European-style expressions have greatly enriched modern Chinese.

2.3 Use of Punctuation, Annotations, Numbers, and Comments

Translating is an interpretive and dialogic activity. Schereschewsky combined Jewish Midrashim with traditional Chinese commentaries: employing Jewish exegetical methods together with Chinese hermeneutic techniques, making notes in the margins, and arranging biblical passages in the traditional vertical versions of classical Chinese texts. The Mandarin version of the Song of Songs uses pauses and periods to break a sentence. The font is large, which is suitable for ordinary readers at a low level of literacy. The Easy Wenli version uses pauses without periods. The chapter numbers and verse divisions are indicated using the ancient Chinese chronological method known as the Ten Heavenly Stems and Twelve Terrestrial Branches (*tian gan di zhi* 天干地支), which makes it easy for readers to consult the Bible. On every page, the paragraphs or sentences are interspersed with annotations. These comments and cross-references construct an intertextuality that is suitable for highly literate and cultured readers.

As Raoul David Findeisen observes, "In the intercultural transfer for which translation always and still is the 'king's way,' the lexical field related to the material world often presents one of the greatest obstacles. This may be even more poignant in the case of the huge distance in time and space that Chinese writers had to overcome in order to translate the Song of Songs."[9] In other words, the translation of words and phrases with a highly specific cultural referent is a challenging task. Therefore, Schereschewsky tried to translate the original names of the plants, fruits, types of wood, animals, fabrics, and even currencies into Chinese and added notes to explain specialized terms (geographic locations, people, history, proverbs, and colloquial idioms, as well as images and their symbolic meanings) in order to avoid the embarrassment of cultural misunderstanding. For example, the Easy Wenli Song of Songs 8:11–12 reads: 尔得一千 (*er de yi qian*, 'every one for the fruit thereof was to bring a thousand pieces of silver'); 守者可得二百 (*shou zhe ke de er bai*, 'those that keep the fruit thereof two hundred'). Above all, they demonstrate Schereschewsky's erudition and his profound familiarity with the biblical text and the Jewish commentary tradition.

3 Flexible Translation Techniques in the Chinese Context

An analysis of Schereschewsky's approach to translation illuminates his contribution to translation theory, the intercultural nature of Bible translation in general, and the specific intercultural dialogue that is still occurring between the Jewish and Chinese cultures.

3.1 Being Faithful to the Original Hebrew Text

Lamin Sanneh writes, "That mission [i.e., the Christian mission of evangelization] was not the instrument for sifting the world into an identity of cultural likeness, with our diversities being pressed into a single mold in preparation for some millennial reckoning. So obedience to the gospel was distinguished from loyalty to a universal cultural paradigm. Translatability presupposed cultural pluralism

---

9 Findeisen, "Two Chinese Versions of the Song of Songs (1930/32)," 133.

by assuming that linguistic variety was needed for the word of God."[10] In China, Christianity is a translated religion; the Christian Bible had to be translated into Chinese before it could be understood or accepted by the Chinese people. In other words, the translation of the Bible in different countries or places is subject to the local language, history, culture, literature, religion, and ideology. If the history of Bible translation is a condensed history of world culture, by the same token, the history of Chinese Bible translation is a condensed history of nearly one thousand years of cultural exchange between China and the West from the Tang dynasty to the present. Compared with Catholicism, Protestantism places more emphasis on the translation of the Bible, especially the translation of God's Word into the local language. Starting in the early nineteenth century, Protestant missionaries undertook to render the Bible into Chinese in order to place the "Word of God" into the hearts of the people. Thus, the impetus for Protestant Bible translation emanated from the religious mission to convey the biblical message to the Chinese people. Nevertheless, Christian Bible translators faced challenges of transformation during the process of translation from the source language to the target language. George Steiner points out: "The schematic model of translation is one in which a message from a source-language passed into a receptor-language via a transformative process."[11] The translation and reception of the Bible are always influenced by the translator's linguistic ability, ideology, religious sect, and knowledge of religious teachings, as well as by the expectations of target-language readers.

Eugene Nida articulates the translation principle of "dynamic or functional equivalence," whereby the message of the source text is made understandable to readers in the target language ("sense for sense" or "literary translation," or *yiyi* 意译).[12] Another conservative method of translation is "formal equivalence" (*xingshi duideng* 形式对等), for which the source language is more important than the target language, and whereby an attempt is made to convey the form and content of the source text to target-language readers ("word for word" or "literal translation," or *zhiyi* 直译). Schereschewsky's translation practice accords with both of these translation theories. By stressing faithfulness while simultaneously employing a clear and idiomatic style, Schereschewsky employed both literal

---

[10] Lamin Sanneh, *Translating the Message: The Missionary Impact on Culture* (Maryknoll, NY: Orbis Books, 1990), 170 and 205.
[11] George Steiner, *After Babel: Aspects of Language and Translation* (London: Oxford University Press, 1975), 28.
[12] Jast Oliver Zetzsche: *The Bible in China: The History of the Union Version or the Culmination of Protestant Missionary Bible Translation in China* (Sankt Augustin: Monumenta Serica Institute, 1999), 349.

and literary translation, adapting his approach to his audience's literacy level. The Mandarin Version was a literal translation for a lower-class audience; the Easy Wenli Version was a literary translation for elite readers. Schereschewsky believed, on the one hand, that the translator must attempt to transpose the source text not only into the target language but also into the target culture – and, on the other, that the translator must be sufficiently well acquainted with the source text and the source language in order to find cultural and linguistic equivalents that will be appropriate for his translation.[13] These two translation strategies may seem incompatible or contradictory, but the good translator will make a choice according to different circumstances and achieve a perfect balance between the two. Schereschewsky's goal was to give Chinese readers an understanding of the original Hebrew text that would be as accurate as possible.

3.2 Respecting China's Literary Tradition and Ethnic Characteristics

Far from demanding cultural conformity, missionaries encouraged cultural pluralism by means of translation. Schereschewsky profoundly respected the Chinese civilization. He insisted that translators must possess a deep familiarity not only with the source text but also with the target culture and its customs in order to find equivalent expressions suitable for both cultures and languages. He also declared that "the mind, the spirit, and the mode of thinking of the nation" must be made the translator's own. Like the apostle Paul, who drew on two cultures to preach his message, who was "to Jews a Jew, and to the Greek a Greek," the missionary to China must be able to speak to the Chinese as though he were Chinese himself.[14] For Schereschewsky, the aim of the mission was the creation of a native and thoroughly Chinese Christianity. He argued that nothing must be done to destroy Chinese "ethnic characteristics"; "foreign traits" must not be grafted onto the Chinese character. Dislocating the Chinese "from all their social and civil articulations with the body politic in which they were born" must be avoided: "Instead of weaning him from the dress, the dwellings, the food, the habits and customs, the family circle and the civil obedience due from him. . ., his whole status should be preserved intact."[15] In the introduction to the 1875 Old Testament, he wrote,

---

[13] Eber, *The Jewish Bishop and the Chinese Bible*, 167.
[14] "Report of S. I. J. Schereschewsky," *SM* 25 (August 1860): 290–296. The report is dated April 5, 1860.
[15] "Consecration of the Missionary Bishop of Shanghai," *Spirit of Missions* 42 (December 1877): 672.

"The original Holy Scripture was written by the Jews (*youtai*, 犹太). Afterward all Western countries (*qinxi*, 秦西) translated [it] into each language. The present translation into Mandarin (*guanhua*, 官话) is profound in meaning and is prepared in accordance with the original. [I] . . . did not dare add or subtract one word."[16] Later, he wrote, "It is possible to be faithful to the original without being slavishly literal."[17] He believed that it was important to reproduce the style and poetry of the Bible and to preserve "biblical diction" in Chinese, especially the unique characteristics of Hebrew poetry.[18] He had a deep appreciation for the Chinese language and a highly unusual grasp of its complexities. Already, during the initial stages of the translation work, he was ". . . resolved to adhere to the Hebrew original as much as the nature of the Chinese language . . . will possibly admit. I believe that the Hebrew text is to be preferred to any version old as it may be."[19] Schereschewsky was more sensitive than other nineteenth-century Bible translator to the problems of Chinese cultural and linguistic factors. In the Easy Wenli Version, Song of Songs 8:6 reads as follows: 因爱强如死、由爱而生之妒心、酷如示阿勒（示阿勒有译黄泉有译阴府有译坟墓）、爱情之烈、如火如巨焰（因爱强如死由爱而生之妒心酷如示阿勒）(*yin ai qiang ru si, you ai er sheng zhi du xin, ku ru shi a le [shi a le you yi huang quan, you yi yin fu, you yi fen mu], ai qing zhi lie, ru huo ru ju yan [yin ai qiang ru si you ai er sheng zhi du xin ku ru shi a le]*, 'For love is strong as death; jealousy is cruel as the grave: the coals thereof are coals of fire'). Schereschewsky transliterated the Hebrew word *sheol* into the Chinese 示阿勒 (*shi a le*) according to the Hebrew pronunciation. Notes in brackets indicated the Chinese meaning of these characters: 黄泉 (*huang quan*, 'netherworld'); 阴府 (*yin fu*, 'hell'); and 坟墓, (*fen mu* 'tomb'). These notes allowed Schereschewsky to precisely explain the Hebrew term's meaning. In contrast, *sheol* was translated as 墓 (*mu*, 'tomb') and 阴间 (*yin jian*, 'grave') in Schereschewsky's Mandarin Version and in the later Union Version.

---

16 *Jiuyue quanshu* (Peking, 1875). The full English title is *The Old Testament in the Mandarin colloquial, translated from the Hebrew by the Reverend J. I. S. Schereschewsky, D.D. of the American Episcopal Mission, and printed for the American Bible Society at the press of the ABCFM.*
17 Schereschewsky, "Translation of the Scriptures into Chinese," *Records of the General Conference of the Protestant Missionaries of China, 1890* (Shanghai: American Presbyterian Mission Press, 1890), 41.
18 Schereschewsky, "Translation of the Scriptures into Chinese," 42.
19 DFMS, RG64-28, Schereschewsky, letter to S. D. Denison, July 21, 1865.

3.3 Multiple Interpretations and Intercultural Communication

Professor Even-Zohar is a pioneer of polysystem theory. In his terms, a "polysystem" is "a multiple system, a system of various systems which intersect with each other and partly overlap, using concurrently different options, yet functioning as one structured whole, whose members are interdependent."[20] A "polysystem" is multidimensional, able to accommodate multiple taxonomies established in the realm of literature (between high and low literature), translation (between translation and non-translation), social relationships (between dominant and dominated social groups), and canonicity (between canonized and non-canonized texts).[21] Even-Zohar's polysystem theory provides a way for us to examine the tension and balance between the Hebrew scriptures and and Schereschewsky's Chinese Bible translations. For example, Schereschewsky's mission, translation work, and other publications were supported by the American Bible Society as he began to create "Chinese Christianity" as a distinct cultural identity, which it continues to be. In contrast to the majority of Western missionaries of his time, he sought to achieve an intercultural understanding of indigenous cultures and mother-tongue speakers, especially in China vis-à-vis the modern West. Unfortunately, his reputation suffered when he refused to join a new Bible translation group in 1890, and his first vernacular Bible translation was gradually replaced by later versions.

Polysystem theory helps to account for the ways in which the process of translation is subject to the influence of the recipients' cultural tradition and native language system. Due to his Jewish-Christian cultural background, outstanding linguistic talent, and indomitable will, Schereschewsky became the first person to translate the Bible into vernacular Chinese. At the same time, we should not neglect the essential help of some Chinese and Japanese Christian teachers or workers. Schereschewsky's Chinese colleagues Lian Yinghuang (连应煌), Yu Baisheng (余包生), Zhang Zhijie (张志杰), Jin Shihe (金世和), and Ye Shandang (叶善荡) rendered him particularly valuable assistance. A successful Bible translator often relies on colleagues who are unknown to the public and pass through history leaving hardly a trace behind.

Although full play may be given to the translator's subjectivity, the cultural context of the target language must regulate the translator's understanding of his own activities and decision-making process. Both of Schereschewsky's biblical versions, which place special emphasis on guides, notes, and references, greatly

---

20 Itamar Even-Zohar, "Polysystem Studies," *Poetics Today*, 11, no. 1 (Spring 1990): 11.
21 Even-Zohar, "Polysystem Studies," 12–20.

benefit from his training in classical Jewish texts, his gift for language, and his flexible handling of ideology throughout the process of translation. Schereschewsky always places his notes within the text so that they directly follow the words or phrases which they elucidate. In many cases, his explanations are based on Rashi's commentary or other midrashic materials. They attest to Schereschewsky's intimate acquaintance with the Old Testament and its Jewish commentary tradition.

Moreover, Schereschewsky's notes add a new dimension to the biblical text. His annotations to the Song of Songs provide more than a theological revelatory interpretation of this love poem by means of metaphor. Without them, the translation of obscure passages would lead to misunderstandings or embarrassment. His extensive comments and annotations on the translation compensate for the ambiguity and flexibility of the source language (Hebrew) as well as the target language (Chinese). These notes allow the translation to become a teaching tool for newly converted readers. In a word, they constitute a skillful combination of the Jewish Talmudic and midrashic traditions with the ancient Chinese tradition of textual annotation.

4 Jewish-Chinese Dialogue between Two Ancient Civilizations

Susan Bassnett writes, "Language . . . is the heart within the body of culture, and it is the interaction between the two that . . . [is important]. In the same way that the surgeon, operating on the heart, cannot neglect the body that surrounds it, so the translator treats the text in isolation from the culture at his perils."[22] This quote illustrates that translation is not based on cultural universality. The divine words of the Hebrew Bible can be translated into Chinese only if the translator is intimately familiar with both cultural contexts: that of the ancient Hebrew text and that of his contemporary auditors in late nineteenth-century China. Indeed, Schereschewsky deeply understood the European Jewish, European Christian, and Chinese Confucian cultures. His admiration for the Chinese civilization convinced him that becoming Christian would not entail complete Westernization for the Chinese people, and that a Chinese-style Christianity could be developed in China. His two Bible versions, which reflect the translatability, readability, sinicization, and indigenization of the Sacred Word, also reveal Schereschewsky

---

22 Susan Bassnett, *Translation Studies*, rev. ed. (London and New York: Routledge, 1991), 14.

himself as a vanguard of the literary dialogue between the Jewish and traditional Chinese cultures. Irene Eber praises him highly: "More than any other early translator of scripture, Schereschewsky recognized and tackled the problem of Chinese cultural and linguistic factors in the expression of foreign ideas."[23]

Schereschewsky's Bible translations have had an important impact on the history of the Bible in Chinese. He brought a deeper knowledge of biblical Hebrew than his missionary colleagues to the endeavor, and his translating modes exhibit adaptability and openness. Moreover, his familiarity with the Jewish commentary tradition made a difference in his reading of the Hebrew text and his translations into Chinese. Both the Mandarin Version and the Easy Wenli Version exhibit cross-cultural hermeneutics that link classical Chinese traditions with Jewish scriptural exegesis and may contribute to our understanding of the ongoing dialogue between these two ancient civilizations. Of course, in using different literary forms to translate the Bible, his purpose was to promote the mission of Protestantism in China and to convert more Chinese readers and listeners to Christianity. In particular, the vernacular version of the Bible promoted his Protestant missionary work, enabling ordinary Chinese people to understand the Bible's words and thus convert to Christianity. Yet we can see in retrospect how his multicultural and multireligious background as a *Jewish* Christian makes his achievements all the more profound.

It is worth mentioning that the Union Version for Protestants was published in 1919,[24] forty-five years after the appearance of Schereschewsky's 1875 translation. The 1919 translation, which draws on Schereschewsky's 1875 Mandarin version, omits many of the annotations and reference marks found in earlier versions. As its authority became increasingly well-established, the Union Version gradually overshadowed Schereschewsky's pioneering work. This strange phenomenon was pointed out by the Slovak Sinologist Marián Gálik: "In any case, the Union Version was much more successful. Its translators, however, did not acknowledge their debt to Schereschewsky's translation."[25] As Irene Eber states,

---

23 Eber, "Translating the Ancestors: S. I. J. Schereschewsky's 1875 Chinese Version of Genesis," *Bulletin of the School of Oriental and African Studies, University of London*, 56, no. 2 (1993): 233.
24 In the late nineteenth century, a group of Protestant missionaries decided to translate a Union Version of the Bible. The General Conference took place in Shanghai, May 7–20, 1890. Long conferences followed in different cities in China over the following 29 years. The whole New and Old Testaments were translated by different translators, including Calvin W. Mateer, Chauncey Goodrich, Henry Blodget, Griffith John, John Reside Hykes, Henry M.Woods, Federick William Baller, Alfred G. Jones, Spencer Lewis, and so on. The whole Mandarin Union Version was finally published in 1919.
25 Marián Gálik, "Three Western Books on the Bible in China," *Influence, Translation, and Parallels: Selected Studies on the Bible in China* (Sankt Augustin: Monumenta Serica Institute, 2004), 142.

"A superficial comparison of both Bibles reveals the extent to which the later version was indebted to the former. Still, questions must be asked whether the Union translators were as sensitive to the languages – both Hebrew and Chinese – as Schereschewsky and the Peking Translation Committee had been."[26] As my article makes clear, there is evidence that the Union translators borrowed from Schereschewsky's translation. Recently, a growing number of academic studies on the close relationship between Schereschewsky's 1875 translation and the 1919 Union Version of the Bible for Protestants have demonstrated that Irene Eber and Marián Gálik's opinion is accurate.[27]

The sacred mission of translating the Bible in China gave Jewish-born Protestant missionary Schereschewsky a new understanding of the meaning of existence and the value of life. It was in China, in the Chinese Bible, that his wandering finally found refuge in spiritual conversion and the great mission. It is a miracle that Schereschewsky's great contribution built a bridge between the Jewish-Christian and Chinese cultures in terms of language, faith, religion, literature, and education. He left behind a rich and astonishing legend that endures to this day. Today, in the twenty-first century, strengthening this friendly bond between the Jewish and Chinese peoples can only be a worthwhile endeavor. Globalization, moreover, requires us to keep an open mind, to listen to others, and to enrich ourselves through continual dialogue and participation – this is the dream of Schereschewsky, who dedicated his whole life to Chinese Bible translations. Whenever we open a Chinese Bible translation, we should remember Schereschewsky's fruit and its cultural harvest, illuminated by "Light and Truth."[28]

---

[26] Eber, "Remarks On the Intercutural Nature of Bible Translation," in *Talking Literature: Essays on Chinese and Biblical Writings and Their Interaction*, eds. Raoul David Findeisen and Martin Slobodnik (Wiesbaden: Harrassowitz Verlag, 2013), 73–74.
[27] For related research on this issue, see Jast Oliver Zetzsche, *The Bible in China: The History of the Union Version or the Culmination of Protestant Missionary Bible Translation in China* (Sankt Augustin: Monumenta Serica Institute, 1999).
[28] "Light and Truth" was the motto of St. John's University in Shanghai.

References

Bassnett, Susan. *Translation Studies*. London and New York: Routledge, 1991.
Domestic and Foreign Missionary Society. China Records, 1835–1951. The Archives of the Episcopal Church. Austin, Texas.
Eber, Irene. *The Jewish Bishop and the Chinese Bible: S. I. J. Schereschewsky, 1831–1906*. Leiden and Boston: Brill, 1999.
Eber, Irene. "Translating the Ancestors: S. I. J. Schereschewsky's 1875 Chinese Version of Genesis." *Bulletin of the School of Oriental and African Studies* 56, no. 2 (1993): 219–233.
Eber, Irene. "Remarks On the Intercutural Nature of the Bible Translations." Translated by Hegui Guan. *Journal for the Study of Biblical Literature* 11 (2015): 136–149.
Even-Zohar, Itamar. "Polysystem Studies." *Poetic Today* 11, no. 1 (1990): 9–26.
Findeisen, Raoul David. " 'God Was Their Souls' Love, Women Their Bodies' ': Two Chinese Versions of the Song of Songs (1930/32)." In *Talking Literature: Essays on Chinese and Biblical Writings and Their Interaction*, 123–138. Wiesbaden: Harrassowitz Verlag, 2013.
Gálik, Marián. "A Comment on Three Western Books on the Bible in Modern and Contemporary China." In *Influence, Translation, and Parallels: Selected Studies on the Bible in China*, 135–144. Sankt Augustin: Monumenta Serica Institute, 2004.
Sanneh, Lamin. *Translating the Message: The Missionary Impact on Culture*. Maryknoll, NY: Orbis Books, 1990.
Schereschewsky, S. I. J. "Consecration of the Missionary Bishop of Shanghai." *Spirit of Missions* 42 (December 1877): 672.
Schereschewsky, S. I. J. "Translation of the Scriptures into Chinese." In *Records of the General Conference of the Protestant Missionaries of China*, 91–92. Shanghai: American Presbyterian Mission Press, 1890.
Schereschewsky, S. I. J. "Report of S. I. J. Schereschewsky." *Spirit of Missions* (August 25, 1860): 290–296.
Schereschewsky, S. I. J., trans. *Jiu Yue Quan Shu* 旧约全书 [The Old Testament in the Mandarin Colloquial]. Peking: American Bible Society, 1875.
Schereschewsky, S. I. J. and the Peking Translation Committee, trans. *Qian Wen Li Jiu Xin Yue Sheng Jing* 浅文理旧新约圣经 [Easy Wenli Old Testament and New Testament Version]. Shanghai: American Bible Society, 1902.
Steiner, George. *After Babel: Aspects of Language and Translation*. London: Oxford University Press, 1975.
Zetzsche, Jast Oliver. *The Bible in China: The History of the Union Version or the Culmination of Protestant Missionary Bible Translation in China*. Sankt Augustin: Monumenta Serica Institute, 1999.

II Jews in Modern China

The eight essays in Part II, "Jews in Modern China," cover a number of topics in the modern and contemporary periods. Xu Xin's opening essay, "Jewish Communities and Modern China: Encounters of Modern Civilizations," presents an overview of the history of the Jewish Diaspora in modern China, from the mid-nineteenth to the twenty-first century. Ai Rengui's essay, "When the Muscular Jews Came to the Far East: Jewish Sports and Physical Culture in Modern China, 1912–1949," considers the establishment of athletic groups by Ashkenazic Jewish residents and refugees in Shanghai and other cities in China. Maisie Meyer discusses the Baghdadi Jews who established trade and commerce in Shanghai starting in the mid-nineteenth century and explores their interactions with and interventions on behalf of the Ashkenazic Jews who came later. The next four essays in Part II deal with the Jewish refugees from central and eastern Europe who found shelter in Shanghai from Nazi antisemitism from 1938 through 1949. Wang Jian surveys the demographic challenges in determining the "Exact Number of Jewish Refugees in Shanghai," Nancy Berliner presents a study of "Jewish Refugee Artists in Shanghai," Yang Meng writes on the theater produced in "Wartime Shanghai," and Marc B. Shapiro illuminates the survival of the students and faculty of the Mir Yeshiva in Shanghai during the war. Finally, Samuel Heilman explores the Lithuanian Hasidic Chabad movement's current efforts to establish religious outreach programs for contemporary Jews living in the People's Republic of China.

Xu Xin
6 Jewish Communities and Modern China: Encounters of Modern Civilizations

The Chinese and Jewish cultures are both great civilizations. Both developed in ancient times and have endured until today, keeping continuous recorded accounts of their origins. Both have had a significant impact on world history: the Jews on the West, the Chinese on the Far East. Unfortunately, before the modern era, these two major societies seldom met. As a result, little was known about Jewish culture in China. The first direct and meaningful Chinese encounters with Jews took place at the end of the nineteenth century and the beginning of the twentieth, chiefly due to the ongoing arrival of Jews in China. In time, various Jewish communities were established in modern Chinese cities.

The Jewish Diaspora in China is a unique experience for world Jewry, as China is the only country in East Asia that has had Jews living in its society for a millennium or longer. But a significant distinction exists between Jews in pre-modern China (before 1840) and those in modern China (since 1840). Those who arrived before the modern era integrated into Chinese society and consequently lost many of their distinctive features, but those who have come during the modern era have remained foreigners.

The earliest documentary evidence of Jews in China survives from the Tang dynasty (618–907 CE).[1] During that time, a dozen Jewish communities appeared in Chinese cities such as Quanzhou, Guangzhou, Hangzhou, Ningbo, Yangzhou, Xi'an, Peking, Luoyang, Nanjing, and Ningxia. However, with the exception of the Kaifeng Jewish community, pre-modern Jews in China left behind very few materials for us to reconstruct their lives and histories. By the eighteenth century, they had all but vanished.[2] The Kaifeng Jewish community, established between

---

[1] The earliest available evidence is a business letter dating from 718 CE, written in the Judeo-Persian language and found in Dandan Uiliq, an important post along the Silk Road in Northwest China. The text contains 37 lines and was written on paper, a product then manufactured only in China. From this fragment, we learn that a Persian-speaking Jew was trading commodities. He wrote to a fellow Jew, who was obviously also a trader, and asked him for help in disposing of some sheep of inferior stock that he had the misfortune to possess. See D. S. Margoliouth, "An Early Judæo-Persian Document from Khotan, in the Stein Collection, with Other Early Persian Documents," *Journal of the Royal Asiatic Society of Great Britain and Ireland* (October 1903): 735–760.

[2] Most likely they were totally assimilated into Chinese society. See Xu Xin, *The Jews of Kaifeng, China: History, Culture, and Religion* (Hoboken, NJ: KTAV, 2003), 154–165.

960 and 1126 CE in the capital city of the Song dynasty, survived until the mid-nineteenth century, when their last rabbi died without a successor. Without regular attendance, the synagogue gradually diminished.³ By then, one could claim, the community had virtually ceased to exist as such, although individual Jewish descendants still live in the city to this day.

But before the Jewish communities established in pre-modern China had entirely disappeared, additional Jewish immigrants settled in China, initiating a new era for Jews and Chinese alike.⁴ The new arrivals came in several waves. First, Sephardic Jews, originally based in Baghdad and Bombay, sought business opportunities in newly opened Chinese treaty cities such as Hong Kong and Shanghai during the second half of the nineteenth century. By the beginning of the twentieth century, they had built up solid Jewish communities in those coastal cities. Second, during the early twentieth century, an influx of Ashkenazi Jews – mainly from Russia and other eastern European countries – initially arrived in Harbin and contiguous zones in Northeast China and later moved south. Although a few came in search of better economic opportunities, the majority were fleeing from pogroms, wars, and revolutions in Russia. The third wave consisted mainly of European Jewish refugees from Nazi Germany and Austria. From 1937 through 1940, about 20,000 Jewish refugees arrived in Shanghai. This wave also included some 1,000 Jews from Kobe, Japan. Among these, all the teachers and students of the Mir Yeshiva, some 400 in total, had previously escaped Poland through Vilna, obtained transit visas to Japan from Sugihara Chiune (the Japanese consul in Kovno), and finally made their way to China in the early 1940s. In Shanghai, they continued their studies in the Beth Aharon Synagogue, the only place of worship with space enough to hold the entire Yeshiva. Overall, from 1845 through 1945, more than 40,000 Jews arrived in China seeking business development or a safe haven, which at last made it possible for a significant number of Chinese to encounter them directly.⁵

---

3 Xu Xin, *The Jews of Kaifeng, China*, ch. 6, pp. 151–165.
4 Modern Chinese history began in the second half of the nineteenth century, when China was forced to open its doors to Western powers. From 1725 (when the Chinese emperor ordered all foreign missionaries to leave China) to 1840, China – apart from the South – was more or less closed to foreigners. However, after China's defeat in the Opium War with Great Britain (1839–1842), the Treaty of Nanjing (1842) and its supplementary protocols (1843) obliged the Chinese government to surrender Hong Kong to the British and open five major port cities to British traders and settlements. This soon led to the establishment of territorial enclaves under the British flag. Other imperial powers followed suit, and many foreign adventurers subsequently came to China – among them, Jews.
5 Pan Guang 潘光, ed., *Youtairen zai Zhongguo* 犹太人在中国 (Beijing: Wuzhou Chuanbuo Chubanshe, 2005), 26–52.

The end of World War II and the surrender of Japan brought new hope for Jews in China. For the European refugees, the first positive changes were the complete resumption of communication with the outside world, the flow of much-needed money into the community, and their newfound freedom of movement. Many found opportunities to rejoin their relatives abroad and/or to live in societies to whose lifestyles and cultures they were more accustomed. It was natural for them to leave – after all, they had only come to China in the first place because they did not have any other choice. The United States, Canada, and Australia became their new destinations if visas could be obtained. However, most countries had yet to widely open their doors to Jewish refugees. The founding of the State of Israel offered a new alternative. In 1948, shortly after its establishment, Israel opened an office in Shanghai to welcome Jews to Israel. About 10,000 Jews found a new home there.

On the other hand, China had been home to the Sephardim and the Russians for a generation or more. Many considered staying. Some began to invest, while others started to rebuild their businesses. However, their hopes were short-lived. In 1946, civil war broke out between the Nationalists and the Communists. Well-established Jewish families in Shanghai, such as the Sassoons and the Kadoories, began to transfer their businesses elsewhere: the Sassoons to the Bahamas, the Kadoories to Hong Kong.

By 1949, the year of the Communists' rise to power, most of the Jews in China had already migrated elsewhere. Only a few thousand had chosen to stay. By the end of 1950s, the Jewish Diaspora in modern China had virtually disappeared. In 1966, at the start of the Cultural Revolution, only a few elders and revolutionaries – such as Israel Epstein and Sydney Shapiro, who were affiliated with the Chinese Communist Revolution – remained. Those who were left eventually passed away.[6]

Nevertheless, the fact that Jews resided in China does not mean that the Chinese had any great awareness of their presence before the modern era. The majority of the Chinese knew very little. Until the beginning of the nineteenth century, they simply referred to Jews as Blue Hat *Hui hui* ('people who came from the West to China'), or *Tiao-jin-jiao* ('sect that plucks out the sinews'). Both names are based on certain customs of the Kaifeng Jews. No one, not even the most knowledgeable scholars in China, had any suspicion that the Jews in Kaifeng might represent a larger religious population who were scattered in many countries, held common beliefs, and shared a similar lifestyle.[7]

---

[6] See also Xu Xin 徐新, *Yixiang Yike: Youtairen Yu Jinxiandai Zhonggou* 異鄉異客：猶太人與近現代中國 [Aliens in a strange land: Jews and modern China] (Taipei: National Taiwan University Press, 2017), ch. 2, pp. 45–57.

[7] Hong Jun, historian, diplomat, and author of the very first scholarly essay on the Jews of Kaifeng, wrote, "I learned from the Westerners that now in Kaifeng of Henan, China, there are

The current Chinese term for Jews is *You tai* (犹太), which is a relatively modern one. It dates from 1823, when Robert Morrison of England, one of the Protestant missionaries to China in the early nineteenth century, published a translation of the Bible into classical Chinese. The term he coined, *You tai*, entered popular circulation and gradually became the standard Chinese term for Jews today.

The first significant encounter between Chinese and Jews occurred in the second half of the nineteenth century, after China, having been defeated in the First Opium War (ca. 1840–42), was forced to open its doors to the West. At the time, the only sources of knowledge about Jews available to the Chinese were:

1. Westerners who came to China on missionary, commercial, trade, or diplomatic ventures;
2. Chinese travelers who gleaned new information from studying or working abroad in the Western world;
3. Chinese scholars and intellectuals who, seeking inspiration to modernize their country, were interested in foreign issues and exposed to foreign literature or documents; and
4. Jews arriving in China in the modern era.

The first three sources offered fascinating accounts of the following topics:
- How the Jews survived throughout their history
- How the Jews revived (politically, economically, and culturally) since the Haskalah and their emancipation
- The uniqueness of the Jewish people
- What the Jews achieved in the sciences, in finances, and in society

From their earliest contacts, Chinese writers saw Jewish culture as a gold mine of wisdom and Zionism as a model for Chinese nationalism. Sun Yat-sen, founding father of modern China, made several references to the Jewish Diaspora in his famous lecture series "On the Three People's Principles." He said:

> Chinese nationalism disappeared when China was conquered by foreigners [the Manchus]. But China was not the only nation that had been conquered. The Jewish people also lost their country... Though their country was destroyed, the Jewish nation has existed to this day....What is the reason why other nations such as the Jews, who lost their country two thousand years ago, could still preserve their nationalism, while our China was conquered only three hundred years ago but Chinese nationalism has entirely disappeared?[8]

---

still Jews." See his "Study of the Names of Religions in the Yuan Period," *Annotations to the Chinese Translation of the Yuan Annuals* 29 (1897): 7.

[8] Sun Yat-sen, "On the Three People's Principles: Nationalism," lecture 3, *Selected Works of Sun Yat-sen* (Beijing, 1956), 620–621.

The same issue was addressed by Yu Songhua, a well-known Chinese intellectual in the 1930s, who also hoped to draw inspiration from the Jewish experience:

> Looking at the Jews, what should we ask ourselves?
>
> From ancient times to the present, prominent figures have come forth in large numbers among the Jews; we have had some great figures in our history, but have had no outstanding personage in modern times. Should we feel ashamed, compared with the Jews and with our own ancestors?
>
> Jews are a people without a country and a people who have been despised everywhere, but they are still struggling very hard, never discouraged by difficulties and setbacks, to carry on the restoration movement. So those people who do have their own countries should strive even harder and resolve to make their countries become strong. . . .If our Chinese fellow countrymen could have the same enthusiasm and determination which Jews displayed in their resurgent movement, to exploit our natural resources and to promote our national culture, I believe our achievements would be much greater than that of the Jews.[9]

The Yiddish literature that was introduced to Chinese readers in the 1920s was basically a modern achievement of European Ashkenazi Jews. Yiddish writers such as Shalom Aleichem and Isaac Peretz, whose stories were newly translated and published in Chinese literary magazines, inspired Chinese writers to write their stories differently.[10] A new era of modern Chinese literature had begun.

The fourth source – Jews themselves – had a completely different impact on Chinese society. They arrived at a time when China, its isolation broken, was beginning to embrace the process of modernization that had already begun in the West a hundred years earlier. Moreover, they had already experienced the Jewish Enlightenment, Haskalah, and integrated with the rest of the modernized West. Well-versed in the rules and regulations of international trade, familiar with modern business strategies, and experts in the means, channels, and privileges of international trade, they took full advantage of their newly-acquired social status to find a place in the early modern economic life and social development of China. As a result, Chinese intellectuals discovered that the influence and contributions of the Jewish people had always been outstanding in the fields of economy, commerce, science, and culture.

In Shanghai, one of the first modern cities in China, foreign businessmen, including Jews, established companies specializing in imports and exports, built modern factories, invested in real estate, and established modern banking systems.

---

9 Yu Songhua, "Jews and the Jewish Resurgent Movement," *Dongfang Zazhi* 24, no. 17 (1927): 25.
10 Irene Eber, *Voices from Afar: Modern Chinese Writers on Oppressed Peoples and Their Literature* (Ann Arbor: Center for Chinese Studies, University of Michigan, 1980).

Frontrunners in real estate, they not only benefited greatly from the appreciation of land prices from 1900 to 1930 but also gave the city a new look. The spectacular buildings they constructed changed the skyline of the city – and reflected their keen business sense. Before 1949, Shanghai held a total of 28 buildings that were over ten stories high. Of those buildings, six were owned by the Sassoons' companies.[11]

Silas Hardoon was a real-estate genius who knew how to increase land value by upgrading transit conditions. He invested 600,000 ounces of silver to pave what was then the Nanjing Road with expensive wood, making it the first fully paved road in modern Shanghai. Because the Nanjing Road was no longer muddy in the long rainy season, more people began shopping there – especially wealthy women in their long, beautiful gowns. In fact, it became the premier shopping street in Shanghai. The value of real estate on both sides of the road, much of which was owned by Hardoon, rapidly increased.[12] At the time of Hardoon's death, he owned 24 office buildings, 544 residential buildings, 812 townhouses, 4 hotels and restaurants, and 3 warehouses.[13] Unsurprisingly, he was considered the real-estate king of modern Shanghai. Decades later, in the 1990s, China's reform and opening-up policy promoted the re-emergence of Shanghai's real estate business. At one colloquium, the participants proposed that the city needed "socialist Hardoons."[14]

This was far from the only Jewish contribution. The first public bus line in Shanghai was created and operated by the Arnold brothers in 1924; the passenger line along the Yangtze River was also first operated by Jews.[15]

Many Jewish businessmen were also philanthropists. In addition to their own donations, Hardoon and his co-religionists raised millions of dollars in aid for the sufferers of famines (which were frequent) and on behalf of other charitable causes through their fundraising events. By doing so, they not only helped the suffering Chinese, but also introduced the traditional Jewish charity concept to China.[16]

---

11 Xu Xin, *Yixiang Yike: Youtairen Yu Jinxiandai Zhonggou*, ch. 2, pp. 45–57, 205.
12 Xu Xin, *Yixiang Yike: Youtairen Yu Jinxiandai Zhonggou*, 206.
13 Xu Xin, *Yixiang Yike: Youtairen Yu Jinxiandai Zhonggou*, 206–207.
14 For instance, a national conference was held in Shanghai in 1997. One of the topics was how to increase the value of land to boom real estate of Shanghai. Hardoon used to be criticized as a capitalist. Now many scholars believe that his strategies to develop the economy, especially the real estate industry, are meaningful and valuable in socialist China.
15 Xu Xin, *Yixiang Yike: Youtairen Yu Jinxiandai Zhonggou*, 207. See also Tang Peiji et al., *Jews in Shanghai* (Shanghai: Sanlian Shudian, 1992), 91–99.
16 Xu Xin, *Yixiang Yike: Youtairen Yu Jinxiandai Zhonggou*, 208.

In Harbin, too, Jews had a far-reaching influence on economic life, especially industry, commerce, and real estate. Besides serving the local market, they aimed at the world market. Due to their efforts, furs and soybean oil became popular global commodities.[17]

S. Soskin, an important member of the Harbin Jewish community, served as vice president of the Harbin Trade Fair. Many buildings constructed by Jewish architects and engineers almost hundred years ago still stand along Harbin's Main Street.[18]

Jews were among the first Westerners to introduce European arts, technologies, and modern professions such as medicine, engineering, and journalism to Northeast China in general and Harbin in particular. The earliest Western-style pharmacies, movie theaters, and modern hotel industries were all first run by Harbin Jews. The Hôtel Moderne, opened by Joseph Kaspé in 1913, was the largest in Harbin at the time of its completion. The Huamei Western Restaurant, the Harbin Cigarette Factory on the West Bank of the Ashi River, and the Acheng Sugar Factory (the first institutional sugar producers in China) were also founded and operated by Jewish entrepreneurs.[19] There is no doubt that the Jews have made indelible contributions to the formation and development of Harbin and improvement of the city's international reputation.

The Harbin Jews also introduced European art, music, ideas, medicine, engineering, and journalism to the city.[20]

Jewish refugees established various arts organizations in Shanghai for artists, musicians, painters, and Yiddish-language performers, whose concerts, operas, and operettas were welcomed by local residents. From 1940 to 1943, each opera was performed over 60 times,[21] greatly enriching Shanghai's cultural life. As a result of these literary events, Shanghai became one of the few cities in the world to have its own Yiddish-language theater.[22]

The association of Jewish artists and art lovers also held many exhibitions. Of the Jewish painters who used their brushes to capture the social features of Shanghai in wartime, Friedrich Schiff and David Bloch enjoyed a great reputa-

---

17 Qu Wei 曲伟 and Li Shuxiao 李述笑, eds., *Youtairen zai Haerbin* 犹太人在哈尔滨 [The Jews in Harbin] (Beijing: Shehui Kexue Wenxian Chubanshe, 2003), 28–63.
18 Qu Wei and Li Shuxiao, eds., *Youtairen zai Haerbin*, 42.
19 Qu Wei and Li Shuxiao, eds., *Youtairen zai Haerbin*, 66–100.
20 Qu Wei and Li Shuxiao, eds., *Youtairen zai Haerbin*, 44–63.
21 Tang Yading, *Cultural Life of the Shanghai Jewish Communities (1850–1950)* (Shanghai: Music College Press, 2007), 90. See also Wang Jian 王健, *Shanghai Youtairen Shehui Shenghuo Shi* 上海犹太人社会生活史 (Shanghai: Shanghai Cishu Chubanshe, 2008), 193–207.
22 Wang Jian, *Shanghai Youtairen Shehui Shenghuo Shi*, 203.

tion. Born in 1908 in Vienna, Austria, Schiff came to China in 1930 and lived in Shanghai for nearly two decades. In commemoration of the fortieth anniversary of the establishment of diplomatic relations between China and Austria in 2011, the Austrian consulate general in Hong Kong organized a traveling exhibition: "Schiff's View of the Clouds: Modern Shanghai by Austrian Painter Schiff," showcasing the masterpieces of this Austrian Jewish painter.[23]

David Bloch (1910–2003), from Bavaria, Germany, often went deep into the city streets to observe life. His watercolors and woodcuts, including portrayals of the Jewish ghetto in Hongkou, depicted the state of affairs in Shanghai with exaggerated brushstrokes, in which the situation of Jewish refugees persecuted by the Japanese occupation authorities can still be clearly seen.[24]

The prosperity and cultural development of modern Chinese cities such as Shanghai, Harbin, and many others have everything to do with Jews. Modern and contemporary Jewish artists have conquered the hearts of many Chinese with their superb craftsmanship, artistic appreciation, and creative ability. Chinese partners benefitted a great deal from doing business with Jewish entrepreneurs.

It is also worth mentioning the role played by Jewish musicians such as Aaron Avshalomov, Alfred Wittenberg, Walter Joachim, and Arrigo Foa, who not only enriched Shanghai's cultural life with their performances, but also trained a large number of young Chinese classical musicians at the Shanghai Art Institute. Their students later became the best of contemporary Chinese musicians.[25]

Alfred Wittenberg's contribution to modern Chinese music deserves special attention. Wittenberg arrived in Shanghai on February 25, 1939. Because of his outstanding talents as a violinist, his fame soon spread among Chinese musicians and music-lovers such as Tan Jizhen, Ma Sihong, Yang Bingjun, and Mao Chuen, who were already accomplished violinists at the time. Zhang Guoling, Dou Lixun, Situ Xingcheng, and others aspired to study with him in the hope of receiving further training in their field. All became famous musicians in China during the 1960s. Today, Wittenberg is called "the Professor of professors."[26]

The Jewish-Chinese connection has stimulated the study of Jewish and Israeli culture in China. Almost all Chinese scholars working in this field today are familiar with the history of the Jewish Diaspora in modern China. In Shanghai, the Jewish Refugees Memorial Museum in the former Beth Moshe synagogue (once

---

23 Pan Guang, ed., *Youtairen zai Zhongguo*, 177.
24 Xu Buzeng 许步曾, *Xunfang Youtairen: Youtai Wenhua Jingying zai Shanghai* 寻访犹太人：犹太文化精英在上海 (Shanghai: Shanghai Shehuikexue Chubanshe, 2007), 101–121. See also Pan Guang, ed., *Youtairen zai Zhongguo*, 177.
25 Xu Buzeng, *Xunfang Youtairen: Youtai Wenhua Jingying zai Shanghai*, 40–57.
26 Xu Buzeng, *Xunfang Youtairen: Youtai Wenhua Jingying zai Shanghai*, 57–72.

used by the Jews confined to the former Hongkou Ghetto District) preserves the history of Jews in China in the form of historical photos and artifacts. In Harbin, the Heilongjiang Academy of Social Sciences has made Harbin Jewish history a key research topic, published a significant number of research results, organized a photography exhibition on the subject of Jews in Harbin, and held international academic seminars. The Heilongjiang provincial administration and the Harbin municipal government have made the restoration of the Harbin Jewish heritage a major project, one they have combined with the further development and transformation of Harbin.[27]

Finally, in the past decade or so, hundreds of books on Jewish life in China have been published in Chinese. Many, written by Jewish refugees themselves, recount their survival of European antisemitism, their lives in China, and their friendships with Chinese people.[28] The understanding of China among Jews today is directly linked to the records of these twentieth-century Jewish refugees in China. From the perspective of outsiders, their memoirs offer a kaleidoscopic view of customs, social conditions, and daily life in wartime China (especially in Shanghai, Harbin, and Tianjin).

In short, it is no exaggeration to say that the Jews who came to modern China in the nineteenth and twentieth centuries made outstanding contributions to the early development of coastal Chinese cities. The rise of China's modern science and culture – from art, architecture, and education to medical care, newspapers, and magazines – were all the results of the Jewish Diaspora. To a certain extent we can say that it is through this encounter with Jews that China finally entered the modern era. The role played by Jews in China cannot be overestimated.

References

Eber, Irene. *Chinese and Jews: Encounters Between Cultures*. London: Vallentine Mitchell, 2008.
Eber, Irene. *Passage Through China: The Jewish Communities of Harbin, Tientsin and Shanghai*. Tel Aviv: Beth Hatefutsouth, 1986.
Eber, Irene. *Voices from Afar: Modern Chinese Writers on Oppressed Peoples and Their Literature*. Ann Arbor: University of Michigan, Center for Chinese Studies, 1980.
Eber, Irene. *Wartime Shanghai and the Jewish Refugees from Central Europe: Survival, Co-existence, and Identity in a Multi-Ethnic City*. Berlin: De Gruyter, 2012.

---

27 Xu Buzeng, *Xunfang Youtairen: Youtai Wenhua Jingying zai Shanghai*, 57–74.
28 Pan Guang, ed., *Youtairen zai Zhongguo*, ch. 6, pp. 210–228. See also Xu Xin, *Yixiang Yike: Youtairen Yu Jinxiandai Zhonggou*, 218.

Hong Jun. "A Study of the Names of Religions in the Yuan Period." *Annotations to the Chinese Translation of the Yuan Annuals* 29 (1897): 6–19.

Kranzler, David. *Japanese, Nazis and Jews: The Jewish Refugees Community of Shanghai, 1938–1945.* New York: Yeshiva University Press, 1976.

Margoliouth, D. S. "An Early Judæo-Persian Document from Khotan, in the Stein Collection, with Other Early Persian Documents." *Journal of the Royal Asiatic Society of Great Britain and Ireland* (October 1903): 735–760.

Pan Guang 潘光 and Wang Jian 王健. *Yigeban shiji yilai de Shanghai Youtairen* 一个半世纪以来的上海犹太人. Beijing: Shehui kexue wenxian chubanshe, 2002.

Pan Guang 潘光, ed. *Youtairen zai Shanghai* 犹太人在上海. Shanghai: Shanghai Huabao Chubanshe, 1995.

Pan Guang 潘光, ed. *Youtairen zai Zhongguo* 犹太人在中国. Beijing: Wuzhou Chuanbuo Chubanshe [China Intercontinental Press], 2005.

Qu Wei 曲伟 and Li Shuxiao 李述笑, eds. *Youtairen zai Haerbin* 犹太人在哈尔滨. Beijing: Shehui Kexue Wenxian Chubanshe, 2003.

Song, Anna 宋安娜, ed. *Youtairen zai Tianjin* 犹太人在天津. Beijing: Wuzhou Chuanbuo Chubanshe [China Intercontinental Press], 2004.

Sun Yat-sen. "On the Three People's Principles: Nationalism," lecture 3, *Selected Works of Sun Yat-sen.* Beijing, 1956. 620–621.

Tang Yading 汤亚汀. *Shanghai Youtai Sheqiu de Yinle Shenghou* 上海犹太社区的音乐生活. Shanghai: Shanghai Yingle Xueyuan Chubanshe, 2007.

Wang Jian 王健. *Shanghai Youtairen Shehui Shenghuo Shi* 上海犹太人社会生活史. Shanghai: Shanghai Cishu Chubanshe, 2008.

Xu Buzeng 许步曾. *Xunfang Youtairen: Youtai Wenhua Jingying zai Shanghai* 寻访犹太人：犹太文化精英在上海. Shanghai: Shanghai Shehuikexue Chubanshe, 2007.

Xu Xin 徐新. *Yixiang Yike: Youtairen Yu Jinxiandai Zhonggou* 異鄉異客：猶太人與近現代中國 [Aliens in a strange land: Jews and modern China]. Taipei: National Taiwan University Press, 2017.

Xu Xin 徐新. "二十世纪五十年代后期在华犹太人状况简述" [Jewish life in the second half of the 1950s in China]. *Shehui Kexue* 4 (2000): 72–76.

Xu Xin 徐新. *The Jews of Kaifeng, China: History, Culture, and Religion.* Hoboken, NJ: KTAV, 2003.

Yu Songhua. "Jews and the Jewish Resurgent Movement." *Dongfang Zazhi* 24, no. 17 (1927): 27–34.

Ai Rengui
7 When the Muscular Jews Came to the Far East: Jewish Sports and Physical Culture in Modern China, 1912–1949

During the first half of the twentieth century, the Jewish body image experienced fundamental changes. Under the ideal of Muscular Judaism, many Jews turned to sports and other physical activities to rebuild the Jewish body, and as this fashion spread from Europe to other parts of the Jewish Diaspora, it developed as a global Jewish phenomenon. Jews in the Far East were no exception. To a large extent, Jewish sports in China were an Ashkenazi phenomenon, for the majority of their participants were Ashkenazim from Europe. Since 1912, when the first Jewish sports club in China, the JRC (Jewish Recreation Club), was founded in Shanghai, Jews in China participated in football, boxing, handball, tennis, track and field, and so on. These activities were supported by Maccabi, Betar, and other Zionist organizations with the goal of organizing young Jews through sports and military training. Jews in China also organized Maccabi sports meetings, joined the great Games of China during the 1930s and 40s, and acquired great influence in the Far East. Through a variety of sports, Jews in China trained their physical strength, reshaping the Jewish body image in China with the dream of Jewish national revival. But with the end of the Second World War and the founding of the State of Israel, a large number of Jewish refugees left China, and as a result, Jewish sports also declined in China. From the Jewish perspective, Jewish sports in China were an important branch of Diaspora nationalism, one that reflected the worldwide influence of Zionism; from the Chinese perspective, the development of Jewish sports in China was closely linked to the changes in Chinese society over the course of modern history. Examining the rise and fall of Jewish sports in modern China will enable us to better understand the evolution of Jews in China as well as China's social changes in the modern era.

1 Jewish Sports in China as an Ashkenazi Phenomenon

Around 1840, by which time the Kaifeng Jewish community on the banks of the Yellow River had been gradually assimilated, the gunboats of the British Empire opened the gates of the Qing Empire, which made it possible for foreigners – including

https://doi.org/10.1515/9783110683943-010

Jews – to enter China again. Unlike pre-modern and early modern Jews, who had entered China mainly through the Silk Road and other land routes, these modern Jewish immigrants followed the footsteps of the British colonists, expanding eastward by sea. They mainly settled in the trading ports on the coast of Southeast China, locations that offered attractive business opportunities. As Jewish immigrants continued to arrive in these areas, they began to form substantial communities in Hong Kong, Shanghai, Harbin, Tientsin, and other important foreign trade ports in China.[1]

Modern Jewish immigration to China was mainly divided into four waves. First, after the Opium War in 1840, Sephardi Jews came to China from cities in the Middle East and South Asia such as Baghdad and Bombay and mostly settled in trade ports such as Hong Kong and Shanghai. Second, in the late nineteenth and early twentieth centuries, Ashkenazi Jews, fleeing the pogroms in Russia, traveled to Russia's spheres of influence in Northeast and North China (such as Harbin, Tientsin, Dalian, Manchuria, and Qingdao). Third, from 1933 to 1941, Ashkenazi Jews from Germany and Austria, seeking temporary asylum from Nazi persecution, took refuge in Shanghai. Fourth, with the start of China's Open Door Policy in 1978, many Jews came to China for business, work, and study, primarily settling in coastal cities with developed economic and cultural properties, such as Beijing, Shanghai, Guangzhou, Shenzhen, and Yiwu.[2]

Many of these modern Jewish immigrants have played important roles in China's economic, political, and cultural fields. In addition to celebrities such as Silas Aaron Hardoon, Jacob Rosenfeld, and Israel Epstein, and families such as the Sassoons and the Kadoories, four large Jewish community centers emerged in modern China: Hong Kong in the South, Shanghai in the East, Harbin in the Northeast, and Tientsin in the North. This chapter in Chinese and Jewish history, in which China became the center of the Jewish Diaspora in the Far East, is one that cannot be ignored.

In 1912, the establishment of the Jewish Recreation Club in Shanghai signaled the beginning of Jewish sports in modern China. Their participants were mainly distributed among Shanghai, Harbin, Tientsin, Dalian, Qingdao, and other cities. Shanghai and Harbin were the two main gathering places, while the gatherings in Tientsin, Dalian, and Qingdao were established by the Harbin branch. In the early twentieth century, these sports activities were initiated by the Ashkenazim from Russia, and by the 1930s, with the influx of Ashkenazi Jewish refugees from

---

[1] Jonathan Goldstein, "The Sorkin and Golab Theses and Their Applicability to South, Southeast, and East Asian Port Jewry," *Jewish Culture and History* 4, no. 2 (2001): 179–196.
[2] Zhang Qianhong and Ai Rengui, *Youtai Wenhua* 犹太文化 [Jewish culture] (Beijing: People's Publishing Press, 2013), 352.

central Europe, they continued to develop rapidly. After the end of the Second World War, when the Soviet Red Army entered Northeast China in 1945, the Harbin Jewish youth organizations Betar and Maccabi were banned, and Harbin Jews were forced to stop their sports activities. By 1949, with the outbreak of the Chinese Civil War and the founding of the State of Israel, most Jews – especially Ashkenazim – had left the country. This led to the decline of Jewish sports in China.

From an ethnic perspective, Jewish sports in modern China were primarily an Ashkenazi phenomenon, connected with the two waves of Russian and central European Ashkenazi immigrants during the early twentieth century and World War II. They were also an external phenomenon, driven forward by the constant influx of Jewish immigrants, who were themselves set in motion by European antisemitism. Jewish sports were relatively small in China, but thanks to Zionist organizations such as Betar and Maccabi, they brought together elements of Jewish sports from around the world. Their purpose was to promote Jewish physical renewal and national rejuvenation. As such, they formed an important part of the Zionist movement in China and as well as Jewish sports among international Jewry.

2 Ashkenazim and the Rise and Development of Jewish Sports in China

In 1912, under the impetus of a group of Ashkenazi Jews from Russia, the Jewish Recreation Club (JRC) was established in Shanghai to improve the physical fitness of Jewish youth and to improve the public image of the "weak" Jewish body.

Why did Jewish sports appear in Shanghai during this period? It was mainly because Jewish immigrants brought the concept of Zionism and Jewish sports to China. The modern Zionist movement that had emerged at the end of the nineteenth century had been mainly aimed at rebuilding the Jewish nation-state in Palestine. The early Zionist leader Max Nordau had put forward the idea of "Muscular Judaism,"[3] which promoted national regeneration by changing the Jewish physical condition through sports and exercise. In the eyes of many Zionists, sports became one of the powerful ways of cultivating the "New Man"

---

[3] Max Nordau, "Jewry of Muscle (June 1903)," in *The Jew in the Modern World: A Documentary History*, eds. Paul Mendes-Flohr and Jehuda Reinharz (Oxford: Oxford University Press, 2011), 616–617; Todd S. Presner, *Muscular Judaism: The Jewish Body and the Politics of Regeneration* (New York: Routledge, 2007), 1–3.

through body-building and nation-building.⁴ Under the influence of Max Nordau, sports quickly became popular in the early twentieth-century Jewish world, and a number of Jewish sports clubs were established in various places. Under the influence of this ethos, Jewish immigrants who came to China also took part in sports.

From a Chinese perspective, Shanghai's status as a trading port with concessions to many Western countries had made the city a window through which Western thought could enter China. Shanghai was also the starting point of modern Chinese sports. In the late nineteenth and early twentieth centuries, the phrase "sick man of East Asia" always referred to China. The Chinese government had been forced to sign a series of unequal treaties (which are also an important symbol of national humiliation for modern China). In order to change the "sick" image of the Chinese body, the Jing Wu Athletic Association (精武体育会), an international martial arts organization, was founded in Shanghai, China, on July 7, 1910 (though some sources date its founding to 1909). Its founder, martial artist Huo Yuanjia, died not long afterward. As one of the first public martial arts institutes in China, Jing Wu was intended to create a structured environment for martial arts instruction and military training, as opposed to the secretive training that had been common in the past.⁵ Driven by the Jing Wu Athletic Association, Shanghai established many new sports organizations. This social atmosphere played an important role in promoting the emergence and development of Jewish sports in Shanghai.

In the beginning, the Jewish Recreation Club, chaired by J. B. Katz, had only eleven members. The membership fee was three dollars per month.⁶ By the mid-1920s, with the increasing number of Ashkenazi Jews entering Shanghai, the club comprised over one hundred members. Located on the upper floor of the Ohel Moishe Synagogue, the Jewish Recreation Club provided its members with football, tennis, table tennis, international chess, checkers, and billiards facilities.⁷

After the October Revolution of 1917, a large number of Ashkenazi Jews arrived in Northeast China, especially Harbin, Dalian, and Tientsin, which led to the development of Jewish sports in these cities. In 1921, the Harbin Jews founded the Maccabi Sports Association, organized Jewish youth to participate in sports

---

4 Ai Rengui, "Suzao Xinren: Xiandai Youtai Minzu Goujian De Shentishi" 塑造"新人"：现代犹太民族构建的身体史 [Cultivating the 'New Man': The body-building and nation-building of modern Jewish people], *Lishi Yanjiu* 历史研究 [Historical research] 5 (2020): 182–185.
5 Brian L. Kennedy and Elizabeth Nai-Jia Guo, *Jingwu: The School that Transformed Kung Fu* (Berkeley, CA: Blue Snake Books, 2010), ch. 1.
6 Ossie Lewin, ed., *Almanac – Shanghai, 1946/47* (Shanghai: Shanghai Echo, 1947), 70.
7 *Israel's Messenger*, February 5, 1926.

activities, established the Hebrew Gymnasium, and held a large-scale sports meeting. The 1930s were a period of vigorous development for Jewish sports in Harbin. The Harbin Jews carried out sports activities such as track and field, boxing, swimming, water sports, ball games, and ice sports under the auspices of Betar and Maccabi. With a large number of outstanding athletes in track and field, swimming, speed skating, boxing, and ball games, they left a record in Harbin history and promoted the development of sports in Northeast China.

Like the Jewish community of Harbin, the Tientsin Jewish community first emerged at the turn of the century with the influx of Jewish refugees from Russia. The Jewish Club KUNST was founded in 1928 as a sports institution for the Tientsin Jews. In addition to a theater that could seat five hundred people, there were billiards rooms and chess rooms. KUNST often held plays, lectures, concerts, and dance performances. In 1937, its new building was completed. At the time, KUNST had about six hundred members. The land purchase and construction fees totaled about 110,000 yuan, while the club's annual budget was estimated to be more than 40,000 yuan.[8] KUNST was also known as the "Jewish congregation."

After Hitler came to power in Germany in 1933, thousands of German and Austrian Jews were forced to flee their homes. In light of the tense international situation, many other countries set up immigration restrictions on Jewish refugees. Shanghai was the only city in the world where Jews could enter without a visa. By the end of 1938, approximately fifteen thousand Jews had arrived in Shanghai.[9]

With the increasing numbers of European refugees, Shanghai Jewish sports reached a greater degree of formal organization (Figure 7.1). The Jewish Recreation Club played a major role in this process: "It (JRC) served to unite disparate Russian Jewish refugees in Shanghai and became a centre of creative Jewish spiritual and cultural life . . . a Jewish defence league was organised in the club premises with the stated purpose of fighting antisemitism, helping victims of discrimination, and developing friendship between Jews of different countries."[10] In 1935, the Jewish Recreation Club was reorganized under the chairmanship of S. J. Moalem, who mobilized European Jewish refugees to attend various sporting events and competitions in Shanghai, including cricket, rugby, football, tennis, bowling, boxing, and

---

8 Fang Jianchang, "Benshiji Sansishi Niandai Zhongguo Gedi Youtairen Gaimao" 本世纪三四十年代中国各地犹太人概貌 [An outline of Jews in China during the 1930s and 1940s], *Jindaishi Yanjiu* 《近代史研究》 [Modern Chinese History Studies] 6 (1997): 65.
9 David Kranzler, *Japanese, Nazis and Jews: The Jewish Refugee Community of Shanghai, 1938–1945* (New York: Yeshiva University Press, 1976), 31.
10 Rena Krasno, *Strangers Always: A Jewish Family in Wartime Shanghai* (Berkeley, CA: Pacific View Press, 1992), 166.

even gambling. In February 1939, the Jewish Recreation Club issued an initiative calling on European Jewish refugees to attend the sports organized by the club. After the outbreak of the Pacific War, the activities of the Jewish Recreation Club were affected. But with the help of E. S. Tuczynski, the Japanese occupation authorities agreed that the club could use a stadium to continue its activities.[11]

Figure 7.1: A sports class at the Jewish Youth Association School; Shanghai, China. (Photograph courtesy of the Yad Vashem Photo Archive.)

3 Zionist Youth Organizations in China and Their Physical Culture

As a modern nationalist movement, Zionism emerged in Europe at the end of the nineteenth century. By the early twentieth century, the international migration of Jews had also set off a Zionist craze in China. In 1900, only three years after the

---

[11] Wang Jian, *Shanghai Youtairen Shehui Shenghuoshi* 上海犹太人社会生活史 [A social history of Shanghai Jews] (Shanghai: Shanghai Dictionary Press, 2008), 264.

First Zionist Congress at Basel, the Palestine Foundation Fund was founded in Shanghai by Eli Kadoorie; in 1903, the Shanghai Zionist Association was established with N. E. B. Ezra as its secretary-general. It became one of the first three Zionist organizations in Asia (the other two were located in Iraq and Turkey), and sent representatives to Basel to attend the sixth Zionist Congress. In 1904, the Shanghai Zionist Assocation established *Israel's Messenger*, a newspaper that promoted the idea of Zionism and became "the official mouthpiece of the Shanghai Zionist Association."[12] Its reports on the activities of the Shanghai Jewish community and Zionist movement had an important influence on the Far East. In 1916, the Zionist organization Kadima established a branch in Shanghai, also known as the Shanghai Zionist Organization.

With the impetus of the Balfour Declaration (November 2, 1917), the Chinese Zionist movement recovered and began to expand its influence. Its most important act was to resume the publication of *Israel's Messenger*, which had been suspended since 1910. With *Israel's Messenger* as their platform, Chinese Jews promoted the Balfour Declaration among the Chinese and other Asian governments and celebrities, calling on them to support Zionism. With their unremitting efforts, they procured the support of Sun Yat-sen, the great leader of the Chinese Revolution. On April 24, 1920, Sun Yat-sen sent a letter to N. E. B. Ezra, the editor-in-chief of *Israel's Messenger*, expressing his sympathy and support for the Zionist movement. That same year, the Shanghai Zionists established a Jewish settlement in Palestine, the "China Jewish Colony"; the following year, the Shanghai Zionists established a second settlement – named after Laura Kadoorie, the late wife of Eli Kadoorie – in Palestine.

The Harbin Jews were not far behind. The year of the Balfour Declaration, the Neurei Zion Association was established for the promotion of the Zionist idea among Jews of Northeast China with lasting consequences. From March 25 through March 29, 1919, the first Zionist Congress in the Far East was held in Harbin. Organized by the local Jewish community, the Congress was attended by Jews from Northeast China, Shanghai, and Tientsin. After the meeting, the Palestinian Far East Bureau was established in Harbin. The official newspaper *Siberia-Palestine* (later renamed *Jewish Life*) was also established. In addition, Harbin Jewish support for the Zionist movement was put into action. The Harbin Jews decided to make *aliyah* to send volunteers to Palestine: "In order to call on Diaspora Jews to return to Palestine and become the 'first pioneers of Palestine,' the Harbin Zionist organization and the Palestinian Far East Bureau have

---

[12] Tang Peiji et al., *Shanghai Youtairen* 上海犹太人 [The Jews of Shanghai] (Shanghai: Shanghai Sanlian Press, 1992), 240.

done an active job. It was decided to send the first batch of 50 people in March 1921 . . . And make a decision to provide loans to non-rich immigration volunteers. . . . They established an immigration foundation and issued a call to all Jews to donate."[13] The Harbin Jewish community sent more than one hundred immigrants to Palestine.

Among the Chinese Jews engaged in sports, there were mainly two Zionist youth organizations: Maccabi, which was relatively mild, mainly devoted to sports and cultural activities; and Betar, which engaged in military training. Emphasizing strict discipline among its members, this semi-military organization was more radical and more popular among youth groups.

3.1 Maccabi in China

The Maccabi Association was the main sports organization of the Jews worldwide. The Maccabi Associations of China, which were mainly established by Ashkenazim from Russia, originated in Harbin in the 1920s. Later, with the influx of European Jewish refugees, they also emerged in Shanghai (Figure 7.2).

The Harbin Maccabi Association was a branch of the Jewish youth organization Maccabi and another youth organization under the Harbin Zionist Association. In June 1921, at the proposal of David Raskov, the Harbin Jews established the Maccabi Association and elected H. Golitberg as the first chairman. The board members, including Lev I. Leymanshteyn, Strizhevski, I. L. Rappoport, and L. Kotovich, etc., actively carried out Jewish sporting activities and promoted Jewish national culture.[14] The Harbin Maccabi Association was committed to sports to improve the physical condition of Jews. On October 9, 1921, the Harbin Jews held the Maccabi Games, which included 60-meter, 100-meter, 200-meter, and 600-meter sprints, as well as discus, shot put, long jump, high jump, pole vault, and volleyball.[15] Due to the emigration of the community, the activities of Harbin Maccabi in 1925 were suspended for some time. With the support of Joseph Gleberman from the Harbin Jewish community, Dalian established its own Maccabi Association.

With the influx of European Jewish refugees in China in the late 1930s, the Harbin Maccabi Association resumed its activities. In 1939, at the proposal of

---

[13] Teddy Kaufman, "Memoirs of Teddy Kaufman," in *Harbin Youtairen* 哈尔滨犹太人 [The Jews in Harbin], eds. Qu Wei and Li Shuxiao (Beijing: Social Sciences Academic Press, 2004), 311.
[14] Fu Mingjing, Zhang Tiejiang, and Han Tianyan, *Harbin Yu Shijie Youtairen* 哈尔滨与世界犹太人 [Harbin and world Jewry] (Harbin: Heilongjiang People's Press, 2007), 130.
[15] Teddy Kaufman, "Memoirs of Teddy Kaufman," in *Harbin Youtairen*, 314.

Figure 7.2: Members of the Maccabi Sports Association; Harbin, 1922. (Photograph from Pan Guang, ed., *The Jews in China* [Beijing: China Intercontinental Press, 2005], 75.)

Harbin Jewish community leader Abraham Kaufman, the Harbin Maccabi Association was reorganized, and Y. Z. Janovic was elected as the new chairman.[16] Teddy Kaufman, former president of the Israel-China Friendship Association and the Association of Former Residents of China in Israel, joined Harbin Maccabi in 1939 as its secretary. The influx of European Jewish refugees into Shanghai had also directly promoted the establishment of the Maccabi Association in Shanghai. Many refugees had been members of their local Maccabi Associations when they were in Europe. The Shanghai Maccabi Association was founded in Hongkou and located at the Ohel Moishe Synagogue on the Ward Road.

3.2 Betar in China

Like Maccabi, Betar was a Jewish youth organization. It had come to China with the Revisionist Zionists. In May 1927, at the proposal of David Slavkov and others, the

---

16 Qu Wei and Li Shuxiao, eds., *Harbin Youtai Jianming Cishu* 哈尔滨犹太简明辞书 [The concise Harbin Jewish dictionary] (Beijing: Social Sciences Academic Press, 2013), 193–194.

Harbin branch of HaShomer HaTzair was established. Like the Revisionist Zionist youth organization Betar, HaShomer HaTzair was mainly dedicated to cultural and athletic activities. In May 1929, a new branch of Betar was established on Artillery Team Street in the Butou District of Harbin, with L. I. Pyastunovich as its first leader. Subsequently, after contact with the Betar headquarters, the Harbin branch of HaShomer HaTzair joined the Harbin branch of Betar, which rapidly increased the latter's membership to more than 150 people. It accounted for about half of the Jewish youth in Harbin. Betar's Harbin branch founded the bi-weekly Russian magazine *Ha-Degel* (meaning 'the flag,' 1932–1942). This magazine, whose circulation was between three hundred and five hundred copies, was widely welcomed by Jews in Harbin. The sports organized by Betar's Harbin branch did not stop until the end of World War II, and a large number of Harbin Jews attended its activities. Mordechai Olmert, the father of former Israeli Prime Minister Ehud Olmert, was one of the leaders responsible for organizing the activities of Betar members in Harbin. The best boxer and long jumper in the organization, he set a record in long jump which lasted for ten years.[17]

In 1929, almost at the same time as the Harbin Jews, the Revisionist Zionist Alliance in China appeared in Shanghai. In 1931, Betar established a branch in Shanghai, which was mainly a project of Revisionist Zionist youths from Harbin and Tientsin. Its first leader was Lela Kotovitch from Tientsin. Membership rose from ten to nearly 100 within a year. In 1933, the English weekly journal *Jewish Voices*, sponsored by Shanghai Betar, was founded. *Jewish Voices* became the main newspaper of the Revisionist Zionists in China and throughout the Far East. By 1936, the Shanghai branch of Betar had somewhere between 400 and 500 members as well as 2,000 supporters.[18] From 1937 to 1941, about 30,000 Jewish refugees arrived in Shanghai from central European countries such as Germany, Austria, and Poland. Among these refugees, many young people were members of Betar and had already been engaged in Jewish sports in Europe (Figure 7.3).

Betar's branches in China actively organized their members to immigrate to Palestine and deliver military-trained Revisionists there. In 1930, Betar's Harbin branch began to apply for visas to go to Palestine. In March 1931, the first members of the Betar's Harbin branch, Eliyalhu Rankin,[19] R. Levina, R. Lifshitz, I. Soroviyi,

---

17 Qu Wei and Li Shuxiao, eds., *Harbin Youtai Jianming Cishu*, 125.
18 Pan Guang and Wang Jian, *Yigeban Shiji Yilai de Shanghai Youtairen* 一个半世纪以来的上海犹太人 [A history of Shanghai Jews through one and a half centuries] (Beijing: Social Sciences Academic Press, 2002), 137.
19 Among them, Harbin Betar's leaders, Nathan Germant and Eliyalhu Lankin, immigrated to Palestine in 1936 and became important members of the Jewish underground military organization Irgun. In June 1948, these two Jews (who had lived in Harbin) planned the famous Altalena Affair.

Figure 7.3: The Shanghai Betar exercising in 1935. (Photograph courtesy of Leo Hanin.)

and G. Mordokhovich, became pioneers of Chinese Jewish immigration to Palestine. Lela Kotovich, the founder of Betar's Shanghai branch, left Shanghai in 1934 to go to Palestine.[20]

Betar's branches in China actively organized athletic activities among Jewish youth – especially activities that could be combined with military training to improve Jewish self-defense, promote and practice Revisionist Zionism, and rebuild the Jewish state by force: "Here, the Jewish youth decided to organize themselves. They vowed to learn the techniques of self-defense, and they were eager to integrate themselves into the past history of the nation. They enthusiastically pursued defensive sports, athletics and team games."[21] In 1932, through

---

[20] Pan Guang and Wang Jian, *Yigeban Shiji Yilai de Shanghai Youtairen*, 137.
[21] Yaacov Liberman, *My China: Jewish Life in the Orient 1900–1950* (Jerusalem: Gefen Publishing House, 1998), 33.

the active efforts of Betar's Shanghai branch, the Shanghai Volunteer Corps (SVC) established a Jewish company, which consisted of 120 former military-trained Betar members. N. S. Jacobs became its commander; R. B. Bitker (a decorated veteran of the Russian army) and M. Talan were the company's sergeants.[22]

Figure 7.4: Members of Betar Harbin at an athletics display at the Harbin sports stadium, China, 1934. (Photograph reproduced from the Beth Hatefutsoth Photo Archive, courtesy of Vera Shtopman, Israel.)

With the influx of European Jewish refugees, the number of participants in Betar sports increased (Figure 7.4). With the deterioration of Jewish-Arab relations in Palestine and the outbreak of the Second World War, the military color of these athletic activities intensified. After the Japanese occupation of the whole of Shanghai in December 1941, especially after the establishment of the Hongkou Ghetto in February 1943, the Betar members, mainly Russian Jews, continued to participate in sports and military training.[23] In order to avoid any possible suspicion or intervention by the Japanese authorities, their military training was conducted secretly, in the form of sports competitions (such as football, tennis, swimming, etc.) on public occasions.

---

22 Irene Eber, *Wartime Shanghai and the Jewish Refugees from Central Europe* (Berlin:De Gruyter, 2012), 23; Martin Sugarman, "*Hagedud Ha-Sini*: The Jewish Company of the Shanghai Volunteer Corps, 1932–1942," *Jewish Historical Studies* 41 (2007): 185.
23 In *Laihua Youtai Nanmin Ziliao Dangan Jingbian* 来华犹太难民资料档案精编 [Sources on Jewish refugees in China], ed. Pan Guang (Shanghai: Shanghai Jiao Tong University Press, 2017), 4:93.

4 Winning Recognition Through Competition: Jews and non-Jews on the Playing Fields

The athletic activities of the Jews in China were mostly competitive sports, such as boxing, football, or track and field. Jews in Shanghai, Tientsin, Harbin, and other cities participated in various sporting activities organized by their local governments – even the big Games in the Far East. They accomplished many extraordinary achievements, and a number of outstanding athletes emerged. With the influx of European Jewish refugees in the 1930s, excellent athletes, such as boxers and professional football players who had participated in the Olympic Games, came to Shanghai and other places, highlighting the Jewish advantage in many sporting activities. These sports were attended by both Jews and non-Jews. This was an important manifestation of the Jewish participation in Diaspora life, and also a way for Jews to prove the normality of the Jewish body in order to win recognition through competition.

4.1 Jews and Competitive Sports

The Harbin Jews had an outstanding performance in track and field. There were many Jewish athletes who joined the local competitive sports and set the sports records for Harbin. Track and field athlete Jacob S. Matelin set two records for sprint in Harbin and Northeast China in 1910. He was elected as the president of the Harbin Sports Association.[24]

Boxing emphasizes confrontation and helps to develop endurance, agility, and bodily functions. The Betar branches of Harbin, Shanghai, Tientsin, and other places were focused on cultivating the fighting spirit of Jews. As a result, they were admired for their boxing teams. In 1929, Betar's Harbin branch established the first boxing team, and then Shanghai and Tientsin also formed their own boxing teams. Betar hired experienced boxing coaches to train talented Jewish youths. Since 1930, Betar has held national Betar internal boxing championships every year in Harbin and Tientsin. There have been senior coaches and outstanding boxers, such as G. Mordokhovich and others.[25]

Football was also a competitive sport that was loved by Chinese Jews. It had an important development in Tientsin and Shanghai. The Tientsin Jewish

---

[24] Zhang Tiejiang, *Zhongguo Dongbei Youtairen Yanjiu* 中国东北犹太人研究 [Studies on Jews of Northeast China] (Harbin: Heilongjiang People's Press, 2013), 334–335.
[25] Zhang Tiejiang, *Zhongguo Dongbei Youtairen Yanjiu*, 342.

football team participated in the local football league. Jewish football rose to a high level in Shanghai. The football team of the Shanghai Jewish Recreation Club had always been in the ranks of the C-class teams in the Shanghai Football League. It only scored in the B-class in 1933. However, with the participation of some professional football players and European Jewish refugees, the Shanghai Jewish Recreation Club's team was greatly improved. After 1935, it entered the A-class of the Shanghai Football League. In order to give more Jewish youths the chance to play and thereby select more promising young athletes, the Shanghai Jewish Recreation Club organized the Jewish Football League. Originally held at the Jingzhou Road stadium, it was moved to the newly built Zhaofeng Road stadium in 1940. The Shanghai Jewish Football League was divided into three levels: A, B, and C. The A-League stipulated that only eight teams could participate: AHV, Embankment, Shanghai Jewish Chronicle, Huishan, Hakua, Barcelona, United, and Maccabi.[26] The most successful team of the Jewish League was the AHV (*Alte Herren Verein*, or 'Old Men's Club'). Most of its members were older players who had once been active in the sport in Germany and Austria. Some, already retired from soccer, nonetheless began playing again in Shanghai. The AHV won the Jewish League championship in 1941–1942, 1943–1944, and 1944–1945 (Table 7.1).

Table 7.1: Winners of the Jewish League Championship, 1940–1945.

1940–1941	1941–1942	1942–1943	1943–1944	1944–1945
Embankment	Alte Herren Verein	Barcelona	Alte Herren Verein	Alte Herren Verein

4.2 Jews and the Big Games

Jews in China (Shanghai, Tientsin, Harbin, etc.) participated in various athletic activities held by local governments. The Harbin Jews actively participated in local, regional, and even national and international sporting events, and they frequently visited the Manchurian Games. In 1933, in the Manchuria National Athletics Open Championship, Harbin Betar athlete Boris Triguboff won the championship in the 200-meter final with 26 seconds. In the 800-meter final, he won the runner-up with two minutes and 12 seconds. In 1934, at the Manchuria National Athletics Open Championship, Harbin Betar athlete Osi Freer won the second place in the 100-meter final with 12.1 seconds. In the

---

26 Wang Jian, *Shanghai Youtairen Shehui Shenghuoshi*, 265–256.

1,500-meter final, Harbin Betar athlete David Bregel won the runner-up with four minutes and 54.8 seconds. Harbin Betar athlete Liva Taler won the championship with a score of 41.47 meters in the javelin final.[27]

As more and more Jews began to participate in sports, the Jews of China also organized large-scale sporting events, such as the Betar Games and the Maccabi Games, indicating that the Jewish Diaspora in China was part of worldwide Jewish sports. As Yaacov Liberman pointed out, "Betar's colorful parades on the streets of Harbin, Shanghai and Tientsin, as well as its members' achievements in athletic competitions and team tournaments, contributed greatly to the prestige and honor of all Jews in China."[28] In 1934, the Tientsin Jewish community organized the Betar Games among the Betar branches of Shanghai, Tientsin, and Harbin. The competitions included discus, javelin, shot put, high jump, long jump, and many others. The track races included 100 meters, 200 meters, 400 meters, 800 meters, and 1,500 meters. The ball games included basketball and volleyball. The team of Shanghai won first place, with Harbin coming in second and Tientsin third. On April 23, 1939, under the auspices of the Jewish Children's Welfare Fund, the first Shanghai Jewish Games, or the Maccabi Games, were held at the Jingzhou Road stadium, with the aim to prepare for the Maccabiah Games in Palestine.

By participating in various large-scale competitions in China, Jewish sports teams gradually gained recognition and even took on the same status as other national teams – which was very rare for the Jews in the Diaspora. We learn from the records of the *Shun Pao* [Shanghai News] that the Shanghai Jews participated in the International Football Championships: "Four teams (China, Jewish, British, Japan) joined the International Football Championships of the Far East Games. These four teams divided into two groups. One was the Chinese team versus the Jewish team. These two teams played yesterday, and China won a 7–0 victory. The other group, the British team versus the Japanese team, will play at 4:30 this afternoon. The winners of these two teams will decide the championship tomorrow."[29] From this report, we can see that the Jewish people, though stateless, could join the Far East Games in the name of a country. The Jewish team was deemed a national team (Figure 7.5).

---

27 Zhang Tiejiang, *Zhongguo Dongbei Youtairen Yanjiu*, 341.
28 Yaacov Liberman, *My China: Jewish Life in the Orient 1900–1950*, 33.
29 Luo Zhenguang et al., *Youtai Nanmin yu Shanghai: Chenfeng Wangshi* 犹太难民与上海：尘封往事 [Jewish refugees and Shanghai: Dust-laden past] (Shanghai: Shanghai Jiao Tong University Press, 2015), 117.

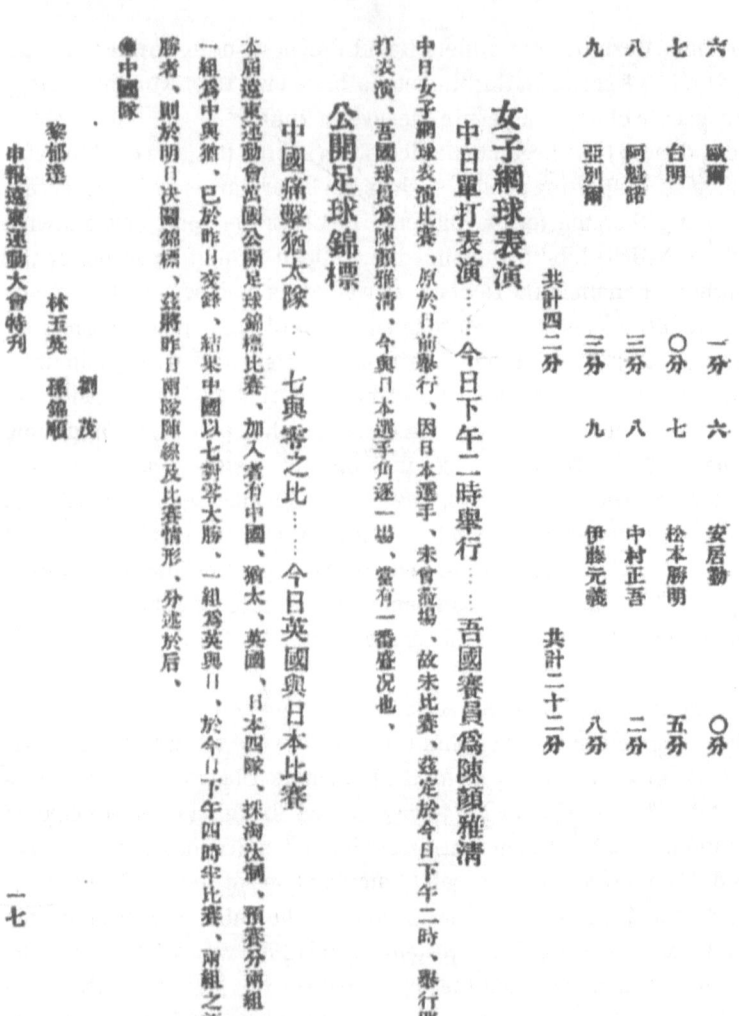

Figure 7.5: A Jewish team participated in the International Football Championship of the Far East. (Photograph from *Shun Pao* [Shanghai News].)

Conclusion: Constructing the Jewish Identity in the Diaspora Through Sports

In August 1945, Japan was defeated, and the Japanese forces left China. Many Jewish refugees left Shanghai, Harbin, and Tientsin for Palestine, the United States, Canada, and Australia. The establishment of the State of Israel in 1948 provided a national home for world Jewry, which greatly contributed to the departure of many Jews from China. During the Cold War's confrontation between the East and the West, the Jews who stayed in China were met with unprecedented shocks and challenges. In addition to Hong Kong, several major Jewish communities that had existed for a century in China quickly withered and died. With the departure of a large number of Jewish immigrants and the demise of the Jewish communities in China, Jewish sports in China also came to an end. Although Jewish sports only existed in China for a short time (1912–1949), they have left behind important historical legacies.

First, sports among Jews in China became an expression of their Jewishness as part of the worldwide phenomenon of modern Jewish sports. As sports had played a large role in the lives of many Jews, it is no surprise that they continued to remain significant to those who managed to escape European antisemitism. When they came to China, sports were used for cultivating the strength of Jews. In particular, Jewish sports in wartime Shanghai demonstrated the strength of Jewish identity in the face of adversity, notwithstanding the Nazi threat (see "Final Solution in Shanghai," by Nazi officer Josef Albert Meisinger). Athletic activities not only promoted the identity of the Jewish community, but also brought a glimmer of joy to the Jewish refugees who had lost their laughter in hard conditions for a long time: "It shines a warm glare in their grey exile."[30]

Second, sports among Jews in China became a weapon to combat antisemitic stereotypes. In the eyes of antisemites, the Jewish body was weak, effeminate, and ugly. Since the rise of Jewish sports in the late nineteenth and early twentieth centuries, Jews everywhere have sought with their sporting prowess to destroy this myth. As Peter Levine has written, "Despite its reputation as a disreputable sport, no other activity provided such a clear way to refute stereotypes of the weak, cowardly Jew that the anti-Semites employed to deny Jewish immigrants and their children full access to American opportunities. Nor did any other sport that the Jews engaged in provide better connection to an historical tradition of Jewish physical strength and power employed on behalf of Jewish protection and survival in a hostile world."[31] So Jews in Harbin, Shanghai, and Tientsin, though facing no antisemitism in China, joined sports in order to prove the normality of the Jewish body.

Last but not least, sports among Jews in China reflect a strong pro-Zionist inclination. Many Jewish sports activities in China were organized by Zionist organizations such as Betar and Maccabi. Betar, committed to militant Zionism,

---

30 *Shanghai Jewish Chronicle*, February 7, 1944, 2.
31 Peter Levine, *Ellis Island to Ebbets Field: Sport and the American Jewish Experience* (New York: Oxford University Press, 1992), 162.

was active in training Jewish youth for possible future military engagements: "The pioneers who helped to create the Harbin Betar, and in later years the Betar branches in Tientsin and Shanghai, were all, without exception, true Zionists – dreamers of a Jewish homeland and patriots of a national rejuvenation . . . This generation of Betar leaders, living far away from centers of Zionism and Revisionism, nurtured themselves on Jabotinsky's feuilletons and latest articles. Soon, they converted words and dreams into action and reality."[32] Many of the Jewish athletes in China were committed Zionists, and their sports activities went beyond fighting for exercise. They usually combined sports with military training to prepare struggle for the dream of national independence and revival.

References

Ai Rengui. "Suzao Xinren: Xiandai Youtai Minzu Goujian De Shentishi" 塑造"新人"：现代犹太民族构建的身体史 [Cultivating the "New Man": The body-building and nation-building of the modern Jewish people]. *Lishi Yanjiu* 历史研究 [Historical research] 5 (2020): 173–197.

Eber, Irene. *Wartime Shanghai and the Jewish Refugees from Central Europe*. Berlin: De Gruyter, 2012.

Fang Jianchang. "Benshiji Sansishi Niandai Zhongguo Gedi Youtairen Gaimao" 本世纪三四十年代中国各地犹太人概貌 [An outline of Jews in China during the 1930s–1940s]. *Jindaishi Yanjiu* 近代史研究 [Modern Chinese history studies] 6 (1997): 48–68.

Fu Mingjing, Zhang Tiejiang, and Han Tianyan. *Harbin Yu Shijie Youtairen* 哈尔滨与世界犹太人 [Harbin and world Jewry]. Harbin: Heilongjiang People's Press, 2007.

Goldstein, Jonathan. "The Sorkin and Golab Theses and Their Applicability to South, Southeast, and East Asian Port Jewry." *Jewish Culture and History* 4, no. 2 (2001): 179–196.

Kennedy, Brian L. and Elizabeth Nai-Jia Guo. *Jingwu: The School that Transformed Kung Fu*. Berkeley, CA: Blue Snake Books, 2010.

Kranzler, David. *Japanese, Nazis and Jews: The Jewish Refugee Community of Shanghai, 1938–1945*. New York: Yeshiva University Press, 1976.

Krasno, Rena. *Strangers Always: A Jewish Family in Wartime Shanghai*. Berkeley, CA: Pacific View Press, 1992.

Levine, Peter. *Ellis Island to Ebbets Field: Sport and the American Jewish Experience*. New York: Oxford University Press, 1992.

Lewin, Ossie, ed. *Almanac–Shanghai, 1946–1947*. Shanghai: Shanghai Echo, 1947.

Liberman, Yaacov. *My China: Jewish Life in the Orient, 1900–1950*. Jerusalem: Gefen Publishing House, 1998.

Luo Zhenguang et al. *Youtai Nanmin yu Shanghai: Chenfeng Wangshi* 犹太难民与上海：尘封往事 [Jewish refugees and Shanghai: Dust-laden past]. Shanghai: Shanghai Jiao Tong University Press, 2015.

---

32 Yaacov Liberman, *My China: Jewish Life in the Orient 1900–1950*, 33.

Mendes-Flohr, Paul and Jehuda Reinharz, eds. *The Jew in the Modern World: A Documentary History*. Oxford: Oxford University Press, 2011.

Pan Guang and Wang Jian. *Yigeban Shiji Yilai de Shanghai Youtairen* 一个半世纪以来的上海犹太人 [A history of Shanghai Jews through one and half centuries]. Beijing: Social Sciences Academic Press, 2002.

Pan Guang, ed. *Laihua Youtai Nanmin Ziliao Dangan Jingbian* 来华犹太难民资料档案精编 [Sources on Jewish refugees in China]. 4 vols. Shanghai: Shanghai Jiao Tong University Press, 2017.

Presner, Todd S. *Muscular Judaism: The Jewish Body and the Politics of Regeneration*. New York: Routledge, 2007.

Qu Wei and Li Shuxiao, eds. *Harbin Youtairen* 哈尔滨犹太人 [The Jews in Harbin]. Beijing: Social Sciences Academic Press, 2004.

Qu Wei and Li Shuxiao, eds. *Harbin Youtai Jianming Cishu* 哈尔滨犹太简明辞书 [The concise Harbin Jewish dictionary]. Beijing: Social Sciences Academic Press, 2013.

Sugarman, Martin. "*Hagedud Ha-Sini*: The Jewish Company of the Shanghai Volunteer Corps, 1932–1942." *Jewish Historical Studies* 41 (2007): 183–208.

Tang Peiji, et al. *Shanghai Youtairen* 上海犹太人 [The Jews of Shanghai]. Shanghai: Shanghai Sanlian Press, 1992.

Wang Jian. *Shanghai Youtairen Shehui Shenghuoshi* 上海犹太人社会生活史 [A social history of Shanghai Jews]. Shanghai: Shanghai Dictionary Press, 2008.

Zhang Qianhong and Ai Rengui. *Youtai Wenhua* 犹太文化 [Jewish culture]. Beijing: People's Publishing Press, 2013.

Zhang Tiejiang. *Zhongguo Dongbei Youtairen Yanjiu* 中国东北犹太人研究 [Studies on Jews of Northeast China]. Harbin: Heilongjiang People's Press, 2013.

WANG Jian
8 Tracking the Exact Number of Jewish Refugees in Shanghai

The year 2015 marks the seventieth anniversary of the victory of the World Anti-Fascist War and China's Anti-Japanese War. Seven decades ago, after eight years of arduous fighting, the Chinese people achieved great victories in their resistance against the Japanese invasion and made great contributions to the final victory of the World Anti-Fascist War, including the rescue of about 30,000 European Jewish refugees who had been persecuted by the Nazis during the war.

Although the Chinese people were themselves suffering from the persecution of the Japanese fascists, they were still concerned with the Jewish refugees in Europe. As early as May 13, 1933, the China League for Civil Rights (headed by Madame Sun Yat-sen) submitted a protest to R. C. W. Behrend, the German consul in Shanghai, strongly condemning Hitler's anti-Jewish atrocities. Others in the delegation included Doctor Tsai Yuan-pei, vice-chairman of the committee; Yang Ching, general secretary; Lin Yu-tang of the *China Critic*, chairman of publicity; Lo Shun, a well-known Chinese author; Agnes Smedley, author of the book *Daughter of Earth* as well as many magazine articles on China; and Harold Isaacs, editor of the *China Forum*.[1] In February 1939, Sun Ke, then president of the Legislative Yuan of the Republic of China, proposed to establish a Jewish settlement in Yunnan, China, and to resettle Jewish refugees there. From 1933 to 1941, Shanghai accepted a large number of Jewish refugees. The Simon Wiesenthal Center, which specializes in Holocaust studies, points out that the number of Jewish refugees accepted by Shanghai was higher than that of Canada, Australia, New Zealand, South Africa, and India.[2]

However, there are different views on the exact number of Jewish refugees who came to Shanghai. Opinions vary among the Jewish refugees themselves. Some accuse the Chinese media of exaggerating the number of refugees rescued. This article intends to discuss the number issue by examining the reports from *Israel's Messenger*, a newspaper that was very popular in the Jewish community in China at the time.

---

[1] *Israel's Messenger*, June 2, 1933.
[2] Alex Grobman and Daniel Landes, *Genocide: Critical Issues of the Holocaust* (Los Angeles: Simon Wiesenthal Center, 1983), 299.

1 The Number of Jewish Refugees in Shanghai before World War II

Jewish refugees began to arrive in Shanghai in 1933. Although Hitler had already begun his rise to power in Germany, the nature of the threat he posed was not widely understood, and relatively few German Jews left the country during this period. Of these, the majority took refuge elsewhere in Europe. The few who came to Shanghai did so because they had family or professional connections here. The first group of German Jews to arrive in Shanghai in 1933 consisted of approximately 12 families and at least 100 people.[3] *Israel's Messenger* observed:

> The Lloyd Trestino liner S.S. *Conte Verde*, which reached here on the 6th ultimo, brought the first batch of eminent Jewish professors and medical men who intend to make China their future home. No less than 26 highly skilled and qualified scientists and doctors, together with their families, are at present in the city and will either settle here or find fields for their labours in other parts of the country. These future residents of China form a section of the large number of Germans who, following the adoption of an Aryan policy by the present stupid Government of Germany, were forced to leave their adopted country. Seeking new fields for endeavour and finding the countries of Europe already more than well-stocked with men of their professions these men turned to China. Others are expected to follow in their footsteps this month on the *Conte Rosso*. They are all men of long experience.[4]

By the end of that year, about 30 German Jewish doctors had immigrated to Shanghai, many of them famous physicians who later opened their own private clinics in the concessions. Their arrival brought new vitality to the Shanghai Jewish community. Richard Loewenberg, who opened a medical practice at the famous Denis Apartments, came with strong recommendations from well-known personages. He had attended the University of Göttingen and studied at the Universities of Freiburg and Hamburg. From 1923 to 1926, he had been an assistant doctor for internal disease in the Hospital of the Deutsch-Israelitische Gemeinde; from 1927 to 1929, he had worked as an assistant doctor in the department of nervous diseases at St. George Hospital; since 1929, he had been an assistant doctor at the Psychiatric University Clinic in Hamburg-Friedrichsberg. He had also authored various valuable medical works. Another famous Jewish doctor who traveled with his family from Germany to Shanghai was Hugo Jakubowski, a dentist and specialist in mouth and jaw surgeries who had passed his governmental examinations in 1912. During the war, he had served as a captain, manning a tooth and jaw

---

3 Alvin Mars, "A Note on the Jewish Refugees in Shanghai," *Jewish Social Studies* 1 (October 1969): 286.
4 *Israel's Messenger*, December 1, 1933.

station in the fighting field, and had been decorated with an Iron Cross. As a result of his experience during the war, Jakubowski had gained a tremendous amount of expertise, which later distinguished him in his civil practice. During his career as a dental and jaw surgeon after the war, he had been appointed head of the Bergstuecken Hospital's dental department and was also active in the Berlin Public Health Department.[5]

Between 1933 and the summer of 1938, a total of approximately 1,000 to 1,500 Jews arrived in Shanghai. Pan Guang believes that, in the strictest sense, the Jews who came to Shanghai in this period should be considered expatriates rather than refugees. These early pioneers, who were mainly educated professionals, achieved success without difficulty, settling in the International Settlement and French concession in Shanghai.[6] However, I would argue that because Hitler's antisemitic movement began in early 1933, the Jews who fled to Shanghai at that time were already aware of the Nazi threat and therefore – like those who came later – should be categorized as refugees.

August 1938 witnessed an intensification and escalation of the Nazi persecution of Jews. After the annexation of Austria and Czechoslovakia, Germany posed an increasing threat to other European countries. As a result, many Jews fled Germany and central Europe for their lives. The following are reports from *Israel's Messenger* in September and November 1938:

> The first batch of refugees since the *Anschluss*, consisting of 15 Austrian Jews, arrived in Shanghai on August 15 aboard the *Conte Biancamano*. Further batches will arrive shortly and will be looked after by the Austrian Refugee Committee, a local organization set up for this purpose. It is distressing to note that the men and women who have arrived in this city were well-to-do people in Vienna and the fact they have each been allowed 20 marks for travelling expenses is a telling commentary on how the Jews are being plundered of their entire earthly possessions before being set adrift in the world.

> Ten more Austro-Jewish refugees, including a woman and two children, arrived in Shanghai on the August 28 from Anschlussed Austria via Italy. The group was met by the Austrian refugees who arrived in Shanghai a fortnight ago. These pioneer refugees took charge of the newly arrived batch, who came by the Conte Rosso, and directed them to pre-arranged lodgings.

> The arrivals were in the same plight as the 15 who preceded them. Permitted to take not more than 20 marks – the equivalent of one pound sterling – from Germany, they landed in Shanghai with insufficient funds to pay even for transportation to their assigned lodgings after the incidental expenses on the boat were met.

---

5 *Israel's Messenger*, January 14, 1934.
6 Pan Guang, "Jewish Refugees in Shanghai during World War Two," *Quarterly Journal of the Shanghai Academy of Social Sciences* 2 (1991): 114.

Another contingent of Jewish refugees from Europe, six in number, arrived in Shanghai on September 11, aboard the ss. Victoria. One of the refugees is a doctor from Germany. The remaining five persons, four men and one woman, are all from Vienna. Three of the Viennese are commercial people while the fourth man is described as being an engineer. The woman is the wife of one of the commercial men.[7]

A further batch of Jewish refugees from Germany and Austria arrived in Shanghai on the 18th ult., by the Conte Biancamano. Of the 25 who arrived, 19 were men, five women and one a child. Few of the refugees could speak English and most of them were financially distressed.[8]

2 A Dramatic Increase in the Number of Jewish Refugees in Shanghai after Kristallnacht

After Kristallnacht in November 1938, German and Austrian Jews struggled to escape from the Nazis in increasing numbers. But by that time, the Nazis were systematically depriving Jews of their property. As a result, these new refugees arrived in Shanghai with only small amounts of money and personal belongings.

According to a group of 187 Jewish refugees who arrived in Shanghai in December of that year, many of them had been business tycoons in Germany and Austria, worth millions of pounds, but when they were forced to leave their countries, each of them was allowed to carry only ten pounds' cash in addition to their travel expenses. Any cash exceeding that amount would be confiscated if found. The Chinese and foreign newspapers in Shanghai, especially *Israel's Messenger*, recorded the experience of these Jewish refugees who landed at Wayside Dock:

> Very little arrived as a matter of fact because most of the luggage of the travelers from Berlin was detained at the German frontier to be examined for possible currency smuggling, so that the majority of those arriving had nothing but the original hand-luggage which they had taken along for their two days trip from Berlin to Trieste. They were informed that their other luggage would reach here with the next steamer.

> At least one of those arriving bore vivid evidence of his detention in a concentration camp, his forehead being heavily bandaged. Questioned as to the origin of his injury, he refused to make any statement but a bystander informed the representatives of the "North-China Daily News" that he had been hit across the head at the concentration camp at Buchenwalde, in which, incidentally, most of the Germans who arrived had been detained prior to their departure, for periods varying from three years to ten weeks ... the arrivals are mostly from Germany, only about 30 per cent coming from Austria.[9]

---

7 *Israel's Messenger*, September 20, 1938.
8 *Israel's Messenger*, November 11, 1938.
9 *Israel's Messenger*, December 16, 1938.

On December 15, 1938, some 250 Jewish refugees from Germany and Austria arrived aboard the Lloyd Triestino liner *Victoria*.[10] It was reported that the largest group of foreign émigrés to arrive in Shanghai since the White Russian influx of 1918–1922 had landed on December 20, 1938, when 524 German-Jewish men, women, and children made port on the *Conte Biancamano*. A total of 526 had originally been expected, but a few had disembarked in Hong Kong or Manila en route to Shanghai.[11]

On December 31, 1938, 400 German Jewish émigrés arrived on the *Potsdam* and the *Conte Rosso*. Originally, only 300 had been expected. Seventy had been expected to disembark from the *Potsdam*, but when the ship arrived, there were approximately 120. The *Conte Rosso*, instead of landing 240 as planned, brought 280. Among this latest group of émigrés, there were 28 children.[12]

Over the next few months, more and more Jewish refugees poured into Shanghai. On January 29, 1939, some 420 arrived aboard the Lloyd Triestino liner *Conte Verde* and were temporarily placed in the Embankment Building and the Beth Aharon Synagogue. At that point, there were 2,305, of whom 400 were already self-sufficient, while 1,905 required the care of the rescue committee.[13] The following are news reports from January through May 1939:

> More than 85 German-Jewish emigres arrived in Shanghai with the Messageries Maritimes vessel Athos II on the 10th inst. It is reported that these emigres did not leave Germany legally, but fled across the border into France, proceeding to Marseilles, thence to Shanghai. They are being temporarily accommodated at the Embankment Building.
>
> More than 850 Jewish emigres will arrive in Shanghai on February 21 aboard the Conte Biancamano. This will bring the total number of emigres here to 3,155.[14]
>
> Some 85 additional Jewish refugees from Germany and Austria arrived here on the 24th ult., by the Scharnhorst.
>
> An additional 450 German and Austrian Jews arrived here aboard the Lloyd Triestino liner Conte Rosso on the 5th inst.
>
> As has been the custom on previous occasions, a large number of members of the committee looking after the new arrivals here were at the Customs Jetty and saw them through the usual customs formalities, whilst a large number of trucks were drawn up at the entrance, to take care of the luggage.

---

10 *Israel's Messenger*, January 20, 1939.
11 *Israel's Messenger*, January 20, 1939.
12 *Israel's Messenger*, January 20, 1939.
13 *Israel's Messenger*, February 17, 1939.
14 *Israel's Messenger*, February 17, 1939.

> The arrivals were housed in the Embankment Building, where a section of the building has been put at the disposal of the Refugee Committee, whilst some of the bachelors found accommodation in the new home on Ward Road and which can accommodate up to 1,200 persons.
>
> More than 4,500 German Jewish refugees are today residing in Shanghai, and these fugitives of Nazism continue to trickle into this city in batches ranging in numbers from 15 to 800.
>
> Registered with the Jewish Refugees Committee here are 3,945 emigres, but the process of registration is not yet complete. Hundreds of refugees who have landed here have not even come near the committee, since they are able to look after themselves with funds received from friends or relatives either in Shanghai or abroad.[15]
>
> It is reported that on the eve of the Passover, April 3 1939 more than 400 refugees from Europe landed in Shanghai.
>
> Over 220 emigres arrived on the April 24, 1939 aboard the Hakusaku Maru and the Gneisenau, and 850 more arrived on the Conte Biancamano on April 25, 1939. This brings the total number of Jewish refugees here to 8,400.[16]

Over the next few months, more and more Jewish refugees continued to disembark in Shanghai. Another 440 German Jewish refugees arrived on the *Conte Rosso* on May 8, 1939. Of these, the majority had come from Berlin, Vienna, and Hamburg. On May 14, an additional 738 German Jews arrived at Wayside Dock. The *Scharnhorst* arrived in Shanghai on May 19, carrying 155 men, women, and children. Once again, families were predominant; this group included 45 couples with a total of 24 children. The following are news reports from *Israel's Messenger* over the course of that year:

> Shanghai's Jewish emigré community was boosted by 308 men, women and children, who arrived on the May 22, 1939, by the Lloyd Triestino liner Victoria. Another 465 emigres arrived here on June 4, 1939 aboard the Lloyd Triestino liner Conte Verde. Most of them were accommodated in the Kinchow Road camp, whilst others were taken to Ward Road, Chaoufoong Road, Wayside Road and the Embankment Building. The total number of refugees here is estimated to have reached 10,506.[17]
>
> The Italian liner, Conte Biancamano, brought in 827 emigres, while the French boat, Chenonceaux of the Messageries Maritimes brought 35 more on June 27, 1939, bringing the total number of European refugees in Shanghai to over 12,000. All have been accommodated in camps situated in the eastern sector of Wayside and Yangtzepoo, except 100 who have found private quarters.[18]

---

15 *Israel's Messenger*, March 17, 1939.
16 *Israel's Messenger*, May 5, 1939.
17 *Israel's Messenger*, June 9, 1939.
18 *Israel's Messenger*, July 14, 1939.

Another batch of 265 emigre men, women and children, arrived in the s.s. Victoria on August 7, 1939, and were taken to the various centers in the Wayside district, bringing the total number of European refugees in Shanghai to over 16,000.[19]

At the same time, additional information has reached Shanghai from Manchuria, where it is believed that large numbers of refugees are making their way to the Far East, via Siberia. If these people are unable to find employment in such places as Harbin, Mukden and Dairen it is more than likely that they will proceed to Shanghai, as has been the case in the past with so many White Russian emigres. For example, about 50 emigres made the long journey across Russia on the Trans-Siberian Railway on December 14,1939, in the s.s. Sansho, a Japanese coastal freighter from Dairen.[20]

As these news reports reveal, from August 1938 through early August 1939 – within the span of a year – the number of European Jewish refugees who arrived in Shanghai was over 16,000, far exceeding those who originally lived in Shanghai. The total number of Sephardi Jews and Ashkenazi Jews (mainly from Russia) was 6,000, accounting for a little more than one-third of the refugees.

3 The Refugees who Arrived in Shanghai after the Restriction in August 1939

Although the Jewish refugees' relatives in Shanghai had done their utmost to help them, it was expected that at least 12,000 refugees would arrive there by the end of 1939, exerting considerable pressure on the city's aid system. Due to limitations on resources such as manpower and finances, problems had arisen among the Jewish refugees. In May 1939, an epidemic of scarlet fever spread through the refugee camp, infecting about 200 people. More than 150 patients were sent to an emergency hospital on Chaofoong Road (now Gaoyang Road); the rest received treatment in other hospitals in the concessions.

The Shanghai Jewish community did not anticipate that Nazi Germany would ultimately adopt a policy of genocide against the Jews in Europe. Instead, they were frustrated by their own situation in Shanghai and deeply worried that the increasing influx of Jewish refugees would exceed the city's rescue capacity. Therefore, community leaders recommended restricting the number of refugees. At the same time, they repeatedly called on Jewish groups in other countries to increase their acceptance of and assistance to refugees from Europe. As early as December

---

19 *Israel's Messenger*, August 16, 1939.
20 *Israel's Messenger*, January 20, 1939.

20, 1938, Michel Spearman, chairman of the Committee for the Assistance of European Jewish Refugees in Shanghai (CAEJR) and general manager of the International Savings Society, and Ellis Hayim, director general of the CAEJR, met with G. Godfrey Phillips, the British consul general and secretary and commissioner of the Shanghai Municipal Council (SMC), to discuss the refugee problem in Shanghai. In his report to C. S. Franklin, chairman and secretary general of the SMC, Phillips noted, "I obtained the impression that both these gentlemen were extremely anxious . . . I formed a strong impression that they would very much welcome any practical means to limit the number of the Jewish refugees who are admitted here."[21] Some of the Russian Jews holding non-professional, low-qualification, and low-paying occupations were also worried that the newcomers would take their jobs by accepting lower wages and even hours of unpaid work. On May 25, 1939, Sir Victor Sassoon and Ellis Hayim once again complained that the CAEJR's relief activities were under great pressure because of the shortage of funds and the increasing number of refugees. They pointed out that the Japanese were now their last hope for effective negotiations with the Germans and guaranteed that local Jewish communities in general would understand restricting the numbers of newly arriving refugees would improve the lives of those who were already in Shanghai.[22]

Meanwhile, the increasing influx of refugees had greatly affected daily life in the concessions by bringing more chaos, which caused mounting discontent among the residents and concern among the concession authorities. Rumor had it that the Chinese bus company run by the Sassoon family was considering replacing its White Russian employees with Jewish refugees, which stirred panic and antisemitic sentiment among the Russians. One twelve-page pamphlet was titled: "A Warning to all Chinese, Japanese and Gentiles alike." Its sub-title read: "The Chosen People have invaded Shanghai! Be prepared to resist an Economic Invasion!"

Since most of the refugees took up residence in the district of Hongkou – which was also home to the majority of the Japanese citizens living in Shanghai – housing rents there rose drastically and business competition grew fierce. The Japanese residents strongly urged their government to take action to protect their interests. On July 1, 1939, a joint committee comprised of Colonel Yasue from the Ministry of the Army, Captain Inuzuka from the Ministry of the Navy, and Consul Ishiguro Shiro from the Ministry of Foreign Affairs in Shanghai submitted a report

---

21 SMAF, reel 4, U001/4/2971, File no. K38/1,0240-0245. G. Godfrey Phillips to the Chairman and the Secretary-General of the SMC on "Jewish Refugees," December 20, 1938.
22 AJMFA, "Joint Report of the Investigation on the Jewish Issue in Shanghai," July 7, 1939, S9460-3, 1238.

titled "Emergency Measures for Managing the Shanghai Jewish Refugees" to Tokyo. They suggested preventing Jewish refugees not only from residing or doing business in the area but also from entering it.[23] Following the entry of 64 Jewish refugees who arrived in Shanghai on July 16 aboard the Nippon Yusen Kaisha liner *Suwa Maru*, no additional Jewish refugees would be allowed to reside in Hongkou.[24]

The Japanese government was also concerned that restricting the numbers of newly arriving Jewish refugees might cause complaints among the American and British Jews and, as a result, affect the implementation of the Fugu Plan.[25] However, when Shanghai Jewish community leaders asked the Japanese authorities to implement restrictions, Japan seized the opportunity to do so, emphasizing that this new policy was undertaken at the request of the Committee for the Assistance of European Jewish Refugees in Shanghai (CAEJR).

It was in this context that on August 10, 1939, the Japanese Ministry of Foreign Affairs officially ordered the Consulate General in Shanghai to inform the German and Italian consuls general that the Japanese government would prevent Jews from entering Shanghai after that date. The Foreign Ministry also warned Japanese shipping companies to stop transporting Jewish refugees to East Asia.[26] The following news report summarized the position of the Japanese government:

> The spokesman replied that that portion of the International was controlled by the Japanese – who could legislate as they pleased – by reason of military conquest. No spokesman would admit that the Powers would admit this right, but the naval spokesman pointed out that the Japanese had notified the Consular Body of the procedure which they proposed to adopt.

---

[23] AJMFA, "Emergency Measures for Managing the Shanghai Jewish Refugees," July 1, 1939, S9460-3, 1224–1226.
[24] *Israel's Messenger*, September 12, 1939.
[25] The Fugu Plan, proposed by the Japanese government after its occupation of Northeast China, was officially titled "Research and Analysis of the Introduction of Jewish Capital." The plan involved the establishment of a Jewish settlement in the Chinese territories under Japanese occupation. This settlement was expected to accommodate 30,000 Jewish refugees at first and gradually expand. The cost of its construction was expected to be provided by the American Jewish consortium. Fulfilment of the plan demanded 100 million US dollars to cover construction expenses, a promotion campaign in the United States and other Western countries, invitations to Jewish celebrities from all over the world to visit the settlement, investments from Jewish financiers, and improvement in Japan's relations with the United States and other Western countries. The fugu is a delicious yet highly poisonous fish, and the Japanese took it as a metaphor for the Jews: the assimilation of Jewish immigrants was, for them, a lucrative enterprise but also a dangerous one. Similarly, the chef must rid fugu of its toxins before serving it as a meal.
[26] AJMFA, Consul General Miura to Foreign Minister Arita, August 10, 1939, S9460, 1413–1418; JACAR: B04013207600, 0156-0158. "Emergency Measures for Managing the Shanghai Jewish Refugees," August 10, 1939.

The spokesman adduced further that more arrivals of refugees, who intended to open businesses would threaten the livelihood of those residing in the occupied portion of the area, which included Chapei – this was the viewpoint, he added, of the Jewish committee. The committee did not want a further influx of refugees. The spokesman, in continuing, said that the Jewish people living in the area, excluding those in camps, were about one-tenth of the Japanese residing there and the authorities feared friction between the two communities.[27]

A memorandum from the Japanese Naval Landing Party Headquarters also made it clear that Jewish refugees arriving after August 21 would not be allowed to reside in Hongkou. Out of humanitarian considerations, the Japanese occupation authorities had so far imposed no restrictions on the placement of refugees in areas under the Japanese occupation. However, the occupation authorities decided to reduce the flow of refugees into Hongkou because the Battle of Shanghai in 1937 had caused severe damage to the district, reducing the availability of housing there. Considering the interests of all parties concerned, the writers of the memorandum advised suspending Jewish immigration until a study of the feasibility of any future resettling of immigrants could be completed. Moreover, they required that all refugees residing in Japanese-occupied Hongkou as of August 22, 1939 register with the Directory of Jewish Refugees and send copies of their registration to the Japanese authorities through the CAEJR. Once the Japanese authorities had confirmed the registration's accuracy, they would return one copy to the refugees. Only those with returned copies would be allowed to live in the area north of the Suzhou Creek. In the event that they failed to register, they would not be permitted to stay.[28]

On August 14, the Shanghai Municipal Council of the International Settlement also notified the CAEJR, the consular body, and the three leading shipping companies that they had made a decision to forbid any additional European refugees from entering the International Settlement. A Council official observed:

> Jewish refugees who have already fled to the comparative security of Shanghai to escape molestation in their homelands are now numbered at 16,000. About 5,000 more were expected to arrive here before the end of the year, and as a result of the Japanese ban, would have been compelled to [reside] South of the Creek. With the hospital situation already acute, the burden of 5,000 more dependent people thrown on the resources of the city would be indeed a difficult one to bear. An outbreak of any epidemic, for instance, would be disastrous: When scarlet fever struck the refugees living North of the Creek a few months ago it was coped with quite successfully because there was ample space with which to provide an

---

27 *Israel's Messenger*, September 12, 1939.
28 *Israel's Messenger*, September 12, 1939; AJMFA, Memorandum, August 9, 1939, S9460-3, 1424–1426; Consul General Miura to Foreign Minister Arita, August 10, 1939, S9460, 1406–1407.

emergency hospital while the refugees themselves cared for their sick compatriots. A similar epidemic among thousands of refugees living South of the Creek would be quite different as there is hardly a single vacant building which might be used as a hospital, in the entire city and the hospitals are filled to capacity.

The official added:

> This sudden decision on the part of the Council was not taken in conjunction with the decision of the Japanese authorities to restrict the influx of refugees North of the Creek. Reports of these restrictions laid down by the Japanese, however, forced the Council to prohibit the entry of thousands of emigres into the area South of the Creek. We've already done more than our share here in Shanghai, but the point has been reached where Shanghai cannot absorb any more refugees.[29]

Following the decision of the Shanghai Municipal Council to curtail the immigration of Jewish refugees, the French consul general also issued an ordinance prohibiting any additional Jewish refugees from taking up residence in the French concession. All shipping companies in Shanghai were notified of the new ruling.

On August 9, the Shanghai Jewish Organization notified the German Jewish Council in London that immigration from Europe to Shanghai must be stopped. On August 14, the German Jewish Council in London informed the American Jewish Joint Distribution Committee (JDC) of this fact. Shipping companies in Germany and Italy posted notices announcing that China's economic prospects were bleak in the hopes of discouraging Jews who had applied to seek refuge in Shanghai. It is not difficult to imagine the frustration that local Jewish refugees must have felt after the two bans appeared in the Shanghai newspapers on August 16. Those who had relatives in Europe or on their way to the city were the hardest hit. Those who had booked tickets for Shanghai immediately after August 14 had some difficulty convincing the shipping companies to return their deposits. Later on, the Hebrew Immigrant Aid Society (HIAS) was informed that four ships scheduled to depart from August 14 to August 21 carrying 631 passengers would still be allowed to land. Understandably, the Jewish refugees in Shanghai were still worried. Jewish community leaders, hoping to change the relevant regulations, conducted secret negotiations with all of the various administrative authorities in the city. An agreement was finally reached with the Municipal Council of the International Settlement and made public on October 22.

The new agreement stated that even though the Municipal Council had announced in August that it had banned any European Jewish refugees from entering the International Settlement, this ban did not apply to people who met the following conditions: adults with disposable funds of no less than 400 dollars

---

[29] *Israel's Messenger*, September 12, 1939.

or other foreign currencies of the same value; children under the age of 13 with 100 dollars or the equivalent; immediate relatives or fiancés of current Shanghai Jewish residents who could also produce proof of disposable funds; and those who had contracted for employment in Shanghai. Shipping and rail companies and other travel agencies would be held responsible for determining that their clients met these requirements. Refugees would be required to submit their applications via CAEJR to the Municipal Council, which would review the applications before passing them on to the occupation authorities. In this way, Jewish community leaders created a new opportunity for European Jewish refugees to enter Shanghai. However, these regulations only applied to the International Settlement under the control of the Municipal Council, not to Japanese-controlled Hongkou or to the French Concession. The Japanese deleted the article involving 400 dollars and said they would consider applications case by case. According to CAEJR, the vast majority of these refugees were denied entry into Hongkou and the French Concession. A letter written in January 1940 by a Japanese diplomat in China reveals that the Japanese government was highly displeased with the Municipal Council for having changed the rules and issuing too many entry licenses to the refugees. The Japanese occupation authorities had issued only 25 until then.[30]

Therefore, even though the administrative authorities in Shanghai had issued orders to restrict the influx of the European Jewish refugees in August 1939, many Jewish refugees were still entering Shanghai through various channels. Their numbers, however, sharply decreased. From August 1939 to June 1940, when Italy had been at war with Britain and France for almost a year, it was estimated that a maximum of around 1,000 Jewish refugees arrived in Shanghai both by land and by sea. On August 28, 1939, approximately 619 refugees, who had been allowed to leave Italy before the restriction was announced on August 14, arrived in Shanghai aboard the *Giulio Cesare*.[31] After the outbreak of the Second World War on September 1, the refugees still at sea faced even more uncertainties. Meanwhile, more than 100 German Jews were forced to leave Hong Kong and Singapore for Shanghai due to Britain's declaration of war on Germany.

Since then, only some ships docked in Shanghai sporadically, unloading refugees from Europe. On January 22, 1940, the *Conte Biancamano* arrived in Shanghai. In contrast to most of the previous refugees who had made their homes in Shanghai, the latest refugees were financially fairly well-off. Of these, the majority

---

30 David Kranzler, *Japanese, Nazis and Jews: The Jewish Refugee Community of Shanghai, 1938–1945* (New York: Yeshiva University Press, 1976).
31 *Israel's Messenger*, September 12, 1939.

moved into the International Settlement after proving that they had 400 dollars in their possession. A few obtained special permission from the Japanese authorities to make their homes in Hongkou. Many did not come directly from Germany but had been staying in Italy for a considerable time. They paid for their passage and produced the cash deposit with funds they had received from abroad. On February 9, another 161 arrived on board the *Conte Rosso*.[32]

On April 4, about 100 refugees arrived on the *Conte Verde*, mainly from Germany, Austria, Hungary, Czechoslovakia, and Poland. All, of course, had proof of funds.[33] On May 9, 211 Jewish refugees arrived on the *Conte Rosso*. Most of these new arrivals came from Berlin, Bolesław (renamed Wrocław after the World War II), Danzig, and Czechoslovakia in order to reunite with their families.[34] On June 6, the *Conte Verde* arrived with 263 émigrés on board – mostly German, but with some Austrians and a significant portion of Czechoslovakians. Some had had difficulty in Geneva before they could go on board. On May 6 and 7, the immigrants who had booked places aboard the *Conte Verde* were sent back to Munich from Brenner, which was then the German-Italian frontier, because the Italian authorities at the frontier believed that it was too dangerous for the *Conte Verde* to set sail. However, thanks to the initiative of the Committee of Munich, they left Munich again on May 8 and arrived in time to board the ship before its departure. About 90 percent of these new arrivals had 400 dollars each; the remaining 10 percent had settlement permits.[35] On June 10, Italy declared war on Britain and France, and France was soon defeated and surrendered. Since then, Britain and Germany engaged in intense sea and air warfare on the Atlantic Ocean and the Mediterranean Sea. The fighting spread to the Balkans and North Africa, thus cutting off all sea routes from Europe to Shanghai.

At the same time, western European countries such as France, the Netherlands, Belgium, and Luxembourg and Balkan countries such as Yugoslavia and Greece successively fell into the hands of the Nazis. The Baltic countries also faced the Nazi threat and later were annexed into the Soviet Union. The German occupation forces launched a campaign to persecute the Jews in eastern Europe, driving more Jews to flee, though their chances of success were severely reduced. Many attempted to reach Shanghai by land. After June 1940, around 2,000 refugees came to Shanghai via Soviet Siberia, Northeast China, North Korea, and Japan.

After the German invasion of the Soviet Union in June 1941, this land route was also cut off. No additional refugees could leave Europe for Shanghai. Nevertheless,

---

[32] *Israel's Messenger*, March 20, 1940.
[33] *Israel's Messenger*, April 19, 1940.
[34] *Israel's Messenger*, May 17, 1940.
[35] *Israel's Messenger*, June 14, 1940.

some who had previously left Europe and had later been detained in the Soviet Union, Northeast China, or Japan did manage to set foot in Shanghai. Most of these were Polish and Lithuanian Jews, who amounted to more than 2,000 all together. The war and the immigration restrictions that had been implemented by a number of countries denied them other safe havens.

It is worth mentioning the difficult journey of more than 1,100 Polish Jewish refugees, including more than 400 faculty and students from the Mir Yeshiva and Lublin Yeshiva, who fled to Lithuania before and after the German invasion of Poland in 1939. They escaped from Europe by obtaining Japanese transit visas that allowed them to go to the Dutch colony Curaçao via Japanese territory. After the annexation of Lithuania by the Soviet Union, the Soviet government permitted them to leave the country. With the assistance of a Soviet travel agency, they managed to reach Vladivostok by train through Siberia, paying $200 each. From Vladivostok, they sailed to Kobe, Japan, where they stayed for more than half a year. However, their application for visas to enter the United States was unsuccessful. Later, with the help of Zorach Warhaftig, Commissioner of the Palestinian Jewish Agency, they were granted permission to enter Shanghai. They arrived in several groups over the second half of 1941. *Israel's Messenger* reported:

> Another batch of 296 European Jewish refugees arrived in Shanghai on August 22, 1941, in the Asama Maru from Kobe and Yokohama. This number included 255 Polish Jews and sixteen German Jews. The refugees, who had left war-torn Europe almost one year ago and who had visas to stay in Japan for only two weeks, had remained there for ten months. Among the newly arrived there were a number of rabbis and they were all taken to the Synagogue in Museum Road.[36]

These may well have been the last Jewish refugees who came to Shanghai before the Pearl Harbor incident on December 7. After the outbreak of the Pacific War, it was impossible for Jewish refugees to enter Shanghai.

Conclusion

According to the CAEJR Annual Report of 1940, there were 23,310 Jewish refugees in Shanghai registered in CAEJR in 1940, which was then spending the sum of $3.26 million in assistance.[37] Afterward, that number altered slightly: some refugees were transferred from Siberia, Korea, and Japan; some traveled to other

---

36 *Israel's Messenger*, September 19, 1941.
37 *Israel's Messenger*, February 21, 1941.

countries. For example, in 1940, 102 German Jewish refugees journeyed to France via Saigon to join the French Foreign Legion and fight against the Nazis.[38] In 1941, twenty-nine Polish Jewish refugees who had arrived in Shanghai via Japan departed for Palestine, where they would take up colonization work under the auspices of the Zionist Organization.[39]

In summary, during the Second World War, at least 25,000 Jewish refugees stayed in Shanghai for a long time. This figure matches the statistics of the Simon Wiesenthal Center, a world authority for the study of the Holocaust.[40] If we take into account the Jews who finally went to other countries from 1933 through 1941 or just stayed in Shanghai for a short time, the number would be even greater – roughly 30,000.

Therefore, it is no exaggeration to say that Shanghai was the largest international metropolis that saved the greatest number of Jewish refugees during the Second World War.

References

Diplomatic Archives. Ministry of Foreign Affairs of Japan. Tokyo.
Grobman, Alex, and Daniel Landes. *Genocide: Critical Issues of the Holocaust*. Los Angeles: Simon Wiesenthal Center, 1983.
Israel's Messenger. January 1934 – September 1941.
Kranzler, David. *Japanese, Nazi and Jews: The Jewish Refugee Community of Shanghai, 1938–1945*. New York: Yeshiva University Press, 1976.
Mars, Alvin. "A Note on the Jewish Refugees in Shanghai." *Jewish Social Studies* 31, no. 4 (1969): 286–291.
Pan Guang. "Jewish Refugees in Shanghai during World War Two." *Quarterly Journal of Shanghai Academy of Social Sciences* 上海社会科学院学术季刊 2 (1991): 113–121.
Shanghai Municipal Archives Files.

---

38 *Israel's Messenger*, March 20, 1940.
39 *Israel's Messenger*, September 19, 1941.
40 Grobman and Landes, *Genocide*, 299.

Maisie MEYER
9 The Global Reach of Shanghai's Baghdadi Jews

The global reach of the Baghdadi Jews of Shanghai negates Rudyard Kipling's famous assertion: "Oh, East is East, and West is West and never the twain shall meet."[1] The evolution of this insular community to one with international involvement in commercial enterprises is truly remarkable.

Large numbers of Jews began to leave Baghdad in the early 1830s to escape persecution, conscription, and frequent epidemics of plague. Many of them traveled to Bombay, where David Sassoon was recruiting Baghdadi Jews to launch a vast commercial empire. His son Elias would later pioneer the settlement of Baghdadi Jews in Shanghai after the 1845 Treaty of Nanking ended the infamous Opium Wars and Shanghai became a so-called treaty port, open to foreign trade and settlement. Initially, Jews left their families in Baghdad for lengthy periods in order to take advantage of China's lucrative trading opportunities. They were undeterred by the arduous seventy-day journey from Bombay to Shanghai, during which the ships were occasionally grounded for days, the cargo thrown overboard, and the passengers obliged to sit through the night with guns at the ready in case of pirates. It was also frequently necessary to end the voyage and disembark into small sampans well before the ships had reached their destination.

Biographical accounts collected in my book, *Shanghai's Baghdadi Jews: A Collection of Biographical Reflections* (Hong Kong: Blackman Books, 2015), illustrate the remarkable global reach of these peripatetic migrants. They wandered with their families from one Baghdadi Jewish settlement to another – notably in Bombay, Calcutta, Rangoon (Yangon), Singapore, Hong Kong, and Batavia (Djakarta in the Dutch East Indies) – in search of a livelihood before eventually settling in the foreign concessions of Shanghai. Shaul Ghazal, to avoid conscription into the Turkish Army, migrated with his wife and three sons to first to Burma, then to Malaysia. When seven-year-old Silas Isaiah Jacob was stoned in an anti-Jewish riot in Baghdad, his mother traveled with her three sons to Shanghai via Bombay. During their stay in Bombay, Silas worked as a clerk for the Sassoon firm. Catherine Levy Hardoon's family migrated to Basrah, Turkey, and Calcutta, and stayed in Bombay for about two years before settling in Shanghai. Nineteen-year-old Maurice Dangoor's trade in diamonds took him to France, England, and Holland.

---

[1] Rudyard Kipling, "The Ballad of East and West," in *Barrack-Room Ballads, and Other Verses* (London: Methuen Publishing, 1889).

He returned to Baghdad during World War I and then traveled to Germany, where a Baghdadi friend encouraged him to depart for Shanghai, which at the time was experiencing an economic boom. Sassoon Reuben's quest to expand his import-export business led him from Egypt to Syria, Lebanon, Bombay, Kobe (in Japan), and ultimately Shanghai.

Shanghai's Baghdadi Jews emerged out of the cocoon of the *mahala* (Jewish neighborhood). From lowly beginnings, with astonishing speed, panache, and entrepreneurial vision, several became pre-eminent figures within the foreign community and movers and shakers in financial and commercial circles. The end of the nineteenth century witnessed Baghdadi Jews achieving a high profile in banking, public utilities, the stock exchange, industrial development, and, most conspicuously, in real estate. Benjamin David Benjamin (1844–1889), the largest shareholder of the Hong Kong and Shanghai Banking Corporation and one of the largest residential property holders, allegedly owned more than a quarter of the International Settlement.

Shanghai's Baghdadi Jews were extraordinarily forward-thinking in outlook and contributed in a large measure to Shanghai's character and reputation as a cosmopolitan city. Their ability to communicate in English identified them with the British oligarchy that held power in the foreign enclave, while their common commercial interests further cemented their status as valued partners of the British elite and even as members of the administration. Gradually, they sacrificed – at least in part – their own traditions and culture on the altar of pragmatic (or perhaps opportunistic) alignment with all-powerful Imperial Britain. Their slavish Anglicization and conviction that everything British was worthy of emulation moulded the very structure of their lives. A thoroughly English education, running the whole gamut of ballet, piano, deportment, and elocution classes, generated strong British affinities, which continued over four generations. As Rebecca Toueg explains, they considered themselves to be both completely Baghdadi and completely British and were accepted in British society and British clubs (Figures 9.7 and 9.8).[2]

Several were educated in boarding schools and universities in England. George and Dick Hayeem made the adventurous journey to London via Siberia with an entourage of thirty-nine Baghdadis. After endless preparations for the packing of kosher food, they boarded a steamer for Dairen, where they traveled by train to Harbin, Manchuli (then under Japanese rule), Moscow, Warsaw, Berlin, Baden-Baden, and Paris.

---

[2] Rebecca Toueg, "Isaac Hayim Toeg (1888–1980)," in Maisie J. Meyer, *Shanghai's Baghdadi Jews: A Collection of Biographical Reflections* (Hong Kong: Blackman Books, 2015), 244.

Leah Jacob was born in Shanghai to a middle-class family. Her father was of Baghdadi origin, her mother Russian. She recalled: "Guests from all over the world graced our table. No formal schooling could possibly give us the education that so extended our horizons." There was constant interaction among the Judeo-Arabic-speaking Jews who had settled in a string of trading posts in Southeast Asia. Ezekiel Sion Jacob (1889–1938) would regularly sail to Kobe, Japan, to perform circumcisions for the small community of Baghdadi businessmen who lacked this facility. Eventually he was dubbed the "China Clipper," a pun on the name of the transpacific seaplane service. Baghdadi Jews were constantly traveling back and forth between Shanghai and Kobe, often in order to find employment or a spouse by visiting their relatives. "In this way," Flower Elias observes, "their horizons stretched far beyond the confines of their homes, for 'home' to them was not a house, but anywhere the family dwelt."[3]

The astonishing extent of their global reach, though manifest throughout a wide cross section of the community, is best exemplified by Sir Eleazer Kadoorie, Nissim Ezra Benjamin Ezra, Silas Aaron Hardoon, and Sir Ellice Victor Elias Sassoon.

1 Eleazer ("Elly") Silas Kadoorie (1865–1944)

Eleazer ("Elly") Kadoorie was descended from one of Baghdad's foremost families, who had been "merchant farmers" in an era when the currency for trade was livestock. He traveled to Hong Kong via Bombay to serve as a clerk at E. D. Sassoon and Company, on the paltry salary of 37 rupees a month. After being sent to Wei-hai-wei and Ningbo in North China, he branched out on his own, becoming a successful broker in Hong Kong.

In 1910, Elly decided he had enough money to retire in England. He placed his sons Lawrence and Horace (Figure 9.1) in school in London and bought a house, with a view to living in a grand style. Ultimately, a telegramme informing him that his partners were squandering the firm's money compelled him to return to Hong Kong, while his sons remained in school. He would never recover the lost funds. Four years later, the family had to extend their summer holiday in Canada unexpectedly, due to the outbreak of the First World War. They lived in in Europe and England from 1921 to 1924, while their family residence, Marble Hall, was under construction. The family made a broad circle of friends and entertained

---

[3] Flower Elias and Judith Elias Cooper, *The Jews of Calcutta: The Autobiography of a Community, 1789–1972* (Calcutta: Jewish Association of Calcutta, 1974), 46.

dignitaries, including King Faisal of Iraq and the Emperor Haile Selassie of Ethiopia, at their London residence. Elly was knighted in 1926. Clearly, he was respected far beyond the borders of Southeast Asia.

Figure 9.1: Sir Elly Kadoorie with his sons Lawrence (left) and Horace (right). (Photograph courtesy of the Hong Kong Heritage Project.)

In Shanghai, the iconic Marble Hall was well known to a wide spectrum of visitors from around the world: high-ranking British officers, Zionist emissaries, and men of letters, among them the famous Bengali poet Rabindranath Tagore in May 1924[4] and the Panchen Lama – second only to the Dalai Lama in spiritual authority within Tibetan Buddhism – in July 1924.[5] The Panchen Lama brought along

---

4 *Israel's Messenger*, May 4, 1924, 2.
5 *Israel's Messenger*, July 4, 1924, 4.

his Tibetan orchestra, complete with mountain trumpets. During World War II, Marble Hall maintained the international character of its hospitality and served as the meeting place of representatives of the Allied Nations.

The Kadoorie family sponsored hospitals, relief organizations, and educational programs for all creeds in Iraq, Iran, Syria, Turkey, India, Palestine, China, and Hong Kong. Sir Elly donated land to the Jewish National Fund to set up a library for the Hebrew University, paid for the establishment of two Kadoorie Agricultural Schools in Palestine (one for Arabs and one for Jews), and erected the Kadoorie Synagogue in Oporto, Portugal. Sir Elly pioneered the first educational facilities for girls in the Middle East, irrespective of creed, at a time when women were only educated at home. In memory of his wife, he founded Baghdad's renowned Laura Kadoorie School, which provided religious and secular education to about 1,200 girls, in 1922. The Kadoories might justifiably claim to have started a "women's lib" movement, since former pupils of the school, rather than acquiescing to their parents' arrangements, demanded that their future husbands should also be educated.

The Kadoorie family probably has been and still is the largest single benefactor in East Asia over the last several decades. The British and Chinese governments have recognized their outstanding generosity. They played a significant role in the post-war economic restoration of Hong Kong and are currently involved in nearly every sphere of commerce. The Kadoorie Agricultural Aid Association has trained over 3,000 Gurkha soldiers, who have since returned to Nepal and started farming on their own; several are teaching agricultural courses at the resettlement centers. The Kadoorie Farm and Botanic Garden continues to flourish as a center for biodiversity conservation, nature education, and sustainable living.

2 Silas Aaron Hardoon (1851–1931)

With no formal education but exceptional business acumen, Silas Aaron Hardoon worked his way up from clerk to manager in the Sassoon firm and later set out on his own, investing in rental properties with huge success. His pagoda-roofed home with its 40-acre garden was managed by a vast retinue of servants. With his Eurasian Buddhist wife, Eliza Roos (Figure 9.2), he adopted eleven children of various nationalities and brought them up as Jews (Figure 9.3). He donated the iconic Beth Aharon Synagogue, which was valued at $300,000 – at a very conservative estimate – and would be worth 3 million today.

Figure 9.2: Silas Aaron Hardoon with his wife, Eliza Roos; Shangahi, ca. 1925. (Photograph courtesy of Leo Hardoon.)

Figure 9.3: Silas Aaron Hardoon's adopted children; Shanghai, 1930s. (Photograph courtesy of Leo Hardoon.)

When Hardoon died in 1931, he left his entire fortune to his wife: a staggering 15 million dollars. This caused a furor among Shanghai's Baghdadis. The enormous sum attracted claims from Hardoon's numerous relatives and so-called relatives:

> From Baghdad to Bombay to Basra to Jerusalem to Shanghai, wires are kept hot with claims of relatives of the late Silas Aaron Hardoon, who, in leaving the greatest hoard of gold ever gathered by one person in the Far East, instigated a flood of litigation that threatens to tie up the huge fortune for many months.[6]

Hardoon's will aroused considerable global interest, not least in the Zionist Organization, which was expecting to receive substantial sums. In honor of the Zionist envoy Ariel Bension, Hardoon and his wife had hosted receptions for as many as four hundred guests. Bension was gratified, stating: "I am also especially thankful to our host and hostess, for not only giving us this historical opportunity of forming a committee for the promotion of culture in Palestine, but also in helping us in this great cause."[7] Clearly, the Organization was disappointed. A Reuters correspondent in Jerusalem noted:

> A claimant to the huge estate of the late Silas Aaron Hardoon, real estate magnate of Shanghai, has appeared here. He is a Palestinian Jewish nephew of the late Mr. Hardoon and he claims to be entitled to a third share of the $5,000,000. He has telegraphed a claim to the British Supreme Court in Shanghai.[8]

The HBM Supreme Court for China became the arena for the sensational legal battle for Hardoon's 15-million-dollar estate (which would be valued at several billions today). From June 1932 to February 1933, the lengthy court proceedings – with illustrious British legal representation – dominated local newspaper columns and were followed with great interest in Baghdad, Palestine, and Britain. The judge, Sir Peter Grain, commented, "Individuals styling themselves 'Hardoon' appear to be arriving from all parts of the world, all claiming to be related to the late Mr. Hardoon."[9] He delivered one of the longest and most important judgments ever given in the court in favor of Hardoon's wife, with costs. Israel Cohen, general secretary of the Jewish Agency for Palestine, reflected ruefully on how much Hardoon might have done to benefit Jews.

---

6 *Israel's Messenger*, "Hardoon Will Case Enters Another New Stage," December 1, 1931, 1.
7 Ariel Bension, *Israel's Messenger*, March 7, 1925, 7.
8 Reuters, published in the local papers in Jerusalem on December 7, 1931, and in *Israel's Messenger*, "Hardoon Will Case Enters Another New Stage," December 17, 1931, 1.
9 *Israel's Messenger*, "Plaintiff Was a Relative," July 1, 1932, 6.

3 Nissim Ezra Benjamin Ezra (1881–1936)

Nissim Ezra Benjamin Ezra (Figure 9.4) was the editor of *Israel's Messenger*, the journal of the Baghdadi Jews in Shanghai, which was published between April 22, 1904 and October 17, 1941. Its social and personal columns recorded the community's global holiday destinations. Frequent vacations in Europe had become *de rigueur* among the wealthy Baghdadis. Several, like their British peers, referred to their holidays in Britain as "going home." In addition to local news, *Israel's Messenger* featured editorials and articles on events in other Baghdadi communities in the East and on issues affecting world Jewry generally – reinforcing links between Jewish communities in the East and West. Some 10–20% of its publications were sent to Jewish communities in China and abroad, in the Philippines, India, Persia, Baghdad, and the British, French, and Dutch Indies.

Figure 9.4: Nissim Ezra Benjamin; Shanghai, ca. 1925. (Photograph courtesy of Rose Jacob Horowitz.)

Israel's Messenger received "Little Bouquets," as Ezra called compliments, from readers as far afield as Singapore, Batavia, Java, Kuling, Johannesburg, London, Cardiff, and Edinburgh, among them Shigemitsu Mamoru, Japan's vice-minister for foreign affairs; Rabbi Doctor Bernard Drachman of New York; and the editors of the *Indiana Jewish Chronicle* and the *Jewish Guardian* (London).

Ezra was instrumental in influencing three independent Asian countries – Siam (Thailand), China, and Japan – to recognize the Balfour Declaration of 1917 in favor of a Jewish national homeland in Palestine. Although Siam and China could hardly have been regarded as influential powers at the time, this was a significant political achievement – their cooperation was crucial, as unanimous approval was needed to validate the Declaration. Ezra publicized the statements of approval from several political figures, among them Doctor Sun Yat-sen, whose statement he sent to the Hebrew University of Jerusalem, where it is preserved to this day.

In 1925, Ezra wrote to Viscount Uchida Yasuya, the Japanese foreign minister, suggesting that he send a Japanese consul to Palestine to promote trade between the two countries. Shigemitsu Mamoru was keen to establish a close commercial relationship between Palestine and Japan. Ezra encouraged tourism, highlighting Palestine's potential as the world's great health resort. Undaunted by the arduous journey, several Shanghai Jews visited the Holy Land. Isaac A. Toeg, Isaiah Cohen, and David Silman Somekh (the largest shareholder in the Maccabean Land Company, formed in 1908), purchased land there. Jacob E. Salmon visited Palestine twice and, on his return to Shanghai in 1932, initiated the Eres Yisrael Tree Fund. He reported:

> I met my friend, Mr. Ezra Shahmoon, and his charming bride at Rammat Gan, near Tel Abib [sic]. His enthusiasm is without bounds and, if he had the choice, he would settle here for good. Another friend of mine hailing from Baghdad, Mr. Manashih Bechor, invited me to his orange plantation at Hadar.[10]

Ezra sent a petition to the League of Nations, drawing international attention to the oppression of Jews in Baghdad. He campaigned from 1909 to the mid-1930s to have Shakespeare's *The Merchant of Venice* excluded from the curriculum of Shanghai's public schools and to prevent it from being staged. He advised Neville Laski, president of the Board of Deputies of British Jews, of the "vital necessity" of approaching Cambridge University to have the book proscribed from their curriculum. Laski responded: "There are so many urgent matters, that we feel it would be improper for us to indulge in a campaign in this country."

There were no boundaries to Ezra's global reach. He was involved in world affairs was not merely as a bystander but as an active participant.

---

10 Ezra, "Tel-Abib [sic] Has Its Charm," *Israel's Messenger*, June 2, 1933, 9.

4 Sir Ellice Victor Elias Sassoon (1881–1961)

Six of the eight sons of David Sassoon, the patriarch of Baghdadi Jews in India and China, emigrated from Bombay to London in the second half of the nineteenth century. They entered the very heart of the British ruling circles and became close friends of the Prince of Wales, later King Edward VII. Within a generation, the Sassoons established an extensive commercial empire boasting eminent merchants, industrialists, politicians, scholars, and courtiers, whose influence endures.

Sir Ellice Victor Elias Sassoon (1881–1961; Figure 9.5), the grandson of Elias Sassoon, who had pioneered the settlement of Baghdadi Jews in Shanghai in 1845, was born in his parents' honeymoon suite in Italy while they were *en route* from England to India. His father, Sir Edward Elias Sassoon, was born in Bombay and settled in England. Victor lived in China until the age of seven, when he went to Harrow School in England and then to Trinity College, Cambridge, where he received a second-class honors degree.

Figure 9.5: Sir Ellice Victor Elias Sassoon, Third Baronet, GBE; Shanghai, ca. 1935. (Photograph courtesy of Evelyn, Lady Barnes.)

During the First World War, Victor served in the Royal Flying Corps. Although a plane crash left him with a limp and acute attacks of pain in his hip, he remained in service until the end of the war, first serving in the RFC as a purchasing commission officer in France and later attached to the United States Army and Navy

Air Forces. Afterward, he became a patron of aviation in England and India and president of the Royal Air Force Association of Shanghai in the 1930s (Figure 9.6).

Figure 9.6: Caricature: "Sir Victor Sassoon, the new president of the Royal Air Force Association of Shanghai." (Image from the *North China Herald*, April 9, 1939.)

Victor became the third holder of the Bombay baronetcy on the death of his brother Jacob in 1916. Unable to communicate with his father (who, he believed, favored his younger brother Hector), Sir Victor decided to take care of the family's interests in India, including fourteen textile mills, which employed over 20,000 native workers. E. D. Sassoon and Company Merchants and Bankers was registered in India in 1918 as a private limited company. Sir Victor, as chairman, chose Bombay as his headquarters. However, the rise of Indian nationalism convinced him that there was little scope for foreign entrepreneurs in India. He caused a stir among British bankers and politicians worldwide when he announced his intention to make Shanghai the focus of the firm's activities.

He honored the terms of his father's will, which obliged him to spend several months of each year in India, and would travel about twelve hundred miles to England and back to enjoy a summer racing season. In 1941, the *Memphis Daily News* reported: "Sir Victor Sassoon, the British Baronet, has made his headquarters in Shanghai for fourteen years, while spending about half the time traveling in India, the U.S. and the rest of the world."[11]

Sir Victor crossed the Atlantic more than a hundred times over the course of his travels. By 1936, he had visited every continent. He visited European capital cities to buy factories and machines and to recruit engineers and specialists to join his effort to industrialize China. In January 1935, the Budapest press announced the arrival of "Asia's Rothschild, [who] holds in his hands the greater part of Shanghai's economic life . . . he is leader of Asia's finance, commerce and industry."[12]

Sir Victor's worldwide contacts in government and banking circles equipped him to play the role of a roving ambassador for England. His social circle included Winston Churchill, then under-secretary of the Treasury, with whom he often took shooting lessons. Queen Elizabeth II wrote two letters (which I have in my possession) congratulating Sir Victor on his horses winning races. In the West, he was regarded as an authority on political affairs in Southeast Asia and was frequently interviewed and profiled by the media, as in the following example:

> Abroad was Sir Victor Sassoon, number one Capitalist in the Far East, notably Shanghai, where his firm is all-powerful. Real estate banking, shipping, hotels; you name the business, Sir Victor is in it. Monocled [sic], quietly dressed in blue coat and grey slacks, pausing in San Francisco for only a night. He will leave for London via New York: the usual trip every two years. "What's happening in my part of the world? Well, you step over there and ask."[13]

His outspoken anti-Japanese comments in the press and on Western radio stations received extensive coverage in Tokyo and Shanghai. His statements were

---

[11] Ward Archer, "Shanghai's Richest Man Visits Memphis after Auto Accident," *Memphis Daily News*, April 8, 1941, 4.

[12] Quoted in *Israel's Messenger*, "Sir Victor Sassoon in Budapest Buys Factories and Transports them to China," January 4, 1935, 6.

[13] *San Francisco Chronicle*, "Sir Victor Sassoon, number one Capitalist in the Far East," June 9, 1939, 2.

tactless, if not blatantly dangerous, considering the fact that thousands of victims of Nazi persecution had found refuge in Shanghai, which was then under Japanese control. Leaders of the Shanghai Jewish community, infuriated with Sir Victor, tried to assure the American public that the Japanese authorities were supporting the refugees in every possible way.

Throughout his life, Sir Victor combined business with pleasure. A photograph of him with Marlene Dietrich accompanied the announcement of his arrival in Hollywood, which read:

> British Aviation Leader Arrives – Sir Victor Sassoon Credited with Helping Keep Royal Air Force Powerful.
>
> Sir Victor, here for a short stay from China, is having himself a whirl and, at the same time, trying to buy more bombers and ambulances for England.[14]

During his stay in Hollywood, Sir Victor made a significant financial contribution to the British war effort:

> The most expensive raffle in the history of such an event will be held in Hollywood shortly. The prize will be a 425-carat sapphire, contributed by Sir Victor Sassoon for the benefit of Britain's war relief. Each ticket in the raffle will cost $1,000 and the sale will be limited to members of the motion picture colony, who can afford it.[15]

Cinematography was Sir Victor's hobby. He was invited to have lunch with Motion Picture executives at the Samuel Goldwyn Studio and permitted to film several scenes of a movie, featuring Bette Davis, with his 6mm camera. He also shot his own films of Marlene Dietrich. It was even rumored that he might be planning to invest in Hollywood. The leading member of the Nazi Party, Hermann Goering, considered him significant enough to condemn him on the radio as a "mischievous Hollywood playboy." In New York, the FBI insisted on giving him two bodyguards, believing he might be a target of the Nazi Bund or Japanese gunmen.

Soon after the outbreak of World War II, Sir Victor contributed enormous sums to the British War Fund in the East and West. He made donations to Archibald McIndoe, who had achieved international fame for his pioneering work with plastic surgery on fighter pilots who had been grotesquely burned in the RAF Battle of Britain.

Sir Victor contributed generously to Jewish charities and institutions. His donations to Jewish refugee relief were reputedly the largest in the East. In 1938, he purchased 10,000 square miles of land in Brazil and investigated the possibility

---

14 *Los Angeles Examiner*, "British Aviation Leader Arrives," October 20, 1940, 2.
15 Leonard Lyons, "The Lyons Den," *Los Angeles Daily News*, 23 April 1941, 2.

of establishing a colony of refugees from Nazi Europe, stating, "I am all for the Jews living in a colony together, where the Jews do everything from being sweeper to president."[16]

Sir Victor continued to commute regularly between Shanghai, Bombay, Hong Kong, London, and the United States for fourteen years. For several months each year, he stayed in his suite at the London Ritz and conducted his business there. He launched a new private banking company and switched his fortune, which was estimated at £15 million (roughly £675 million today), from the sale of property from East to West. When a reporter inquired if it were true that he was the third richest man in the world, Sir Victor replied, smiling, "I never contradict that, because it's good for credit." Upon further questioning, he said, "If China goes, I'll be way down. If India goes, I shall be around asking for a job."[17] He estimated he was worth about $10 million after the war.

Sir Victor was sixty-five years old when the German forces surrendered in Italy in April 1945, concluding the Pacific war. With the loss of its extra-territorial rights, Shanghai lost its attraction for him. Sir Victor dejectedly sailed off to the United States at the end of 1948, aware that the commercial empire his grandfather Elias had painstakingly established nearly a century before was disintegrating. He ruefully noted, "I gave up India and China gave me up." He registered E. D. Sassoon Banking in Nassau in the Bahamas and took up residence there in 1949.

When asked why he never married, Sir Victor would reply, "I promised at least fifty women that I wouldn't and can't bring myself to disappoint that many."[18] He finally plucked up his courage, at the age of seventy-eight, and shook the world with surprise when he married his devoted thirty-nine-year-old nurse, Maude Evelyn Barnes, on April 1, 1959: "The marriage of the richest bachelor in the world, a titled Englishman to his American nurse, was one of the noteworthy news stories of the century."[19]

Sir Victor poured vast sums into horse breeding. He was one of the top breeders in Britain, owning more than 200 horses. The famous old gold and peacock-blue Sassoon colors made racing history by winning an astonishing series of four victories within eight years in the prestigious British Epsom Derby. Sir Victor famously proclaimed that the derby was the only race greater than the Jewish race.[20] His

---

16 *The Jewish Tribune* (Bombay), "Sir Victor wants Jews to Live in a colony together," July 1938, 10.
17 *Los Angeles Examiner*, "Fortune in India," March 28, 1942, 3.
18 *Los Angeles Times*, February 5, 1941, 1.
19 *Los Angeles Times*, February 5, 1941, 1.
20 *Los Angeles Times*, February 5, 1941, 2.

success – at least, according to his own assessment – was entirely the result of horse racing: "Neither business affairs, nor politics, nor an aristocratic descent would have made me famous. My fame is due to the fact that I own the best racing horses of the century."[21] (His ancestors must have been spinning in their graves.) Sir Victor died in Nassau, after a heart attack, on August 12, 1961, five months short of his eightieth birthday. His global reach surpassed that of any other Shanghai Baghdadi Jew. Renowned in society, commerce and finance, and politics worldwide, he was one of the truly international personalities of his era.

Figure 9.7: A party in D. E. J. Abraham's garden, Shanghai, ca. 1938. (Photograph courtesy of David Dangoor.)

---

21 *O Globo* (Rio, Brazil), "One of the Most Famous Thoroughbreds of the Century Among Us," November 5, 1953.

Figure 9.8: Baghdadi Jews on a boating excursion on the Huangpu River, Shanghai, ca. 1938. (Photograph courtesy of Rebecca Toueg.)

Coda: Exodus in Search of New Homes

In the aftermath of the Communist conquest of Shanghai in 1949, the Chinese population regarded all foreigners as "foreign entrepreneurs," with the evident connotation of "despised imperialist parasites." The government condemned property owners as exploiting capitalists. The liberal and cosmopolitan metropolis, where capitalism and Western influences had dominated for a century, gradually lost its vitality and its appeal for Baghdadi Jews, who felt compelled to relocate due to the volatile political situation. Unable to take their assets out of the country, they virtually left Shanghai as refugees. Their global reach is further illustrated in the resilience with which they adapted to their new environments.

The year 1948 witnessed an exodus of Shanghai Jews to the newly founded State of Israel, where eventually about half the community settled. Among them was Joe (Yaacob) Jacob, who helped to establish Israel's English news service and whose faultless diction was a byword among his listeners. After serving as consul general in Ottawa and Washington, Joe was appointed minister of information in London and at the United Nations. Even in retirement, he continued to work as an editor for the Foreign Ministry and became a sub-editor at the *Jerusalem Post*.

After military service in the Israeli army, the journalist Sasson Jacoby became one of the founders of a cooperative agricultural settlement comprising a mixed group of Russian Ashkenazim, Sephardim, South Africans, Dutch, and a few Israelis. One Hannah Levy became his wife. He served as news editor for the *Jerusalem Post* for forty years.

In 1946, after applying to train as a nurse in England, Cissy Jacob acquired a UK passport, obtained free passage on board a troop ship, and worked as a nurse in London for three years. Having studied English history and literature at the Shanghai Jewish School, she found it easy to adapt to life in England. After qualifying as a nurse in 1947, she emigrated to Montreal, where she married William Flegg (who was born in Heidelberg). In 1948, the couple settled in Jerusalem, Israel. Cissy (Jacob) Flegg's parents were accepted at Montefiore College in Ramsgate, England in 1949. For six years, her parents and four siblings lived in one of the ten cottages on the Montefiore estate, where the trust fund provided a small income and paid their living expenses. Her siblings attended the local school in Ramsgate until they emigrated to New York.

Isaac Hai's parents sent him to London in 1926 to further his studies. He became a barrister, renowned judge, and professor of law at University College London. During World War II, he served as a captain in the British Army. In 1972, he was knighted for his work in civil procedural law.

On their arrival in London at the end of 1949, Isaac Abraham's family were initially accommodated in the Jews' Temporary Shelter and eventually allocated a Council house. Isaac enrolled as a yeshiva student for the first ten years: first in Gateshead, County Durham; then in B'nei B'raq, Israel; and finally in Etz Haim, London. After serving as headmaster of a parochial school in North London, he taught Jewish subjects in several schools. He took early retirement and became the director of the Sephardi Kashrut Authority. On relinquishing the post, he was appointed registrar of the Sephardi Beth Din in April.

Brothers Abraham and Isaac Jacob embarked from Shanghai on a converted American army transport ship, the SS *General Gordon*, on what turned out to be an excruciatingly circuitous journey of fifty-five days to Israel via Honolulu, San Francisco, and New York. After arriving in Israel, they made their way to Haifa, where 18-year-old Isaac was conscripted to serve in the army for three years. The rest of the family was transferred to a transit center and then lived for a year in a *ma'abara* (tent settlement) in Binyamina and built their own home in Shikun Olay Sin [Settlement of Immigrants from China] before finally settling in the United States.

Several others also settled in the US. In May 1949, Matook Rahamim Nissim could not buy passage to Hong Kong, as there were very few transport ships. Instead, he went on board an American military ship and agreed to work in the galley, although he did not even know what a "galley" was. It was illegal to take currency out of China, so his *amah* sewed gold bars – each weighing about ten ounces, for a total of twenty pounds – into a vest. He deposited them with the National City Bank in Hong Kong together with a donation of US dollars that he had smuggled in a box of cigars for the Jewish Sephardi Association. In 1950, he spent two weeks working on the Magic Carpet Operation airlifting Yemenite Jews to Israel. The Magic Carpet Operation, which brought 49,000 Yemenite Jews to the newly established State of Israel, required traveling to Khartoum (Anglo-Egyptian Sudan), Tripoli, Tripolitania (Libya), and several locations in the Middle East. He stayed in Paris before returning to Hong Kong for about three years and, in 1952, finally emigrated to the United States.

Teenager Leah Jacob and her sister Ritchie traveled to San Francisco on student visas. The journey took seventeen days with stops in Yokohama and Honolulu. On their first Sabbath in San Francisco, they attended the Magain David, the only Sephardic synagogue in the city, where Ritchie met her husband-to-be, Joe Safdie, on her first Sabbath. Their parents and 12-year-old brother Jack traveled to Hong Kong with two suitcases each, but, due to their Chinese National Stateless status, the British authorities did not permit them to stay for even a single day. Fortunately, Macau, an open Portuguese port on the Chinese mainland, had no such restriction. They took the ferry, a three-hour ride, across the China Sea, and stayed in Macau as the only Jews for eighteen years.

Stephen Sopher's voyage to São Paulo in 1950 took sixty-three days. During that time, the ship docked at Manila, Batavia (Jakarta), Singapore, Mauritius, Durban, Cape Town, Buenos Aires, Montevideo, and many other ports. He obtained a position at the Geological Survey of Canada and enrolled at the same time at Carleton University in Ottawa. His research in paleomagnetism contributed to the concept of continental drift. Representing the Canadian Chamber of Commerce at an event held in Rio de Janeiro, he had the honor of sitting next to Pierre Trudeau, the Canadian prime minister.

When the Moalem family disembarked in Sydney in June 1950, customs officers questioned them closely, sarcastically commenting on how well they spoke English for Chinese-born people. Because the White Australia Policy was in effect at the time, every member of the family had to roll up their sleeves so that the official could check the color of their skin.

In 1951, Clive Jackie Levy's International Red Cross travel documents allowed him a one-way trip to Australia, which took three days and two nights by train to Hong Kong via Canton. Finally, he walked a few hundred yards to the border between Communist China and the New Territories and caught a train to Hong Kong, where he had a memorable reunion with his *amah*, Ah-say, who gave him some money, as he had left Shanghai with only five pounds. After this reunion, he went on to Sydney, where his brother met him at the wharf. Within a week he became an apprentice in a gold-refining firm. He went on to work as a "freelance traveler" selling expanding watchbands made in China and Hong Kong, and later became the representative at a large wholesale jewelry company selling diamonds and watches. In 1953, he visited his brother Saul, who had carved out a name for himself in the Japanese financial market. He owned the sales agency for Johnny Walker whiskey and French champagne and wines, as well as the franchise to supply American PX stores in Vietnam. When Clive returned to Sydney, he worked in the Post Office and the News Agency and later purchased his own taxicab, which enabled his to become a prosperous gentleman of leisure.

The adopted Hardoon children settled as far afield as Argentina, Australia, and America in 1953. Leo, with help from the Jewish Agency, traveled to a *kibbutz* in Israel, where he met his Canadian wife. The couple settled in Toronto. Maple traveled to the Channel Islands, married Melville Doron there in 1954, and settled with him in Israel. Reuben and George settled in Hong Kong. Catherine and Silah Charlie Hardoon departed from Shanghai in 1949 via Hong Kong, intending to apply at the American Consulate for permission to travel to the Philippines and acquire residency in Manila (where there was also an American Consulate). However, they changed their plans and applied for American visas instead. As a result, Charlie's brother, who lived in Paris, was able to have their passports renewed at the Iraqi Consulate in France, which enabled them to travel to San Francisco.

Among the few of Shanghai's Baghdadi Jews who emigrated to Iraq was Renée Dangoor, who won the title of "Beauty Queen of Baghdad 1947." She married Naim Dangoor, the grandson of the Chief Rabbi of Iraq, and later settled in London.

There is thus compelling evidence to illustrate that the reach of Shanghai's Baghdadi Jews was quite extensive.

References

Archer, Ward. "Shanghai's Richest Man Visits Memphis after Auto Accident." *Memphis Daily News*, April 8, 1941.
Elias, Flower and Judith Elias Cooper. *The Jews of Calcutta: the Autobiography of a Community 1789–1972*. Calcutta: Jewish Association of Calcutta, 1974.
Ezra, Nissim Ezra Benjamin. "Tel-Abib [sic] Has Its Charm." *Israel's Messenger*, June 2, 1933.
Bension, Ariel. *Israel's Messenger*, March 7, 1925.
Israel's Messenger. "Hardoon Will Case Enters Another New Stage." December 1, 1931.
Israel's Messenger. "Hardoon Will Case Enters Another New Stage." December 17, 1931.

Israel's Messenger. "Plaintiff Was a Relative." July 1, 1932.

Israel's Messenger. "Sir Victor Sassoon in Budapest Buys Factories and Transports them to China." January 4, 1935.

Israel's Messenger, May 4, 1924.

Israel's Messenger, July 4, 1924.

Kipling, Rudyard. "The Ballad of East and West," in *Barrack-Room Ballads, and Other Verses.* London: Methuen Publishing, 1889.

Leonard Lyons. "The Lyons Den." *Los Angeles Daily News.* April 23, 1941.

Los Angeles Examiner. "Fortune in India." March 28, 1942.

Los Angeles Examiner. "British Aviation Leader Arrives." October 20, 1940.

Los Angeles Times, February 5, 1941.

Meyer, Maisie J. *Shanghai's Baghdadi Jews: A Collection of Biographical Reflections.* Hong Kong: Blackman Books, 2015.

O Globo (Rio, Brazil). "One of the Most Famous Thoroughbreds of the Century Among Us." November 5, 1953.

San Francisco Chronicle. "Sir Victor Sassoon, number one Capitalist in the Far East." June 9, 1939.

The Jewish Tribune (Bombay). "Sir Victor wants Jews to Live in a colony together." July 1938.

Nancy BERLINER

10 Jewish Refugee Artists in Shanghai: Visual Legacies of Traumatic Moments and Cultural Encounters

The population of Shanghai in the 1940s was probably at least 96 percent Chinese.[1] Although the Jewish community represented mere droplets in this vast urban sea, Jewish refugee artists contributed an abundance of new cultural riches to Shanghai society.

Works by three European Jewish artists, Friedrich Schiff, David Ludwig Bloch, and Paul Fischer, all living in Shanghai during the turbulent 1940s, not only reflect their own lives and struggles, but also depict the Shanghai neighborhoods that they observed around them. Their works are visual records of the various lifestyles of Jewish refugees, other foreigners, and local Chinese residents in Shanghai during the 30s and 40s. Moreover, they reveal Shanghai's radical transition from the lively 30s to the desperate 40s.

Contemporary classical musicians in Shanghai often note that their professional heritage inevitably goes back to a European Jewish refugee who had escaped Nazi Europe and lived in Shanghai during the 1940s.[2] While visual art by refugees may not have such clear lines of descent, their work, appearing in exhibitions, magazines, newspapers, and even large-scale murals, attracted and affected both foreign and local audiences during their lifetimes. Today, their images continue to communicate stories, perspectives, and traumas. The complex realm that was 1940s Shanghai remains a testament to the universality of painful challenges in human history.

---

[1] To get a sense of the small percentage of foreigners residing in Shanghai in the 1940s, we can look at the 1942 census of the International Settlement. On March 27, 1942, the Shanghai *Municipal Gazette* (page 34) reported the entire population of the International Settlement as a total of 1,585,673 persons, 57,434 (less than 4%) of whom were not Chinese.

[2] Personal conversations in Shanghai, 2015. See also Pan Guang, *A Study of Jewish Refugees in China (1933–1945)* (Shanghai: Jiao Tong University Press, 2019), 68: "Among Jewish refugees, at least 13 taught at the Shanghai Conservatory of Music, cultivating a large number of Chinese musicians, many of whom later became masters and pioneers in the Chinese music community." And Zhou Qingyang, "Interactions Between the Chinese and the Jewish Refugees in Shanghai During World War II," *Penn History Review* 25, no. 2 (April 5, 2019): 72.

https://doi.org/10.1515/9783110683943-013

1 Friedrich Schiff (1908–1968)

Friedrich Schiff, born in Vienna, raised in a family of passionate art-lovers,[3] and a graduate of Vienna's High School of Applied Arts and Academy of Fine Arts, was the first of the three to arrive in Shanghai.[4] The year was 1929. He arrived not as a refugee but as a talented young man who happened to be of Jewish ancestry (his maternal grandfather was a cantor at the Central Synagogue in Budapest,[5] but his father had converted from Judaism to Catholicism), looking to spread his wings in a cosmopolitan metropolis. The city of Shanghai was still awash in luxury, privilege, and decadence. The Cathay House Hotel – built by Victor Sassoon, an heir of the Baghdadi Jewish Sassoon family – had just opened, and Noel Coward, writing his play *Private Lives*, was ensconced therein. Charlie Chaplin would come to stay in a few years. The city was expanding, with new roads, residential buildings, and factories. European dress, bars, restaurants, and jazz were in vogue among foreigners and Chinese who could afford such a lifestyle. The Japanese had not yet invaded. Members of the budding Communist Party noticed the suffering of Chinese laborers in the textile factories, but many in the growing capitalist economy focused on their own incomes and pleasures.

Judging by his illustrations of city life, Schiff was surely exhilarated to be in Shanghai during the early 1930s.[6] At first, he looked to earn money by painting portraits. Photographs of two portraits published in an August 1930 Shanghai newspaper announced his recent arrival in Shanghai and his interest in finding work along those lines.[7] The portraits reveal an artist working in a contemporary European style, eschewing classical naturalism for a hint of cubism. Before long, Schiff no longer needed to rely on portrait painting for a living. His talents were quickly recognized by both Chinese and foreign interests. As a book illustrator and a cartoonist for Chinese- and English-language newspapers and magazines,

---

[3] Schiff's father, Robert Schiff, was a well-known artist in Vienna. Pan Guang, *A Study of Jewish Refugees in China (1933–1945)*, 304.
[4] Gerd Kaminski, *Der Blick durch die Drachenhaut: Friedrich Schiff: Maler dreier Kontinente* [The view through the dragon's skin: Friedrich Schiff, a painter from three continents] (Vienna: Eigenverlag, 2001), and Matthias Messmer, *Jewish Wayfarers in Modern China: Tragedy and Splendor* (Lanham, MD: Lexington Books, 2011), 155.
[5] Messmer, *Jewish Wayfarers in Modern China*, 154.
[6] In 1983, a reprint of much of his Shanghai work was published in Austria. Kaminski, *China Gemalt: Chinesische Zeitgeschichte in Bildern Friedrich Schiff* (Vienna: Europa Verlag, 1983). In 1998, the Shanghai Library held an exhibition of 120 of his works. In February and March of 2002, another exhibition, Friedrich Schiff: In Shanghai Berühmt, In Wien Vergessen [Famous in Shanghai, forgotten in Vienna] was held in Vienna at the Historisches Museum der Stadt Wien.
[7] *The China Journal of Science and Arts*, August 1930.

Schiff (known by his Chinese name Xu Fu, or 许福) portrayed the cosmopolitan life he saw around him. Leaping from the pages of *Shanghai* (1940),[8] illustrated by Schiff and written by his long-time book partner Ellen Thorbecke,[9] are thin Chinese women dancing in high heels and colorful, sleeveless, tight-fitting *qipao* (旗袍), with slits traveling high up their thighs; American sailors lolling at a bar, chatting with a blonde in a low-cut dress; and a well-dressed, fedora-clad European gentleman relaxing in a rickshaw pulled by a fleet-footed, buck-toothed Chinese man, who is portrayed as though he were completely untroubled by his burden. Shanghai was an exotic, easy playground for even those non-Chinese visitors and residents with moderate incomes. *I Love Chinese*, another book illustrated by Schiff, reveals the emotions the city stirred up for him and many others at that time. Their love for Shanghai, however, did not necessarily manifest any deep sympathy for the Chinese workers who made their comfortable lives possible. In another book by Schiff and Thorbecke, a poem called "Maskee"[10] showcased a European and American stereotype of Chinese women as only eager for a moneyed lifestyle. Called "Miss Shanghai," the verse rattled:

Me No Worry
Me No Care!
Me go Marry
Millionaire!

If he die –
Me no cry!
Me go marry
Other guy!!

Schiff's time in Shanghai was decidedly a professional success for him. In addition to his cartoons for Chinese- and English-language periodicals, book illustrations, and commercial commissions – such as designing graphics for the KPM (Koninklijke Paketvaart-Maatschappij) Dutch shipping line – he also taught and even opened his own institution, the School of Applied Art, where students could take classes in advertising, fashion, design, sculpture, woodcarving, handweaving, and life drawing.[11] The Woman's World column from an undated *China Press*

---

8 Ellen Thorbecke, *Shanghai*, with sketches by Schiff (Shanghai, 1940).
9 Thorbecke (1902–1973) was a Dutch writer and photographer who moved to China in 1931, following her diplomat husband and working as a journalist and correspondent for German newspapers. She met Schiff at one of his exhibitions in Shanghai.
10 The word *maskee* was a Chinese pidgin expression meaning 'never mind.' N. B. Dennys, *Journal of the Straits Branch of the Royal Asiatic Society* 2 (December, 1878): 172.
11 A printed pamphlet advertising the school is found in Bloch's archive at the Leo Baeck Institute.

newspaper clipping published photos from a masquerade party held there, familiarly nicknaming the host "Freddy."[12] His talent – evident from his striking graphic designs – was in high demand. Hotels and clubs, such as the glamorously-appointed Cercle Sportif Français, a French social club built in the Art Deco style in 1926 (now the Okura Garden Hotel), hired him to paint murals. A view of the Cercle Sportif's card room pictured on an old postcard shows two floor-to-ceiling paintings, possibly by Schiff.[13] Dizzying abstract shapes and forms depict an overhead view of human figures enjoying bar life. Another undated newspaper clipping shows Schiff painting a mural of elegantly-dressed European gentlemen and scantily-clad European women toasting cocktails at the Maskee Night Club.[14] Schiff was busy – his creations were in high demand, and he was deeply involved in the highlife of Shanghai.

As time passed, and the 30s became the 40s, Shanghai changed. The Japanese invaded. War arrived. And more Jews from Europe began pouring in. Schiff's attitude and artwork would change as well.

2 David Ludwig Bloch (1910–2002)

David Bloch's woodblock print of a European refugee sitting on a steamer trunk candidly conveys a difficult tale (Figure 10.1). The subject's face is unseen. His head rests on his hands, which are perched on the handle of a cane. His body slumps, exhausted. The eyeglasses lying on a book hint that he is an intellectual or a person of some substance who has lost almost everything. The leather handle of his trunk is torn from rough travel. Several details offer clues, for those in the know, that the scene is set in Shanghai. Smoke pours from a factory; along the river is the telltale skyline with the triangular pinnacle of Sassoon House; a rickshaw is passing by. Next to the subject stands an enamel cup, which may contain a food distribution from an aid group, and the ubiquitous Chinese rattan-covered thermos for hot water. But the scene is also intended to reflect a universal situation. "D. P. Nobody Anywhere," reads the inscription on the traveler's luggage, using the then-common abbreviation for "displaced person." Though they may never

---

[12] "Fancy Dress Party," The Woman's World, in *The China Press*, clipping from the Österreichisches Institut für China- und Südostasienforschung [Austrian Institute for China and Southeast Asia Research], http://www.china-kultur.at/content/Detail.aspx?CatalogItemID=29215.
[13] "Cercle sportif français: Salle des cartes / Card-Room; A. Léonard, P. Veysseyre, Architectes," http://shanghailander.net/wp-content/uploads/2012/05/CFS-cardroom.jpg.
[14] Lacks, "Decorations at the Maskee," clipping from Österreichisches Institut für China- und Südostasienforschung, http://www.china-kultur.at/content/Detail.aspx?CatalogItemID=29203.

Figure 10.1: *Mr. Nobody, Shanghai,* by David Ludwig Bloch, 1947. (Photograph courtesy of the Leo Baeck Institute at the Center for Jewish History.)

have seen Bloch's work, many Chinese inhabitants of 1940s Shanghai were also refugees from war-torn and impoverished regions of the country.

Shanghai newspapers in English, German, Chinese, and Yiddish were all raving about David Ludwig Bloch's work in the early 1940s: "Shanghailanders last month witnessed one of the most unique one-man art exhibitions ever held in this city. Holding the Spotlight at the Shanghai Art Gallery on this occasion was Artist David Ludwig Bloch who festooned critics with a brilliant collection of watercolors and woodcuts. Under Artist Bloch's careful hands, all the incidents which are crowded in his hectic life are displayed in a series of illustrations, telling eloquently, though without words, the tragedy, pathos and humor that make up his daily occupation."[15] "The colors, the composition," effused one Chinese newspaper. "Distinct, elegant and smart."[16]

Unlike the sophisticated Viennese Friedrich Schiff, David Ludwig Bloch (born in the small town of Floss, Bavaria, on March 25, 1910) did not travel to Shanghai to explore its rich opportunities and fast-paced lifestyles. Instead, he arrived as a refugee in the spring of 1940. Despite the rise of Hitler and the drive to rid Europe of the Jewish people, Shanghai was an open port, allowing an influx of stateless people – and Bloch was determined to survive.

Bloch had already encountered numerous challenges from his earliest days. An illness, possibly meningitis, had left him deaf at about one month old.[17] By the age of one year, he had lost both his parents. His mother, Selma Ansbacher Bloch, died from an infection contracted during childbirth. His father, Simon, was struck down by a heart attack at a spa in Italy soon afterward. The young, orphaned Bloch was raised by his grandparents. At age fifteen he became an apprentice – later, an employee – at a porcelain decoration workshop. His finely limned designs reveal a bright eye, a confident hand, and a creative mind. Thanks to Bloch himself, much of his design work from that time still exists. He saved his watercolor designs, carrying them to China when he fled, and later transporting them to the United States. In 1934, after honing his skills at the Plankenhammer porcelain factory near his hometown of Floss,[18] he applied to and enrolled at the State Academy for Applied Art in Munich, where he learned the techniques of woodblock carving and printing. Though few woodblock prints from Germany

---

[15] *ASIANA Magazine*, Shanghai, January 1943, 46.
[16] Wen Zhaotong, "Bai Lu Hei Watercolor Paintings," *Xinwen Bao*, November 27, 1941 (10th month, 9th day of the 30th year of the Republic of China), 13.
[17] Telephone conversation with Bloch's older son, Dean Bloch, April 2020.
[18] According to an article on Bloch in the January 1974 issue of *Decal Data*, held as a clipping in the Leo Baeck Institute archives.

survive, Bloch clearly had a talent for the craft.[19] The academy, though, forced him out because of his Jewish background. Later, he lost a job as a decorator at the Sallinger department store in Straubing, again because he was Jewish.

After Kristallnacht (November 9, 1938), Bloch's situation worsened. Along with over 10,000 other Jewish men, he was deported to the Dachau concentration camp. After a month, many of those prisoners, including Bloch, were released. Sensing that the worst was yet to come, Bloch booked a ticket to Shanghai with financial assistance from a cousin in the United States. That cousin, Louis Bloch, would help finance Bloch's life for the following decade.

With much of his life's work in his suitcases, David Bloch embarked from Venice. As the ship made its way to Asia, he made visual records of the route. Those rich watercolors – which he saved – depict cities that seem like scenic postcards, not urban centers on the verge of entering a world war. In Venice – "Venedig, April 1940," as he captioned it – he painted a pedestrian bridge spanning a canal, with ancient buildings reflected in the water. A tree-lined boulevard with handsome houses facing the sea and a turquoise-domed mosque in the distance represent Port Said on April 16, 1940. An arid desert mountain rises up at the edge of a quiet port in Aden, April 1940. Skiffs sail across a pale blue sea in Bombay, April 1940. Then, by May, he was in Shanghai.

Despite the challenging circumstances of his arrival, Bloch, like Schiff, must have been astonished upon encountering Shanghai's fast-paced decadence and seedy atmosphere. In a pencil sketch, he depicts the infamous Zhu Baosan Road (located between today's Yan'an East Road and Jinling East Road, close to the Bund) – a short block known as "Blood Alley" in English because of frequent brawls among young foreign sailors. A local newspaper described the densely packed lane in 1938:

> The world's "wettest" and most lawless block is probably located in the down-town section of the French Concession. It fronts on Avenue Edward VII and is bounded by Rue Chu Paosan, Rue du Consulate and Rue Petit. By actual count there are 17 low-class bars and cabarets in this district, all of them catering to the sailor trade.[20]

Bloch's 1941 sketch offers specifics with textual notations at the bottom of the sheet. On the right, he has written: "Famed 'Blood Alley.' French concession. The street full of bar [sic], music, dance, taxi girls, prostit. [sic], etc." On the left, he

---

[19] In the Alfred Dreifuss archive of the Akademie der Künste in Berlin, there are two early woodcuts by Bloch. One, from 1933, depicts the Floss synagogue; another, from 1935, portrays a newspaper seller. Neither are as sophisticated as the later Shanghai works.
[20] *The China Weekly Review*, "Blood-Alley Should be Made into a Retail District," September 10, 1938, 39.

lists the bars: "New Ritz, Mummy, Chalston [sic], New Royal, Cristal, Salmein, Frisco, Fantasia." Rickshaws await customers; a man, his arm around a woman, strolls down the middle of the street; and the presence of two policemen, one with a club in hand, suggests that street fights and other kinds of mayhem are ever-present risks.

Once settled in Shanghai, Bloch continued painting and making woodblock prints. Very soon, he was holding one-man exhibitions. In December 1940, only eight months after his arrival, he took part in a six-person exhibition at a gallery in the Shidai Gongsi [Modern Company] on Jing'an Temple Road (known in English at the time as Bubbling Well Road and today as Nanjing West Road). The following year, he presented a solo exhibition at the same gallery, according to a Chinese-language review in the *Xinwen Bao* [News Post] in 1941.[21] The exhibition – of watercolors and woodblock prints – included fifty watercolors, about which the reviewer raved. Of these, almost half had been completed in Europe before Bloch's arrival in Shanghai. A year later, there was another solo exhibit at the Shanghai Art Gallery (Shanghai Hualang), 212 Nanjing Road.

For his December 1942 exhibition at the Shanghai Art Gallery, Bloch created a clever woodblock-printed poster. The text was written on three different painter's palettes: one white, one green, and one black. Each palette conveyed the same information in a different language (Chinese, Japanese, and English): "Exhibition of watercolors and woodcuts by D. L. Bloch will be held at the Shanghai Art Gallery, 212 Nanking Road from 10 AM to 6 PM commencing on Wednesday December 16th continuing to Sunday December 20th."[22]

The three differently colored palettes – white, green and black – were a visual pun on Bloch's Chinese name and an indication of how quickly he had absorbed and integrated himself into Shanghai society and culture.[23] Bloch had

---

[21] Wen Zhaotong, "Bai Lu Hei Watercolor Paintings," 13. Bloch saved many reviews of his work in Chinese, English and German.

[22] The poster is in the private collection of Dean Bloch.

[23] This exhibition is also a fascinating window into the complex relationship among the various cultures in Shanghai in the early 1940s. The Shanghai Art Gallery was owned by Satomi Hajime, also known as the "Opium King" in China, who had hired a Japanese art dealer to come to Shanghai manage the gallery. Bloch had visited the gallery at least as early December 1940, just seven months after his arrival in Shanghai, to see an exhibition of modern Japanese paintings. A Japanese-language newspaper, published in Shanghai for the Japanese living there, quotes Bloch, referring to him as a "famous European artist," as being surprised at the excellent accomplishments of the Japanese artists in contemporary European mediums and styles. His early visit to the gallery and praise for Japanese art may have been the beginning of a relationship that led to the eventual one-man exhibition in 1942. For more information see Ohashi Takehiko (大橋毅彦), "Bōmei yudayajin bijutsuka D. L. Bloch kara miru bunkateki atsureki to yūwa no shoos" 亡命ユ

taken on a Chinese name consisting of the three characters *bai* 白, *lu* 绿, and *hei* 黑. The sounds approximate the phonation of "Bloch." *Bai*, which is a Chinese family name and was therefore appropriate, also means 'white.' *Lu* and *hei* mean, respectively, 'green' and 'black,' so Bloch's name was White, Green, Black – thus the color palettes in his poster.

Adopting a practice common to all Chinese artists, Bloch had elegant seals carved with his Chinese name, which he stamped in red on all his works. Seal carving was itself an art form, not just for the carving technique but also for the visually stimulating compositions of Chinese characters, which had to fit into the shape of the seal. While reviewing the red impressions made by seals on Bloch's paintings and woodcuts, I have found that Bloch used at least four seals of different designs: three squares and one rectangle.[24]

The unnamed Chinese journalist who reviewed Bloch's exhibition praised the watercolors, rarely seen in China, as unique and elegant, but was less enthusiastic about the woodcuts. Using traditional Chinese art criticism terms, he called the watercolors 'expert' (*shan*) and the woodblock prints 'competent' (*neng*). A German Jewish writer, on the other hand, hailed Bloch's woodcuts of rickshaw pullers as "unique and ravishing," and compared him to Maxim Gorky and China's celebrated cultural hero Lu Xun (1881–1936).

In 1942, the Shanghai publishing company Taiping Shuju published sixty of Bloch's rickshaw woodcuts in a small book called *Huang Bao Che*[25] – with text in Chinese and Japanese only. This intimate and powerful collection of astutely observant woodblock prints depicting the harsh lives of rickshaw pullers was accompanied by short verses written by the Japanese poet Kusano Shinpei (1903–1988). Kusano had studied at Lingnan University in the 1920s. In the early 40s, he was working in Shanghai for the Japanese-backed puppet government.[26] Accord-

---

ダヤ人美術家 D·L·ブロッホから見る文化的軋轢と融和の諸相 [Aspects of cultural friction and harmony: From the perspective of D. L. Bloch, a Jewish refugee], *Ritsumeikan gengo bunka kenkyū*『立命館言語文化研究』30, no. 1 (October 2018): 51–60. I am indebted to Hiroki Takezaki for his assistance in tracking down and reading this article.

24 The Leo Baeck Institute in New York City has a large collection of woodblock prints by and archival materials from David Bloch.

25 As described in the Kedem Auction House catalogue for Auction 47, on September 8, 2015: "[64] leaves (sheets folded into two, unopened, printed on one side), 21 cm. Woodcuts: Approx. 7x5 cm – 9x12 cm."

26 Kusano's participation was described in an undated Chinese-language newspaper review of Bloch's first one-man exhibition ("Bai Lu Hei Yizhan," by Ding Shan). The clipping of the article is among Dean Bloch's archives. A recent article by a Japanese scholar discusses the collaborative publication: Tatsumi Tamura 田村立波, D.L.ブロッホと草野心平の共著である詩画集『黄包車』について [On the poetry and painting collection rickshaw by D. L. Bloch and Kusano

ing to the Japanese scholar Ohashi Takehiko, Bloch did not know Kusano, and it was the publisher who decided to marry the texts to the images.[27] The pages of the small (10.5 cm x 10.5 cm) book illustrate the unimaginable burdens of rickshaw pullers. They strain under the weight of hauling clients and their packages, including trees and even bicycles. In place of a human passenger, the seat of one rickshaw is filled with another rickshaw. The pullers get into fights with other pullers. They relax for a moment with their comrades at a stall selling bowls of noodles. Through the sixty images – which took the artist over a year to complete – Bloch bequeaths a degree of respect and dignity to these struggling men.[28]

Bloch's papers, archived at the Leo Baeck Institute, include a typed manuscript review of *Rickshaw* by the German Jewish writer Willy Tonn, a Sinologist who had come to Shanghai in 1939 to further his knowledge of Asia and who had established an academy where Jewish refugees could learn about Chinese culture and history. In this essay, Tonn applauds Bloch for his minimal but powerful use of lines – which he equates with Chinese aesthetics – and his profound empathy for the Chinese working people:

> Besides being rather scarce, such art publications – normally texted in English – take little, if any, interest in rickshaws, and none at all in the hard life of the rickshaw-puller and his vehicle; instead, they would rather portray in a more or less caricaturistic vein, the lofty "master," puffing away at his big cigar and proudly floating on his wheeled throne dragged on and on by a sweating nonentity. . . .
>
> For the first time the rickshaw is visualized here from where the puller stands. Hard his life, strenuous his daily existence, and yet, all hardships are, as it were, subdued by a good-natured humor and a never-flagging eagerness to toil: therein lies the puller's force. Signalled, and not articulated here are the straits and sufferings of the rickshaw-men, who unrecognizably scurry along and plunges into the crowd, "faceless" and unheeded.
>
> A product of the masses – D.L. Bloch, the artist, has opened the field in presenting him to the public in a solicitous and yet harmonious manner; a work comparable to "Ah Q" by Lu Hsuen [Lu Xun], that Maxim Gorky of China. Lu Hsuen's function in Chinese literature might one day well be assigned to Bloch's *Rickshaw* in the domain of fine arts. Both have fared in the depth and touched the core of life and they also knew how to mould their experiences – without flaw or crack – to artistic consumption.[29]

Shinpei], *Bulletin of Eastern Japan International University* 東日本国際大学研究紀要24, no. 1 (March 2019): 175–191. Ohashi's article (see footnote 24) proposes that Kusano was in Shanghai producing Japanese nationalist propaganda but that although the text for Huang Bao Che was subtly anti-American, Bloch had no idea his images were being used for this purpose.
27 Ohashi, 55.
28 *ASIANA Magazine*, Shanghai, January 1943, 46.
29 The typed manuscript is in the private collection of Dean Bloch.

Travelers arriving from European metropolises – where roads in the 30s and 40s were crowded with automobiles, buses, trolleys, and, occasionally, horse-drawn carriages – would have been overwhelmed by the sight of the myriad rickshaws that greeted every boat pulling into the harbor of Shanghai.

By the time Bloch arrived, the rickshaw – originally imported from Japan – had become almost synonymous with many foreigners' visions of Shanghai. There were at least 80,000 people pulling rickshaws in the city in the late 1930s. According to some estimates, over 340,000 people (10% of the population) were involved in some manner in the industry.[30]

Bloch's selection of the rickshaw puller as a symbol of suffering in a dysfunctional social system in China was not unique.[31] The writer Lao She (Shu Qingchun, 1899–1968) had already shone a light on rickshaw pullers in one of his most famous novels, *Luotuo Xiangzi* (published in 1937; often translated into English as *Rickshaw Boy*). During the early twentieth century, the constant flow of poor peasants from the countryside to the big cities meant a growing force of cheap labor. Companies would rent out the rickshaws to the migrants, who would make pennies a day. It was a hard and strenuous life.

A quick comparison between Schiff's and Bloch's rickshaw pullers illustrates the distinct divergence between their lives in China. Schiff, oblivious to the pullers' struggle, drew a self-satisfied foreigner being pulled by a happy-go-lucky, smiling Chinese man. Bloch's rickshaw pullers are emaciated, exhausted, and human. Perhaps it was his own experiences of deafness and displacement that deepened Bloch's empathy for the struggling masses in China.

In addition to the rickshaw pullers, Bloch also gave visual voice to the harsh conditions in which many other Chinese in Shanghai existed. His follow-up series of woodblock prints, released in 1943, focused on beggars. One print[32] depicts a Shanghai resident's shelter within a large water or sewer pipe, with a fabric sheet across the front to offer a measure of privacy. Two bamboo poles, supported by a tree on one side and two posts on the other, form a rack for hanging laundry, shoes, and an umbrella. Next to the mammoth pipe, there are a small bamboo chair, a tub, and a scrubbing board. On the opposite side is the "kitchen": a portable stove, a pot, a round fan (to keep the fire burning), and homemade charcoal balls (made from coal-dust waste). These numerous and highly specific details seem

---

[30] Zhou Fang, "The Wheels that Transformed the City: The Historical Development of Public Transportation Systems in Shanghai, 1843–1937" (PhD diss., Georgia Institute of Technology, 2010).
[31] David Strand, *Rickshaw Beijing: City People and Politics in the 1920s* (Oakland: University of California, 1993).
[32] Seen in the home of Dean Bloch on August 21, 2018.

to reflect Bloch's deep respect for the dweller's ingenuity and humanity. Other images in the book show people without limbs managing to walk or crawl with the aid of homemade crutches. In one print, a blind beggar kneels on the ground, holding a long staff. Beside him, on the ground, is a tin for collecting coins. In tiny letters, Bloch has inscribed the tin with the brand name "Maxwell" – an ironic jab at the importation of expensive coffee. Despite his subjects' disabilities, Bloch has preserved their individuality and dignity. He was keenly aware that there were those living in more meager situations than his own.

Not all of Bloch's works focused on the lives of the most unfortunate. There are also colorful streetscapes that capture ordinary people and typical buildings in 1940s Shanghai. One of his masterworks is a 48-inch-long, multi-colored woodblock print of Shanghai's bustling street life in which men sit drinking casually at a teahouse, an itinerant barber works on trimming a client's hair, and children play at kicking a shuttlecock. There are shops selling soy sauce, wine, oil, rice, coffins, flowers, watches, dentures, and coal; there are fortune tellers, a money exchange, a tailor, a shoe repair, and an eye doctor. Laundry hangs from second-floor balconies, a mop dangles next to the wall of a house, and fish are drying on a rope strung from a second-floor window. A butcher climbs onto his counter, straining to reach an animal's leg for a customer waiting with her basket. A high-walled pawn shop has the giant character for PAWN written on the exterior. A young woman in a *qipao* walks into a silk and brocade store, which is next to the tea store, near the laundry and dyeing shop. On a giant billboard, a hand points toward a downtown bar café. Last but not least, below the billboard, there is a corner store with a clever sign in Chinese and English: "Hand-colored Woodcut by D. L. Bloch." Unsurprisingly, Bloch has placed his iconic rickshaw and puller in front of the shop.[33]

Schiff and Bloch were not the only Jewish artists to have arrived in Shanghai from Europe. Many others had fled. Like the musicians and dramatists, they gathered together and supported one another. In 1942, the visual artists formed ARTA (the Association of Jewish Artists and Lovers of Fine Art) with the mission of exhibiting and assisting in the sales of works by Jewish artists. Bloch created a woodblock printed poster for at least one of the ARTA exhibitions. Within the shape of a painter's palette, Bloch wrote, in German, "The first art exhibition of Jewish painters and graphic artists living in the district." Held from March 5 through March 15, 1944, at the SJYA (Shanghai Jewish Youth Association) School,

---

[33] One copy of this print is held at the Leo Baeck Institute in New York (object no. 83.153); another, in the United States Holocaust Memorial Museum in Washington, D.C. (object no. 2002.532.1).

627 East Yuhang Road, just inside the west end of the ghetto,[34] this exhibition included 103 paintings.[35] According to a review in one of the most popular of Shanghai's Jewish weeklies, *Our Life* (originally published in Russian as *Nasha zhizn* and eventually printed in three languages: Russian, English and Yiddish), the works represented "all manners of art from oils to water-colours to pencil, pen, crayon etc [sic] and a diversity of these ranging from European landscapes to studies of émigré life in Shanghai and scenes of Chinese life."[36] One review of the exhibition, by Alfred Dreifuss, mentioned some of the writer's favorites: "Ernst Handel's 'Going Home,' Fredden-Goldberg's 'Iron Mill' and 'Shanghai Street,' and Bloch's inimitable flowers: 'Anemones' and 'Water Lilies.'" Dreifuss remarked on the uniqueness of such an exhibition in Shanghai and the quality of the work despite the harsh conditions under which the artists were living: "The general impression of the Exhibition was that Shanghai has never yet seen such an excellent display of good paintings, graphic works and drawings which inclusion is extremely important taking into consideration the fact that all the artists work and live in extremely difficult conditions." Dreifuss praised Bloch as "a master of small and big forms," adding, "He is an exceptionally gifted artist. We extremely enjoyed his 'Between Vienna and Shanghai,' his superb flowers and especially his Chinese motives. A very dramatic picture is his 'Bund.' Woodcuts are his favorites and he is extremely good in them. I even don't know which of them to mention first (rickshaws – potpourri)."[37]

While in Shanghai, Bloch created over 300 woodcuts.[38] Could his work have been spurred on by Chinese artists of the time? Bloch had studied woodblock carving at the State Academy for Applied Art in Munich, but no pre-Shanghai prints of his are extant. Upon his arrival in Shanghai, he may have come across some examples of contemporary Chinese woodcut artists' work.

---

[34] See the hand-drawn map now housed at the Ghetto Fighters House Archives in Israel, catalog no. 12886, https://www.infocenters.co.il/gfh/multimedia/GFH/0000007782/0000007782_1_web.jpg.

[35] Horace Kadoorie, a successful Baghdadi Jew living in Shanghai since the 1920s, had established the SJYA in 1937.

[36] A.G., "Arta's Second Exhibition," *Our Life*, May 26, 1944. Quoted in *Jewish Refugees in Shanghai 1933–1947: A Selection of Documents*, ed. Irene Eber, vol. 3 of *Archive of Jewish History and Culture* (Gottingen: Vandenhoeck & Ruprecht Gmbh, 2018), 537, document 137. Eber notes that A.G. is probably Anna Ginsbourg.

[37] Alfred Dreifuss, "First Jewish Artists' Exhibition in the Designated Area," *Our Life – Unser Lebn*, March 10, 1944, 10.

[38] A book of his work was published in Barbara Hoster and Malek Roman, eds., *David Ludwig Bloch: Holzschnitte / Woodcuts, Shanghai 1940–1949* (Abingdon-on-Thames: Routledge, 1997).

Lu Xun (1881–1936), the heralded leftist writer and thinker, often called the founder of the modern woodcut movement in China, had advocated for woodcuts in China to focus on class struggle and provoke change. Woodcuts by European and Soviet artists – such as Kathe Kollwitz, Vladimir A. Favorsky, and Frans Masereel – that drew attention to the under-served masses in Europe deeply influenced his thinking. Moreover, as he often noted, woodcuts were already a "people's art" in China, a traditional and popular medium that provided inexpensive New Year's decorations for those who could not afford the fine arts. Lu Xun organized exhibitions of European woodcuts and, in August 1931, arranged for a class of Chinese artists to study woodblock printing with the Japanese artist Uchiyama Kakechi.[39] Though he was not officially a party member, Lu Xun's mission was taken up by the Communist Party, and woodblock printing became a primary art form among left-leaning Chinese artists.

In Bloch's archives at the Leo Baeck Institute in New York City are pages torn from the December 1942 issue of the Chinese magazine *Chang Jiang Hua Kan* [The Yangze Painting Periodical]. They feature black-and-white woodblock prints by Chinese artists primarily depicting toiling peasants and workers: a man shoveling rocks; bare-chested farmers hoeing and plowing fields; another farmer threshing a sheaf of wheat, banging it against a make-do harrow; and a young woman, in simple peasant clothes, with a handkerchief on her head, hoping for better days, kneeling beside a smoking censer in a work titled "Silent Prayer." Among the many images he would have seen while in Shanghai, Bloch chose to save this magazine fold-out and carried it with him throughout his life.

3 Paul Fischer (1891–1982)

Shanghai was home to other Jewish refugee artists, who also noticed the rickshaw pullers and other Chinese inhabitants living in humbled circumstances. The cover of a set of hand-colored postcards entitled "Shanghai Sketches," created by the artist Paul Fischer, features the iconic barefoot rickshaw puller braving the rain as he hauls his customer – hidden, protected from the storm, behind a patched fabric curtain – splashing through puddles. The booklet – probably produced for the tourist or foreign market – depicts food peddlers carrying their merchandise on poles over their shoulders; a paper collector dressed in rags, tongs in his hand

---

39 Caroline Corban, "Lu Xun (1881–1936) and the Modern Woodcut Movement," *Bowdoin Journal of Art* 1 (2015), https://www.academia.edu/13157636/Lu_Xun_1881_1936_and_the_Modern_Woodcut_Movement.

and a basket on his back; pallbearers carrying a coffin, followed by mourners; a simple vegetable seller; and more rickshaw pullers, all weighed down under the burdens they bear.[40]

Though only a few works by Fischer are still extant, Alfred Dreifuss, in his review of the first ARTA exhibition, implies that he was productive while in Shanghai: "Mr. Paul Fischer. Well-known in Shanghai for his 'Ex libris' presented many graphics. First of all, we should mention his 'Reading Man,' 'Rat Catcher,' a good colour-balanced painting 'Yellow Flowers.' Fischer is a lover of small forms, which he masters extremely well."

Fischer, born in 1891 in Vienna, where he graduated from the High School of Applied Arts, had been a private student of David Kohn (1861–1922),[41] a royal artist at the Habsburg court. Despite this comfortable Viennese upbringing, he depicted his underprivileged subjects with deep sympathy. In China, he had become well aware of the challenges of living in humbled circumstances. A watercolor he painted displays the details of a refugee's home in Shanghai – his own home. The bedroom holds a sleeping cot, a coal stove, a wash basin, and a burner for heating a kettle. A laundry line extends diagonally across the space. The four walls encompass a bedroom, a washroom, a closet, and a kitchen. The walls are crumbling, the mirror on the wall is cracked and broken, the stool has a split stretcher, and some of the clothing hanging from the laundry line has been patched. The makeshift "table," on which the kettle, a cup, and an enamel plate are sitting, is a wooden crate labeled "B. N. Shanghai via Genoa." It captures the difficult lives of Jewish refugees in Hongkou.

Coda: After the War

Fischer created this portrait of his home in 1949, most likely after his difficult circumstances were in the past. With the end of the war, European Jewish artists' work began to shift. Instead of focusing on the Chinese scenes around them, many seem to have turned inward, concentrating on their own experiences. The catalogue for the YIVO-sponsored Exhibition of Jewish Artists in 1946 lists nine watercolors by Bloch, including "Jom-Kipur," "Refugee camp," and "Refugee camp

---

40 Paul Fischer, *Shanghai Sketches* (Shanghai: The New Star Company, 1947).
41 Catalogue for the Exhibition of Jewish Artists at the Shanghai Jewish School, December 22–29, 1946, sponsored by YIVO.

kitchen and Ward Rd. camp theatre," and two works by Handel Ernst (b. 1893), "Refugee at home" and "Refugee at work."[42]

Schiff, too, seems to have risen above his often-sardonic attitude. Among his sketches at the Österreichisches Institut für China- und Südostasienforschung [Austrian Institute for China and Southeast Asia Research] in Vienna are sensitive and skillfully limned portraits of the unfortunate members of Chinese society. One pencil drawing, captioned "On the Bund, Shanghai. Refugees pouring into the Settlement," seems to depict Chinese from the countryside flooding into city for safety, only to be bombed by Japanese planes attacking from above. A colored ink sketch portrays a beggar in patched clothes humbly stretching out his hand toward a vendor of steamed buns who is trying to ignore him. In an interview, years after he had left China, Schiff professed a clear awareness of the profound and disturbing poverty he had seen: "This city and the life in it consist of the sharpest contrasts: here are luxury apartment houses equipped with all the achievements of modern technology, with central heating and their own swimming pool, which is reserved only for the tenants and their guests. Right next to it, coolies live in the most primitive dwellings. People are born under the thatched roofs of the sampans, the narrow houseboats that crowd in their hundreds on the shore, and they die on the narrow deck without having known any other home. In this Shanghai people live in misery unimaginable for our terms and there is also hardly any wealth imaginable."[43]

Most poignant among Schiff's productions is a small book he produced with Danish journalist Paula Esklund: *Squeezing Through: Shanghai Sketches, 1941–1945*.[44] This booklet, bound Chinese-style with red threads, recounts the harsh conditions experienced by the inhabitants of Shanghai during those four years. Shortages, racketeering, endless lines for buying bread, cigarettes, and rice – all are illustrated by Schiff's scant but deeply affecting ink sketches. The book devotes a section to the arrival of Jewish refugees, noting that the Japanese restricted them to two square miles in Hongkou, and the subsequent creation of "a miniature European city among ruins... cafes and restaurants serve first-class coffee and cakes." A series of scenes, drawn by Schiff, narrate the daily frustrations and humiliations Jews had to go through in order to receive a pass from the

---

[42] These works, unfortunately, have not yet been located. The catalogue for the YIVO-sponsored Exhibition of Jewish Artists at the Shanghai Jewish School (December 22–29, 1946) is currently in the collection of Dean Bloch.

[43] As noted in Kaminski, *China Gemalt* [Painted China] (Europa Verlag, 1983), 12, and translated in Matthias Messmer, *Jewish Wayfarers in Modern China: Tragedy and Splendor* (Lanham, MD: Lexington Books, 2012), 155.

[44] Printed by the Hwa Kuo Printing Company, 1945, location unidentified.

Japanese officials to leave the ghetto. Schiff's willingness to participate in this inexpensive production, so unlike his earlier commercial work, seems to signal a recognition on his part of the suffering the Jews had endured. "The emigrants look sad," the text reads, "but they have a sense of humor... [The Jew belongs] to a strong race. Through the centuries his system has developed anti-toxins to hardships. He wants to survive. And he did."

In 1947, Schiff left Shanghai and settled in Argentina, where he continued his artistic career.[45] There, he continued to paint and began lecturing on his experiences in China. In 1954, seeking better medical care for his daughter, he moved again, this time returning to to Vienna, where he was able to find a job as a graphic designer at Unilever. His early death at age 60 cut short his career, but Chinese and European interest in his work has continued to this day. At least three major exhibitions – held in Vienna in 1988, 2002, and 2011[46] – as well as a thorough scholarly volume[47] and a dedicated website[48] have disseminated his work and preserved his legacy.

Fischer's later history has still not been explored or recorded. He seems to have moved to San Francisco – his drawings of cable cars occasionally appear for sale online – but little is known of his post-Shanghai life or artistic production.

Bloch married a Chinese woman and traveled with her to the United States, where he found a job as a lithographer. They raised two children. His artistic endeavors never slowed. He continued sketching, painting, and creating woodcuts. There were numerous exhibitions of his work in the United States, as well as

---

[45] In 1954, he returned to Austria in search of medical assistance for his daughter stricken with polio. In Austria, he found employment as a graphic artist with Unilever, but unfortunately passed away at the age of 60. From Österreichisches Institut für China- und Südostasienforschung [Austrian Institute for China and Southeast Asia Research], http://www.china-kultur.at/content/index.aspx?CatalogItemID=29168.

[46] In 1988, Gedächtnisausstellung Friedrich Schiff was held at the Künstlerhaus in Vienna. *Friedrich Schiff: In Shanghai Berühmt, In Wien Vergessen* [Famous in Shanghai, forgotten in Vienna], at the Historisches Museum der Stadt in Vienna, February 14 to March 31, 2002. A third exhibition of Schiff's seventeen years in China, "A Look through the Dragon Skin," was held in Hong Kong and Vienna in May 2011, but no location is cited (http://en.cnicif.com/html/2013-10/13692.html).

[47] Gerd Kaminski, *Der Blick durch die Drachenhaut: Friedrich Schiff: Maler dreier Kontinente* [The view through the dragon's skin: Friedrich Schiff, a painter from three continents] (Vienna: Einverlag, 2001).

[48] Schiff-Galerie, http://schiff-galerie.at/ueber-friedrich-schiff.php.

articles, a book,[49] and even a documentary film.[50] A Japanese scholar is currently working on another book.[51] In 1977, after a trip back to Dachau, his artistic output focused almost solely on his Dachau experience and the horrors of the Holocaust[52]: the experiences that sent him to Shanghai and drove him to create powerful, emotional tributes honoring the victims and celebrating survival. Like Schiff's sketches, Bloch's work continues to resonate with contemporary audiences looking to understand the Holocaust, its ramifications, and its relevance to the world today.

References

A. G. (probably Anna Ginsbourg). "Arta's Second Exhibition." *Our Life*. May 26, 1944. 537.
ASIANA Magazine. Shanghai. January 1943. 46.
The China Journal of Science and Arts. August 1930.
The China Weekly Review. " 'Blood-Alley' Should be Made into a Retail District." September 10, 1938. 39.
Corban, Carolin. "Lu Xun (1881–1936) and the Modern Woodcut Movement." *Bowdoin Journal of Art* 1 (2015). https://www.academia.edu/13157636/Lu_Xun_1881_1936_and_the_Modern_Woodcut_Movement.
Decal Data, January 1974. Leo Baeck Institute, New York.
Dennys, N. B. "Pidgin English." *Journal of the Straits Branch of the Royal Asiatic Society* 2 (December 1878): 168–174.
Dreifuss, Alfred. "First Jewish Artists' Exhibition in the Designated Area." *Our Life – Unser Lebn*. March 10, 1944.
Eber, Irene, ed. *Jewish Refugees in Shanghai 1933–1947: A Selection of Documents*. Gottingen: Vandenhoeck & Ruprecht, 2018.
Hoster, Barbara and Malek Roman. *David Ludwig Bloch: Holzschnitte / Woodcuts, Shanghai 1940–1949*. Abingdon-on-Thames: Routledge, 1997.
Kaminski, Gerd. *Der Blick durch die Drachenhaut: Friedrich Schiff: Maler dreier Kontinente* [The view through the dragon's skin: Friedrich Schiff, a painter from three continents]. Vienna: Eigenverlag, 2001.
Kaminski, Gerd. *China Gemalt: Chinesische Zeitgeschichte in Bildern Friedrich Schiff* [China painted: Chinese contemporary history in Friedrich Schiff's pictures]. Vienna: Europa Verlag, 1983.
Kedem Auction House catalogue. Auction 47. September 8, 2015.

---

49 Barbara Hoster and Malek Roman, eds., *David Ludwig Bloch: Holzschnitte / Woodcuts: Shanghai 1940–1949* (Abingdon-on-Thames: Routledge, 1997).
50 *Who is David Bloch?* directed by Wang Shuibo (2018; a Zen and Revolution Film Production), as yet unreleased.
51 Ohashi Takehiko, professor at Kansei Gakuin University.
52 Many of these Dachau works are reproduced in Vivian Alpert Thompson, *A Mission in Art: Recent Holocaust Works in America* (Macon, GA: Mercer University Press, 1988), 20–27.

Map of the Jewish ghetto in Shanghai (photograph). Ghetto Fighters House Archives, Israel. Catalog no. 12886. https://www.infocenters.co.il/gfh/multimedia/GFH/0000007782/0000007782_1_web.jpg.

Messmer, Matthias. *Jewish Wayfarers in Modern China: Tragedy and Splendor*. Lanham, MD: Lexington Books, 2011.

Österreichisches Institut für China-und Südostasienforschung [Austrian Institute for China and Southeast Asia Research], Vienna.

Pan Guang. *A Study of Jewish Refugees in China (1933–1945)*. Shanghai: Jiao Tong University Press, 2019.

Shanghai Municipal Gazette. March 27, 1942. 34.

Strand, David. *Rickshaw Beijing: City, People, and Politics in the 1920s*. Oakland: University of California, 1993.

Takehiko, Ohashi 大橋毅彦. "Bōmei yudayajin bijutsuka D. L. burohho kara miru bunkateki atsureki to yūwa no shoos" 亡命ユダヤ人美術家 D·L·ブロッホから見る文化的軋轢と融和の諸相 [Aspects of cultural friction and harmony: From the perspective of D. L. Bloch, a Jewish refugee]. *Ritsumeikan gengo bunka kenkyū* 立命館言語文化研究 30, no. 1 (October 2018): 51–60.

Tatsumi Tamura 田村立波. "D. L. burohho to kusa yashin hira no kyōcho de aru shi gashū" D. L. ブロッホと草野心平の共著である詩画集『黄包車』につい [On the poetry and painting collection 'Rickshaw' by D. L. Bloch and Kusano Shinpei]. 東日本国際大学研究紀要 [Bulletin of Eastern Japan International University] 24, no. 1 (March 2019): 175–191.

Thompson, Vivian Alpert. *A Mission in Art: Recent Holocaust Works in America*. Macon, GA: Mercer Univsity Press, 1988.

Thorbecke, Ellen and Friedrich Schiff. *Shanghai*. Shanghai: North China Daily News and Herald, 1940.

Wen Zhaotong. "Bai Lu Hei Watercolor Paintings." *Xinwen Bao*. 10th month, 9th day of the 30th year of the Republic of China (November 27, 1941). 13.

Zhou Fang. "The Wheels that Transformed the City: The Historical Development of Public Transportation Systems in Shanghai, 1843–1937." PhD diss., Georgia Institute of Technology, 2010.

Zhou Qingyang. "Interactions Between the Chinese and the Jewish Refugees in Shanghai During World War II." *Penn History Review* 25, no. 2 (2018): 50–88.

Yang Meng
11 Drama in Wartime Shanghai

This essay[1] examines the exile culture of German-speaking Jewish refugees in Shanghai during the Shoah through two plays: *Die Masken fallen* and *Fremde Erde*, which were the only two dramatic works by Jewish refugees to be published in Shanghai during the post-war period and can thus be regarded as representative of the exile culture in Shanghai. Their publication after the war has distinguished them from all other plays that were written during the Jewish exile in Shanghai.

According to research by Michael Philipp, the colorful exile culture of the German-speaking Jewish refugees in Shanghai had no other significant influence on the host country, on Europe, or on the larger world.[2] Nevertheless, the social resonance of these dramatic works during wartime and their lasting importance in the memory of the survivors are noteworthy.

Of all cultural activities among the Jewish refugees in Shanghai, their theatrical life was exceptional. During this period of exile (1933–ca. 1949), around 30 new pieces (including some operettas) were written either in Shanghai or en route to Shanghai, far more than in other locations. Such productivity would have been remarkable for a community of around 20,000 people in peacetime, let alone war; even for a university with 20,000 students, this would have been an extraordinarily high level of cultural activity. Even if the production quality was not first class, these endeavors still signify a flowering of cultural activities and represent one aspect of Jewish exile in Shanghai.

Michael Philipp's *Nicht einmal einen Thespiskarren* provides a bird's-eye view of the theatrical pieces produced in Shanghai.[3] From titles such as *Brennende Sehnsucht* (by Max Brandt-Bukofzer), *Die geschiedene Frau* (Adolf Breuer), and *Ohne Permit nach Shuschan* (Desiderius Grün and Erwin Engel), it can be perceived that most of the plays produced in Shanghai were not philosophical or abstract but realistic and concrete. Many were comedies, while some were simply about Shanghai. Only two of them have been republished after the war. Many are now kept in the Vienna Library in the city hall. In addition to the plays listed

---

[1] This essay is supported by the National Social Science Fund of China (Grant no. 20BSS058).
[2] Michael Philipp, "Exiltheater in Shanghai 1939–1947," *Handbuch des deutschsprachigen Exiltheaters 1933–1945*, ed. Frithjof Trapp et al. (Munich: Saur, 1999), 1:457–476.
[3] Michael Philipp, *Nicht einmal einen Thespiskarren: Exiltheater in Shanghai 1939–1947* (Hamburg: Hamburger Arbeitstelle für Deutsche Exilliteratur, 1996), 198–199.

above, there were performances of well-known pieces such as *King Oedipus* in November 1939 and *Nathan der Weise* in January 1940.⁴

1 The Two Playwrights

Die Masken fallen [The masks fall] and *Fremde Erde* [Foreign land] are the two most successful German-language plays that were staged during the exile in Shanghai. In addition, they are the only ones that were published after the war. Both were published under the names of Hans Wiener and Mark Siegelberg. "Wiener" is one of two pseudonyms – the other being "Schubert" – for Hans Morgenstern, who was born in Vienna in 1905. Morgenstern was, like Siegelberg, Jewish.

In both plays, the language is rather simple. The authors' choice of words is influenced by Austrian German, such as *Stubenmädchen, Semmel, i wo*, et cetera.

Prior to his exile in Shanghai, Morgenstern had worked as a commercial clerk in Vienna and had been successful in Austria as the playwright of *Vorstadtkomödie*. In 1938, he was deported to the Dachau concentration camp but was able to escape to China the following year. In Shanghai, he took the name "Wiener" to express his affiliation with his native city. During his exile, he wrote four comedies (*Marriage on a Split Account, Heart on a Leash, In a Small Bank*, and *Divorce Reason Love*) and a libretto for an operetta (*Music around Barbara*). He also wrote for a German-language newspaper, the *Shanghai Jewish Chronicle*, and for the radio station XGDN. He worked as a salesman for various Chinese and Russian companies until 1941. In 1965, he died in his native city, Vienna.⁵

Many of the comedies that he wrote in exile continued in the Viennese theatrical tradition. However, these pieces gained no significance in the post-war period, whereas *Die Masken fallen* and *Fremde Erde* were the only ones to be republished after the war.

Morgenstern's co-author, Mark Siegelberg, was born in Kiev in 1895. Prior to his career as a playwright, he had studied in Bern and Vienna, and worked as a

---

4 Helmuth F. Braun, "Man hat nicht so das Fremde gesucht...: Emigrantenkultur in Shanghai," in *Heimat und Exil: Emigration der deutschen Juden nach 1933*, eds. Stiftung Jüdisches Museum Berlin und Stiftung Haus der Geschichte der Bundesrepublik Deutschland (Frankfurt am Main: Jüdischer Verlag im Suhrkamp Verlag, 2006), 135.
5 Siegelberg, Mark and Hans Schubert (pseud. of Hans Morgenstern), *Die Masken fallen – Fremde Erde: Zwei Dramen aus der Emigration nach Shanghai 1939–1947*, eds. Michael Philipp and Wilfried Seywald (Hamburg: Schriftenreihe der Hamburger Arbeitsstelle für Deutsche Exilliteratur, 1996), 18.

journalist for several Austrian newspapers. From 1938 to 1939, he was interned in the Dachau and Buchenwald concentration camps. Like Morgenstern/Wiener, he was able to flee to Shanghai in 1939. On his way to China, he began to write the autobiographical novel *Schutzhaftjude 13877*, which was published in Shanghai in 1940. The protagonist of this novel shares his first name, "Paul," with the main character in the play *Die Masken fallen*. During his time in exile, Siegelberg worked for the information service of the British Legation in Shanghai until December 1941, when he fled to Australia. There, the play *Die Masken fallen* was translated into English and given the English title *The Masks Drop*. In July 1942, a radio play "created" (German: *erstellt*) by Catherine Shepherd under the title *Tickets to Shanghai*[6] was broadcast in Melbourne. That same year, *The Face of Pearl Harbor* was printed. This play, which is called *Das zweite Gesicht* [The second face] in German, is about the situation in Shanghai before the Pacific War.[7] It was republished in 2017 by Thomas Sommadossi.[8]

2 *Die Masken fallen* [The masks fall]

Die Masken fallen is divided into five acts. According to the stage directions – "location: Austria, time: March 1938" – the action of the play takes place during the Anschluss, or the annexation of Austria by the German Reich. Christine, an Aryan woman, wants to leave her Jewish husband, Doctor Paul Brach, because she has fallen in love with an Aryan man, Ludwig Huber. Paul, a journalist in Vienna, is – like the two co-authors – later deported to a concentration camp because of his Jewish origin. To help Christine to separate from her husband, Huber turns to the lawyer Doctor Forstner, an old friend from school and a supporter of the National Socialist ideology. However, when Christine learns the terrible truth about the concentration camps, she decides to suspend the divorce and help Paul escape. Despite several attempts – she even purchases two ship tickets to Shanghai – her plan fails. Paul can only be released on condition that Christine signs the divorce and becomes engaged to Ludwig. The last scene takes place at the train station, where Paul arrives from the concentration camp and is on the way to Shanghai with the ticket that Christine has bought. Paul's father wants to give Christine the ticket and thus commits suicide by throwing himself

---

6 Siegelberg and Schubert, *Die Masken fallen – Fremde Erde*, 18.
7 Siegelberg and Schubert, *Die Masken fallen – Fremde Erde*, 141.
8 Siegelberg, *Das zweite Gesicht* [The face of Pearl Harbor], ed. Tomas Sommadossi (Munich: Iudicium, 2017).

in front of a train at the station. In the end, Christine promises him to follow her divorced husband to Shanghai.

This drama takes up the topic of "mixed marriage" to portray an Aryan woman standing up for her Jewish husband. It also addresses the historical experience of many Shanghai refugees: by November 1940, around 100 men had fled directly from the Buchenwald or Dachau concentration camps to Shanghai.[9] Many of the Jewish men in the audience had – like the characters of Paul Brach and his father – been interned in concentration camps, and their Aryan wives – like the character of Christine – had tried to acquire the papers that would allow them to flee to Shanghai together. After Kristallnacht in 1938, Shanghai was the only place of refuge for many Jewish exiles, as no visas were required to enter the city. Travelers leaving Germany had to show their *Ausreisepapiere* ('departure papers') or, alternatively, prove that they were able to leave the country. Tickets for a ship to Shanghai were considered acceptable proof. In contrast to the *Ausreisepapiere*, these tickets were relatively easy to obtain.

Directed by Karl Bodan, *Die Masken fallen* premiered on November 9, 1940, at the British Embassy in Shanghai, exactly two years after the November pogrom. When the German consul general threatened reprisals against Jews who were still living in Germany if the play was not canceled, the Jewish Refugee Committee in Shanghai attempted to prevent the performance in order to avoid provocation.[10] Moritz Speelman, the committee chairman, criticized the planned production in a letter to the editor of the *North-China Daily Tribune*: "My Committee feels very strongly that at a time like the present, anything provocative of discussion should be avoided in this city."[11] The co-authors, Mark Siegelberg and "Hans Wiener" (i.e., Hans Morgenstern), responded with their own letter to the editor:

> We like [sic] to declare that so far as we are informed none of the Committee's members has ever read our play *Die Masken fallen* . . . We are astonished, indeed, that an organization responsible for weal and woe of so many thousands of people is attacking a play which its leaders cannot know, and the only purpose of which is to do service to the understanding between man and races.[12]

---

[9] Georg Armbrüster, Michael Kohlstruck, and Sonja Mühlberger, "Exil Shanghai: Facetten eines Themas," in *Exil Shanghai 1938–1947: Jüdisches Leben in der Emigration* (Teetz: Hentrich and Hentrich, 2000), 147.
[10] Helmuth F. Braun, "Man hat nicht so das Fremde gesucht. . .: Emigrantenkultur in Shanghai," 135.
[11] Moritz Speelman, "Die Masken fallen: Refugee Committee Painted," *North-China Daily Tribune* 2, no. 11 (1940), in *Nicht Einmal einen Thepsiskarren*, 100.
[12] Siegelberg and "Hans Wiener" (pseud. of Hans Morgenstern), "Die Masken fallen: Authors' Reply," *North-China Daily Tribune*, November 1940.

One reader also reacted to the committee's decision:

> To call such a work a provocation which should be avoided, seems so much more amazing as, according to all information, the chairman and vice-chairman of the Jewish Committee are Dutch and British citizens. Nevertheless, they are not ashamed to struggle against the performance of a play directed against the same people who have destroyed Rotterdam and are bombing London every day. Jews who fear that something might provoke the Nazis are indeed, rather difficult to comprehend.[13]

Yet the long arm of the Gestapo could reach even as far as Shanghai. The premiere remained the only performance until after the war. It was not until April 1946 that the second production, directed by Robert Weiss-Cyla, took place in Shanghai, with actress Lily Flohr reprising the role of Christine. The response was still enormous.[14]

When Siegelberg came to Australia, the play was translated into English and read at a private home in Melbourne in late 1942. The title was translated literally as *The Masks Drop*.[15] In July 1942 it was broadcast as a radio play in Melbourne under the title *Tickets to Shanghai*. Its message also resonated with Australians:

> No more vivid impression of the brutality of Nazidom could have been given . . . I think the Melbourne players felt deeply conscious of the importance of the message they had to convey and they gave their very best.[16]

Even after the war, this piece was appreciated for its relevance – not only as an expression of the Zeitgeist, but also as a timeless political masterpiece.

3 *Fremde Erde* [Foreign land]

Fremde Erde is divided into four acts. The action of the play takes place in Shanghai in April 1941, which corresponds to its premiere on April 8, 1941, about half a year after the premiere of *Die Masken fallen* in November 1940. Unlike *Die Masken*

---

13 Dutch (pseud.), "Die Masken fallen: An Amazing Protest," *North-China Daily Tribune*, November 1940.
14 Georg Armbrüster, Michael Kohlstruck, and Sonja Mühlberger, "Exil Shanghai: Facetten eines Themas," in *Exil Shanghai 1938–1947: Jüdisches Leben in der Emigration*, ed. Armbrüster, Kohlstruck, and Mühlberger (Teetz: Hentrich and Hentrich 2000), 157.
15 Siegelberg and Schubert, *Die Masken fallen – Fremde Erde*, 18.
16 Catherine Shepherd to Mark Siegelberg on July 10, 1944, quoted by Michael Philipp and Wilfried Seywald, introduction to Mark Siegelberg and Hans Schubert (pseud. of Hans Morgenstern), *Die Masken fallen – Fremde Erde*, 18.

fallen, which portrays the events in Austria before the exile, *Fremde Erde* deals with the problems commonly faced by European Jewish émigrés in Shanghai: downward social mobility and the existential predicament of living in a foreign country. The main characters are a Jewish couple. The man, Robert Melzer, is a doctor in Austria, but when he arrives in Shanghai, he finds himself obliged to sell soap from door to door. His wife, Anny Melzer, takes a job as a barmaid and earns some money by providing special services to an educated Chinese man so that her husband will have the means to establish a clinic. When her husband learns that the money did not come from the sale of a pearl necklace but from "love wages," he separates from his wife and gives up his practice. Only when he realizes that his wife was acting solely out of love for him does he return to her.

Working as a barmaid was a common activity for women expatriates in Shanghai at the time. It was by no means unusual for women to take care, pragmatically, of economic maintenance while their husbands floundered. For many men, exile meant a long unemployment and an abrupt decline in socioeconomic circumstanes. This often led to a reversal of gender roles in their families, sometimes with profound psychological consequences. *Fremde Erde* addressed these changes within traditional family structures and the emergence of the modern family during that turbulent time.

In contrast to *Die Masken fallen*, *Fremde Erde* included some Chinese characters, though they were marred by the authors' anti-Chinese prejudice. At the time, it was common for German-speaking expatriates to give their Chinese environment hardly any attention at all.

Fremde Erde, also written by "Wiener" (pseud. of Morgenstern) and Spiegelberg, was unique in its depiction of the figure of a wealthy, educated Chinese man, Mr. Loo, who, having spent his youth in Germany, speaks fluent German. Perhaps the author intended this role to be performed by a German-speaking Jewish refugee. Not only was the character of Mr. Loo crucial to the narrative, he also exhibited various Chinese features – politeness, helpfulness, and warm-heartedness – which reflected the image of China as perceived by the Jewish exiles. However, a certain contradiction can be detected: On the one hand, the Jewish refugees were victims of racist persecution by the Nazis; on the other, their own prejudice vis-à-vis the Chinese is clearly visible in their writings.

Unlike Mr. Loo, the vast majority of Chinese people at that time were not rich, had not traveled to Europe, and spoke no German. Those who had done so belonged to a rather unusual circle within Chinese society. Why did the author design the figure of Mr. Loo in this way? Was the German-speaking Chinese character only included in the play so he could be played by a refugee? Although he uses his money to purchase a relationship with Anny, his entire demeanor is portrayed positively. Between the lines, it is clear that he is fond of Anny and respects her.

The racism in this play deserves further study. It is noteworthy that, despite his wealth and education, Mr. Loo feels inferior to Anny because he is Chinese:

> Loo: . . . I'm not a European, just a simple Chinese . . .
>
> Anny: . . . none of this has anything to do with the fact that you don't happen to be a European, Mr. Loo.[17]
>
> Vally: . . . I think he's offended because he says you don't like him because he's Chinese . . .[18]
>
> Loo: [. . .] I'm afraid I couldn't bridge the gap between our races. What was business to your wife meant much, much more to me.[19]

The Jewish refugees were considered Europeans, whereas the Chinese – even successful businessmen – were the objects of stereotyping. Is this passage the result of sensitive observation of social hierarchies in Shanghai? Or does it reflect the authors' own point of view?

Interestingly, the couple's eating habits remain unchanged in their new environment. No Chinese dishes – for example, rice soup or rice cakes – ever appear in the drama, only Western and especially Austrian food. In the stage directions for the first act, their breakfast is described as follows: "He prepares coffee on a spirit stove."[20] The main character, Robert, eats "Semmeln [the word for bread in Austrian German] and margarine"[21] for breakfast. As we can see from their eating habits, they do not accommodate themselves to Chinese customs.

However, the characters do use a few typical Chinese words. For example, Robert uses the Chinese term *typhoon*:

> You see, Anny, on this foreign earth we still fail. It is not easy to take root in the emigration. And if we don't support each other, one for the other, the next typhoon will destroy us.[22]

Anny's reply – "We've already seen our typhoon!"[23] – demonstrates her hope for the future despite the challenges she faces in exile to her family life.

Like *Die Masken fallen, Fremde Erde* offers a highly realistic depiction of its sociohistorical context. Brothels and entertainment venues were abundant in Shanghai before the war, and many women, especially refugees, worked as barmaids. According to the research of Dicker and Embacher / Reiter, the bound-

---

[17] Siegelberg and Schubert, *Die Masken fallen – Fremde Erde*, 134.
[18] Siegelberg and Schubert, *Die Masken fallen – Fremde Erde*, 101.
[19] Siegelberg and Schubert, *Die Masken fallen – Fremde Erde*, 117.
[20] Siegelberg and Schubert, *Die Masken fallen – Fremde Erde*, 87.
[21] Siegelberg and Schubert, *Die Masken fallen – Fremde Erde*, 87.
[22] Siegelberg and Schubert, *Die Masken fallen – Fremde Erde*, 137.
[23] Siegelberg and Schubert, *Die Masken fallen – Fremde Erde*, 137.

ary between service work and sex work was fluid.[24] Parents and husbands of the women who prostituted themselves had to accept the situation and may even have participated, like the couple Vally and Robert Jablonsky in *Fremde Erde*. After the war, most of the then-former bartenders and prostitutes would return to their normal lives as members of the middle classes in the United States, Europe, and Australia.

Hardly any women in exile in Shanghai were known as artists.[25] The women in this "undesirable" place – Shanghai – tended to follow one of three models: some continued their traditional roles as wives and mothers, despite the difficult conditions; others bore a double burden as both homemakers and breadwinners, since their husbands were no longer able to support their families; still others opted for a role reversal. The "classic German housewife" had to be independent and to develop new life strategies. In Germany, many women saved their husbands from the concentration camps despite enormous difficulties. In Shanghai, they watched their husbands experience a radical social decline. Some even became mere "house-husbands." After the war, many women fell back into their conventional roles, which is why researchers do not use terms such as "emancipation" to describe the situation during the war.[26] The change in gender roles, which arose out of necessity and lasted only during the exile, is one reason why most of the Jewish refugees remained silent about their experiences in Shanghai for a long time after the war. Many chose not to tell even – or perhaps especially – their own children.

Conclusion

During the years of exile in Shanghai, about thirty German-language scripts were written, mainly between 1938 and 1945. About half of the plays dealt with the fate of Jews in central Europe, the escape from the Third Reich, and everyday life in exile in Shanghai. Michael Philipp has found that, unlike the two dramas analyzed here, the other half were purely for entertainment. This preference for comedy probably corresponded to an unspoken wish on the part of the refugees to return through

---

24 Embacher, Helga and Margit Reiter, "Geschlechterbeziehungen in Extremsituation: Österreichische und deutsche Frauen im Shanghai der dreissiger und vierziger Jahre," in *Exil Shanghai 1938–1947: Judisches Leben in der Emigration*, eds. Georg Ambrüster, Michael Kohlstruck, and Sonja Mühlberger (Teetz: Hentrich and Hentrich, 2000), 133–146. See also Rachel Fabritius, "Frauen im Shanghaier Exil (1933–45)," *Berliner China-Hefte* 24 (May 2003): 76–93.
25 Fabritius, "Frauen im Shanghaier Exil (1933–45)," 88.
26 Fabritius, "Frauen im Shanghaier Exil (1933–45)," 91.

the theater to bourgeois life before the Third Reich. Comic performances put the troubled, uncertain present aside and equipped the refugees with new strength to face the future.[27]

The similarities between *Die Masken fallen* and *Fremde Erde* are numerous. Both pieces dealt realistically with the experiences of the Jewish refugees in Shanghai; both were written by Austrian authors and linguistically influenced by Austrian German; and both were composed and premiered in Shanghai. In both plays, the leading women's roles were characterized by self-sacrifice and support for their respective husbands. Both narratives are driven by the development of the main characters; both suggest that Nazism continued to have a profound effect on the lives of the refugees during their exile in Shanghai. Neither play exhibits any trace of Judaism in the religious sense; neither makes any reference to the fate of children or adolescents in Europe or in Shanghai. Both can be seen as historical documents, as representations of the Zeitgeist, whose value went beyond mere entertainment.

It should be noted that both pieces were criticized for their focus on the private lives of their characters and for what their detractors perceived as the lack of explicitly anti-fascist messaging. The two authors and their supporters responded to these accusations by claiming that the political arises precisely from the personal – and, further, by arguing that the private lives of these particular characters reflected the human condition in the twentieth century. On the other hand, openly anti-fascist cultural work met with sustained resistance in Shanghai. While the lack of references to the younger generation or to religious customs can easily be explained away by the backgrounds of the two then-childless, relatively non-religious Jewish authors, we cannot rule out the possibility that threats of reprisals by the Nazis or restrictions by the Japanese authorities in Shanghai might have played a role. Other potential factors include the political disinterest of the majority of Jewish refugees, their desire for entertainment, and perhaps their assumption that anti-fascist propaganda in Asia would have been cut off from Europe and the rest of the world.

Can these pieces be understood as political? Admittedly, the theatrical performances given by the exiles in Shanghai had no impact on Chinese culture or even on post-war Germany or Austria. Their crucial importance lies in their having given artists the opportunity for individual self-expression in a strange and frightening new environment[28] and in having offered opportunities for the discussion of taboo

---

[27] Hans-Christof Wächter, *Theater im Exil: Sozialgeschichte des deutschen Exiltheaters 1933–1945* (Munich: C. Hanser, 1973), 227.
[28] Michael Philipp, "Exiltheater in Shanghai 1939–1947," 476.

topics. They made a valuable contribution to the social and cultural identities of the German-speaking Jewish refugees in Shanghai. It is for this reason that they were successful in their own time and have remained with us to this day as the only two timeless theatrical works from wartime Shanghai.

References

Armbrüster, Georg, Michael Kohlstruck, and Sonja Mühlberger. "Exil Shanghai: Facetten eines Themas." In *Exil Shanghai 1938–1947: Jüdisches Leben in der Emigration*, 12–21. Teetz: Hentrich and Hentrich, 2000.

Braun, Helmuth F. "Man hat nicht so das Fremde gesucht . . . : Emigrantenkultur in Shanghai." In *Heimat und Exil: Emigration der deutschen Juden nach 1933*, 134–142. Stiftung Jüdisches Museum Berlin und Stiftung Haus der Geschichte der Bundesrepublik Deutschland. Frankfurt am Main: Jüdischer Verlag im Suhrkamp Verlag, 2006.

Dutch (pseud.). "Die Masken fallen: An Amazing Protest." *North-China Daily Tribune*. November 1940.

Embacher, Helga and Margit Reiter. "Geschlechterbeziehungen in Extremsituation: Österreichische und deutsche Frauen im Shanghai der dreissiger und vierzieger Jahre." In *Exil Shanghai 1938–1947: Judisches Leben in der Emigration*, edited by Georg Ambrüster, Michael Kohlstruck, and Sonja Mühlberger, 133–146. Teetz: Hentrich and Hentrich, 2000.

Fabritius, Rachel. "Frauen im Shanghaier Exil (1933–45)," in *Berliner China-Hefte* 24 (May 2003): 76–93.

Philipp, Michael. "Exiltheater in Shanghai 1939–1947." In *Handbuch des deutschsprachigen Exiltheaters 1933–1945*, edited by Frithjof Trapp et al., 1:457–476. Munich: Saur, 1999.

Siegelberg, Mark. *Das zweite Gesicht* [The face of Pearl Harbor]. Edited by Tomas Sommadossi. Munich: Iudicium, 2017.

Siegelberg, Mark and Hans Schubert (pseud. of Hans Morgenstern). *Die Masken fallen – Fremde Erde: Zwei Dramen aus der Emigration nach Shanghai 1939–1947*. Edited by Michael Philipp and Wilfried Seywald. Hamburg: Schriftenreihe der Hamburger Arbeitsstelle für Deutsche Exilliteratur, 1996.

Siegelberg, Mark and Hans Wiener (pseud. of Hans Morgenstern). "Die Masken fallen: Authors' Reply." *North-China Daily Tribune*. November 1940.

Speelman, Moritz. "Die Masken fallen: Refugee Committee Painted." *North-China Daily Tribune* 2, no. 11 (1940). In *Nicht Einmal einen Thepsiskarren: Exiltheater in Shanghai, 1939–1947*, edited by Michael Philipp, 100. Hamburg: Hamburger Arbeitstelle für Deutsche Exilliteratur, 1996.

Wächter, Hans-Christof. *Theater im Exil: Sozialgeschichte des deutschen Exiltheaters 1933–1945*. Munich: C. Hanser, 1973.

Marc B. Shapiro
12 The Mir Yeshiva and Its Shanghai Sojourn

The Mir Yeshiva, founded in 1815 in the Belarusian city of Mir, is the world's oldest yeshiva.[1] With some 8,500 students at its Jerusalem branch, it is also the largest yeshiva in the world. The Mir, as is well-known among Orthodox Jews, was the only yeshiva that escaped Europe during the Holocaust together with virtually its entire student body. This escape came about because of a fateful decision, one that was not taken by the other great European institutes of Torah learning.

On September 19, 1939, at the beginning of World War II, the Soviet Union seized Vilnius (known to Jews as Vilna), which was then under the control of Poland. For its own political reasons, the Soviet Union transferred the city, with its large Jewish population, to Lithuania. While Poland was divided between Germany and the Soviet Union, Lithuania still existed as an independent country until June 1940, albeit "hosting" Soviet military bases and thousands of Soviet troops. At the same time, much of "Jewish Lithuania," now inside Polish borders, was occupied by the Soviet Union.

Understandably, many Jews made their way from Soviet-occupied Poland to Lithuania, in particular Vilna, where, despite economic difficulties, they could practice Judaism without any government interference. Some twenty yeshivot also made their way to Vilna, including the Mir Yeshiva, which came with its administration and students. There were great hopes that the Mir students would be able to continue the study of Torah undisturbed in what was still a free country.[2]

R. Hayyim Ozer Grodzinski, the undisputed leader of the Lithuanian Torah world, lived in Vilna. He would die on August 9, 1940, but until then, he remained at the forefront of everything having to do with the yeshivot. Before the Soviet

---

[1] Although I have added a number of footnotes, the essay preserves the oral form in which it was delivered.
   For a good deal of online material about Mir, both the city and the yeshiva, see Reeva Kimble's online directory at https://darkwing.uoregon.edu/~rkimble/Mirweb.
[2] For the yeshivot in Vilna, see A. Bernstein et al., eds., *Yeshivat Mir: Ha-Zerihah be-Fa'atei Kedem* (Bnei Brak: Merkaz Prager, 1999), 1:108. R. Avraham Zvi Hirsch Komai was one of the instructors at the Mir Yeshiva, yet he did not come to Vilna, but instead remained with his community, as he was also the rabbi of the city of Mir. See Bernstein et al., *Yeshivat Mir*, 3:1064–1065. In November 1941, he was murdered by the Nazis together with the rest of the Jewish residents of Mir. I published one of his only surviving responsa in Jehiel Jacob Weinberg, *Kitvei ha-Gaon Rabbi Yehiel Yaakov Weinberg*, ed. Shapiro (Scranton, 1998), 1:255–265.

occupation, when he was asked whether the yeshivot or individual yeshiva students should take advantage of opportunities to leave Lithuania, he replied that they ought to remain where they were. At the time, it seemed a sound assumption that Lithuania would remain a safe place for Jews, and his advice – to stay put – seemed like a reasonable position. Even after the Soviet occupation, he opposed submitting requests for an exit visa, as he feared that such requests would lead to deportation to Siberia.[3]

In the yeshiva world, leaders like Grodzinski are given enormous authority not only in halakhic matters but in all areas, and their authoritative opinions are termed *Da'as Torah*. It is therefore quite significant that R. Eliezer Judah Finkel

---

[3] See my Seforim Blog post, October 18, 2017; Zorach Warhaftig, *Refugee and Survivor: Rescue Efforts during the Holocaust* (Jerusalem: Yad Vashem, 1988), ch. 14; Shalom Zvi Shapira, "Yeshivat Mir be-Golat Shanghai," *Beit Yaakov* 170–171 (March–April 1974): 5; Efraim Zuroff, *The Response of Orthodox Jewry in the United States to the Holocaust* (New York: Yeshiva University Press 2000), 49, 63, 95; Hillel Levine, *In Search of Sugihara: The Elusive Japanese Diplomat Who Risked his Life to Rescue 10,000 Jews From the Holocaust* (New York: Free Press, 1996), 242–243; Zvi Yavrov, *Ma'aseh Ish* (Bnei Brak, 1999), 2:24; Samuel Iwry, *To Wear the Dust of War* (New York: Palgrave Macmillan, 2004), 52. Grodzinski even told the communal rabbis who had fled to Vilna from German and Soviet-occupied territory to return to their communities. R. Abraham Dov Ber Kahana Shapiro, the rabbi of Kovno, R. Elhanan Wasserman, and R. Isaac Zev Soloveitchik disagreed with Grodzinski in this matter. See Dov Eliakh, *Be-Sod Siah* (Jerusalem: Machon Moreshet ha-Yeshivot, 2018), 249; Shimon Yosef Meller, *De-Haziteih de-Rabbi Meir* (Jerusalem, 2018), 2:222–223. See also Bernstein, *Yeshivat Mir*, 1:392. In 1940, R. Abraham Isaiah Karelitz, the Hazon Ish, told R. Joseph Kahaneman that his son, Jacob, who had a certificate to enter Palestine, should remain in Vilna. Unfortunately, he was later murdered by the Nazis. See Aharon Sorasky, *Ha-Rav mi-Ponovezh* (Bnei Brak: Makhon Hayei Yahadut Lita, 1999), 2:81–82. The question of whether to flee German-occupied territory for territory under Soviet rule also did not have a simple answer. R. Isaac Zev Soloveitchik told people to remain under the Germans and not cross into Soviet territory. See Israel Schepansky, *She'erit Yisrael* (New York, 1997), 24 (third pagination). R. Simcha Zelig Reiger of Brisk stated that there could be no Torah ruling on this topic, since the matter was so unclear as to which was the best choice. See Yecheskel Leitner, *Operation: Torah Rescue* (Jerusalem, 1987), 44.

In discussing Grodzinski's opposition to people leaving Lithuania, R. Yehezkel Levenstein stated: "If someone acts crooked and is successful, that which is crooked does not become straight. However, if it is God's will, even something crooked can succeed." See Shapira, "Yeshivat Mir be-Golat Shanghai," 5 (Shapira personally heard Levenstein's statement). What he meant by this is that even though in the end the Mir Yeshiva was able to leave Soviet-occupied Lithuania, cross the Soviet Union, and enter Japan, it does not mean that they made the "right" decision at the time, based on the knowledge then available. It was only through God's providence that such an apparently mistaken step ended up being successful. After quoting this passage, Zorah Warhaftig added: "But might we not learn from the outcome of the affair that our action [in encouraging the yeshivot to leave Lithuania] was in the first place 'straight' and right in the eyes of the Lord? Surely, in the religious context, too, the facts may speak for themselves." *Refugee and Survivor*, 143.

chose to ignore Grodzinski's opinion and the outlook of so many other heads of yeshivot (*roshei yeshivah*), and began arranging the travel documents that would enable the yeshiva students to go to Japan.[4]

The evidence we have shows that Finkel's personal opinion was that even after Lithuania was occupied by the Soviet Union, it was best to stay put rather than taking the dangerous step of trying to secure exit visas. This was also the opinion of R. Yehezkel Levenstein, the *mashgiach ruhani* (spiritual guide) of the Mir Yeshiva. It was only after student pressure – R. Leib Malin is specifically mentioned in this regard[5] – that the yeshiva administration agreed to request permission from the Soviet authorities to travel to Japan.[6] This is an interesting case where yeshiva students, who are trained to have great respect for Torah scholars, nevertheless chose a different path from that of their leaders. It is only because of the students' dissent that the Mir Yeshiva was able to escape Soviet-occupied Lithuania.[7] By the time the other yeshivot realized that there was no future in Lithuania, it was too late for almost all of their students. However, the heads of certain yeshivot, and other important – and thus well-connected – rabbis, including R. Isaac Zev Soloveitchik, were still able to leave.

The Mir Yeshiva's escape was made possible by the famous Sugihara visas, the fascinating details of which have been told numerous times and thus do not need to be repeated here.[8] What is important for our purposes is that the issuance

---

[4] See also Shimon Goldman, *From Shedlitz to Safety*, trans. Elchonon Lesches (Brooklyn, 2004), 98–99; David Mandelbaum, *Giborei Hayil* (Bnei Brak, 2012), 1:196; Chaim Dalfin, *Lakewood and Lubavitch* (Brooklyn: Jewish Enrichment Press, 2018), 205 n. 21. Zorah Warhaftig notes that among the heads of yeshivot, R. Aharon Kotler was the most opposed to any attempt to leave Lithuania in order to travel to Japan. See the recollections of Warhaftig in *Ha-Aretz*, October 8, 1999, section 2, p. 6. See also the recollections of Eliezer Portnoy in Levine, *In Search of Sugihara*, 242–243.

[5] See Bernstein, *Yeshivat Mir*, 1:223–224, 390–394; Ira Epstein, "Shanghai Sanctuary: A Story of Survival in the Midst of the Holocaust for Twenty Five Thousand Jews who Fled to Shanghai, China" (unpublished master's dissertation, Southern Connecticut State University, 2002), 13, 15.

[6] See Joseph D. Epstein, "Yeshivat Mir," in Samuel K. Mirsky, ed., *Mosdot Torah be-Eiropah be-Vinyanam u-ve-Hurbanam* (New York: Histadruth Ivrith, 1956), 123; Shapira, "Yeshivat Mir be-Golat Shanghai," 5; Zuroff, *Response of Orthodox Jewry*, 95–97.

[7] Only a small number of students whom the authorities regarded as Soviet citizens were not able to leave with the rest of the yeshiva. See Warhaftig, *Refugee and Survivor*, 141; Epstein, "Yeshivat Mir," 124. See also Bernstein, *Yeshivat Mir*, 1:326. There were also some students who for one reason or another did not wish to make the journey to Japan, or even apply for the exit visa, and unfortunately they were murdered. See Bernstein, *Yeshivat Mir*, 1:269; Mandelbaum, *Giborei Hayil*, 1:197 n. 6.

[8] See Levine, *In Search of Sugihara*; Warhaftig, *Refugee and Survivor*, ch. 11; Gao Bei, *Shanghai Sanctuary: Chinese and Japanese Policy toward European Jewish Refugees during World War II*

by Sugihara of the Japanese transit visas allowed the Mir Yeshiva, with around three hundred students,[9] to pass through the Soviet Union and Japan en route to its supposed destination, Curacao. The visas only allowed the students and teachers a temporary stay in Japan, where they arrived in January and February 1941. Finkel, the *rosh yeshiva*, did not join the yeshiva on its journey. Instead, he traveled on his own to Palestine so that he could work on obtaining the certificates that would allow the yeshiva to also enter the Holy Land.[10]

In reality, there was never any intention for the yeshiva to continue on from Japan to Curacao. Despite the information stamped in the passports[11] by the helpful Dutch consul that no visa was required for entry to the Dutch island, in actual fact, access to Curacao could only be granted by a landing permit from the governor, which had not been received.[12] The plan was for the yeshiva to remain in Japan until the next step was figured out. This soon became difficult, as the Japanese government had started pressuring the yeshiva community to leave. Since there appeared to be nowhere the yeshiva as a whole could emigrate to, what were they to do?

In the end, the yeshiva did not have to make a decision, as the Japanese government ordered the community to leave Kobe, where they had settled, and go to Shanghai, which at that time was under Japanese control. In Shanghai, the yeshiva community would join approximately 20,000 Jewish refugees, most of whom were from Germany and Austria.[13] Their time in Japan was short, but it was of historical significance, as it led to a great halakhic debate about where the dateline should be placed in accord with halakhah. While most halakhic author-

---

(Oxford: Oxford University Press, 2013), 112–126; Meron Medzini, *Under the Shadow of the Rising Sun: Japan and the Jews During the Holocaust Era* (Boston: Academic Studies Press, 2016), ch. 10.
9 Regarding this number of students, see Bernstein, *Yeshivat Mir*, 1:199, 224, 270, 297, 344, 2:597, 611, 674; Epstein, "Yeshivat Mir," 123. Other sources put the number around 250, and as mentioned below, that was the number of Tractate *Gittin* printed in May 1942.
10 Epstein, "Yeshivat Mir," 124; Bernstein, *Yeshivat Mir*, 3:1023. See also ibid., 1024, for a letter from Finkel in which he states that the doctors forbade him from traveling to Japan.
11 Polish citizens were actually issued a "safe conduct pass" in lieu of a passport by the Polish Government-in-Exile's consulate in Kovno, which worked out of the British consulate. This is because the Soviet Union no longer recognized the validity of the Polish passports. See Elchonon Yosef Hertzman, *Escape to Shanghai*, trans. Chaim U. Lipshitz (Brooklyn: Maznaim, 1981), 21; Levine, *In Search of Sugihara*, 165–166. See also David Kranzler, *Japanese, Nazis and Jews: The Jewish Refugee Community of Shanghai, 1938–1945* (Hoboken, NJ: KTAV, 1988), 338 n. 12.
12 Bernstein, *Yeshivat Mir*, 1:376–382; David Kranzler, *Japanese, Nazis and Jews*, 312; David Kranzler and Eliezer Gevirtz, *To Save a World* (New York: CIS Publishers, 1991), 92.
13 Regarding the Shanghai Jewish community, see most recently Steve Hochstadt, ed., *A Century of Jewish Life in Shanghai* (New York: Touro University Press, 2019).

ities believed that Saturday in Japan was to be celebrated as Shabbat, which was in fact the practice of the local Kobe Jewish community, the famed Hazon Ish, R. Abraham Isaiah Karelitz, believed that Shabbat in Japan was on Sunday. His opinion was sent to Kobe by Finkel,[14] and this led Rabbi Levenstein to appear at Saturday morning services wearing tefillin. He announced that Shabbat was to be observed the next day, in accord with the Hazon Ish's opinion, and this then became the practice of the Mir students.[15] However, there were other refugees and yeshiva students in Kobe, and many of them continued to observe Shabbat on Saturday:

> These *halachic* disputes, with their resulting problems, led many refugees to set aside a two-day Sabbath for various degrees of Sabbath observance! Also, while one group of scholars would recite Kiddush, welcoming the Sabbath, on Saturday night, another group simultaneously observed the *havdala* ceremony, in farewell to the departing Sabbath![16]

Once the yeshiva left Kobe for Shanghai in September 1941, the dispute ceased to be a practical matter, though Yecheskel Leitner, who was one of the Mir students, informs us that some of his colleagues were still in Japan when Yom Kippur arrived on the evening of September 30. Of this group, "some of them observed two days of complete Yom Kippur fasting, while the others kept the fast for just one day and on the other day followed certain *halachic* modifications for fasting under such circumstances."[17]

While Shanghai would become the salvation of the Mir Yeshiva, it is certain that no one ever intended this as the yeshiva's place of refuge. Indeed, when the yeshiva was still in Europe, Rabbi Levenstein had told Leitner, who wanted to

---

14 See R. Leib Malin's letter in Bernstein, *Yeshivat Mir*, 2:616. He further mentions that uncertainty over which day to fast while on the ocean led some not to leave Shanghai at that time. Regarding this group of sixteen Mir Yeshiva students, who gave up their spots on a ship to the United States (they had visas to enter Canada), see Zuroff, *Response of Orthodox Jewry*, 185.
15 Shapiro, "Yeshivat Mir be-Golat Shanghai," 5. Bernstein, *Yeshivat Mir*, 2:504–507, states that it was a Friday morning when Levenstein announced to the students that the yeshiva would follow the Hazon Ish's opinion.
16 Leitner, *Operation: Torah Rescue*, 84. See also Goldman, *From Shedlitz to Safety*, 122–123; Bernstein, *Yeshivat Mir*, 2:492, 498–501.
17 *Operation: Torah Rescue*, 84. See also Mandelbaum, *Giborei Hayil*, 1:242 n. 37; Vera Schwarcz, *In the Crook of the Rock – Jewish Refuge in a World Gone Mad: The Chaya Leah Walkin Story* (Boston: Academic Studies Press, 2018), 76. Similarly, I heard from a teacher of mine who was a student at the Mir Yeshiva in Shanghai, the late Rabbi Abraham Shlomowitz, that some students fasted on both days, eating less than the biblically forbidden amount on one of the days. See also Bernstein, *Yeshivat Mir*, 2:510, 846. For Shlomowitz's testimony of his experiences during the war, see Abraham Shlomowitz, interview by Joseph J. Preil, April 20, 1993, United States Holocaust Museum, https://collections.ushmm.org/search/catalog/irn507651.

escape to Shanghai by himself, that he should not do so. Levenstein said that Shanghai was not the sort of place where an individual on his own could maintain a Torah lifestyle.[18] Not only was Shanghai – and all of China for that matter – regarded as a place where real idolatry was practiced,[19] but Shanghai was also known as a center of prostitution,[20] in which, incidentally, Jewish women were involved.[21]

In a recent book about the experience of the Mir Yeshiva in Shanghai, the author speaks about the great contrast between the city, which contained every evil imaginable, and the yeshiva, which was an oasis of Torah and spirituality.[22] Chaim Dovber Gulevsky, a yeshiva student from Kletzk who escaped to Shanghai, also referred to the sexual immorality the yeshiva students were obliged to confront in the city, describing it as "the lowest level of impurity."[23] Despite this, Levenstein was deeply opposed to any of the Mir students leaving Shanghai – as he had earlier been opposed to their leaving Japan – for he worried that it could lead to the end of the yeshiva.[24] This was not a theoretical concern, as a number of the students indeed had opportunities to leave, having received visas to the United States, Canada, and Paraguay. Yet almost all of them chose to remain with the yeshiva.[25]

---

18 Leitner, *Operation: Torah Rescue*, 91.

19 See Bernstein, *Yeshivat Mir*, 2:573.

20 Gail Hershatter, *Dangerous Pleasures: Prostitution and Modernity in Twentieth-Century Shanghai* (Berkeley: University of California Press, 1997); Christian Henriot, *Prostitution and Sexuality in Shanghai: A Social History, 1849–1949*, trans. Noel Castelino (Cambridge: Cambridge University Press, 2001).

21 See, for example, James R. Ross, *Escape to Shanghai: A Jewish Community in China* (New York: Free Press, 1994), 72. Ross, ibid., adds, "In Europe, the idea of a Jewish prostitute was unthinkable. Here in Shanghai, the old moral standards could not hold." Yet this statement is far from correct. According to an 1872 survey, Jewish women were very much part of the prostitution business in eastern Europe. For example, 17 percent of known prostitutes in Warsaw were Jewish, 27 percent in Cracow, and 47 percent (!) in Vilna. In 1889, Jewish women were 22 percent of the licensed prostitutes in the Pale of Settlement. See Edward Bristow, *Prostitution and Prejudice: The Jewish Fight Against White Slavery 1875–1939* (New York: Schocken, 1982), 21, 63.

22 Bernstein, *Yeshivat Mir*, 2:570–571.

23 *Perah Shoshanah Adumah* (New York, 1988), 186.

24 Shapira, "Yeshivat Mir be-Golat Shanghai," 5; Bernstein, *Yeshivat Mir*, 2:619, 622, 643. Levenstein was, at least at first, also opposed to Finkel, the *rosh yeshiva*, leaving the students in order to travel on his own to Palestine. See Shapira, "Yeshivat Mir be-Golat Shanghai," 4.

25 Bernstein, *Yeshivat Mir*, 2:517, 615. Three Mir students left Shanghai for the United States on December 4, 1941, with a scheduled stopover in Manila. Due to the outbreak of war between the United States and Japan, they were stranded in the Philippines and were interned by the Japanese authorities for over three years. This story has recently been told by Mordechai Buchie Soroka, *A Mirrer in Manila* (Jerusalem: Feldheim, 2018).

Prior to the arrival of the refugees in Shanghai, there was an established community of Sephardic Jews, who had begun to arrive in the city in the nineteenth century. There was also a community of Ashkenazi Jews under the leadership of a Lubavitch rabbi, Meir Ashkenazi, who had resided in Shanghai since 1926. He would remain in the city until 1949, when he moved to Brooklyn (where he died in 1954). Obviously, the arrival of the Mir Yeshiva had a great impact on Orthodox life in the city. Yet it is noteworthy that *Or Torah mi-Mizrah*, which appeared in 1941 and was the first Torah work issued by the refugees in Shanghai, had nothing to do with the Mir Yeshiva. It was published by a student at a newly-created yeshiva called Yeshivat Mizrah ha-Rahok, which was under the direction of Rabbi Ashkenazi (Figure 12.1).[26]

Ashkenazi would later serve as *rosh yeshiva* for the small Lubavitch yeshiva, Tomkhei Temimim, which was established in Shanghai.[27] The students at this yeshiva had escaped from Europe the same way the Mir students did, with Sugihara visas.[28] It seems that after the Lubavitch students arrived in Shanghai and Ashkenazi began to focus on the Tomkhei Temimim yeshiva, Yeshivat Mizrah ha-Rahok ceased to exist, as I can find no references to it after 1941. Although

---

[26] *Or Torah mi-Mizrah*, 9. Kranzler, *Japanese, Nazis and Jews*, 428, confuses this yeshiva with the Shanghai Yeshiva Ketanah which was for younger and less advanced students.

[27] Regarding this yeshiva, see Shalom Dovber Levin, *Toldot Habad be-Polin, Lita ve-Latvia* (Brooklyn: Kehot, 2011), ch. 59, and https://tinyurl.com/yy34ueuj.

[28] Regarding their escape, see Levin, *Toldot Habad be-Polin, Lita ve-Latvia*, ch. 57. New information has recently come to light about how some of the money sent to Shanghai from Vaad ha-Hatzalah in the United States came with instructions to exclude the Lubavitch yeshiva students. Some have viewed this as a continuation of the difficult relationship between Lubavitch and the Lithuanian yeshiva world that existed in Europe. It is reported that there was a case before a *beit din* after the war, where Rabbi Ashkenazi was charged with disregarding the instructions that Lubavitch students not receive aid sent from Vaad ha-Hatzalah. (Ashkenazi won the case.) See *Ha-Rav Mordechai Shmuel Ashkenazi* (Israel, 2017), 193–194; Dalfin, *Lakewood and Lubavitch*, ch. 3. See also ibid., 137–143, for more on the Lubavitch students in Shanghai. For a telegram from Ashkenazi to Vaad ha-Hatzalah in which he states that he distributes funds sent to him equally to all yeshiva students, including Lubavitch and Hakhmei Lublin, see https://sites.google.com/view/meirashkenazitelegram/home. This telegram, which is found in the Vaad ha-Hatzalah Collection, Yeshiva University Archives, was called to my attention by David Safier. I do not wish to opine as to whether Vaad ha-Hatzalah had any justification for excluding Lubavitch students from its aid. I would only suggest that perhaps the organization's leadership assumed that the special fund for Shanghai aid established by R. Joseph Isaac Schneersohn, the Lubavitcher Rebbe, was sufficient to take care of the Lubavitch students. It is also likely that they felt that the Rebbe's fund hurt Vaad ha-Hatzalah's fundraising efforts. See Dalfin, *Lakewood and Lubavitch*, 27; Goldman, *From Shedlitz to Safety*, 140–141. Ross, *Escape to Shanghai*, 125, provides no source to justify his statement that Mir and other yeshiva students argued that the German and Austrian Jews were "less worthy of rescue" because they were not Orthodox.

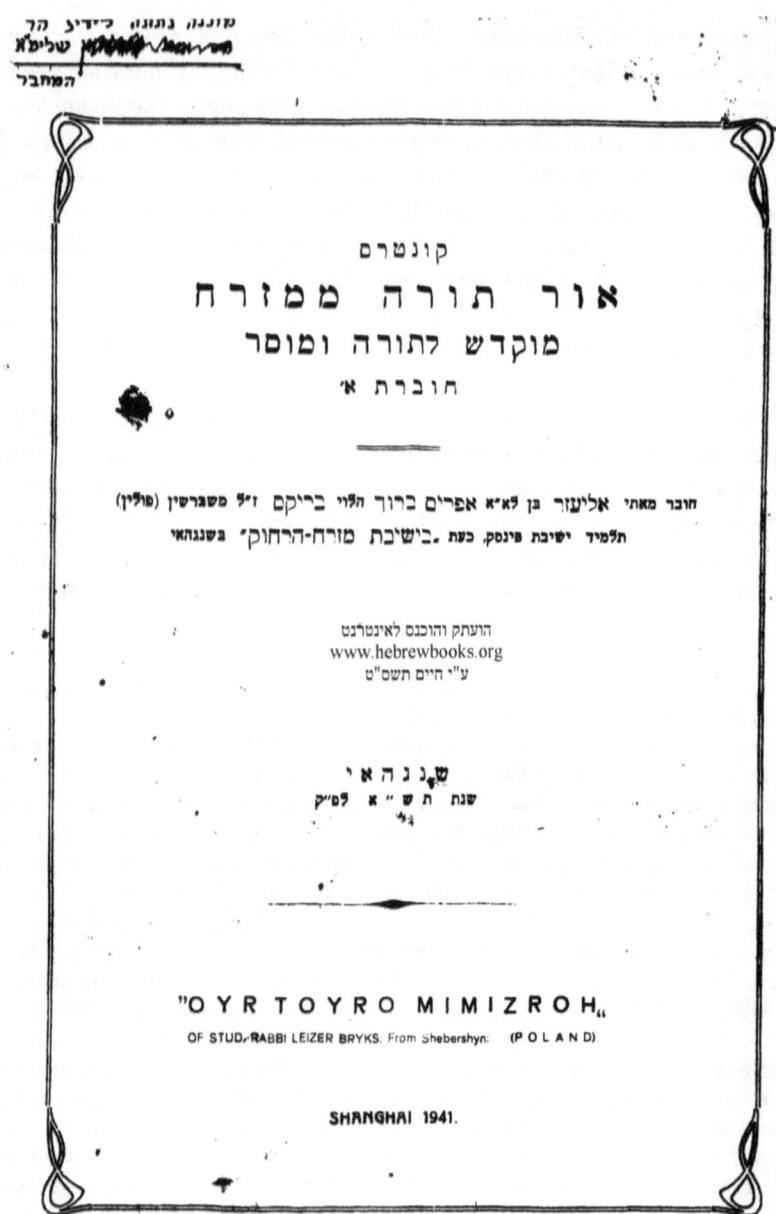

Figure 12.1: Title page of *Or Torah mi-Mizrah*. (Image from HebrewBooks.org.)

R. Chaim Shmulevitz, the son-in-law of Finkel and acting *rosh yeshiva* of the Mir Yeshiva in Shanghai, invited the approximately thirty Lubavitch students to join his yeshiva, the Lubavitchers preferred to remain as a separate group.[29] There were also students from Yeshivat Hakhmei Lublin who succeeded in escaping to Shanghai, where they reestablished their yeshiva, as well as individual students from other yeshivot such as Telz, Kletzk, and Kamenetz who had the foresight to get the Japanese transit visa that also allowed them to escape.[30] As Joseph Zeitin correctly noted, the remote community of Shanghai became "the most active place of rabbinic studies in the years of World War II."[31]

Thanks to Ashkenazi, the Mir students were given permission by the Sephardic community to use the Beth Aharon synagogue.[32] This synagogue, which had opened in 1927 (and would be demolished in 1985), was built by the famous Iraqi-born Jewish businessman Silas Aaron Hardoon. Hardoon was an important figure in Shanghai society and, at the time of his death, perhaps the richest person in East Asia. He is remembered today, among other things, for having funded the construction of the original Nanjing Road in Shanghai. Unusually for his time, he married a Chinese Buddhist woman (whose father may have been Jewish). While Hardoon showed no interest in Judaism, he was not totally alienated from his people and built the synagogue in memory of his father.[33]

The synagogue was built in a part of the city that did not have many Jews and was designed for future Jewish growth in that area.[34] However, from the time of its opening it remained virtually empty, and getting a minyan was difficult. A large kitchen had been included when the synagogue was built, but there was never any need for it. From the perspective of the Mir leadership and students, it was as though the building had been constructed through divine providence, in order to

---

29 S. D. Raichik, "From Kobe to Shanghai," available at http://www.chabadofla.com/templates/articlecco_cdo/aid/1409452/jewish/From-Kobe-to-Shanghai.htm. Regarding Shmulevitz's activities in Shanghai, see Yosef Buxbaum, ed., *Sefer ha-Zikaron le-Maran ha-Gaon Rabbi Chaim Shmulevitz* (Jerusalem, 2000), 64–78.
30 Bernstein, *Yeshivat Mir*, 2:829–833. Some of these yeshiva students joined the Mir Yeshiva in Shanghai. See ibid., 2:462, 834, 3:920–924.
31 "The Shanghai Jewish Community: An Historical Sketch," *Jewish Life* 41 (Oct. 1973): 63–64.
32 Bernstein, *Yeshivat Mir*, 2:574. The relationship between Ashkenazi and the Mir Yeshiva was very good, and he is always portrayed by the Mir students in a positive manner. Understandably, however, the Mir Yeshiva leadership wished to remain independent rather than being placed under his control. See Ross, *Escape to Shanghai*, 124.
33 Regarding Hardoon, see Chiara Betta, "Silas Aaron Hardoon and Cross-Cultural Adaptation in Shanghai," in Jonathan Goldstein, ed., *The Jews of China* (Armonk, NY: Routledge, 1999), 1:216–229.
34 Bernstein, *Yeshivat Mir*, 2:580.

serve the yeshiva when the time came.³⁵ Initially, the yeshiva students also slept in the synagogue. Only later, when money was sent from the United States, were they able to rent rooms. Although after Pearl Harbor there was no way to send money directly from the United States to Shanghai, money could still be sent via neutral countries, and this allowed the yeshiva to survive. It must be noted that money was needed not just for the yeshiva, but also for the boys' and girls' day school that had been established.³⁶

We have a description from one of the Mir students, Zvi Kahana, who was later a *rosh yeshiva* in Israel, of how he and his friends felt when they arrived in Shanghai. They had no idea what to expect in the new city, and were told that they would be living in the Sephardic synagogue. The students, by and large, had never had any contact with Sephardic Jews. Some of them actually believed that the local Jews were Chinese, "just like the Chinese people who carried our luggage to the buses, or perhaps Jews from the Ten Tribes."³⁷ Kahana also mentions how shocked the students were to see how cruelly people treated the rickshaw runners, even kicking them.³⁸ Mir student Abraham Wainhaus recounted his own initial shock on arriving in Shanghai:

> I will never forget the first morning I went out and saw the bodies of dead children left out because they had died of starvation or had frozen overnight . . . Then we had to get used to riding rickshaws. Imagine, using a human being as an animal. We were not trained for that, it is not the Torah way . . . But you get used to it after a while. You realize that it helps a poor man make a living.³⁹

Rabbi Levenstein actually instructed the uneasy students to use the rickshaw, because (as Wainhaus mentioned) if they refrained from doing so, they would deprive the rickshaw runner of his chance to make a living. He told the students to give a large tip if possible, and to act decently towards the runner.⁴⁰

Another description of the yeshiva during its Shanghai period describes how the "sound of Torah" went out from the building and made an impression on all the people outside. The area surrounding the yeshiva was the busiest part of the city with lots of bustle, and this was countered by the sound of Torah study all

---

35 Epstein, "Yeshivat Mir," 128.
36 See the pictures of teachers and students in Bernstein, *Yeshivat Mir*, 2:842, 845.
37 *Yeshivat Mir*, 2:567.
38 See also Mandelbaum, *Giborei ha-Hayil*, 2:31.
39 Vera Schwarcz, "Who Can See a Miracle? The Language of Jewish Memory in Shanghai," in Goldstein, ed., *The Jews of China*, pp. 287–288.
40 Kranzler, *Japanese, Nazis and Jews*, 433.

hours of the day.⁴¹ The general consensus of those who were in Shanghai was that this period was one of great growth in the study of Torah.⁴² R. Shmuel Berenbaum, who was later to become *rosh yeshiva* of the Mir Yeshiva in Brooklyn, described the yeshiva's time in Shanghai as "glorious days,"⁴³ and R. Leib Malin stated that despite the move to Shanghai, when it came to devotion to Torah study nothing had changed.⁴⁴ The students followed the same pattern as in Europe, where everyone had studied the same tractate. While the yeshiva was still in Kobe, they were sent a few hundred copies of Tractate *Kiddushin* by R. Abraham Kalmanovitz in New York.⁴⁵ Kalmanovitz, who in 1926 had been appointed honorary president of the Mir Yeshiva, was the one who had raised the money that allowed the yeshiva to leave Europe for Japan, and he remained the crucial lifeline for the yeshiva throughout its years in Shanghai.⁴⁶ (After the war, he established the branch of the Mir Yeshiva in Brooklyn and served as its *rosh yeshiva*.)

When it was time to move on to the next tractate to be studied, they could no longer have it shipped from the United States due to the war. Having no other choice, the yeshiva decided to print its own copies (Figure 12.2). In May 1942, there was a big celebration at the Jewish club in Shanghai in honor of the printing of 250 copies of Tractate *Gittin*. This was the first of over one hundred religious texts – which came to tens of thousands of copies – that were printed in Shanghai. These books included the entire Talmud (except for *Yevamot*⁴⁷), the *Mishnah*, *Mishneh Torah*, and various medieval and more recent works, including R. Israel Meir Hakohen's classic halakhic text, the *Mishnah Berurah*.⁴⁸

---

41 Epstein, "Yeshivat Mir," 128.
42 See Bernstein, *Yeshivat Mir*, 2:807 (letter of Shmulevitz), 824, 3:910; Shapira, "Yeshivat Mir be-Golat Shanghai," p. 5. Regarding a small *mussar va'ad* in the Mir Yeshiva that met every week in the evening after ma'ariv, see R. Reuven Melamed, *Melitz Yosher: Bereshit* (Bnei Brak, 1989), 9.
43 Meir Shulavitz, "Kavim li-Demuto shel ha-Gaon Rabbi Nahum Partzovitz," *Yeshurun* 22 (2010): 161.
44 Bernstein, *Yeshivat Mir*, 3:1215–1216.
45 Epstein, "Yeshivat Mir," 129.
46 Regarding Kalmanovitz, see Kranzler and Gevirtz, *To Save a World*, 81–116.
47 The reason for this was because *Yevamot* was the volume they were studying when they left Europe for Japan, and thus the students all had a copy. See Hertzman, *Escape to Shanghai*, 39; Avishai Elbaum, "Defusei Shanghai ve-'She'erit ha-Peletah,' " *Ha-Ma'yan* 40 (Nisan 5760): 77 n. 12. Although, as we have seen, the Mir Yeshiva had been sent copies of *Kiddushin*, these were apparently not enough, and this tractate was also reprinted. The talmudic tractates that were published came from a set of the Talmud that belonged to one of the oldest Jewish Shanghai residents, and the new publication required destroying the original copy. See Hertzman, *Escape to Shanghai*, 80; Epstein, "Yeshivat Mir," 130.
48 See Bernstein, *Yeshivat Mir*, 2: ch. 30; Mandelbaum, *Giborei Hayil*, 2: ch. 17. Regarding Jewish publishing in Shanghai, see Irene Eber, *Wartime Shanghai and the Jewish Refugees from Central*

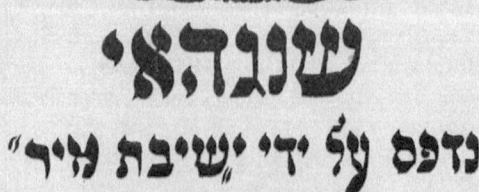

Figure 12.2: Title page from one of the volumes of the Shanghai Talmud. (Image from Wikipedia Commons, https://commons.wikimedia.org/wiki/File:Shanghai_behorot.jpg.)

On February 18, 1943, all Jewish refugees who had arrived in Shanghai since 1937, and were regarded as stateless, were ordered to move into the Hongkou section of the city, an area that was poor and crowded and is what is referred to when people speak of the Jewish ghetto of Shanghai.[49] After the war, the German consul of Tientsin revealed that the internment of the Jews in the ghetto was done at the instigation of the German authorities.[50] At the time, one of the yeshiva students recorded his feelings upon hearing about the order to move into the ghetto: "Here is a nation that for thousands of years did not know what a Jew was . . . It only met him three years ago . . . and it already hates the Jew."[51] He was, of course, speaking about the Japanese, not the Chinese, who were themselves under Japanese control. Quite apart from the fact of internment in the ghetto, there was a widely-believed report, which was also known among the Mir students and continued to be believed after the war, that due to German prodding the Japanese were planning to murder all the Jews of Shanghai by sending them out to sea on ships which would then be sunk.[52]

Europe (Berlin: De Gruyter, 2012), pp. 137ff. Yeshivat Hakhmei Lublin also published books, as did the Lubavitch yeshiva. Agudat Israel published two Yiddish newspapers. See Bernstein, *Yeshivat Mir*, 2:679–682; Jonathan Goldstein, *Jewish Identities in East and Southeast Asia* (Berlin: De Gruyter, 2015), 157. For a list of 104 Torah volumes published in Shanghai (which included three editions of the Passover Haggadah), see Elbaum, "Defusei Shanghai," 79ff. Not all of the Lubavitch publications are included in the list. See Levin, *Toldot Habad be-Polin, Lita ve-Latvia*, 315–316.

49 Kranzler, *Japanese, Nazis and Jews*, 489–491; Joseph Zeitin, "The Shanghai Jewish Community," 61–63. Regarding the ghetto, see also Zhang Yanhua and Wang Jian, *Preserving the Shanghai Ghetto: Memories of Jewish Refugees in 1940s China*, trans. Emrie Tomaiko (Encino: Bridge21, 2016). The information in Marcia Reynders Ristaino, *Port of Last Resort* (Stanford, CA: Stanford University Press, 2001), 197, that the yeshiva students were given an extension and did not move into the ghetto until 1944 is incorrect. The source she cites, Zeitin, "The Shanghai Jewish Community," 64, refers to the location where the students studied, not the students themselves. Regarding the students' move to the ghetto, see Hertzman, *Escape to Shanghai*, ch. 30; Epstein, "Yeshivat Mir," 130–131. Rabbi Ashkenazi was able to arrange for R. Chaim Shmulevitz to remain in his home outside the ghetto. See *A Golden Bridge: Spanning Two Centuries of Masores Hatorah* (n.p.: Yeshivas Mir Yerushalayim, 2017), 1:150.

50 Kranzler, *Japanese, Nazis and Jews*, 488.

51 Bernstein, *Yeshivat Mir*, 2:774.

52 See R. Yehezkel Levenstein, *Or Yehezkel: Mikhtavim* (Bnei Brak, 1976), 355–356; Bernstein, *Yeshivat Mir*, 2: ch. 32. This information was said to have come from Mitsugu Shibata, the Japanese vice-consul in Shanghai. It is also mentioned in Joseph Abraham's description published in Maisie J. Meyer, *Shanghai's Baghdadi Jews* (Hong Kong: Blacksmith, 2015), 98, and in Fritz Kauffmann's recollections after the war, published in Ross, *Escape to Shanghai*, 161. See also Levin, *Toldot Habad be-Polin, Lita ve-Latvia*, 319; Hertzman, *Escape to Shanghai*, ch. 29 (with corrections in Chaim U. Lipshitz, *The Shanghai Connection* [Brooklyn, 1988], ch. 21). Yet in the

The Beth Aharon Synagogue, where the yeshiva was located, was outside the ghetto area, and thus a new site had to be found. The Japanese authorities intended to place the yeshiva in an old building that belonged to the Salvation Army. Yet it was not suitable, and the ensuing tension led to a physical altercation between some yeshiva students and representatives of the Japanese-appointed Jewish organization in charge of the refugees. Thirty-three students were jailed as a result. Fortunately, Rabbi Ashkenazi was able to get them released, supposedly by paying the Japanese to resolve the matter.[53]

For reasons that are not clear, the authorities had a change of mind and permitted the yeshiva to remain in Beth Aharon, with the students receiving a pass so that they could leave the ghetto to go to the yeshiva.[54] Rabbi Levenstein ruled that it was permitted for a non-Jew to carry the Jew's pass on the Sabbath, thus allowing the students to walk to the yeshiva on Friday night and Saturday.[55] The permission for the yeshiva to remain outside the ghetto lasted more than a year, but in autumn of 1944, the students were forbidden from leaving the ghetto to study at Beth Aharon. The yeshiva thus had to relocate inside the ghetto. A new home was found at the Ashkenazic Ohel Moshe Synagogue, which today is the Shanghai Jewish Refugees Museum. This building was smaller than Beth Aharon and was not able to hold all the students.[56] Eventually, the yeshiva moved into a former hotel, which proved sufficient for its needs.[57]

Another difficulty that arose was where to acquire *etrogim* for the holiday of Sukkot. At first, this was not a problem, as there was an etrog tree in the courtyard of a home that had been planted by a family who, decades before, had brought the seeds from Bombay. Unfortunately, this tree was uprooted after Sukkot of 1942, when this family, being British citizens, were put in a civilian prison. In order to prepare for the following year, two Mir students set out with a Chinese guide to

---

record of the conversation with Shibata published in Kranzler, *Japanese, Nazis and Jews*, 478, there is no mention of murder, only the possibility of confining the Jews in a ghetto or sending them to an island. There was also a report that there was a plan to murder the Jews with poison gas. See Eber, *Wartime Shanghai*, 171–172; Hertzman, *Escape to Shanghai*, ch. 33; *Morenu ve-Rabenu ha-Gaon Rabbi Chaim Shmulevitz* (Jerusalem: Degel Yerushalayim, n.d.), 21. Murder of the Jews was certainly desired by the Nazis, but there is no evidence that there was anyone of significance in the Japanese government who was inclined to follow Germany's lead. See Eber, *Wartime Shanghai*, 173.

53 See Kranzler, *Japanese, Nazis and Jews*, 530; Berl Falbaum, ed., *Shanghai Remembered* (Royal Oak, MI: Momentum Books, 2005), 43.
54 Leitner, *Operation: Torah Rescue*, 124.
55 Shapira, "Yeshivat Mir be-Golat Shanghai," 4.
56 Bernstein, *Yeshivat Mir*, 3:879–880.
57 Bernstein, *Yeshivat Mir*, 3:881.

search for an etrog tree. They had been told about a Chinese etrog, and they found what they were looking for near the city of Hangzhou, some 200 kilometers from Shanghai. Yet there was a dispute among the scholars in Shanghai as to whether the fruit – the so-called "Buddha's hand," which looked different than the etrog they were used to – qualified as an etrog upon which one could make a blessing.[58]

In 1944, the first volume of the Torah journal *Meor Torah* was published in Shanghai. Almost all of the articles were written by Mir students.[59] In 1946, the second and final issue appeared. On the last page (p. 62), we find the following:

> With the close of this issue also closes a special era in the life of the yeshiva students in Shanghai. A good number of them have left for Canada and America, and the rest are waiting to leave the city. The story of the *benei ha-yeshivot*, the Mir Yeshiva with all of its students, the rabbis from Poland, and the Orthodox community in Shanghai, was one of growth in the study of Torah ... As we leave the city we stretch out our hands to God with thanks for the past, that he saved us from the horrible destruction and allowed us to occupy ourselves with the study of Torah during this terrible time.

Looking back at the Mir Yeshiva's time in Shanghai, we cannot forget that the students were also part of a larger refugee community, or that they had relationships there, in particular with the Orthodox refugees.[60] A number of refugee boys even began to study in the yeshiva.[61] There were also a number of marriages between yeshiva students and refugee young women.[62] The yeshiva community – and I include in this not only those associated with Mir – was also behind the establishment of schools for boys and girls as well as the opening of a new mikve.[63] The Mir students also had relationships with the local Sephardic community and served

---

58 See Bernstein, *Yeshivat Mir*, 2:605–608; Leitner, *Operation Torah Rescue*, ch. 27; Mandelbaum, *Giborei ha-Hayil*, 2:72. See Chaim Simons, "The Chinese Etrog," at www.chaimsimons.net/chineseetrog.html. R. Abdallah Somekh (1813–1889) was asked about the kashrut of this etrog and ruled that it was kosher. However, his student, R. Joseph Hayyim (the Ben Ish Hai), disagreed with this ruling. See Somekh, *Zivhei Tzedek* (Baghdad, 1899), vol. 2, *Orah Hayyim* no. 37 (second pagination). In Somekh's ruling, he mentions that the question came to him from the city הנבאן , which is how Iraqi Jews wrote "Hong Kong" in Hebrew.
59 In 1945, one issue of the journal *Talpiot* appeared in Shanghai. This was dedicated to "Torah and Hasidism," and included contributions from Mir students. In 1946, Mir students published one issue of a collection of Torah articles entitled *Torah Or*.
60 For recollections of Shanghai, see the videos at www.chinuch.org/audiocategory/Shanghai-Miracle/All.
61 Sigmund Tobias, *Strange Haven: A Jewish Childhood in Wartime Shanghai* (Urbana: University of Illinois Press, 1999), 56, 79.
62 Hertzman, *Escape to Shanghai*, 67.
63 Hertzman, *Escape to Shanghai*, 84–85 (corrected in accordance with the original Hebrew edition [Jerusalem, 1976], 106).

as private tutors for some of the Sephardic youth.⁶⁴ One local man would later recall how the yeshiva "brought new life to our community and raised our religious standards."⁶⁵ A number of Sephardic boys even began studying at the Mir Yeshiva, and some came to the United States after the war to continue their Torah education. It is noteworthy, as well, that the yeshiva students felt comfortable in eating in at least one of these local young people's homes, since most of the local Sephardic Jews' level of religiosity was not at the level of those in the yeshiva.⁶⁶

While some of the young refugees who began attending the yeshiva did so out of conviction, for others there was a more practical reason. Sigmund Tobias later recalled:

> While most of the refugees went hungry the families of the yeshiva students bought milk, butter, bottles of cream, and most of the available kosher meat. They appeared much healthier than the rest of us. It was now taken for granted that the yeshivas were receiving money from America . . . [A] number of the other refugee children who joined the yeshiva had not been observant at all before life became so difficult, nor were most of their parents and families observant even now. My friends and I felt that these boys entered the yeshiva only to eat a little better than the rest of the refugees in Hongkew.⁶⁷

The fact that the Mir Yeshiva, as well as Yeshivat Hakhmei Lublin and the Lubavitch yeshiva, were receiving money from the United States meant that the yeshiva community was better off materially than the other refugees.⁶⁸ Not surprisingly, this led to resentment. Tobias added:

---

64 Maisie J. Meyer, *From the Rivers of Babylon to the Whangpoo: A Century of Sephardi Jewish Life in Shanghai* (Lanham, MD: University Press of America, 2003), 211.
65 Meyer, *Shanghai's Baghdadi Jews*, 184.
66 Meyer, *Shanghai's Baghdadi Jews*, 184, 358; Meyer, *From the Rivers of Babylon to the Whangpoo*, 212; Bernstein, *Yeshivat Mir*, 2:729–730.
67 *Strange Haven*, 79. In an email to me, Tobias clarified that when he wrote of "families of the yeshiva students," he had in mind those students whose families were able to come with them to Shanghai, as well as a few who married while in Shanghai. I would add to this that both Rabbis Shmulevitz and Levenstein had come with their families, and there were also other rabbis with families who were supported with money sent from the United States. None of the discussions of the Mir Yeshiva in Shanghai, including recollections of students, mention anything about families of Mir students who were with them. The same can be said about the students of Yeshivat Hakhmei Lublin and the Lubavitch yeshiva. While it is possible that there were other yeshiva students who had arrived in Shanghai with their parents, it is also possible that Tobias's recollection of this matter is not accurate.
68 Regarding the better conditions that the yeshiva students lived under, see Bernstein, *Yeshivat Mir*, 2:600–601. For reasons that are not clear, the Mir students were also treated better by the Japanese authorities than the other residents of the ghetto. See ibid., 2:782–785, 787, 809, 816–817, 837. Regarding the financial support that came from the United States, see Zuroff, *Response of Orthodox Jewry*, ch. 8. See also ibid., 265–266, where Zuroff mentions how Vaad ha-Hatzalah,

For the first time I began to hear a great deal of anger and resentment at the yeshivas... It had been clear to us that the yeshivas were receiving money from the United States throughout the war. Rumors now circulated that the money had come to Shanghai through neutral Switzerland; every person in the yeshiva community was supposed to have received thirty American dollars every month throughout the war, though no one could be sure of the exact amount... I did not know what to do or say when the peddlers and other refugees imitated the way some yeshiva students showed off their new clothes to each other on high holidays during the war years. Others mimicked overheard conversations among people connected with the yeshivas about buying meat, butter, cream, or other foods that only they could afford. During the difficult war years most of the Jewish refugees, whether they were Orthodox, Conservative, Reform, or not at all religious, often became ill with painful, and sometimes deadly, diseases because they did not have enough food. Many refugees were now saying that the people in the yeshivas were hypocrites who hid their greed with religion, yet did not care if the other Jews in the ghetto lived or died. People wondered if we would have needed the three cemeteries, which were now almost filled with Jewish refugees who had died in Shanghai, if we had had a little more food during the war.[69]

The question anyone who examines the history of the Mir Yeshiva in Shanghai has to ask is: Were the students at all influenced by their surroundings in other than a superficial way? I do not think there is any doubt that the answer is no. This is so for a couple of reasons. First, we must stress that when dealing with an institution as conservative as a yeshiva, it takes a while before one can see evidence of outside influence. Furthermore, this influence will only take place when the yeshiva students speak the local language and see themselves as part of the larger society, as in the United States and Israel today.

---

which in November 1939 was established to save rabbis and yeshiva students, by the end of 1943 had begun to focus on saving all Jews. It is worth noting that Zuroff created a good deal of controversy when, in an interview, he declared that the money sent to support the yeshiva students should have been used to rescue Jews from Nazi-occupied Europe. As he put it, the Vaad ha-Hatzalah, which collected money from American Jews in order to rescue Jews in Europe, should have said to the yeshiva students, "Close your Talmuds and go to work. As long as there is a war and millions of Jews are in danger, we need every dollar to rescue people." See the text of his interview at www.bhol.co.il/forums/topic.asp?cat_id=4&topic_id=1232163&forum_id=771 and in Bernstein, *Yeshivat Mir*, 2:425–426. For strong criticism of Zuroff's book, see David Kranzler, "Orthodoxy's Finest Hour," *Jewish Action* (Fall 2002); and Jonathan Rosenblum, "Anatomy of a Slander," http://www.jewishmediaresources.com/875/anatomy-of-a-slander. See also David Levy's lengthy review, which also deals with the book's reception history, at https://networks.h-net.org/node/28655/reviews/30643/levy-zuroff-response-orthodox-jewry-united-states-holocaust-activities. For a story that the Vaad ha-Hatzalah did not give money to save a hasidic rabbi, employing the excuse that the organization's money was designated only for yeshiva students, see Yuda Strasser and Aharon Perl, *Tzadik Mah Pa'al* (Jerusalem, 2000), 375.
69 *Strange Haven*, 112–113.

The few years that the Mir students were in Shanghai were simply not long enough to speak of any real influence. These students (and the Jewish refugee community in general[70]) never learned Chinese,[71] and all of their official dealings were with the Japanese authorities. (They did not learn Japanese either.[72]) From the recollections of students who were at the yeshiva, the local Chinese are strikingly absent. The Japanese, as the ruling authority, are mentioned, but the Chinese, who were all around them, appear only superficially. Regarding the Chinese sector of the city, Rabbi Elchonon Yosef Hertzman writes, with reference to the diseases rampant in Shanghai: "The Chinese sector was the most contagious, and we feared to enter its district. It was also the most dangerous for robbery and murder. Not one of us ever entered there."[73] This separation from the local Chinese population is also evident with regard to food, as R. Solomon Schwartzman (who was not associated with the Mir Yeshiva) recalled: "The only time I had Chinese food was at a friend's wedding, where the Russian-trained cook made kosher chop suey."[74]

The yeshiva students were no different from most of the refugee population, not to mention the upper-class "white" population, which had little to do with the local Chinese – who were the vast majority of the more than four million residents of Shanghai.[75] The yeshiva students knew that they were in Shanghai only temporarily. They had no interest in putting down roots and never engaged in any sort of cultural, intellectual, or economic relationships with the Chinese. R. Chaim Shmulevitz, writing shortly after the yeshiva arrived in Shanghai, happily mentions that the yeshiva students have "absolutely nothing" to do with the local population, and thus he was not worried that they would absorb any of the city's bad influences.[76]

---

[70] The refugees preferred to learn English so that they would have a chance to immigrate to the United States. See Bei, *Shanghai Sanctuary*, 131.
[71] My teacher, Rabbi Abraham Shlomowitz, recalled that he learned to count a little in Chinese, but that was all.
[72] It is worth noting that Rabbi Zvi Zakheim actually obtained a law certificate from Aurora University, a Jesuit institution in Shanghai that existed from 1903 to 1952. He had earlier received a law degree in Vilna. Zakheim acted as the legal representative of the yeshiva refugees with the Japanese authorities. See Dov Zakheim, "Seven Who Matriculated: Orthodox Rabbis and the Universities They Attended," in Daniel R. Goodman, ed., *Black Fire on White Fire: Essays in Honor of Rabbi Avi Weiss* (Brooklyn: KTAV, 2017), 198, 200.
[73] Hertzman, *Escape to Shanghai*, 99.
[74] Schwarcz, "Who Can See a Miracle?" 293.
[75] Kranzler, *Japanese, Nazis and Jews*, 114. There were, however, some refugees who developed relationships – business and social – with the local Chinese. See Bei, *Shanghai Sanctuary*, pp. 131–133; Kimberly Cheng, "Passing Encounters: German-Speaking Jewish Refugees and Chinese Residents in Wartime Shanghai" (forthcoming).
[76] Bernstein, *Yeshivat Mir*, 2:624.

The Jewish community leadership recognized that the complete separation of the Jewish community from the local population was not a good thing. A school established for refugee children in November 1939 made a point of teaching Chinese, together with English and French. (Only after Pearl Harbor were Japanese and German taught.)[77] In 1942, the three major Jewish communities in Shanghai (Russian, Sephardi, and German) agreed that they would try to create closer relationships between the Jewish community and non-Jewish groups in the city. They spoke about "educat[ing] the Jewish population, especially the newcomers, to a better understanding of the customs and peoples of Japan and China."[78]

However, none of these endeavors had anything to do with the Mir Yeshiva, as its students' efforts were exclusively devoted to Torah study. In speaking about the Mir Yeshiva and its time in Shanghai, it is important to stress how *little* connection there was with Chinese society. It is common for Orthodox writers to describe yeshivot as "islands of Torah," removed from most of the concerns and activities outside their windows. While this is often more hope than fact, in Shanghai it was indeed the case.

References

Bernstein, A. et al., eds. *Yeshivat Mir: Ha-Zerihah be-Fa'atei Kedem*. Bnei Brak: Merkaz Prager, 1999.
Bei Gao. *Shanghai Sanctuary: Chinese and Japanese Policy toward European Jewish Refugees during World War II*. Oxford: Oxford University Press, 2013.
Betta, Chiara. "Silas Aaron Hardoon and Cross-Cultural Adaptation in Shanghai." In *The Jews of China*, edited by Jonathan Goldstein, 216–229. Armonk, NY: Routledge, 1999.
Bristow, Edward. *Prostitution and Prejudice: The Jewish Fight Against White Slavery 1875–1939*. New York: Schocken, 1982.
Buxbaum, Yosef, ed. *Sefer ha-Zikaron le-Maran ha-Gaon Rabbi Chaim Shmulevitz*. Jerusalem, 2000.
Cheng, Kimberly. "Passing Encounters: German-Speaking Jewish Refugees and Chinese Residents in Wartime Shanghai" (forthcoming).
Dalfin, Chaim, *Lakewood and Lubavitch*. Brooklyn: Jewish Enrichment Press, 2018.
Eber, Irene. *Wartime Shanghai and the Jewish Refugees from Central Europe*. Berlin: De Gruyter, 2012.
Elbaum, Avishai. "Defusei Shanghai ve-'She'erit ha-Peletah.' " *Ha-Ma'yan* 40 (Nisan 5760): 75–86.

---

77 Kranzler, *Japanese, Nazis and Jews*, 391.
78 Kranzler, *Japanese, Nazis and Jews*, 484–485.

Epstein, Ira. "Shanghai Sanctuary: A Story of Survival in the Midst of the Holocaust for Twenty Five Thousand Jews who Fled to Shanghai, China." Unpublished master's dissertation, Southern Connecticut State University, 2002.
Epstein, Joseph D. "Yeshivat Mir." In *Mosdot Torah be-Eiropah be-Vinyanam u-ve-Hurbanam*, edited by Samuel K. Mirsky, 87–132. New York: Histadruth Ivrith, 1956.
Falbaum, Berl, ed. *Shanghai Remembered*. Royal Oak, MI: Momentum Books, 2005.
Goldman, Shimon. *From Shedlitz to Safety: A Young Jew's Story of Survival*. Translated by Elchonon Lesches. Brooklyn, printed by the author, 2004.
A Golden Bridge: Spanning Two Centuries of Masores Hatorah. n.p.: Yeshivas Mir Yerushalayim, 2017.
Goldstein, Jonathan. *Jewish Identities in East and Southeast Asia*. Berlin: De Gruyter, 2015.
Gulevsky, Chaim Dovber. *Perah Shoshanah Adumah*. New York, 1988.
Ha-Rav Mordechai Shmuel Ashkenazi. Israel, 2017.
Henriot, Christian. *Prostitution and Sexuality in Shanghai: A Social History, 1849–1949*. Translated by Noel Castelino. Cambridge: Cambridge University Press, 2001.
Hershatter, Gail. *Dangerous Pleasures: Prostitution and Modernity in Twentieth-Century Shanghai*. Berkeley: University of California Press, 1997.
Hertzman, Elchonon Yosef. *Escape to Shanghai*. Translated by Chaim U. Lipshitz. Brooklyn: Maznaim, 1981.
Hochstadt, Steve, ed. *A Century of Jewish Life in Shanghai*. New York: Touro University Press, 2019.
Iwry, Samuel. *To Wear the Dust of War*. New York: Palgrave Macmillan, 2004.
Kranzler, David. *Japanese, Nazis and Jews: The Jewish Refugee Community of Shanghai, 1938–1945*. Hoboken, NJ: KTAV, 1988.
Kranzler, David. "Orthodoxy's Finest Hour." *Jewish Action*, Fall 2002.
Kranzler, David and Eliezer Gevirtz. *To Save a World*. New York: CIS Publishers, 1991.
Leitner, Yecheskel. *Operation: Torah Rescue*. Jerusalem, 1987.
Levenstein, Yehezkel. *Or Yehezkel: Mikhtavim*. Bnei Brak, 1976.
Levin, Shalom Dovber. *Toldot Habad be-Polin, Lita ve-Latvia*. Brooklyn: Kehot, 2011.
Levine, Hillel. *In Search of Sugihara: The Elusive Japanese Diplomat Who Risked his Life to Rescue 10,000 Jews From the Holocaust*. New York: Free Press, 1996.
Levy, David. Review of Zuroff, *The Response of Orthodox Jewry in the United States to the Holocaust*. Published at H-Judaic, February 2002. https://networks.h-net.org/node/28655/reviews/30643/levy-zuroff-response-orthodox-jewry-united-states-holocaust-activities.
Lipshitz, Chaim U. *The Shanghai Connection*. Brooklyn: Maznaim, 1988.
Mandelbaum, David. *Giborei Hayil*. Bnei Brak, 2012.
Medzini, Meron. *Under the Shadow of the Rising Sun: Japan and the Jews During the Holocaust Era*. Boston: Academic Studies Press, 2016.
Melamed, Reuven. *Melitz Yosher: Bereshit*. Bnei Brak, 1989.
Meller, Shimon Yosef. *De-Haziteih de-Rabbi Meir*. Jerusalem, 2018.
Meyer, Maisie J. *From the Rivers of Babylon to the Whangpoo: A Century of Sephardi Jewish Life in Shanghai*. Lanham, MD: University Press of America, 2003.
Meyer, Maisie J. *Shanghai's Baghdadi Jews*. Hong Kong: Blacksmith, 2015.
Morenu ve-Rabenu ha-Gaon Rabbi Chaim Shmulevitz. Jerusalem: Degel Yerushalayim, n.d.
Ristaino, Marcia Reynders, *Port of Last Resort*. Stanford, CA: Stanford University Press, 2001.

Rosenblum, Jonathan. "Anatomy of a Slander." *The Jewish Observer*, August 2005. http://www.jewishmediaresources.com/875/anatomy-of-a-slander.

Ross, James R. *Escape to Shanghai: A Jewish Community in China*. New York: Free Press, 1994.

Schepansky, Israel. *She'erit Yisrael*. New York, 1997.

Schwarcz, Vera. "Who Can See a Miracle? The Language of Jewish Memory in Shanghai." In *The Jews of China*, edited by Jonathan Goldstein, 277–298. Armonk, NY: Routledge, 1999.

Schwarcz, Vera. *In the Crook of the Rock – Jewish Refuge in a World Gone Mad: The Chaya Leah Walkin Story*. Boston: Academic Studies Press, 2018.

Shapira, Shalom Zvi. "Yeshivat Mir be-Golat Shanghai." *Beit Yaakov* 170–171 (March–April 1974): 4–5.

Shulevitz, Meir. "Kavim li-Demuto shel ha-Gaon Rabbi Nahum Partzovitz." *Yeshurun* 22 (2010): 141–214.

Simons, Chaim. "The Chinese Etrog," September 2008. www.chaimsimons.net/chineseetrog.html.

Somekh, Abdallah. *Zivhei Tzedek*. Baghdad, 1899.

Sorasky, Aharon. *Ha-Rav mi-Ponovezh*. Bnei Brak: Makhon Hayei Yahadut Lita, 1999.

Soroka, Mordechai Buchie. *A Mirrer in Manila*. Jerusalem: Feldheim, 2018.

Strasser, Yuda and Aharon Perl. *Tzadik Mah Pa'al*. Jerusalem, 2000.

Tobias, Sigmund. *Strange Haven: A Jewish Childhood in Wartime Shanghai*. Urbana: University of Illinois Press, 1999.

Warhaftig, Zorach. *Refugee and Survivor: Rescue Efforts during the Holocaust*. Jerusalem: Yad Vashem, 1988.

Weinberg, Jehiel Jacob. *Kitvei ha-Gaon Rabbi Yehiel Yaakov Weinberg*. Edited by Marc B. Shapiro. Scranton, 1998.

Yavrov, Zvi. *Ma'aseh Ish*. Bnei Brak, 1999.

Zakheim, Dov. "Seven Who Matriculated: Orthodox Rabbis and the Universities They Attended." In *Black Fire on White Fire: Essays in Honor of Rabbi Avi Weiss*, edited by Daniel R. Goodman, 185–204. Brooklyn: KTAV, 2017.

Zeitin, Joseph. "The Shanghai Jewish Community: An Historical Sketch." *Jewish Life* 41 (October 1973): 54–67.

Zhang Yanhua and Wang Jian. *Preserving the Shanghai Ghetto: Memories of Jewish Refugees in 1940s China*. Translated by Emrie Tomaiko. Encino: Bridge21, 2016.

Zuroff, Efraim. *The Response of Orthodox Jewry in the United States to the Holocaust*. New York: Yeshiva University Press, 2000.

Samuel Heilman
13 Chabad Outreach on the Jewish Frontier: The Case of China

Since at least the fifth of their seven leaders (or *rebbes*), Shalom Dovber Schneersohn, the Lubavitchers (the only remaining Hasidim of the Chabad dynasty) have been deeply attached to their conviction that Judaism is approaching a messianic age. Starting with their first rebbe, Shneur Zalman of Liady, they were persuaded that there was something they not only could but should do to hasten the Messiah's coming. This tenet became the central core of their mission with the sixth rebbe, Yosef Yitzchak, who was convinced that the Messiah's advent was connected to his personal struggles during the Holocaust, the Jewish people's suffering more broadly, and his own subsequent arrival in the spiritual abyss that was America. If he could manage to terrify the American Jews into repenting of their irreligion, the sixth rebbe believed, he could stave off the arrival of a Holocaust in America. After Yosef Yitzchak's death, it was left to his son-in-law and cousin, Menachem Mendel Schneerson, who succeeded him as the seventh rebbe in 1951, to complete this task. But rather than scaring American Jewry or even limiting his mission to them, the seventh rebbe galvanized his Hasidim, recruiting them as *shluchim* or 'emissaries' (which his predecessor had already begun to do during his final years) whose task was to reach out to the Jews wherever they were, both spiritually and geographically, in order to awaken in them a Jewish attachment that – he was absolutely convinced – would (if successful) bring about the coming of the new age. The Messiah, he believed, was his predecessor, but his Hasidim came to identify the figure with Menachem Mendel himself. Originally, the *shluchim* had been emissaries from the rebbe to those of his Hasidim who were at a distance; under Menachem Mendel, they became emissaries to all Jews, in particular those at the very edge of Jewish attachments and affiliation. Finding the targeted Jews and trying to awaken their Jewish consciousness became the central concern of his *rebistvo*, or 'leadership,' and of his Chabad. He did this through a series of campaigns aimed at Jews, especially those most distant from Jewish life and consciousness. These campaigns were meant not to frighten Jews into repentance but rather to charm them into joining his movement to hasten the advent of the Messiah. He tried to convince his Hasidim and the world that if he could inspire even one Jew to perform a public act of Jewish significance, he would change the cosmic balance and thereby "bring the redemption, whose footsteps (*ikvesa dimeshicha*) could now be seen."[1] By building a series of outreach institutions, including a variety of "Chabad Houses," and by sending out emissaries to urge Jews to openly engage in identifiably Jewish acts – from lighting a Hanukkah menorah in the public square or donning *tefillin* ('phylacteries') in the street to making a blessing on a *lulav* and *etrog* ('palm' and 'citron') during the festival of Sukkot or simply placing a mezuah on their doors – modern-day Chabad became a movement. Most of its followers were neither Hasidim nor even necessarily Orthodox Jews.[2] While commitment to Jewish observance was desired, the key was to do something identifiably Jewish. This was a far cry from the intellect and study that was associated with early Chabad Hasidism.[3] And that brings us to China.

There are no publicly available, definitive statistics for the number of Jews living in China today. The Jewish Virtual library put the figure at 2,500 in 2016, less than 0.01% of the national population; the World Jewish Congress lists almost the same number.[4] Among these are some 500 Jews in Kaifeng, whose Jewish bona fides are not universally agreed upon by those whose interest lies in counting Jews. In Harbin, a small community of mostly Russian Jews first established itself in the late nineteenth and early twentieth centuries, reaching about 500 by 1903 and growing exponentially to about 8,000 only five years later.[5] During the Russian revolution, the number of Jews in Harbin who had fled the pogroms, the war, and the revolution rose to between 10,000 and 15,000. Afterward, the population declined. Most of the Jewish community had left Harbin by 1949. In the early 1950s, about 3,500 more embarked for Israel. The last Jew supposedly departed in 1985.

Tiny groups of Russian Jewish expatriates were also to be found in Mukden, Hengdaohezi, Quiqhar, and Manchuria. Most observers, however, consider World War II – when the number of Jews in Shanghai, who arrived there as European Holocaust refugees, peaked at about 30,000 – to represent the Jewish high-water

---

[1] See Samuel Heilman and Menachem Friedman, *The Rebbe: The Life and the Afterlife of Menachem Mendel Schneerson* (Princeton, NJ: Princeton University Press, 2010), 146.
[2] Heilman and Friedman, *The Rebbe*, 167.
[3] Immanuel Etkes, *Rabbi Shneur Zalman of Liady: The Origins of Chabad Hasidism* (Waltham, MA: Brandeis University Press, 2015).
[4] "Vital Statistics: Jewish Population of the World (1882–Present)," Jewish Virtual Library, accessed January 29, 2018, http://www.jewishvirtuallibrary.org/jewish-population-of-the-world. "China," World Jewish Congress, accessed January 29, 2018, http://www.worldjewishcongress.org/en/about/communities/CN.
[5] Irena Vladimirsy, "The Jews of Harbin, China," accessed March 27, 2018, https://www.bh.org.il/jews-harbin/.

mark demographically. By the time of the Communist takeover, a mass exodus occurred.⁶

Given this history, one might assume that organizations dealing in Jewish outreach would not choose to establish much of a presence in China. Nevertheless, a quick look at the Lubavitcher Hasidim's outreach, as documented on the Chabad.org website, reveals that as of 2018, no less than *ten* Chabad-Lubavitch centers are to be found in China⁷: Beijing, Chengdu (Sichuan), Discovery Bay (Hong Kong), Guangzhou, Hong Kong, Kowloon, Ningbo, Shanghai, Shenzhen (Guangdong) (Nanshan), and Yiwu (Zhejiang). A closer look reveals even more. In Shanghai, there is a Chabad Center in the Pudong suburbs, another in town, and a third in Shang Mira Gardens. A plethora of institutions are to be found in Beijing, with two emissary (*shliach*) couples: Rabbi and Mrs. Freundlich and Rabbi and Mrs. Turnheim. Among the services offered are an early childhood center and preschool, kitchen koshering, marriage preparation, holiday programming, and bar and bat mitzvah preparation – the sort of cornucopia of Jewish resources one might expect in communities with far more Jews in them. How is one to explain this?

On the one hand, one could say that Chabad has become so completely absorbed by its outreach mission that its Hasidim increasingly see going on a mission as *the* essential experience. And because all the regions where larger concentrations where Jews are to be found have already been spoken for by the growing cadre of emissaries, they are forced to place *shluchim* even at the farthest reaches of the Jewish world. Moreover, given that Chabad Hasidim remain on a mission to bring about the advent of the Messiah, even those far-off communities must be served. This means, of course, that the Lubavitchers see their residence in China as a temporary, conditional stay while they are on their mission. And if they share their last three rebbes' conviction, that mission is near its end. But why China in particular?

One possibility is that the official counts of Jews in China are lower than the reality, and Chabad therefore is serving far more Jews than people realize. The fact is that there are increasing numbers of Jews who travel to China for business and do not appear in the national Chinese census or other formal counts. Another possible explanation is that Chabad foresees a great influx of Jews to China (even before the coming of the Messiah) and has already started building its institutional infrastructure in anticipation. The simplest explanation is the one that

---

6 Daniel Elazar, "Are There Really Jews in China? An Update," Jerusalem Center for Public Affairs, accessed January 29, 2018, http://www.jcpa.org/dje/articles2/china.htm.
7 "Chabad-Lubavitch Centers in 'China,' " accessed January 29, 2018, http://www.chabad.org/centers/default_cdo/country/China/jewish/Centers.htm.

Chabad has put on its website: "No Jew should ever be lost to the Jewish people, no Jew must ever be lonely."[8] In its ideological view of its mission, no number of Jews is too few for Chabad to provide a full complement of Jewish services.

Another, more deeply rooted explanation, comes from the origins of the Chabad mission. From the beginnings of the *Uforatzto* campaign, an effort by their seventh rebbe to spread his message to the four corners of the globe, the Lubavitchers have been on a mission to transform Jewry and indeed the world one Jew at a time. The cliché that for every Jew there are at least two Chabad emissaries has some basis in fact. This religious operation, whose goal is to retrieve Jewry from its alienation and assimilation and inspire Jews to engage in public Jewish acts, will, if successful – as the Lubavitchers have been assured by their last three leaders – hasten the coming of the Messiah. This became a meme for Chabad bringing about a kind of heaven on earth, with the Lubavitchers leading the way through their attachment to God and his divine commandments in line with the Hasidic vision first articulated by Israel ben Eliezer, the Ba'al Shem Tov, who claimed that the Messiah had promised to cease tarrying when the message of spiritual transformation and unity with God had been spread to all Jews.[9]

The Lubavitchers' late rebbe, Menachem Mendel Schneerson, believed that this message of redemption and religious return would resonate particularly powerfully in a place like China, which at least on its face would seem a less than optimal locale. The current Chinese government has at best an ambivalent attitude toward Judaism within its borders.[10] If the Lubavitchers could retrieve the most wayward Jews in a country whose attitude toward Judaism was complex, this would, their rebbe assured them, not only end the existential loneliness of all Jews (and their God, and their rebbe, who both pined for their return, like a king whose son the prince had gotten lost far from the palace), it also would bring salvation and redemption to all Jews and the world. What could more dramatically symbolize the far reaches of the globe and the lost Jews than China – a locale so far beyond the pale that it was never mentioned in any sacred Jewish text?

The Chabad community in Shanghai, headed by second-generation *shaliach* Shalom Greenberg and his wife Dina, who arrived in 1998, offers a view of Chabad in microcosm. When I first met Greenberg, just months after his arrival, I asked him, "Why China?" In his warm and sincere reply, he told me that as the

---

[8] "Our Mission," accessed April 30, 2021, https://www.chabad.org/library/article_cdo/aid/32812/jewish/Our-Mission.htm.
[9] Heilman and Friedman, *The Rebbe*, 2–3. See also fn. 4, p. 283.
[10] See for example, Hiddai Segev, "China's Ambivalent Attitude Towards Judaism," July 2, 2018, Middle East Institute, accessed September 14, 2018, http://www.mei.edu/content/map/china-s-ambivalent-attitude-towards-judaism.

children of *shluchim*, he and his siblings had agreed to the following challenge: they would each travel to the most distant point on the Jewish periphery and see who could best succeed in Chabad's mission. For his brother, the posting was Anchorage, Alaska; for Greenberg, it was Shanghai. When I first encountered him, he was domiciled in a small apartment in Shanghai Center and could barely find enough Jews to make a minyan. He was nearly arrested at Sukkot time when neighbors reported him to authorities, who accused him of building "an underground church."[11] In 1999, on the all-important Ninth of Av, when Jews traditionally mourn the destruction of the Holy Temple in Jerusalem and the subsequent exile, on the very date when (the rabbis had prophesied) the Messiah would return to end that exile, Greenberg could not even gather enough Jews to fully commemorate the holy day. But the Greenbergs persevered.

When I returned in 2018, Chabad had several locations in Shanghai. Shalom and Dina Greenberg had a large headquarters at a villa in Shang Mira Gardens, where they had built a nursery school and a mikve. On Sabbaths they held not one but two services, each with over sixty worshippers. They had even opened a restaurant, while one of Shalom's brothers had established a center in the Pudong Chabad house across the Huangpu River in the Shanghai suburbs. There was also a third location in the downtown area. Presidents of Israel had visited. Chabad was serving the Jews who were increasingly passing through China. Amos Benjamin, who lived for many years in Shanghai and still serves as a kosher food inspector in East China, explained, "The Shanghai community is really a community of people from everywhere else."[12] As of 2016, the Shanghai metropolitan area alone claimed 2,000 Jews. Obviously, the statistic of a 2,500-person total Jewish population in China is belied by this claim.

By and large, Chabad's operations in China can be explained as part of their efforts not simply to serve a locally based Chinese Jewry but rather to reach a Jewry that is passing through China in order to do business, and which has, in the process, traveled very far away from the Jewish heartland. It also includes the stream of Jewish tourists to China. Chabad's goal is to awaken and nurture among these distant Jews attachments to their Jewish identity even as they find themselves spending extended time – often with their families – in China. Theirs

---

[11] Whimsy Anderson, "Building Bridges & Sukkahs of Understanding in Shanghai, China," accessed September 14, 2018, https://www.chabad.org/library/article_cdo/aid/1431361/jewish/Building-Bridges-Sukkahs-of-Understanding-in-Shanghai-China.htm.
[12] Rhiannon Arnold, "Shanghai's Jewish Community Grows," *Western Independent*, September 22, 2016, accessed January 29, 2018, https://inkwirenews.com.au/2016/09/22/shanghais-jewish-community-grows/.

is a mission of opportunity, narrowly defined and targeted not to the Chinese but to Jews in China.

Perhaps nothing more vividly and symbolically demonstrates this than some of what the Greenbergs do in Shanghai. Their effort is to be *in* but not *of* China. Take, for example, the question of food. As previously noted, Greenberg has opened a kosher restaurant in Shanghai. One might imagine that if Jews in the United States are famous for seeking out and eating Chinese food, a Jewish restaurateur in China might want to stimulate a counter-appetite among Chinese for kosher, Jewish-style food. But that is not the case. The Greenbergs' target audience is not the Chinese but the Jews from elsewhere. As Dina Greenberg explained in an interview, she does not want her children to know what Chinese cuisine tastes like.[13] On the contrary, although they find themselves in Shanghai, she insisted that she wants them to become attached to the "typical" Ashkenazic menu – which is really an eastern European cuisine that has over the years become associated with Jewish eating. What Mrs. Greenberg wants for her children is what she also wants for the Jews they serve. This is not food for the Chinese (although some Chabad centers like the one in Chengdu claim to also offer "authentic Chinese dishes as well"), nor is it even an effort to create a kind of Chinese kosher food (something Jews have found a way to do in places where they are found in large numbers, whether in Jerusalem or New York City).[14] It is a way to make Jews who find themselves in China feel as if they are much closer to – or even enclosed in – a Jewish world.

The connection is not simply gastronomic; it is cultural and religious. Nor is it necessarily for those who already feel that attachment, as Rabbi Greenberg once explained to a fellow Hasid who, visiting the Shanghai center, had suggested that Greenberg was really there to help enable Orthodox Jews to practice their religious and ritual life while travelling through Shanghai and China.

No, Greenberg replied, that was not at all the case. "If I were not here, you would still be eating kosher food that you had brought with you and praying in your hotel room." Then, pointing to the obviously non-Orthodox Jews who were around the Sabbath table and who had just finished attending the Sabbath service, he added, "But if not for me and our Center, none of *these* people would have been doing this." In other words, for the messianic redemption to occur – which was, after all, the ultimate goal of their mission and the reason they were willing to live so far away from the Lubavitcher heartland – Greenberg and his colleagues had to

---

13 Dina Greenberg, interview with Samuel Heilman, August 2002.
14 "Sarah's Kitchen," Chabad Jewish Center of Chengdu, accessed February 6, 2018, http://www.chabadchengdu.com/templates/articlecco_cdo/aid/2436822.

place themselves on the most distant points of the Jewish cultural religious periphery, even in China, and "bring them back" – or, as they might put it in Hebrew, להחזיר אותם בתשובה. And that they would do – one Jewish act at a time.

1 The Chabad Model

How does Chabad establish its connection with other Jews? First, it markets its Judaism as not being unduly burdensome. The Chabad center in Solon, Ohio, shows on its homepage its ultra-modern building, swimming pool, and playground, while claiming it is a place "where being Jewish is fun."[15] The Ningbo Chabad Center presents itself as a Jewish "home away from home."[16] Unlike traditional Jewish communities – in which members make a financial commitment and join a synagogue in order to receive services from the group, the rabbi, and individual fellow members – Chabad provides an alternative business model. In the Chabad way, the *shaliach* offers services and a community free of charge, thereby building a relationship with those who avail themselves of what is being offered. "We hope," the Beijing center proclaims on its website, "you find what you are looking for and come back often."[17] The ensuing sense of obligation this stimulates – as Marcel Mauss[18] explained in his famous essay on the Gift – creates the feeling of a need to repay and thence create a counter-prestation. Chabad fosters this continuing sense of relationship and obligation upon which they can build. As the Chengdu center puts it: "The Chabad Jewish Center of Chengdu does not ask for annual membership dues or require any building fund payments. To help support the efforts of the Chabad Jewish Center of Chengdu, we have created the Chai Club and are inviting you to become our partner."[19] Out of that partnership, the sense of obligation grows. Every "gift" the Chabad *shluchim* bestow on the Jews whom they encounter brings with it the notion of credit and sense of obligation. The goal of Chabad outreach is to create more and more Jewish encounters, to provide more and more services, and to engender more and more opportunities to interact with other Jews under the auspices of Chabad – all in order to create a web of obligations binding all the Jews who arrive in their center to them and

---

15 Chabad Jewish Center of Solon, accessed September 14, 2018, https://www.solonchabad.com/.
16 Ningbo Jewish Center, accessed September 14, 2018, https://www.jewishningbo.org/.
17 Chabad Beijing, accessed September 14, 2018, https://www.chabadbeijing.com/.
18 Marcel Mauss, *The Gift*, first English edition Cohen and West, 1954, (London: Routledge, 1990), 7.
19 "Chai Club," Chabad Jewish Center of Chengdu, accessed February 6, 2018, http://www.chabadchengdu.com/templates/articlecco_cdo/aid/3041162/jewish/Chai-Club.htm.

through them to Judaism as they define it. All this, as the Chengdu center's website declares, "will allow us to continue serving the community's spiritual needs and allow us to reach out like never before."[20] Or, as the Pudong center's website puts it: "Holiday Celebrations are geared so that adult and child, young and old, are able to find a *sense of belonging*..." that will emerge out of the multiplicity of what we might call "moments of connection."[21] Those moments are the building blocks of the wall that encloses the Jews who would otherwise disperse.

2 Moments of Connection

Key to the Chabad mission is understanding when Jews are likely to be open to connecting to other Jews. There are two key moments of connection: either when individuals feel themselves existentially alone and recall a sort of collective consciousness among their Jewish families and communities, or when they have just had children and feel the need to give those offspring a sense of connection to some collective identity. The Jewish holidays – most prominently Passover, Chanukah, and the other family-oriented festivals – become important occasions for awakening these feelings, especially for young families. Even a cursory review of the Chabad houses and their activities (which are often documented with photos) reveals that most of the participants are young families and that these holidays are banner moments of outreach. The development of a preschool or nursery has become a key recruitment tool for Chabad. Nearly all the Chabad centers in China have established such schools.

Of course, having children under one's pedagogic control is doubly useful. In line with Alexander Pope's famous maxim, " 'Tis education forms the common mind, / Just as the twig is bent the tree's inclined," early childhood education is understood as a particularly successful way of transforming people. Following the promise in Isaiah 11:6 of what it will be like in the messianic age, "and a little child will lead them,"[22] the establishment of a preschool is a way of bringing the rest of the family in behind the child. For Chabad, preschools and family events that bring parents with their children are often gateway institutions and part of the messianic mission.

---

20 Ibid.
21 "Family Activities," Chabad of Pudong – Shanghai, accessed February 6, 2018, http://www.jewishpudong.com/templates/articlecco_cdo/aid/2883987/jewish/Family-Activities.htm. My italics.
22 Mechon Mamre, "Isaiah Chapter 11," accessed April 30, 2021, https://www.mechon-mamre.org/p/pt/pt1011.htm.

In China – a culture that, as sociologists Gaye Tuchman and Harry Levine described it, is "utterly alien," its inhabitants perceived as "the most foreign, the most un-Jewish" – these Jewish environments and gateways become even more important.[23] If, in New York, Jews savor visiting Chinatown as "the exotic in the midst of their own community," we might say that in China Chabad arouses the feeling of visiting the Jewish community in the midst of the exotic.[24]

This would seem to make the challenge of succeeding in China the quintessential expression of the Chabad messianic campaign. To borrow from a famous song about New York and apply it to Chabad in China: "If you can make it here, you can make it anywhere." If, even in far-off China, Chabad can find Jews who are attracted by what they offer, then perhaps their rebbe's assurance that "we are now very near the approaching steps of the Messiah . . . and our spiritual task is to complete the process" is not in vain. As of today, they are all still working on it, and the Messiah has not yet arrived.

References

Anderson, Whimsy. "Building Bridges: Sukkahs of Understanding in Shanghai, China." https://www.chabad.org/library/article_cdo/aid/1431361/jewish/Building-Bridges-Sukkahs-of-Understanding-in-Shanghai-China.htm.

Arnold, Rhiannon. "Shanghai's Jewish Community Grows." Posted September 22, 2016. *Western Independent.* https://inkwirenews.com.au/2016/09/22/shanghais-jewish-community-grows/.

Elazar, Daniel. "Are There Really Jews in China? An Update." Jerusalem Center for Public Affairs. http://www.jcpa.org/dje/articles2/china.htm.

Etkes, Immanuel. *Rabbi Shneur Zalman of Liady: The Origins of Chabad Hasidism.* Waltham, MA: Brandeis University Press, 2015.

Heilman, Samuel and Menachem Friedman. *The Rebbe: The Life and the Afterlife of Menachem Mendel Schneerson.* Princeton, NJ: Princeton University Press, 2010.

Mauss, Marcel. *The Gift.* First English edition, Cohen and West, 1954. London: Routledge, 1990.

Segev, Hiddai. "China's Ambivalent Attitude Towards Judaism." July 2, 2018. Middle East Institute. http://www.mei.edu/content/map/china-s-ambivalent-attitude-towards-judaism.

Tuchman, Gaye and Harry Gene Levine, "New York Jews and Chinese Food: The Social Construction of an Ethnic Pattern," *Journal of Contemporary Ethnography* 22, no. 3 (1993): 382–407.

Vladimirsy, Irena. "The Jews of Harbin, China." Museum of the Jewish People. https://www.bh.org.il/jews-harbin/.

---

[23] Gaye Tuchman and Harry Gene Levine, "New York Jews and Chinese Food," *Journal of Contemporary Ethnography* 22, no. 3 (1993): 383, 392.

[24] Tuchman and Levine, "New York Jews and Chinese Food," 394.

III Jews and Chinese

Each of the six essays in Part III, "Jews and Chinese," delineates a significant encounter or exchange between Jewish and Chinese people and their cultures. Communication between peoples and cultures is the key here, and it is made possible through translation, journalism, pedagogy, legal intervention, and scholarship. In "Yiddish Translations of Chinese Poetry and Theater in 1920s New York," Kathryn HELLERSTEIN discusses how modernist Jewish poets and writers in New York City during the 1920s interpreted classical Chinese texts through the act of translating them into Yiddish. BAO Anruo, in "Enemy or Friend: The Image of China in Yiddish Newspapers during the Russo-Japanese War (1904–1905)," explores the ways that Yiddish journalists and editors depicted China as a nation and political entity in the Yiddish press during the Russo-Japanese War. ZHANG Ping, in "To Speak or Not to Speak: Hanoch Levin's *Suitcase Packers* and Cao Yu's *Peking Man* in Light of Cross-Textual Dialogue," performs a cross-cultural analysis of two classic modern dramas: one in Chinese; the other in written in Hebrew, translated into Chinese, and performed successfully several times in twenty-first-century Beijing. LI Dong describes the pedagogical challenges of teaching Jewish American literature to college and university students in China, taking a classic immigrant short story, Anzia Yezierska's "Children of Loneliness" (1923), as his case study. In "Chinese and Ashkenazic Encounters in the American Immigration Regime: Max J. Kohler, Immigration Legal Practice, and the Chinese Exclusion Act," Rebecca KOBRIN tells the exceptional story of the Jewish American attorney Max Kohler, whose belief in freedom and equality led him, as early as 1901, to fight against the renewal of the Chinese Exclusion Act, which severely restricted the number of Chinese people allowed to immigrate to the United States. Our volume concludes with SONG Lihong's essay, "A Homeless Stranger Everywhere: The Shadow of the Holocaust on an Israeli Sinologist," on the intriguing narrative of how the late Irene Eber, born in Germany, became a prominent scholar and professor of Chinese history and culture at the Hebrew University of Jerusalem.

Kathryn HELLERSTEIN

14 Yiddish Translations of Chinese Poetry and Theater in 1920s New York

In the first half of the twentieth century, a significant body of works about China appeared in Yiddish. These works of poetry, drama, translation, fiction, travel writing, journalism, ethnography, and memoir were composed and published or performed in Warsaw, Shanghai, and New York. This essay will examine Yiddish translations published or produced in New York City in the early decades of the twentieth century. At the center of this essay is an elusive text: Moyshe Leyb Halpern's play, *Der krayd-tsrikl* [The chalk-circle], a Yiddish translation of the German play *Der Kreidekreis* [The chalk-circle], which the Weimar Expressionist poet Klabund (pseud. for Alfred Henschke, 1890–1928) had adapted from a nineteenth-century French publication by Stanislas Julien (1797–1873), *Le Cercle de Craie* [The circle of chalk], itself a translation of the Chinese "Hui-lan-chi" [History of the circle of chalk] transcribed by the descendants of Jenghiz Khan.[1] Although Halpern's Yiddish script has been lost, based on other Chinese-to-Yiddish translations from the early twentieth century – specifically, the Yiddish translations by Meyer Shtiker (1905–1983) of Li Bai's medieval Chinese poetry – we can speculate about what kinds of choices Halpern might have made as a translator.

By the nineteen-teens and -twenties, Yiddish literary modernism was thriving in New York City. The poets and writers of avant-garde groups such as di Yunge, 'the Young Ones,' and the Inzikhistn, the 'Introspectivists,' were experimenting in their vernacular, Yiddish, with the aim of expanding the limits of their culture in the face of urban modernity. These young immigrants, most of whom came from the countryside and towns (*shtetlekh*) of eastern Europe, now strove, as American poet Ezra Pound declaimed, to "make it [i. e., literature] new" in the cosmopolitan centers of the United States. They sought to write a new literature in Yiddish, the traditional vernacular of the majority of world Jewry for the past ten centuries. In theme and form, with conscious attention to aesthetics, politics, and secularism, and with unexpurgated expression of repressed emotion, forbidden sexuality, iconoclasm, and blasphemy, these writers produced poetry and fiction that could contend with, compare to, and participate in dialogue with the literatures of the rest of the world.

---

[1] James Laver, introduction to *The Circle of Chalk: A Play in Five Acts Adapted from the Chinese by Klabund,* trans. James Laver (London: William Heinemann, 1929), viii–ix.

Translation figured prominently in this effort to make Yiddish a modern literature, or what today we call a world literature. For example, the final issue of a New York modernist miscellany, *Shriftn* (1925–1926), included a section called "Fun alte kvaln" [From old wellsprings], which featured translations into Yiddish of the Chinese poet Li Tai Po (Li Bai) alongside Yiddish versions of Japanese haiku and Egyptian, Arabic, and American Indian poems, as well as an excerpt from the Finnish *Kalevala* and "The Birth of Buddha."[2] Such an eclectic group of translated works was characteristic of this modernist publication. Earlier issues of *Shriftn* had included translations of Greek and Latin classics, as well as of nineteenth-century Americans like Whitman and Longfellow. These translators intended to break down the perceived provincialism of the Yiddish language, to expand it beyond its Jewish framework, and to open up Yiddish writing to traditions from around the world.

The 1925/1926 translators – David Ignatov, Meyer Shtiker, Hersh Rosenfeld, and A. Almi (pen name for Elihu-Khayim Sheps) – selected and translated these works in the context of American modernism. Their East Asian translations were not the first to appear in American Yiddish. Yehoash (pseudonym of S. Bloomgarden, 1872–1927), best known for his literary translation of the Hebrew Bible into Yiddish, had already published Chinese-themed poems and translations of Chinese stories in the first decade of the twentieth century. And they were certainly not the last: A. Almi published a book-length collection of Chinese philosophy and poetry in 1925,[3] and, in 1930, Bernard Witt translated Lafcadio Hearn's 1887 *Some Chinese Ghosts* into Yiddish as *Khinezishe legenden*.[10] These Yiddish writers were part of a wider Jewish interest in China, exemplified by Martin Buber's converging interests in Hasidism and Chinese philosophy in 1910 and 1911.[4] By importing Chinese poems and reports of Chinese history, culture,

---

2 *Shriftn: A Zamlbukh* 8–9, no. 9 (of 10, each numbered separately) (1925/1926): 1–21 (Japanese and Chinese poems).

In the final issue of *Shriftn*, the section "Fun alte kvaln" [From old wellsprings] includes the following translations: David Ignatov's "Kleyne antologye fun yapanezishe hokis" [Small anthology of Japanese haiku], Meyer Shtiker's "Khinezishe lider (fun Li Tai Po)" [Chinese poems by Li Tai Po], "Indianer lider" [American Indian poems], "Egiptishe lider" [Egyptian poems], and "Arabishe lider" [Arabic poems]; Hersh Rosenfeld's "Di Kalevale," and A. Almi's "Gautama Buddha." See Wikipedia, "Gautama Buddha," http://en.wikipedia.org/wiki/Gautama_Buddha. See also Rachel Rubinstein, *Members of the Tribe: Native America in the Jewish Imagination* (Detroit, MI: Wayne State University Press, 2010), 76.

3 A. Almi (pseud. of Elihu-Khayim Sheps), *Di Khinezsishe filozofye un poezye* (New York: Maks N. Mayzel, 1925).

4 Irene Eber, "Martin Buber and Chinese Thought," *Wegen und Kreuzungen* (2004): 23–25. Reprinted in Irene Eber, *Jews in China: Cultural Conversations, Changing Perceptions*, ed. Kathryn Hellerstein (University Park, PA: Pennsylvania State University Press, 2020), 201–222.

customs, and behavior into Yiddish for their readers in Warsaw and New York, these writers expanded the boundaries of Jewish cultural sensibility.⁵

In contrast to the modernists' highbrow endeavors to bring Yiddish culture into dialogue with the cultures and histories of the larger world, a popular sub-genre featuring Chinese people and subjects developed in the Yiddish theaters in New York City during the 1910s and 1920s. These works comprised a part of what the numerous popular theater companies had begun to offer in the 1890s: "historical operettas and *tsaytbilder*" (literally, 'scenes of the times'), or sensationalized quasi-documentaries about current events, as well as "domestic dramas"⁶ shot through with comedic scenes and interludes.⁷ These comedies, satires, and melodramas entertained large audiences of working-class Jewish immigrants on the Lower East Side. According to a theater advertisement for the Atlantic Garden Theater on the Bowery in New York City, published in the *Morgn-zshurnal* [Jewish Morning Journal] on March 3, 1911, the first Yiddish play about China produced in United States appears to have been Louis Gilrod's *Der prints fun khine* [The prince of China]. It was listed alongside a performance by the "Imperial Japanese Troupe" and "a modern drama in three acts," *Di farshtoysene* [The repudiated woman], by N. Rakov.⁸ Neither the script for *Der prints fun khine* has survived, nor have reviews of the performance. However, we can assume that this 1911 production was a musical comedy from what we know of its author. Louis Gilrod (1879–1930) was a songwriter for the Yiddish vaudeville stage and became a well-known lyricist and actor for the Second Avenue Yiddish theaters. Gilrod wrote satirical, topical lyrics, and co-authored a skit, *Tsar nikolay un tsharli tshaplin* [Czar Nicholas and

---

5 Bernard Witt, trans., *Khinezishe legenden* (New York, 1930), a Yiddish translation of *Some Chinese Ghosts*, by Lafcadio Hearn (1887).
6 Nahma Sandrow, *Vagabond Stars: A World History of Yiddish Theater* (Syracuse, NY: Syracuse University Press, 1977, 1996), 114.
7 Sandrow, *Vagabond Stars*, 91–131.
8 *Jewish Morning Journal*, "Atlantic Garden, Imperial Japanese Troupe No. 2, Der prints fun khine," March 3, 1911, 7, The National Library of Israel and Tel Aviv University, accessed January 27, 2021, https://www.nli.org.il/en/newspapers/tjm/1911/03/03/01/?e=-------en-20--1--img-tx-IN%7ctxTI--------------1. "Louis Gilrod (1879–1930)," Milken Archive of Jewish Music, https://www.milkenarchive.org/artists/view/louis-gilrod/. Steven Lasky, email message to author, refers to the original scan in the Index of Yiddish Periodicals, National Library of Israel, http://yiddish-periodicals.huji.ac.il/Reshimes/Amerike.html. As of January 27, 2021, I have not yet found the *Yidish morgn zshurnal* [Jewish Morning Journal] there. Steven Lasky is the creator of the Museum of the Yiddish Theater on the Museum of Family History website, http://www.museumoffamilyhistory.com/moyt/pih/chalk-circle.htm.

Charlie Chaplin], in 1917.[9] He also composed "A malka af peysekh" [A queen for Passover] for the 1922 musical comedy *Tants, gezang un vayn* [Dance, song, and wine], by Harry Kalmanovitsh, at the famous New York Thomashefsky Theater.[10] One can thus presume that Gilrod's *Der prints fun khine* was likewise a comedic musical entertainment.

It is likely that the Yiddish plays about Chinatown from the following decade were also conceived in this popular vein. The titles of these plays, as well as their prolific productions in American cities up and down the East Coast throughout the 1920s, suggest that they, too, were comedies, satires, or melodramas. For example, in 1922–1923, *Reyzele fun Tshaynataun* [Rose of Chinatown] was performed at the Lenox Theater in Manhattan, at the Liberty Theater in Brooklyn, and later at the People's Theater in Manhattan. In 1925–1926, this same show played in the Folly Theater in Baltimore, Maryland, in the President Theater in Washington, D.C., and in the Shubert Belascoe, also in Washington, D.C. The following season, 1926–1927, *Reyzele fun Tshaynataun* made its way north to the Monument Nationale in Montreal, Quebec, Canada. In 1928–1929, *Reyzele fun Tshaynataun* returned to Brooklyn, to play at the Lyric Theater, and finally, in 1929–1930, *Reyzele fun Tshaynataun* seems to have had its final run at the Lando Theater in Pittsburgh, Pennsylvania. Another play, *Kitty fun Tshaynataun* [Kitty from Chinatown], was staged at the Standard Theater in Toronto, Ontario, Canada, throughout 1923–1924. And on November 27, 1929, *A nakht in Tshaynataun [Chinatoun]* [A night in Chinatown] opened at the Metropolitan Theater in Newark, New Jersey. My source for the information about these productions is an unpublished spreadsheet that Steven Lasky, creator of the website *The Museum of Yiddish Theatre*, compiled from theater advertisements in the Yiddish press. This spreadsheet conveys the data Lasky gathered from these advertisements, which listed the actors and other facts about each performance.[11]

What were these plays? Whether they were original compositions, translations/adaptations of popular American plays in English, *shund* ('trashy') melodramas, racy ethnic comedies, or ethnographic, sensitive dramatic works about interactions between the immigrant populations of Chinese and eastern European

---

9 Neil W. Levin, "Louis Gilrod," Milken Archive, accessed January 28, 2021, https://www.milkenarchive.org/artists/view/louis-gilrod/.

10 Levin, "A Malka af Peysekh," *Great Songs of the American Yiddish Stage*, vol. 13, Milkin Archive, accessed January 28, 2021, https://www.milkenarchive.org/music/volumes/view/great-songs-of-the-american-yiddish-stage/work/a-malke-af-peysekh/.

11 Lasky, "Productions re. Chinatown Plays, in North America, 1920s" (items 1–101), Museum of the Yiddish Theatre, http://www.museumoffamilyhistory.com/moyt, mentioned in email to author, May 9, 2018.

Jews in the urban American melting pot, we do not know. All that survives of these plays are advertisements in the Yiddish press. The plays themselves have vanished: we have none of the scripts, no recordings, and few, if any reviews, as far as I can determine. Even without knowing the substance of these performances, though, we understand from their titles and venues that these works of Yiddish theater about China appealed to audiences of working-class Jewish immigrants in American cities in the early twentieth century. Without the plays themselves or evidence of critical responses to these plays, we cannot know if between 1911 and 1929, Yiddish playwrights, theater companies, and audiences shared an interest in the interactions between the two groups of immigrants, Chinese and Jews, who brushed up against each other in crowded urban neighborhoods, or if they filled their satirical comedies with stereotypes of newly-arrived immigrants, both Jews and Chinese, in an effort to become "real" Americans.

However, we can find a hint of what may well have been the tone and attitude of these plays in another genre of popular Yiddish culture in New York, which also conjured up China from the beginning and into the middle of the twentieth century. In one Yiddish vaudeville song (its title, lyrics, and exact date lost for now), a "henpecked" Jewish husband deserts his family. As Nahma Sandrow writes, "His wife finally tracked him down in Chinatown, which was after all only a few blocks from the Lower East Side; he had grown a pigtail and was working in a Chinese restaurant."[12] To escape from an oppressive home life, this immigrant Jew disguises himself as a member of the neighboring immigrant Chinese population. The sheer unlikeliness of this appropriation of another ethnic identity, when combined with the convenient proximity of urban immigrant neighborhoods, makes for a comedic disparagement of the stereotypical Jewish marriage (i.e., a passive husband and a domineering wife). The song also comments on the notion of American assimilation. Typically, a Jew would shed his Jewishness by trying to join mainstream American culture, but in this song, he chooses to assimilate into yet another tradition-bound ethnic culture: that of Chinese immigrants. Sandrow elaborates on such ethnic assimilation in a vaudeville joke in which immigrant Jews from different regions "react to a cantor's singing by comparing it to characteristic foods," including a Litvak (Lithuanian Jew), who likens the synagogue chanting to "herring and borscht," a Galitisaner (Jew from Polish Galicia), who compares it to "meat and wine," and "a typical American," who describes the cantor's prayers as "sweet like sugar, like chop suey and chow mein, . . . like ham

---

12 Nahma Sandrow, "'A Little Letter to Mamma': Traditions in Yiddish Vaudeville," *American Popular Entertainment: Papers and Proceedings of the Conference of the History of American Popular Entertainment,* ed. Myron Matlow (Westport, CT, and London: Greenwood Press, 1977), 87–95. Thank you to Nahma Sandrow for leading me to her article.

and eggs, like hot dogs *mit* mustard."¹³ The punchline highlights how in America, Jews who describe synagogue music with culinary metaphors have discarded the traditional dietary laws of kashrut to create a mishmash cuisine that includes Americanized Chinese dishes, alongside *treyf* ('non-kosher') diner breakfasts and baseball stadium snacks.

As late as 1950–1951, the Borsht Belt performer Mickey Katz recorded a song called "Chiny Town," for Capitol Records. "Chiny Town" was the B side of the single "Gehakte Mambo" ('Chopped Mambo,' referring to the Latin American rumba-like dance); the record label states, beneath the song title, "Parody of 'Chinatown, My Chinatown' (Jean Schwartz–William Jerome)."¹⁴ The parodied English-language original was written by the Tin Pan Alley team: composer Jean Schwartz, a Jewish immigrant from Hungary, and lyricist William Jerome, a son of Irish immigrants. Schwartz and Jerome composed "Chinatown, My Chinatown" in 1906 and in 1910 added it to the musical revue *Up and Down Broadway*; it became a hit song only in 1915.¹⁵ At least two early recordings were made (in 1914 and 1928); later, between 1933 and 1952, it was recorded at least nine more times.¹⁶ Jerome's lyrics for "Chinatown, My Chinatown" are problematic from a twenty-first century point of view, due to the inclusion of an ethnic slur and the stereotyped imagery of Chinese men, as we see in the lyrics accompanying an undated recording by the popular vaudeville singer and actor, Al Jolson:

> When the town is fast asleep, and it's midnight in the sky
> That's the time the festive chink starts to wink his other eye
> Starts to wink his dreamy eye, lazily you'll hear him sigh

---

13 Sandrow, 92.
14 Mickey Katz, vocalist, "Chiny Town," B side of "Gehakte Mambo," Capitol (1419), 78 RPM, Florida State University Recorded Sound Archives, accessed February 7, 2021, https://rsa.fau.edu/album/2672.
15 Jean Schwartz and W. M. Jerome, "Chinatown, My Chinatown" (New York: Jerome H. Remick, 1910), *Historic Sheet Music Collection* no. 1346, accessed February 7, 2021, https://digitalcommons.conncoll.edu/sheetmusic/1346. See also Wikipedia, "Chinatown, My Chinatown," https://en.wikipedia.org/wiki/Chinatown,_My_Chinatown.
16 The American Quartet with Billy Murray, "Chinatown, My Chinatown," recorded 1914, Library of Congress National Jukebox, accessed February 7, 2021, https://www.loc.gov/item/jukebox-11359/; Art Gillham, recording pianist, "Chinatown, My Chinatown," with Andy Sannella (clarinet, alto sax, flute, guitar, and effects), Murray Kellner (violin), and Rube Bloom (second piano), recorded January 11, 1928, YouTube, accessed July 6, 2021, https://www.youtube.com/watch?v=y0TM1n00ENw; "Chinatown," Musicbrainz, accessed February 7, 2021, https://musicbrainz.org/work/5e66dc31-15fe-3c1b-a5ae-44ac512673b1.

Strangers taking in the sights, pigtails flying here and there
See that broken wall street sport, still thinks he's a millionaire
Still thinks he's a millionaire, pipe dreams banish every care

Chinatown, my Chinatown
Where the lights are low
Hearts that know no other land
Drifting to and fro
Dreamy dreamy Chinatown
Almond eyes of brown
Hearts seems light and life seems bright
In dreamy Chinatown[17]

In addition to the slur and the stereotype of the queue (a Manchurian hairstyle imposed upon all men in China during the Qing dynasty),[18] these lyrics present a version of an American urban Chinatown neighborhood as a refuge for the down-and-out American late at night. This failed American Wall Street mogul, having lost his fortune, escapes from his impoverishment through the "pipe dreams" available in Chinatown. The song alludes to the then-well-known fact that such pipe dreams were fueled by opium. From the 1890s through the 1930s, New York's Chinatown was infamous for its gambling, opium, and prostitution, activities that were controlled by warring "tongs," or secret brotherhoods.[19] Even though most Chinese immigrants in New York worked in legitimate jobs as shopkeepers, cigar-makers, laundry-workers, or domestics, the song conveys a romanticized image from an outsider's point of view. Schwartz and Jerome's "Chinatown" is characterized by longing, dreaminess, and delusion. It is a place where one can encounter "[a]lmond eyes of brown," perhaps of local sex workers, and where "[h]earts seem light and life seems bright" – at least to American tourists, the pleasure-seekers who visit late at night.

Mickey Katz's 1951 "Chiny Town," a parody of Jerome and Schwartz's 1906 Tin Pan Alley hit, replaces the original's jazzy melodic tune and the local color

---

17 Al Jolson, "Chinatown, My Chinatown," https://genius.com/Al-jolson-chinatown-my-chinatown-lyrics and https://genius.com/Al-jolson-chinatown-my-chinatown-lyrics. Variant lyrics are available in a recording by the Mills Brothers, https://www.youtube.com/watch?v=sW1hp-Wof-dE. See also "Chinatown, My Chinatown," released by National Telefilm Associates in 1929, https://www.youtube.com/watch?v=VjFu5XwCVyI. For a history of the song "Chinatown, My Chinatown," see Wikipedia, accessed April 22, 2021, https://en.wikipedia.org/wiki/Chinatown,_My_Chinatown.
18 "Queue (hairstyle)," Wikipedia, accessed April 22, 2021, https://en.wikipedia.org/wiki/Queue_(hairstyle).
19 See for example, Scott D. Seligman, *Tong Wars: The Untold Story of Vice, Money, and Murder in New York's Chinatown* (New York: Viking, 2016).

and longing of the lyrics with crass Yinglish rhymes set to an orientalized tune characterized by Chinese gongs and perhaps a hammered dulcimer (*yangqin*)[20] or a zither (*guzhen*),[21] interspersed with American brass and saxophone. Katz's lyrics mention Chinese food ("Chiny vetshere iz a mekhaye" ['Chinese supper is a pleasure']) in a Yiddish/English dialect that conveys exaggerated warnings ("shpritz di food mit iodine, un es shtikt in boykh ya [vi a] shteyn" ['Spray the food with iodine, and it sticks in your belly like a stone']), as well as a possible allusion to illicit sexual contact ("Chiny mitl [?], Chiny pipik" ['Chinese middle, Chinese bellybutton']).[22]

Katz's 1951 take-off on Schwartz and Jerome's Tin Pan Alley and jazz classic, alongside the vanished vaudeville song about the Jew who fled his family for life disguised as a Chinese man, may well represent the tone of the Yiddish plays about Chinatown: comical, farcical, parodic – a cocktail of stereotypes of both immigrant groups rubbing elbows in New York City.

There is, however, one Yiddish play about China that we know more about, and what we know, although incomplete, suggests a different register of the cultural interplay between the Chinese subject and the Jewish language. This play is the Christmas Eve, 1925 production by the Yiddish Art Theater in New York City of a translation of a medieval Chinese classic. I will preface the discussion of this Yiddish play with a synopsis of the original Chinese drama.

---

20 "Yangqin," Wikipedia, accessed July 6, 2021, https://en.wikipedia.org/wiki/Yangqin.
21 "Guzheng," Wikipedia, last edited July 16, 2021, https://en.wikipedia.org/wiki/Guzheng.
22 Mickey Katz, "Chiny Town," by Mickey Katz and His Orchestra; Mickey Katz; Jean Schwartz; William Jerome, Capitol (1419), Publication date 1951, 78rpm, Novelty. Digitizing sponsor, Kahle/Austin Foundation. Contributor, Internet Archive. https://archive.org/details/78_chiny-town_mickey-katz-and-his-orchestra-mickey-katz-jean-schwartz-william-jerome_gbia0070726a/_78_chiny-town_mickey-katz-and-his-orchestra-mickey-katz-jean-schwartz-william-jerome_gbia0070726a_02_2.3_CT_EQ.flac.

A recording of a different version of this Mickey Katz performance is found on Florida Atlantic University Recorded Sound Archives. However, this item may be a mislabeled recording of a different Mickey Katz song., https://rsa.fau.edu/album/2672.

Here are the lyrics of the alternate version of the Mickey Katz parody, "Chiny Town": "Come on in mayn hoyz / I'm gonna give you feygelekh / Come on in mayn hoyz, mayn hoyzeke man (refrain). / I'm gonna give you bobke-chat un a piece of kalevat / I'm gonna give you chicken-fligl un a lokhshn kigl / come on I'm [for?] two cents plain / I'll give you gribeniz / es shtikt in boykh like farshteyn." These Yinglish lyrics are sung in a thin, whiny voice, addressing an unknown listener. Are the lyrics about Jewish food mixed up with American Chinese dishes? Is the speaker a Chinese restauranteur trying to lure a Jewish customer? The madame in a brothel, doing the same? The recording on the Florida American University Recorded Sound Archive website does not supply a context. This version varies so significantly from the other version I found that it may be a mislabeled entry on the FAU/RSA website.

According to Gwyn Williams, in the preface to the 1953 English volume, *The Story of the Circle of Chalk: A Drama from the Old Chinese*, "This play comes to us from medieval China, from the China of the Yuan or Mongol dynasty, which was established by the splendid Kublai Khan, grandson of Genghis Khan, and which ruled a vast empire of which China was only a part from 1279 to 1368."[23] The playwright was Li Qianfu. My brief discussion of the play is based on the 1953 English translation by Frances Hume, published in London, which was itself a translation from the 1832 French translation by one Stanislas Julien, also published in London.

The Chinese play is a classical "zaju verse play and gong'an crime drama"[24] about corruption and injustice in the countryside, which are corrected by the righteous and honest Pao, the governor of Kai-feng-fu. The plot features Chang Hai-Tang, a girl from an honorable but impoverished family, who is reduced to becoming a courtesan. One client, the wealthy Lord Ma, falls in love with her and takes her as his Second Wife. She soon bears him a son. Ma's First Wife, called in translation "Mrs. Ma," who is childless, poisons her husband in a plot to free herself to marry her lover. Mrs. Ma accuses Chang Hai-Tang, the young Second Wife, of the murder and falsely claims the young son as her own, in order to inherit the whole of Lord Ma's fortune. Her lover, Chao, a functionary in the court system, rigs the trial by bribing the corrupt, greedy judge into condemning the young Second Wife to death and by buying false testimony from the midwives and neighbors who had witnessed the birth of Chang Hai-Tang's son. Second Wife's estranged brother then appears and intervenes on his sister's behalf, before her execution, when the case is sent to the superior Governor Pao. Pao devises a test to determine who is the real mother of the boy. He draws a circle of chalk on the ground, places the child within it, and commands the two women each to pull the boy by one arm toward herself; the one who succeeds in pulling the boy out of the circle will, he says, be proven the real mother. The greedy First Wife forcefully yanks the boy out of the circle two of the three times, because the second wife, unable to voice her innocence, is equally unwilling to hurt her son

---

[23] Gwyn Williams, preface to *The Story of the Circle of Chalk: A Drama from the Old Chinese*, trans. Frances Hume from the French of Stanislas Julien, with illustrations by John Buckland-Wright (London: Rodale Press, 1953), 5. The Chinese title of the play is written on the title page of this volume as *Hui-lan-ki*. The Encyclopaedia Britannica transliterates the title as *Huilanb ji* (https://www.britannica.com/art/Chinese-performing-arts#ref283395). The playwright was: "Li Qianfu, courtesy name Xingdao, who was a 14th century Chinese playwright. His works include Hui Lan Ji, which was used as the basis for Bertolt Brecht's 1948 play *Caucasian Chalk Circle*" ("Li Qianfu," Wikipedia, https://en.wikipedia.org/wiki/Li_Qianfu).

[24] "Li Qianfu," Wikipedia.

by pulling on his frail arm. Governor Pao then reveals that this was his intended test and declares the kind-hearted Second Wife to be the true mother of the boy and innocent of murdering her husband.

In 1924, Alfred Henschke (1890–1928), a prolific Weimar poet, novelist, playwright, and translator, adapted and translated this play into German, publishing it as *Der Kreidekreis* under the pseudonym "Klabund."[25] To render the play into German, Henschke worked from the London 1832 publication of a French translation by Stanislas Julien (1797–1873), *Le Cercle de Craie*, which was a translation of the *Hui-lan-chi* [History of the circle of chalk], published under the princes of the family of Jenghiz Khan, who reigned in China from 1259 to 1368.[26] Klabund's translation was produced in Germany in 1925 and in London in 1929, starring Anna May Wong, Rose Quong, and Laurence Olivier.[27] Thus, Klabund's 1924 German version of Julien's French translation was an adaptation of Li Qianfu's fourteenth-century Chinese classic.

Klabund changes the Chinese drama (via the French translation) in the following ways. First, he converts the four acts of the original into a five-act play. Second, he introduces a suicide (of Chang Hai-Tang's father), an evil capitalist (Mr. Ma), and a love story that frames the action and the outcome. The admirer in the courtesan house sneaks into the young girl's marital bed and makes love to her on the night of her wedding to Mr. Ma. In the end (spoiler alert), this same young man ends up becoming the Emperor, who, incredibly acting as a judge, hears her case, recognizes the imprisoned and condemned Chang Hai-Tang, frees her, and marries her. Third, Klabund introduces twentieth-century revolutionary themes through the character of Chang Ling, Chang Hai-Tang's estranged brother. Fourth, Klabund sprinkles numerous chalk circles throughout the play as symbolic or aesthetic flourishes, in contrast to the single chalk circle test that culminates the classical drama. In sum, Klabund's version adds elements of post-Shakespearean comedy – disguise, intrigue, titillating eroticism, a happy ending through marriage – as well as 1920s issues of social justice, socialist revolutionary rebellion, and a rags-to-riches plot.

What does this have to do with Yiddish renditions of Chinese culture? On Christmas Eve, 1925, Maurice Schwartz's famous Yiddish Art Theater (Yidishe

---

[25] See Sander Gilman, online biography of Klabund. Also "Klabund," *Encyclopaedia Britannica Online*, accessed May 12, 2018, https://www.britannica.com/biography/Klabund.

[26] James Laver, introduction to *The Circle of Chalk: A Play in Five Acts Adapted from the Chinese by Klabund*, translated by James Laver (London: William Heinemann, LTD, 1929), viii–ix.

[27] Steven Lasky, " 'The Chalk Circle,' by Klabund," Museum of the Yiddish Theatre, accessed July 6, 2021, http://www.museumoffamilyhistory.com/moyt/pih/chalk-circle.htm.

Kunst Teater) staged *Der krayd tsirkl* [The chalk circle].[28] The Yiddish Art Theater had been founded in 1918 by Schwartz, a renowned actor, director, and producer, to serve as what scholar Edna Nahshon calls an "outpost of culture" for Jewish immigrant intellectuals on the Lower East Side and to counteract the predominant low-brow popular theater entertainment known as *shund* ('trash'),[29] a category to which the "Chinatown" Yiddish plays most likely belonged. *The Chalk Circle* was translated into Yiddish from Klabund's 1925 German hit by the modernist Yiddish poet Moyshe Leyb Halpern (1886–1932). Although Halpern's script has not been found, we know something about this production from the ephemeral metatexts that have survived it.

First, we have a full-page newspaper advertisement in the Yiddish *Forverts* (January 10, 1926), which includes portraits of all the actors in costume and photos of key scenes from the stage (Figure 14.1). Second, we have a synopsis of the play, in the program for a 1926 Philadelphia production, written by Maximillian Horowitz (or Hurwitz).[30] The synopsis reveals that Halpern (and/or Maurice Schwartz) abbreviated the play from Klabund's five-act expansion back to Li Qianfu's original four acts. In addition, the synopsis ends with the corrected paternity of Chang Hai-Tang's son – not as the child of Mr. Ma, but rather as the offspring of the now-Emperor, the handsome intruder who seduced Chang Hai-Tang on her wedding night.

Horowitz's introduction to his synopsis reads, in a translation by Steven Lasky:

> This extraordinary play, at once realistic drama and fairy tale, is a mordant satire on social and political conditions with a happy, Cinderella-like ending. Though its theme is universal, it reproduces faithfully the life of the East with its sordidness and picturesque quaintness, its brutality and tenderness, its sensuous, [sic] mysticism, its stolid resignation and heroic endurance. There are many lyrical passages of great beauty. The author, whose real name is Alfred Henschke, is a German Jew who, despite his comparative youth (he is only thirty-four), has produced numerous poems, plays, novels and short stories which have won for him a place in the front rank of German writers of today.[31]

---

28 Lasky, " 'The Chalk Circle,' by Klabund," Museum of the Yiddish Theatre.
29 Edna Nahshon, "Maurice Schwartz and the Yiddish Art Theater Movement," in *New York's Yiddish Theater: From the Bowery to Broadway,* ed. Edna Nahshon (New York: Columbia University Press, 2016), 150–173.
30 A footnote to the synopsis of Act Four has it as "Maximilian Hurwitz. Playbill for the Yiddish Art Theatre's production of 'The Chalk Circle.' " The synopsis has been translated by Steven Lasky and is available on the website of the Museum of the Yiddish Theatre (courtesy of YIVO), ttp://www.museumoffamilyhistory.com/moyt/pih/chalk-circle.htm.
31 Maximilian Horowitz (Hurwitz?), program notes for "Der krayd tsirkl," production in Philadelphia, 1926, trans. Steven Lasky, Museum of the Yiddish Theatre.

Despite Horowitz's assertion, Henschke was not Jewish, although because of his political views and the fact that he had been married to a Jewish woman, the Nazis outlawed his work after 1933.[32]

Horowitz's claim that the play presents an accurate depiction of "the East" suggests that a big draw for a Yiddish audience of 1925 and 1926 would have been curiosity about East Asia, particularly China and Japan. The good judge's solution of the chalk circle is Solomonic: Like the biblical King Solomon, who devises a test to determine which of two women is the real mother of a baby, the judge threatens to cut the child in two; the false mother says, "divide it," while the real mother says, "let her have the child," to save her child's life.[33] Following Klabund's play, the synopsis of Halpern's translation states that Halpern changed the emphasis from exalting the fair and honest judge Pao to exposing the messiness of human relations – and the role of chance, luck, and coincidence in resolving injustice, rather than the reason and clarity of a just authority (like Pao, or like King Solomon). This transformation from the Chinese play's restoration of social order to the capriciousness of luck is what makes both the German and the Yiddish translations of Li Qianfu's play modern.

What would have drawn Moyshe Leyb Halpern to translate Klabund's expressionist version of a medieval Chinese play about justice? It is likely that Halpern's initial motivation to translate the play was practical – translation for the Yiddish theater would have been a way to earn money in 1925, and a commission from Maurice Schwartz's Yiddish Art Theater would have assured the translator that his words would contribute to a production of the highest quality.[34] An artist and peripatetic poet, Halpern was always scrambling to make a living to support his wife, Reyzele Barron, and son, Isaac (Ying) Halpern. The eight years Halpern had spent in Vienna, where he was sent at age twelve by his father from his hometown (Zlochev, Galicia) for an apprenticeship in commercial art, made him well-

---

32 Sander L. Gilman, "Klabund (Alfred Henschke) 4 November 1890–14 August 1928," in James N. Hardin, ed., *German Fiction Writers, 1885–1913* (Detroit, MI: Gale Research, 1988), 1:269–275, accessed April 25, 2021, https://babel.hathitrust.org/cgi/pt?id=uc1.32106020063944&view=1up&seq=275&q1=Klabund.

Gilman states that Klabund/Henschke was "married to a Jew," but nowhere suggests that Henschke, himself, was Jewish. I have been unable to locate online Henschke's birth or death records, or his grave in Krosno Odrzańskie, any of which could verify his religious origins.

33 I Kings 3:26–27: "[26] Then spoke the woman whose the living child was unto the king, for her heart yearned upon her son, and she said: 'Oh, my lord, give her the living child, and in no wise slay it.' But the other said: 'It shall be neither mine nor thine; divide it.' [27] Then the king answered and said: 'Give her the living child, and in no wise slay it: she is the mother thereof.'"

34 Edna Nahshon, "Maurice Schwartz and the Yiddish Art Theater Movement," 154.

prepared to translate Klabund's play. By the time Halpern returned to Zlochev in 1907, at age twenty-one, he had developed an interest in German literature, sitting in on university classes to read the classics, frequenting cafés with young writers and artists, and writing his own poems in German.[35] It was upon his return to Zlochev that Halpern was exposed to Yiddish literature and decided to write in Yiddish. In August 1908, he attended the Czernowitz Yiddish language conference, organized by Nathan Birnbaum, and left for the United States. By 1925, Halpern had previously proven his abilities as a translator from German through his contributions to the multi-volume Yiddish translation of the works of Heinrich Heine (New York, 1918). His first book of Yiddish poetry, *In nyu york* [In New York], had been published in 1919. In 1924, Halpern's second poetry collection, *Di goldene pave* [The golden peacock], appeared in Cleveland.[36] From 1922 to 1926, Halpern was employed as a writer by the Communist daily newspaper, *Di frayhayt* [Freedom], but after a political falling-out with the editorial board, he struggled to earn a living.[37] The opportunity to translate Klabund's play for the Yiddish Art Theater offered Halpern immediate income, the possibility of future jobs, and an expanded audience.

Horowitz's synopsis of Halpern's Yiddish translation leaves out the poetry of both the Chinese original and of Klabund's rendition, and the songs that serve different purposes in the medieval original and in the modern rendition. However, it is not just the poetry that is missing from the Yiddish version of *Der krayd tsirkl*, but, in fact, the Yiddish text itself. It seems that the play was never published, and I have not yet located a copy of the script that the actors used in their several productions, although I have looked in a number of archives and collections. My search will continue, in part because Moyshe Leyb Halpern was one of the truly great Yiddish modernist poets. His irreverent wit and merciless satirical weaponry, expressed through a perfect mastery of lyric and narrative poetry, call out for the discovery of his rendition of Klabund's satirical and lyrical German of *The Chalk Circle*. If I find the text, I will examine how Halpern remasters Klabund's German into a Yiddish that the great actors Maurice Schwartz, Bella Bellarina, Ben Zion

---

35 Ruth Wisse, *A Little Love in Big Manhattan: Two Yiddish Poets* (Cambridge, MA: Harvard University Press, 1988), 168–203 and 76–79. See also Kathryn Hellerstein, introduction to *In New York: A Selection*, by Moyshe Leyb Halpern (Philadelphia: Jewish Publication Society, 1982), xi–xxv.
36 Moyshe Leyb Halpern, *Di goldene pave: lider* (Cleveland, 1924).
37 Julian Levinson, "Moyshe-Leyb Halpern," Recovering Yiddish Culture in Los Angeles, part of Mapping Jewish Los Angeles, accessed April 25, 2021, http://scalar.usc.edu/hc/recovering-yiddish-culture-in-los-angeles/moyshe-leyb-halpern. Ruth Wisse, *A Little Love in Big Manhattan*, 168–203.

Katz, and others in the Yiddish Art Theater Troupe could perform to entertain and instruct their audiences in New York, Philadelphia, and elsewhere.[38]

Although Li Qianfu's drama is indisputably a product of its historical moment in fourteenth-century Yuan dynasty China, its political conflict and human dilemmas are so universal that the play has lent itself to expressing the conflicts and dilemmas of diverse Western cultures across the subsequent six centuries. Indeed, the device that determines the just outcome in Li Qianfu's play – that is, the chalk circle devised by the righteous Governor Pao – echoes King Solomon's threatening sword in the ancient text in the Hebrew Bible. Both are created as a means to determine who is the true mother of a disputed child. What makes the play so apt for adaptation are the interwoven stories of side-tracked romantic love, forced marriage and sex, childbirth and birthright, unequal and unfair application of power in social hierarchy, the oppression of girls and women, the role of fate, and the ultimate assertion of moral decency. The twentieth-century versions of Li Qianfu's play in German and Yiddish may be explained according to one model of translation theory.

This theory posits a spectrum that places the domestication of a text at one end and the foreignization at the other. Lawrence Venuti develops this model to argue that the "fluency" of domesticating translation, while creating a readable and approachable work in the target language, makes the translator invisible and erases both the translator's artistry and the otherness of the original work.[39] Domestication pulls the original text as fully into the target language as possible, all but erasing its cultural distinctiveness. Foreignization leaves the original's linguistic and cultural otherness as close to intact as possible within the target language, thus transforming the target language into something that itself seems foreign to its native readers. Reading a foreignized translation reminds readers, through the disruption of their own idiom, that languages are continually chang-

---

38 On December 29, 2020, I searched Yiddish Stage Resources on the website of Digital Yiddish Theatre Project (https://web.uwm.edu/yiddish-stage/resources) without finding Halpern's Yiddish *Der krayd tsirkl*: Yiddish Language Playscripts, Library of Congress, http://lcweb2.loc.gov/ammem/vshtml/vsyid.html; Index to Yiddish Plays, Dorot Division, New York Public Library, https://docs.google.com/spreadsheets/d/1j2d2ds5y2eFlEEV4Z-gzwIHsqmqlEXcI6IqO8OKR-BN8/pubhtml; *The Lawrence Marwick Collection of Copyrighted Yiddish Plays at the Library of Congress: An Annotated Bibliography*, by Zachary M. Baker with the assistance of Bonnie Sohn (Washington, D.C.: Library of Congress, 2004), https://www.loc.gov/rr/amed/marwick/marwick-bibliography.pdf; and the Spielberg Digital Yiddish Library, Yiddish Book Center, https://archive.org/details/nationalyiddishbookcenter?and%5B%5D=Klabund&sin.

39 Lawrence Venuti, *The Translator's Invisibility: A History of Translation* (Abingdon-on-Thames, UK: Routledge, 1995, 2008), 1–42.

14 Yiddish Translations of Chinese Poetry and Theater in 1920s New York — 245

Figure 14.1: "Scenes from 'The Chalk Circle,'" Yiddish *Forverts*, New York, January 10, 1926, 21. (Image courtesy of the Museum of the City of New York.)

ing, flowing constantly against each other, and that reading a translation pulls the reader into that flux. This dualism of domestication and foreignization applies to the Yiddish translations of Chinese literature in the 1920s.

The most famous and extreme example of the domestication in translation and adaptation of Li Qianfu's *Chalk Circle* is by German playwright and poet Bertolt Brecht, who wrote *The Caucasian Chalk Circle* in 1944 and 1945, during the six years of his American exile from Nazi Germany.[40] Commissioned by a Hollywood film star, Luisa Rainer, as a vehicle for her own Broadway appearance, Brecht composed a completely new version adapted from his friend and fellow actor and writer Klabund's 1925 German play.[41] According to scholar James K. Lyon, Brecht utilized many elements of popular American theater and film in his play to appeal to an American audience, including, in Brecht's own words, "certain elements of the older American theatre which excelled in burlesque and shows," or rather, "the American musical and vaudeville [which] contained 'certain primitive epic devices.'"[42] The play never made it to Broadway, but premiered in 1948 at Carleton College in Northfield, Minnesota. It was also performed later that year at the Hedgerow Theatre in Philadelphia, but was not produced again until the 1960s.[43] Yet Brecht's play is the most famous example of how Li Qianfu's drama lent itself to twentieth-century adaptation. Brecht creates a double narrative, setting the frame story among the bombed ruins of two Russian collective farms in the Caucasus Mountains in 1944, during a land dispute, and placing the central story, drawn from Klabund's version of Li Qianfu, in the same location, but during the tenth century, in the midst of the Persian wars.[44] The play unfolds the medieval tale of two women laying claim to a child: Grusha is the kitchen maid who rescues the governor's baby son after the infant's greedy, aristocratic mother forgets him while fleeing the insurrectionists. After Grusha's virtuous soldier-suitor is called off to battle, and she flees into the mountains with the baby, she is forced into marriage with an inappropriate husband in order to escape social censure for claiming to be an unwed mother. These events occur in the chaos of a society overrun by its own rebellious army returning from the Persian war. Azdak, the village clerk, is thrust into the role of judge who literally "sits on the law," commanding "the Statute Book"[45] to be placed beneath him on the judge's chair, and meting out a

---

[40] John Willett and Ralph Manheim, introduction to *The Caucasian Chalk Circle*, by Bertolt Brecht, trans. James and Tania Stern with W. H. Auden (London: Methuen Drama, A & C Black, 2000), vii.
[41] James K. Lyon, "Elements of American Theatre and Film in Brecht's *Caucasian Chalk Circle*," *Modern Drama* 42, no. 2 (1999): 238, Gale Literature Resource Center, accessed April 25, 2021, https://link.gale.com/apps/doc/A58575770/LitRC?u=upenn_main&sid=LitRC&xid=f90b32d6.
[42] Lyon, "Elements of American Theatre and Film in Brecht's *Caucasian Chalk Circle*," 239.
[43] Lyon, "Elements of American Theatre and Film in Brecht's *Caucasian Chalk Circle*," 243.
[44] Lyon, "Elements of American Theatre and Film in Brecht's *Caucasian Chalk Circle*," 244. Bertolt Brecht, *The Caucasian Chalk Circle*, 2–8, 9–97.
[45] Brecht, *The Caucasian Chalk Circle*, 87.

topsy-turvy justice that turns out ultimately to be the righteous justice of the chalk circle. What Brecht achieved with his play – formally, thematically, and aesthetically – was something beyond the limitations of the Broadway hit he'd been commissioned to write, according to James K. Lyon. Brecht's epic play was stylized, and a "Singer" narrated the opening of each scene. As Lyon suggests, however, Brecht's play "went in directions different from those he intended,"[46] for its focus on a solitary woman advocating for a child, without a partner or societal approval, speaks to our own emotions and social and legal concerns in the twenty-first century.

Brecht's brilliant 1945 rendering of Li Qianfu's fourteenth-century *The Story of the Chalk Circle* may suggest what Moyshe Leyb Halpern might have done in his Yiddish version twenty years earlier for the Yiddish Art Theater. Both versions are stylized according to a particular locale. Brecht transported the narrative from China to the Caucasus, in modern Soviet and medieval Persian wartimes. In contrast, Halpern's Yiddish Art Theater version retained the medieval Chinese setting and was staged in an "Oriental" mode, as we can see from the photographs in the *Forverts* broadside, which show actors in distinctly Chinese brocade costumes, wigs, and makeup, on-stage sets of curved roofs and pagodas, the stock images of old-time Chinese architecture. For example, one photo, captioned, "In Chang's Tea-house: Prince Pao falls in love with the orphan Chang Hai'Tang," shows a large structure on stage right with three curtained chambers; in each chamber, there sits a prosperous man who is waiting for a concubine. Center stage stands a narrow pagoda on which hangs a vertical banner with large Chinese lettering, and stage left is a half-visible half-circle gate leading out of the courtyard. The Prince and another figure stand before the pagoda, regarding Chang Hai'Tang, a slender woman in a white robe and an enormous coiffure, who faces away from them.[47] Without the script, we have no way of knowing how Halpern's Yiddish translation conveyed the human story of Klabund's version of Li Qianfu through the sensory cues of medieval China to a New York immigrant audience, or how that audience responded.

Yet even in the absence of Halpern's actual Yiddish words, we can hazard a guess as to what kinds of things Halpern might have done as a translator, by looking briefly at translations by one of Halpern's contemporaries. In my recent study of Yiddish translations of classical Chinese poet Li Bai, I have discovered that Meyer Shtiker, a nineteen-year-old poet associated with the Yunge movement, rendered his beautiful Yiddish versions from a 1922 New York translation of medieval Chinese texts into English by a Japanese immigrant to America,

---

46 Lyon, "Elements of American Theatre and Film in Brecht's *Caucasian Chalk Circle*," 244–245.
47 *Forverts*, "Scenes from the 'Chalk Circle,'" January 10, 1926, 21, http://jpress.org.il/Olive/APA/NLI/?action=tab&tab=browse&pub=FRW#panel=documenthttp://www.museumoffamily-history.com/moyt/pih/chalk-circle.htm.

Shigeyoshi Obata. In the process of re-translating Obata's English translations of Li Bai into Yiddish, Meyer Shtiker reconfigured Li Bai's eighth-century Chinese verse into an expression of the concerns of a Jewish immigrant to New York – dislocation, loss of home, separation from a beloved, and fear of abandonment.

Most notably, Shtiker placed four distinct and unrelated poems by Li Bai together into a sequence as a monologue spoken by a deserted wife. This act of selection and compilation makes the Chinese lyrics into a narrative that would have been instantly recognizable to Jewish immigrants to America: the story of the *agune*, or 'abandoned wife.' The *agune*, a woman in sexual, legal, and social limbo, was a common predicament for immigrant wives. She was frequently invoked by modern Yiddish and Hebrew writers to serve a variety of symbolic or allegorical purposes. By joining together four of Li Bai's poems of longing to form a Jewish immigrant narrative, Shtiker both Judaized the Chinese poems and infused the familiar Jewish story with a new kind of beauty through the Chinese imagery of nature.

Here is Meyer Shtiker's 1925/1926 translation of four poems by Li Bai (Li Tai Po):

Di froy redt

I.
Ven du bist do geven iz ful geven dos hoyz mit blumen.
Itster az du bist nito – pustevet dos leydike gelenger.
Der oygeshtikter tsudek ligt tsunoyfgeviklt afn bet
Ikh ken nit shlofn. Dray yor shoyn az du bist nito.
Der reyakh, vos iz farblibn hinter dir, farfolgt tif alts.

Der reyakh blondzshet um, nor vu bistu gelibter?
Ikh krekhts – gele bleter faln fun di tsvaygn.
Ikh veyn,--der toy blistshet vays afn grinem mokh.

II.
Dos vaser – bloy.
Levone – klor un reyn.
Vayse bushikes flien in levone-shayn.
Her! Di meydlekh kloybn
Vaser-kashtanes fartrakht,
Un geyen zingendik aheym
In der shtiler nakht.

III.
Dos groz fun Yen vakst grin un lang,
Un in Tshin hengen di moylber tsvayglekh bay der tir,
Atsind az mayn harts iz tsebrokhn un krank –
Trakhstu khotsh, mayn tayerer, fun kumen tsurik tsu mir?

O, nit gebetener un fremder frilingsvint –
Nit shpil zikh mit di zaydene forhenglekh atsind!

IV.
Opgeshaydt fun dir zits ikh aleyn
Un klog unter di himlen fun Yeh-lang.
In mayn hoyz balaykhtn fun levone-shayn
Kumt zeltn a shlikhes on fun dir.

In friling flien vilde genz keyn tsofn
Un shtelen op zikh bay mayn tir.
Un kumen shpeter tsurik aher –
Ober nit keyn brivl fun Yu-tshang.

* * * *

His Wife Speaks

I.
When you were here, the house was full of flowers.
Now that you are not – the empty bed lies waste.
The embroidered coverlet lies rolled up on the bed
I cannot sleep. Three years already that you've been gone.
The scent that lingered after you still torments me.

Your scent wafts around, but where are you, beloved?
I sigh – yellow leaves fall from the branches.
I weep – the dew gleams white on the green moss.

II.
The water – blue.
Moon – clear and pure.
White storks fly in the moonlight.
Listen! Dreamily, the girls gather
Water-chestnuts
And singing, walk home
In the quiet night.

III.
The grass of Yen grows green and long,
And in Tshin mulberry branches hang by the door.
Now that my heart is broken and sick –
Do you think, though, my dear one, of coming back to me?
Oh, uninvited and alien spring-breeze –
Do not play with the silken curtains now!

IV.
Separated from you, I sit alone
And lament under the skies of Yeh-Lang.
In my house illuminated by moonlight
A message seldom arrives from you.

In the spring, wild geese fly north
And settle by my door.
And later return there –
But no note from Yu-Tshang.[48]

I will summarize the narrative implied by Shtiker's compilation and translation. In Part I, the wife speaks to her husband, who has been gone for more than three years. She recalls their home as "full of flowers" when he was present and contrasts it with its current desolation: the bed is empty; the embroidered coverlet is rolled up, unused. Unable to sleep, the speaker is tormented by the scent of her absent husband, which still lingers. Night becomes morning, and the season changes from summer to autumn, as leaves turn yellow and fall. The image of dew lying white on green moss suggests winter's approach and the speaker's own encroaching old age. In Part II, the speaker describes a different night scene. This one is dream-like and unburdened by the emotions of Part I. Here, the blue water and pure moonlight provide a setting for the speaker to observe white storks flying past and to hear the songs of young girls out harvesting water chestnuts as they return home. She does not address her absent husband in this section, but rather seems to sublimate her sorrow into the beauty that insomnia allows her to perceive. However, in Part III, the speaker's longing returns in full force. She invokes the names of places: Yen, where green grass grows tall, and Tsin, where mulberry branches blossom with their male and female blooms. It is not clear if Yen and Tsin are located near the speaker or whether they are far-off places that she remembers. In this burgeoning season, the speaker plaintively asks her still-absent husband if he ever thinks of returning to her. As if in response to her invitation, the spring breeze intrudes, "uninvited and alien," stirring the curtain and reminding the speaker that the breeze is not an answer from her husband. In Part IV, yet another year has passed; it is once again a spring night. The speaker is still alone, "[s]eparated from you," and still weeping. In the moonlight, she continues to wait for the infrequent messages her husband sends. The second stanza summarizes in four lines the passing of time from spring, when the wild geese fly north, pausing by the speaker's door, to autumn, when the geese fly south again.

---

[48] Meyer Shtiker, trans., "Di froy redt" [His wife speaks], by Li Tai Po (Li Bai), *Shriftn* 5, nos. 7–8 (1925/1926): 13–14. English translation by Kathryn Hellerstein.

In all that time, "[n]o note from Yu-Tshang." Two names are invoked in Part IV: Yeh-Lang, where the speaker's house is located, and where she laments; and Yu-Tshang, which refers either to the place where her husband has gone, or to her husband himself. These two Chinese names, along with the two place names in Part III – Yen and Tsin – imprint the Yiddish poem, as well as my English translation, with the foreignness that reminds readers that they are reading a translation from Chinese, though indirectly, mediated by another translation. At the same time, the narrative that Shtiker creates by stitching together into a dramatic monologue Li Bai's four discrete poems (which were not originally associated with a female persona) is that of a deserted wife, an *agune*, a Jewish woman waiting in legal and sexual limbo.

By transforming medieval Chinese poetry into twentieth-century Yiddish through Shigeyoshi Obata's English translation, Shtiker made the foreign familiar, the medieval contemporary, and Chinese concerns Jewish. Shtiker, like the other translators in the 1925/1926 issue of *Shriftn*, at once expanded the kinds of texts available to Yiddish readers and imported a poetics to enhance the Yiddish poet's toolbox. Yet, as my colleague in Yiddish studies, Jeffrey Shandler, asked me recently in conversation, of these Yiddish translations that, I argued, make Chinese poems appear to be Jewish, "Is it impossible to engage the diversity of world cultures through Yiddish absent a Yiddish cultural sensibility?"[49] In other words, do Yiddish translations of Chinese literature inevitably render the originals Jewish? How do the forces of domestication and foreignization contend within a Yiddish translation of a Chinese text, and how is a balance of these forces achieved? One could also reverse the question and ask whether and to what extent Chinese translations of Yiddish literature render the originals Chinese. Is it even possible not to domesticate a text to some degree when translating?

From the reading of Meyer Shtiker's translation, we can imagine what Moyshe Leyb Halpern may well have done in his translation of Li Qianfu's play. The female protagonist, the second wife Chang Hai-Tang in both Li Qianfu's fourteenth-century drama, *The Circle of Chalk*, and Klabund's 1924 German adaptation *Der Kraide-Kreis*, is abandoned, betrayed, and abused – if not by her murdered husband, then by the First Wife Frau Ma (Mrs. Ma). This fact encourages me to speculate that Halpern might well have employed the Yiddish/Hebrew term *agune* in his Yiddish translation of Klabund, drawing out themes that would have spoken directly to the Jewish immigrant audience of the Yiddish Art Theater. In the same way that Brecht transformed Klabund's translation of Li Qianfu's *The Circle of Chalk* to speak to the moment in 1945 America, so I argue that Halpern's vanished script may well have

---

49 Email conversation with Jeffrey Shandler, "Yiddish Chinoiserie," April 26, 2018.

played to the concerns of immigrant Jews in the mid-1920s, in theme and tone, if not in costume and set, much as Meyer Shtiker's translations transformed Li Bai's poems into laments of an abandoned wife. I contend, as well, that the *agune*, deserted by her husband and thus perpetually suspended between the status of married and available, was the embodiment for these men, these Jewish immigrant poets, of their own state of suspension between two worlds, between languages and cultures.

References

Almi, A. (pseudonym of Elihu-Khayim Sheps). *Di Khinezsishe filozofye un poezye*. New York: Maks N. Mayzel, 1925.

"Atlantic Garden, Imperial Japanese Troupe No. 2, Der prints fun khine," Theater advertisement in the *Jewish Morning Journal*, March 3, 1911, 7. Accessed January 27, 2021. https://www.nli.org.il/en/newspapers/tjm/1911/03/03/01/?e=-------en-20--1--img-txIN%7ctxTI--------------1.

Baker, Zachary M., with the assistance of Bonnie Sohn. *The Lawrence Marwick Collection of Copyrighted Yiddish Plays at the Library of Congress: An Annotated Bibliography*. Washington, D.C.: Library of Congress, 2004. https://www.loc.gov/rr/amed/marwick/marwickbibliography.pdf.

Brecht, Bertolt. *The Caucasian Chalk Circle*, translated by James and Tania Stern with W. H. Auden. London: Methuen Drama, A & C Black, 2000.

Eber, Irene. "Martin Buber and Chinese Thought," in *Wegen und Kreuzungen* (2004), 23–25. Reprinted in Irene Eber, *Jews in China: Cultural Conversations, Changing Perceptions*, ed. Kathryn Hellerstein (University Park, PA: Pennsylvania State University Press, 2020), 201–222.

Forverts. "Scenes from the 'Chalk Circle.'" January 10, 1926. 21. National Library of Israel. http://jpress.org.il/Olive/APA/NLI/?action=tab&tab=browse&pub=FRW#panel=documenthttp://www.museumoffamilyhistory.com/moyt/pih/chalk-circle.htm.

Gilman, Sander L. "Klabund (Alfred Henschke) 4 November 1890–14 August 1928," in James N. Hardin, ed., *German Fiction Writers, 1885–1913*, 1:269–275. Detroit, MI: Gale Research, 1988. Accessed 25 April 2021. https://babel.hathitrust.org/cgi/pt?id=uc1.32106020063944&view=1up&seq=275&q1=Klabund.

Halpern, Moyshe Leyb. *Di goldene pave: lider*. Cleveland, OH: Farlag Grupe Yidish, 1924.

Hellerstein, Kathryn. Introduction to *In New York: A Selection*, by Moyshe Leyb Halpern, translated by Kathryn Hellerstein. Philadelphia: Jewish Publication Society, 1982.

Horowitz, Maximilian (Hurwitz?). Program notes for "Der krayd tsirkl," production in Philadelphia, 1926. Translated by Steven Lasky, on the Museum of the Yiddish Theatre website (courtesy of YIVO). Accessed July 6, 2021. http://www.museumoffamilyhistory.com/moyt/pih/chalk-circle.htm.

Lasky, Steven. "'The Chalk Circle,' by Klabund." Museum of the Yiddish Theatre. Accessed July 6, 2021. http://www.museumoffamilyhistory.com/moyt/pih/chalk-circle.htm.

Laver, James. Introduction to *The Circle of Chalk: A Play in Five Acts Adapted from the Chinese by Klabund*, translated by James Laver. London: William Heinemann, 1929. viii–ix.

Levin, Neil W. "A malka af peysekh (A Queen for Passover): Louis Gilrod." *Great Songs of the American Yiddish Stage*, Volume 13, Milkin Archive. Accessed January 28, 2021. https://www.milkenarchive.org/music/volumes/view/great-songs-of-the-american-yiddish-stage/work/a-malke-af-peysekh/.

Levin, Neil W. "Louis Gilrod (1879–1930)." Milken Archive. Accessed January 28, 2021. https://www.milkenarchive.org/artists/view/louis-gilrod/.

Levinson, Julian. "Moyshe-Leyb Halpern." Mapping Jewish Los Angeles: Recovering Yiddish Culture in Los Angeles. Last updated December 7, 2015. Accessed April 25, 2021. http://scalar.usc.edu/hc/recovering-yiddish-culture-in-los-angeles/moyshe-leyb-halpern.

Lyon, James K. "Elements of American Theatre and Film in Brecht's *Caucasian Chalk Circle*." *Modern Drama* 42, no. 2 (1999): 238–246. Gale Literature Resource Center. Accessed April 25, 2021. https://link.gale.com/apps/doc/A58575770/LitRC?u=upenn_main&sid=LitRC&xid=f90b32d6.

Nahshon, Edna. "Maurice Schwartz and the Yiddish Art Theater Movement." In *New York's Yiddish Theater: From the Bowery to Broadway*, edited by Edna Nahshon, 150–173. New York: Columbia University Press, 2016.

Rubenstein, Rachel. *Members of the Tribe: Native America in the Jewish Imagination*. Detroit, MI: Wayne State University Press, 2010.

Sandrow, Nahma. " 'A Little Letter to Mamma': Traditions in Yiddish Vaudeville," *American Popular Entertainment: Papers and Proceedings of the Conference of the History of American Popular Entertainment*, edited by Myron Matlow (Westport, CT, and London: Greenwood Press, 1977), 87–95; 92.

Sandrow, Nahma. *Vagabond Stars: A World History of Yiddish Theater*. Syracuse, NY: Syracuse University Press, 1977, 1996.

Schwartz, Jean and Jerome, W. M. "Chinatown My Chinatown." New York: Jerome H. Remick, 1910. *Historic Sheet Music Collection* no. 1346. Accessed February 7, 2021. https://digitalcommons.conncoll.edu/sheetmusic/1346.

Seligman, Scott D. *Tong Wars: The Untold Story of Vice, Money, and Murder in New York's Chinatown*. New York: Viking, 2016.

Shriftn: A Zamlbukh 8–9, sec. 9 (of 10, each numbered separately) (1925/1926): 1–21.

Shtiker, Meyer, trans. "Di froy redt" [The wife speaks], by Li Tai Po (Li Bai), in *Shriftn* 5, nos. 7–8 (1925/1926): 13–14. English translation by Kathryn Hellerstein.

Venuti, Lawrence. *The Translator's Invisibility: A History of Translation*. Abingdon-on-Thames, UK: Routledge, 1995, 2008. 1–42.

Willet, John and Ralph Manheim. Introduction to *The Caucasian Chalk Circle*, by Bertolt Brecht, translated by James and Tania Stern with W. H. Auden. London: Methuen Drama, A. & C. Black, 2000.

Williams, Gwyn. Preface to *The Story of the Circle of Chalk: A Drama from the Old Chinese*, translated by Frances Hume from the French of Stanislas Julien, with illustrations by John Buckland-Wright. London: Rodale Press, 1953.

Wisse, Ruth. *A Little Love in Big Manhattan: Two Yiddish Poets*. Cambridge, MA: Harvard University Press, 1988.

Witt, Bernard, trans. *Khinezishe legenden*. Yiddish translation of *Some Chinese Ghosts*, by Lafcadio Hearn (1887). New York: n.p., 1930.

Musical Recordings

Fleischer, Dave, dir. "Chinatown, My Chinatown." Released by National Telefilm Associates in 1929. https://www.youtube.com/watch?v=VjFu5XwCVyI.

Gillham, Art, recording pianist. "Chinatown, My Chinatown." Andy Sannella (clarinet, alto sax, flute, guitar, and effects), Murray Kellner (violin), and Rube Bloom (second piano). Recorded January 11, 1928. Accessed July 6, 2021. https://www.youtube.com/watch?v=y0TM1n0OENw.

Jolson, Al, vocalist. "Chinatown, My Chinatown." Released by National Telefilm Associates in 1929. https://genius.com/Al-jolson-chinatown-my-chinatown-lyrics.

The Mills Brothers, vocalists. "Chinatown, My Chinatown." Accessed July 6, 2021. https://www.youtube.com/watch?v=sW1hpWof-dE.

Katz, Mickey, vocalist. "Chiny Town." Parody of "Chinatown, My Chinatown," by Jean Schwarz and William Jerome. Capitol (1419). Released in 1951. Digitized by the Kahle/Austin Foundation. https://archive.org/details/78_chiny-town_mickey-katz-and-his-orchestra-mickey-katz-jean-schwartz-william-jerome_gbia0070726a.

Katz, Mickey, vocalist. "Chiny Town," B side of "Gehakte Mambo," Capitol Records, 78 RPM. Florida State University Recorded Sound Archives. Accessed February 7, 2021. https://rsa.fau.edu/album/2672.

The American Quartet with Billy Murray. "Chinatown, My Chinatown." Recorded in 1914. Library of Congress National Jukebox. Accessed 7 February 2021. https://www.loc.gov/item/jukebox-11359/.

Bao Anruo
15 Enemy or Friend: The Image of China in Yiddish Newspapers during the Russo-Japanese War (1904–1905)

At the end of the nineteenth century, motivated by national interest, two of China's neighboring countries, Tsarist Russia and Japan, both turned their attention toward the abundant resources and vast territory of the northeastern region of China: Manchuria, which included the three eastern provinces of Liaoning, Jilin, and Heilongjiang and covered a region of about 36,310 square miles.[1] Though the two countries both coveted the rich natural resources and fertile lands of Manchuria, Russia had a specific aspiration of its own: to gain control of the Far East and the warm-water ports in Manchuria. In the Russian Far East, the only port Russia had was in Vladivostok, which could only be used in summer. However, before Russia could realize its intention of occupying the warm-water ports in the Liaotung Peninsula (辽东半岛), Japan obtained control of the Liaotung Peninsula through the Treaty of Shimonoseki after winning the First Sino-Japanese War (1894–1895). This action severely threatened Russia's objective. With the help of France and Germany, Russia forced Japan to return the Liaotung Peninsula to China in 1895. In this way, Russia positioned itself as a protector of Chinese territorial sovereignty and secretly signed the Convention for the Lease of the Liaotung Peninsula, in which Russia claimed a twenty-five-year lease on Port Arthur (旅顺) from the Chinese government. Moreover, from 1897 to 1903, Russia also built a railroad from Harbin (哈尔滨) to Port Arthur through Mukden (奉天, now 沈阳) in order to strengthen Russian control of Manchuria and to transport cargo through the region. In 1900, under the pretext of protecting Russian consultants and treasury in China during the outbreak of the Boxer Rebellion (义和团运动), Russia sent over 200,000 troops to Manchuria and, after the rebellion was suppressed, kept over 100,000 soldiers there. This occupation greatly threatened the interests of other invasive powers – including Japan. In 1903, Russia refused to withdraw its army from Manchuria as required by a treaty that had been signed with the Chinese government in April 1902. Japan, displeased, sent an emissary to negotiate with Russia. However, the negotiations broke down, and war began.

---

[1] *Los Angeles Herald*, "Size of Manchuria," April 10, 1904, accessed October 6, 2019, https://cdnc.ucr.edu/cgi-bin/cdnc?a=d&d=LAH19040410.2.381.21&e=-------en--20--1--txt-txIN--------1.

https://doi.org/10.1515/9783110683943-019

This costly war between Russia and Japan,[2] with active participation from the other Western powers, was actually a prelude to the two world wars in the twentieth century.[3] Apart from these foreign powers, which benefited greatly from the Russo-Japanese War, another country should be considered: China.[4] During this war, the Empire of China was ruled by the Manchu, whose weak government and army were hardly able to protect the Chinese people and territory from invasion. Although the Empire of China was a third party and did not actively participate in the war, it was inevitably involved and tragically suffered the greatest losses. According to a study that adds up the losses in official counts performed by the Chinese government shortly after the war, the Russo-Japanese War took over tens of thousands of innocent Chinese lives and caused an economic loss of over 40 million *liang* of silver.[5]

No one doubts the terrible Chinese losses from the Russo-Japanese War, or from other wars from the mid-nineteenth through the mid-twentieth centuries. But these wars, especially the British invasion from 1840 to 1842 during the First Opium War, forced China, a culturally and geographically isolated country, to become involved in the world system.[6] This attracted the attention of other nations and peoples, including the Yiddish-speaking Ashkenazi Jews, who represented two completely different images of China in their newspapers during the Russo-Japanese War.

---

2 Ian Nish, *The Origins of the Russo-Japanese War* (London and New York: Longman, 1985), 2: "The Russo-Japanese war was an important war of the twentieth century. Although it was confined to two countries, it was significant because of the vast number of those who took part in it: The Russian forces in the area starting at 100,000 troops and growing in 1905 to 1,300,000 and the Japanese starting with 300,000 and growing in 1905 to roughly triple that strength. The war was equally important because of the bitterness of the fighting and the toll it took of the manhood of both countries: the lengthy siege of Port Arthur ended with a loss of 58,000 killed to the victorious Japanese and a loss of 31,000 to the Russians, while the immense battle of Mukden is estimated to have caused casualties of 85,000 to the Russians as against 70,000 to the Japanese."
3 Nish, *Origins of the Russo-Japanese War*, 2: "Even if the Russo-Japanese war was not a world war, it had repercussions throughout the world. Though the outside powers were not belligerents, they were surely 'involved.'"
4 Although the Kingdom of Korea should also be taken into the picture, this article will not discuss the issue of Korea because its emphasis is on China and, at that time, the Kingdom of Korea was also a tributary state of China. Nish, *Origins of the Russo-Japanese War*, 12.
5 李刚:《日俄战争给中国带来的损失问题研究》,河北大学硕士论文，2008 年。Li Gang, "On the Losses of China in Russo-Japanese War," master's thesis, Hebei University, 2008.
6 宋炳辉:《弱小民族文学的译介与20世纪中国文学的民族意识》,复旦大学博士论文，2003 年，第1页。Song Binghui, "Translation of 'Weak Literature' and the National Consciousness of Chinese Literature in the Twentieth Century," PhD diss., Fudan University, 2003.

Why are Yiddish newspaper reports so important? In her monograph, *Making Jews Modern: The Yiddish and Ladino Press in the Russian and Ottoman Empires*, Sarah Abrevaya Stein discusses the function of newspapers in the Jewish world:

> (The newspapers) were by and large more accessible, and comprehensible than the weeklies and monthlies that preceded them. Further, not only did daily newspapers report on change, but they also served as barometers of the interests and predilections of readers.... While undoubtedly didactic at times, newspapers reimagined their readership by embracing women and men of all ages who were not necessarily well-educated, but who were interested in and who could find pragmatic benefits in the day's news. They seemed to signal a movement away from elite culture and toward a more popular culture.[7]

According to Stein, given the wide availability and affordability of Yiddish newspapers, they could be taken as an instant reflection of the masses' concern and curiosity vis-à-vis historical events as well as their own living situation. In other words, through the prism of newspaper reports about current events, some previously hidden aspects of Russian Ashkenazi Jewish self-understanding can be brought to light. This article will focus on the Jewish people's self-identification at the beginning of the twentieth century through the image of China in Yiddish newspapers published in the United States.

1 News Reports

According to the statistics on the Historical Jewish Press website, during the period of the Russo-Japanese War, 80 news reports mentioned China. These reports can be roughly divided into two categories: first, breaking news reports about the war; second, articles introducing China to a Yiddish readership. Though these articles were written in the same period, the attitudes towards China shown in them were surprisingly different – even diametrically opposed. Generally speaking, the news reports were indifferent, sometimes even hostile, while the introductory articles were milder, even admiring and friendly. Why this discrepancy? How did the Yiddish-speaking Jews view themselves through the prism of China?

The news reports depicted China only as a battlefield. Although their authors did notice the miserable living situation of innocent Chinese people, they did not show much if any sympathy. For instance, in a report titled "Getriben un geyogt"

---

7 Sarah Abrevaya Stein, *Making Jews Modern: The Yiddish and Ladino Press in the Russian and Ottoman Empire* (Bloomington: Indiana University Press, 2004), 5.

(געטריעבען און געיאגט) [Driven and driven away]⁸ published on May 10, 1904, in the newspaper *Di yidishe velt*,⁹ on the arrival of American warships in Niuchuang and the flight of Evgenii Alekseev from Mukden to Harbin, the author also described the actions and mindset of the local, non-military residents:

> Di sivil aynvoyner fun niu-tshwang tsiteren yetst far di khinezer banditen, velkhe zaynen zehr fil in yene gegenden un zey tsuloyfen masenvayz tsuzamen mit di miliyer.
>
> Di banditer hobn fernikhtet a shtik eyzenban tsvishen niu-tshwang, toshio un hartsheng. Es hert zikh, az der keybel tsvishen port arthur un tshifu iz obgeshnitn gevoren.¹⁰

Despite mentioning the local Chinese people's fear of the bandits (土匪), the author paid more attention to the destruction of a small part of the railway that belonged to Russia. In other words, compared to Russia's loss in China, the local residents' fear was nothing.

This article was far from alone in its indifference. In another news report, published in *Di yidishe velt* on May 30, 1904, and titled "Gezeyre uf korn" (גזרה אויף קארן) [Decree on rye],¹¹ the journalist began by describing a specific group of local bandits called *khon-huzen*, the 'red-bearded bandits'¹²: "... arbeten di khon-khuzen, khinezer banditen, tsu ferbitern dem lebn fun tsar's militer in di

---

8 "Getriben un geyogt," *Di yidishe velt*, May 10, 1904, 1.
9 "The Jewish World (Die Iddishe Welt)," Historical Jewish Press, accessed October 6, 2019, http://web.nli.org.il/sites/JPress/English/Pages/AllJPressPage.aspx?p=36: "The Jewish World (Die Iddishe Welt) is a Yiddish-language daily newspaper published in New York in the years 1902–1904."
10 "Getriben un geyogt": "The non-military inhabitants of Niuchuang are trembling now for the Chinese bandits, who are of enormous number in that area and run up to Masenveyz together with the troops. The bandits destroyed a little part of the iron-railway between Niuchuang, Toshio and Hartsheng. It is reported that the cable between Port Arthur and Tshifu was cut off." Except certain terms, all Yiddish translations are of the author's own.
11 *Di yidishe velt*, "Gezeyre uf korn," May 30, 1904, 2.
12 *Khon-huzen* 红胡子 means 'red beard' in Chinese; *huzi*, in a northeastern Chinese dialect, means both 'beard' and 'bandit.' According to some historical material, when this group of bandits pillaged, they would put on bizarre clothes and dye their beards red in order to hide their true appearance and identity. The predecessors of these bandits were the soldiers of Mao Wenlong (1576–1629), an admiral in charge of the navy in the Liaotung Gulf during the Ming dynasty (1368–1644); after he was killed, his seamen disembarked and became bandits. During the Russo-Japanese war, these red-beards took over dispersed territories in Manchuria, equipped themselves with guns and horses, and killed wealthy people to pillage money. Compared to the other bandits, the red-beards were stronger and more cruel. 边羽: "关东'红胡子'考辨", 载于《社会科学辑刊》, 1980 年 01 期, 第 116 页. Yu Bian, "The Origins of the Red-bearded Bandits in Kwantung," *Journal of Social Studies* 1 (1980): 116.

shtet, vos gefinen zikh nokh in rusishe hend."[13] The author saw only the threat posed by the red-bearded bandits to the Russian troops – not their destructive impact upon the local Chinese residents.

If this report were only about the relationship between the Russian troops and the local red-beards, there would have been no need to mention Chinese people in this report. But the Russian strategy of striking these bandits was closely relevant to the local Chinese peasants' lives. The report continued: "Der sheyne-lemeylekh admiral alekseiev hot aroysgegebn an order tsu di khinezer famers fun mandzhuria, dos zey zolen nit zeyen keyn korn oder andere tvues uf zeyere felder. Vayl di khon-khuzen behalten zikh in di korn felder ven di rusishe soldaten vilen zey khapen."[14] The Chinese must not sow rye or other grains in the fields so as to enable the Russian soldiers to catch the red-beards. In order to obey Russia's order, the local Chinese peasants had to stop cultivating their staple crops. What did they eat?

Heedless of this question, the author wrote: "Di rusishe armee in liaoyong hot erhalten orders tsu ferzeyen farsheydene sorten grinsen, um men zol hobn vos tsu esen. Ven ale esenvargen velen oysgeyn. Ot azoy kormet der tsar zayne 2 fisige beheymes mit groz befor men shlakhtet zey oys."[15] The first sentence mentions the Russian army's order to provide the local population with vegetables during famines; the second sentence explains the ultimate goal of the decree: to keep the people alive before they are slaughtered. Obviously, the "two-legged cattle" are a metaphor for the local people – the Tsar can slaughter them like animals. Moreover, although this news report does not mention these vegetables' origin or the reason to keep these cattle, these questions can be answered by consulting other historical materials.

In the spring of 1905, the local municipal Chinese governments of Manchuria promulgated an order regarding the Russian army's deployment: 铁路附近不必种高粱，玉米等类高枝粮食，以免作践，其余低矮之物，仍须照常播种。[16] From

---

13 "Gezeyre uf korn": ". . .the *khon-khuzen*, the Chinese bandits, work to make the life of the Tsar's troops miserable in the city, which finds itself in Russian hands."
14 "Gezeyre uf korn": "The king's minister Admiral Alekseev promulgated an order to the Chinese famers of Manchuria, that they should not sow any rye or other grains in their fields, because the red-bearded bandits hide themselves in the rye fields when the Russian soldiers try to catch them."
15 "Gezeyre uf korn": "The Russian army in Liaoyang had orders to provide different kinds of vegetables, so that the people would have something to eat when all the foodstuffs run out. In this way, the Tsar feeds his two-legged cattle with grass before they are slaughtered."
16 《增祺，廷杰关于日俄开战恐民废时晓谕乡民及时播种布告》，《日俄战争档案史料》，辽宁省档案馆编，辽宁古籍出版社，1995 年，第 313 页。"Zeng Qi, Ting Jie's Announcement about Informing Farmers to Cultivate in Case They Were Discouraged by the War," *Historical*

this order, we can see that the Russian army's deeds in Manchuria as depicted in *Di yidishe velt* were not an isolated case. In regards to the origin of their food, another Chinese source may offer an answer: 俄兵驻境实属堪怜，均将田苗蹂躏，谷稗喂马，所有各屯房间均被人占驻，竟将老幼逐出，所有衣饰、粮草、木器等物尽行烧毁......[17] It is evident that the Russian army's food supply was actually seized from local inhabitants. Although these inhabitants were allowed to plant vegetables, obviously, it was hard for them to get as much energy from crops. Both of these authors, who mentioned Chinese farmers in their reports, were probably aware of the miserable living situation of these poor famers. But they said nothing.

Indifferent to the suffering of the Chinese people, these reporters also distrusted China. This indicates a committed support for Russia. Although the materials discussed below were not originally written by Jewish writers but were instead reprinted and translated from other newspapers, their selection is indicative of the Jewish newspaper editors' attitude toward China. In a report titled "Khina vet zikh nit mishen" (כינא וועט זיך ניט מישען) [China will not get involved][18] published on March 16, 1904, in *Forverts* [The Forward],[19] the author voiced some skepticism of China's promise that it would not become involved in the war – skepticism that was arguably shared by the newspaper's Yiddish-speaking editors. This report was based on two sources, one from Paris and another from Washington. Both mentioned that China had made a promise of being neutral during the war, but both hinted that that promise might be broken. The report from Paris was translated into Yiddish as: "Der korespondent ober – meldet, az der oylem hot in dem keyn emune nit, un ale tseykhens vayzn, az khina vet nit

---

Materials of the Russo-Japanese War, compiled by the Liaoning Archive (Liaoning Ancient Books Publishing House, 1995), 313: "In order to avoid Russian trampling of crops, there is no need to plant high crops like broomcorn and maize near the railway; other short crops should be planted as usual." Except the place names, all Chinese translations in this article are the author's own.

17 《关于俄军在省城周围蹂躏田苗，拆毁房屋，奸淫搜掠等文件》,《日俄战争档案史料》, 辽宁省档案馆编, 辽宁古籍出版社, 1995 年, 第 355 页。"A Document about the Russian Army's Damage of Crops and Houses and Rapes around the Province's Capital City," *Historical Materials of the Russo-Japanese War*, 355: "[The Chinese people who are living] in the places where the Russian army was stationed were pitiful. The Russians trampled crops, fed horses with unhusked rice, took all the rooms in all the towns, drove the elders and children away, and burned all their clothes, rations, animal-feed, and wooden housewares and implements..."

18 *Forverts*, "Khina vet zikh nit mishen," March 16, 1904, 1.

19 *Forverts*, the "largest Jewish newspaper in the world" for many years, was founded in 1897 in New York City by a group of socialist immigrants from eastern Europe. One of its founders was Abraham Cahan, who later became the editor-in-chief and the leading figure in the newspaper for several decades. See "The Forward," Jewish Historical Press, accessed October 6, 2019, http://web.nli.org.il/sites/JPress/English/Pages/FRW.aspx.

oyshaltn un frier oder shpeter vet zi zikh araynshlepn in der milkhome."[20] And the translated news report from Washington said: "Khina hot shoyn eyn mol farzikhert, az zi vet zikh in der milkhome nit mishn. Di itstige tsveyte farzikherung iz gekumen tsulib dem, vos klangen hobn zikh genumen farshpreyten az khina farzamelt a groyse armey arum mandzhuri..."[21] Both parts of the report mentioned China's untrustworthiness.

Another news report, titled "Durkh khina keyn mandzhurie" (דורך כינא קיין מאנדזשוריע) [Through China to Manchuria] and published in the same newspaper on March 25, 1904,[22] escalated from distrust to outright hostility. This report was also a reprint, originally from St. Petersburg. Although mainly about the Liaotung Gulf (辽东湾) and the nearby Russian railway, it also mentioned Japanese soldiers' espionage along the railroad: "Rusland hot zikhere beveyze, az yapanishe soldaten hobn zikh farshtelt far khinezer un zey dreyhn zikh arum der ayzenbahn vos geyt fun mandzhuri in khina."[23] After showing the readers Japanese soldiers' stealthy actions along the Russian railway, this report discussed the possibility of cooperation between China and Japan: "Di rusishe hobn nit keyn shum tsutroy tsu di khinezishe generaln ma un mu, un gloybn, az zey veln zikh fareynigen mit di yapaner."[24] Here, from a Russian perspective, the Japanese soldiers' disguising themselves as Chinese in order to spy on and sabotage their railway was as malicious as China's potential cooperation with Japan. This comparison cast China, though a third party, as an enemy of Russia.

From the news reports examined above, we can see the image of China in the eyes of these Yiddish newspaper writers and editors: for Russia, China was not to be trusted – the Chinese government might cooperate with Russia's enemy (Japan), and Chinese bandits were known to sabotage the Russian railway and harry the Tsar's troops. Although the local Chinese inhabitants were in fact greatly suffering from the war, compared to Russia's interest, China's losses could be ignored. But as we shall see, the informative articles tell a very different story.

---

20 "Khina vet zikh nit mishen": "But the correspondent – declared that the public does not have faith in it [China], and all signs show that China will not hold out and sooner or later will have to enter the war."
21 "Khina vet zikh nit mishen": "China has already assured that it will not get involved in the war. The current second promise [not to go to war] came because of (the) rumors that China assembled a great army around Manchuria..."
22 *Forverts*, "Durkh khina keyn mandzhurie," March 25, 1904, 1.
23 "Durkh khina keyn mandzhurie": "Russia has certain evidence that Japanese soldiers disguised themselves as Chinese and roamed around the railway that goes from Manchuria to China."
24 "Durkh khina keyn mandzhurie": "The Russians do not trust the Chinese generals Ma and Mu, and believe that they will unite with the Japanese."

2 Informative Articles

In contrast to the news reports, the informative articles were aimed at introducing China to a Yiddish readership. For these writers, China was not merely a battle-field but an interesting and exotic country with a long history, rich culture, vast territory, and orderly society of polite and heroic people – totally different from the image shaped by the war reports.

On July 17, 1904, an author named Ben-Rafael (בן־רפאל) published an article titled "Di mandzhurier" [The Manchurians] in *Di yidishe velt*, a Yiddish newspaper that also published reports like those discussed above. Ben-Rafael not only praised the Manchurians' courage and strength, he also showed great pity for the downfall of the empire ruled by these former warriors. Moreover, he used over one-third of the article to expose the Russians' atrocities in Manchuria, which, perhaps surprisingly, was similar to the descriptions in the Chinese news reports.

In the lede, Ben-Rafael wrote: "Goyse heldn amol un feyglinge yetst, zey bazaygn korea, behershn khina un vern zehr a shvakhe folk."[25] This lede exhibits the author's complicated emotions towards the Manchurians, on which he elaborated in the body of the article:

> Ot dieze shvakhe mandzhurier hobn amol bahersht khina un hobn ufn tron in pekin aroyf-gezetst a mandzhurier familiye, vos hersht nokh ad hayom haze iber di 500 milion aynvoner fun khina. Zey hoben onfang 16tn yahr-hundert geshlogn makes retseyekh di koreer un zey zaynen geven azelkhe heldn. Dos yeder eyntsiger mandzhurier flegt zikh mit a boygn lozn in vald uf a yagd uf tigern un lempertn azoy undz ershrokn vi bay undz geyt men shisn hozn oder foygln.[26]

In this paragraph, not only did the author mention the Manchurians' military strength and political power, but he also admired their physical prowess and bravery as hunters, even contrasting them favorably against his own people. How different from the descriptions in the war reports!

Ben-Rafael also described Russian abuses in China: "Di befelkerung fun manchuria hot rusland behandelt ufn shreklikhstn oyfn. Dem tsars soldatn un kozakn hobn fargvaldikt di shehnste froyen un hobn oysgeshlaktet zeyere mener. Hobn beroybt di raykhste shtet un hobn opgebrent file derfer in velkhe zey hobn

---

[25] Ben-Rafael, "Di mandzhurier," *Di yidishe velt*, July 17, 1904, 4: "Great heroes once and cowards now, they defeated Korea, dominated China, and have become a very weak people."

[26] Ben-Rafael, "Di mandzhurier": "Here these weak Manchurians once dominated China and installed on the throne in Peking a Manchurian family, which governs until today over 500 million inhabitants of China. At the beginning of the sixteenth century, they struck murderous blows (on) Koreans and they were heroes. Every single Manchurian was able to hunt tigers and leopards in the forest with a bow. (These animals) frighten us, and we go to shoot hares or birds."

nit gefunen vos tsu roybn. Mandzhuria iz aruntergefaln unter aza shreklikhn yok."²⁷ Unlike the news reports published in the same newspaper, Ben-Rafael's article exposed this cruelty in detail and with compassion. His tone bore a close resemblance to that of a Chinese news report appearing at the same time: 奉天电云俄兵在海城岫岩等处骚扰不堪，民间牛羊及骡马车辆已搜掠一空，近更拘人当苦力转运工作，役同牛马，妇婴之辗转沟壑者尤多，呜呼惨哉.²⁸ Although the Yiddish article and the Chinese report were not identical in content, the pity the authors clearly felt toward the local Chinese people was the same.

Ben-Rafael's article focuses more on pity for China than praise, but other Yiddish writers in this period did not stop at sympathy. One anonymous article, titled "Khina, di fargliverte melukhe" (כינא, דיא פֿארגליװערטע מלוכה) [China, the frozen kingdom] and published on April 15, 1905, in *Forverts*, went a step further in identifying the Jewish people with China. In fact, this article seems to model an ideal future Jewish nation on China. Centering on the key word *mineg*, 'custom,' the author addressed five points about China that are similar to Jewish values.

First, in the lede, the author admired the preservation of ancient Chinese customs in current Chinese people's everyday lives: "Di medine vu men lebt nokh heynt punkt azoy vi men hot gelebt mit toyzender yor tsurik."²⁹ The first paragraph continued on the same theme, introducing the importance of *mineg* in the lives of Chinese people over thousands of years, and suggesting that the paper's Yiddish readership might see a commonality with Jewish tradition: "Khina iz di merkvirdikste medine uf der velt. Es hershn dortn minegim zint toyzender yoren un dize minegim vern nokh haynt gehaltn punkt azoy heylig un vern nokh punkt azoy obgehit . . ."³⁰ The author's admiration is clear.

---

27 Ben-Rafael, "Di mandzhurier": "Russia treated the population in Manchuria in the worst way. The Tsar's soldiers and Cossacks raped the most beautiful women and killed their men. (They) plundered the richest cities and burned down many villages where they did not find anything to rob. Manchuria fell under this terrible burden."
28 《俄兵骚扰电闻》，载于《大公报（天津版）》，1904年3月2日，第2版。*Ta Kung Pao* (Tianjin), "A Telegram on Russian Soldiers' Atrocity," March 2, 1904, 2: "A telegram from Fengtian says Russian soldiers' harassing and wrecking activities caused great damage in Haicheng and Xiuyan; they pillaged all the local residents' oxen, sheep, horses, mules, and carriages; recently, they also forcefully recruited and imprisoned local residents as hard laborers working in shifts for them like oxen and horses; a large number of homeless women, with their babies, drifted from trench to trench; they are living such a miserable life!"
29 *Forverts*, "Khina, di fargliverte melukhe," April 15, 1905, 9: "The country where people live today exactly as they lived thousands of years ago."
30 "Khina, di fargliverte melukhe": "China is the most remarkable country in the world. There customs have ruled for thousands of years, and these customs are still kept sacred today . . ."

Second, the description of the Chinese emperor resembled well-known histories of Jewish kings from the biblical period:

> Der k-ger[31] vert nokh haynt in kh-a[32] batrakht nit nor far dem foter fun di gantse medine, nor oykh far dem zun fun himl. Un derfar vert er gemakht farantvortlekh far yeden umglik vos befalt dos land, vi lemoshl ven es pasirt an erd-tsiternes, ven es geyt nit a tsayt lang keyn regn, oder ven es makhn zikh groyse farfleytsungen.[33]

The author was familiar with one of the common titles of Chinese emperors: 天子 (*Tianzi*, 'Son of Heaven'). Similarly, ancient Jewish kings, such as Saul and David, were chosen by God and, as the *Tanakh* recorded, bore a moral responsibility for any calamities that might befall their nation.[34]

Third, the author drew his readers' attention to the Chinese emphasis on the "law." Though this "law" was not identical to Jewish law, the author's comparison between the Chinese and Jewish commitments to their respective laws is still noteworthy: "Der gantser lebn fun dem khinezer iz fargeshribn fun dem gezets. Er tor zikh anders nit firn vi der gezets hot es im fargeshribn mit toyzender yorn tsurik. Ven the khinezer boyt a hoyz muz er ihr boyen uf a gevisn stil, un fun a gevise groys, vi der gezets shrayb es far."[35] Without mentioning the religious origin of Jewish law, the author claimed that this *gezets*, or 'law,' functioned almost the same way in Chinese society as in Jewish. Regardless of any historical inaccuracies in the author's description of "Chinese law," his argument – that the Chinese, like the Jews, were governed by ancient laws – is striking. In this context, the word *khinezer*, 'Chinese,' could very easily be replaced by *yidn*, 'Jews.'

Fourth, the author asserted that China, too, was monotheistic – and that the Chinese God resembled that of the Jews: "In khina zaynen ferbreytert dray religionen. Di vikhtigste fun zey iz di religion vos iz gegrindet gevorn fun dem barimtn

---

[31] This word is not legible in the original text, but, from the context, it could probably be a variant of the Yiddish word קיניג, 'king.'

[32] This word is not legible in the original text, but, from the context, it could be כינא, 'China.'

[33] "Khina, di fargliverte melukhe": "Today in China, the king is not only considered the father of the whole country, but also the son of heaven. And therefore he is made responsible for every calamity that befalls the country – for example, when an earthquake happens, when there is no rain for a long time, or when there are floods."

[34] For instance, 2 Samuel 21:1 (NIV): "During the reign of David, there was a famine for three successively years; so David sought the face of the LORD. The LORD said, 'It is on account of Saul and his blood-stained house; it is because he put the Gibeonites to death.'"

[35] "Khina, di fargliverte melukhe": "The whole life of the Chinese is prescribed by the law. He does not allow other (things) to guide him, as the law had already prescribed it for him thousands of years ago. When the Chinese builds a house, he must build it in a certain style and of a certain size, as the law prescribed."

khinezishen --[36] un gezetsgeber konfutsius, un velkhe iz oykh di ofitsiele religion fun land un fun der regirung. Dize religion onerkent an eyntsikn got, velkher bashteht fun gayst, fun rukhnies un velkher zitst in himl."[37] Although later in the same paragraph, the author realized the religions in China were only about "morality,"[38] he still mistakenly attributed monotheism not only to Confucianism but also to Buddhism and Taoism as well. None of these three major religions, however, was monotheistic. In Taoism, there were numerous gods, some of whom were represented by stars. Confucianism ordered its believers to keep a distance from god(s) and ghosts and emphasized present life, while Buddhists believed that mortal humans could become Buddhas through meditation and good deeds. This mistake was a consequence of the author's intention of identifying Chinese with Jews and envisioning China as the model for an ideal Jewish "nation."

Fifth, the author discussed the long history of China: "In di khinezishe geshikhte bikher vern dertseylt pasirungen velkhe zoln hobn getrofn umgefer mit finf toyzend yor tsurik. Khina hot nokh ober ekzistirt fil frier."[39] Here, the author found another similarity between the two nations: both had a long history, as well as a longstanding tradition of recording history.

From the example of Ben-Rafael, it is clear that, in the introductory articles, the authors' attitude towards China was positive. Not only did they pity the tragic downfall of a formerly glorious country, they also admired the long history, religious observance, and great warriors of China. Moreover and perhaps more significantly, they identified China as a model for their own future nation. But there was a radical discrepancy between the introductory articles, which portrayed China as a kind of Jewish utopia, and the war reports, which (as we have seen) indifferently described China as an untrustworthy and malicious nation. How can this be?

---

36 This word is not legible in the original text.
37 "Khina, di fargliverte melukhe": "In China three religions are emphasized. The most important one is the religion which was founded by the famous Chinese – and law-giver Confucius, and which is also the official religion of (the) country and of the government. These religions recognize a single god, who exists in mind and in spirituality and sits in heaven."
38 "Khina, di fargliverte melukhe": "Zi lernt nor moral . . ." (It teaches only [about] moral . . .).
39 "Khina, di fargliverte melukhe": "In the Chinese history books, the events, which should have happened approximately five thousand years ago, were told. But China existed much earlier."

Conclusion

From our analysis of the introductory articles, it is not difficult to see that their Jewish authors were creating an image of China that derived from their understanding of Jewish history. China, in these articles, was no longer a real country, devastated by the Russo-Japanese War on the other side of the world, but an imagined Jewish "nation" mingled with the Jewish past, present, and future. The descriptions of China in the introductory articles can be further divided into two categories. First, by emphasizing the similarities (real or imagined) between the Chinese and Jewish peoples, such as their long history, law, monotheism, and tragic downfall, the authors remade China in the image of the Jewish past and present. Second, by contrasting the military strength, political power, and able-bodied population of historical China with the relative powerlessness of then-present-day Jewish communities, they envisioned new possibilities for the Jewish future.[40] They also underscored the vastness of China's geographic territory:

> ... di gantse provints velkhe hot bay 20 million menshen un velkhe iz greser fun mankhe eyropeishe lender, vos shpiln a role als groysmekhte.[41]

> Di erd vert nokh dorten bearbeyt azoy vi es iz forgeshribn gevorn in di alte khinezishe gezets-bikher vos zaynen farpast mit toyzender yorn tsurik. Menshen tsien nokh dem akerayzn anshtot ferd.[42]

Not only did China have vast land, that land was also carefully treasured by the Chinese people. Considering the relationship between China and Jews in the context of contemporaneous Jewish history, the emphasis on and yearning for land can be related to Zionism – the return to the promised land and the establishment of a Jewish regime in Israel. The repeated mentions of Chinese military strength and political power, as well as the admiration of the Manchurian war-

---

[40] According to Warren Rosenberg, the image of Jewish scholars was the stereotype of Jewish men, who were seen as "erudite, comedic, malleable, nonthreatening, part nebbish, part shlemiel." Rosenberg, *Legacy of Rage: Jewish Masculinity, Violence, and Culture* (Amherst: University of Massachusetts Press, 2001), 1.
[41] Ben-Rafael, "Di mandzhurier": "... the whole province which has about 20 million people and which is larger than many European countries, which play a role as great-power."
[42] "Khina, di fargliverte melukhe": "The land there is cultivated in the same way as it was written in the old Chinese law-books that passed through thousands of years. People pull plows instead of horses."

riors' robust bodies, further illustrate this point.⁴³ Thus, the introductory articles can be taken as a Zionist blueprint for the Jewish future through creating a "Jewish" image of China. If this is so, what of the war reports?

If the introductory articles were about solving the Jewish question "there," the war reports indirectly represented a solution to the Jewish question "here." These reports took on the Russian perspective of China, both as a battlefield by which the Russians might profit and as a malicious potential enemy who probably had allied with Japan to fight against them. Although the selected texts were from Yiddish newspapers published in America, the deep relationship between the "old country" and the "new land" may also have sustained the patriotism of these emigrant Jews, a patriotism that had deep roots in the Russification of Russian Jews⁴⁴ and internal Jewish nationalism⁴⁵ in Russia.

Why did these writers articulate these solutions through the figure of China? Admittedly, China was the battlefield of the Russo-Japanese War, which deeply attracted Jewish attention.⁴⁶ But more importantly, they saw parallels between the Chinese and Jewish situations, parallels that could be used to express their hopes and fears at the beginning of the twentieth century.

Chinese intellectuals also recognized and took advantage of the two nations' similarities. In 1904, one of the advocates of the New Culture movement (新文化运动), Chen Duxiu (陈独秀), discovered one similarity between the two oppressed groups:

> As early as 1904, Chen Duxiu discussed the global situation in his article "About the Nation." He talked about issues ranging from the plight of China to nationalism, and divided the

---

43 Ronnie A. Grinberg summarizes Max Handman's view: "Zionists called for the creation of a Jewish state with 'new' and 'muscular' Jews with characteristics that would 'physically mimic those of the gentiles: tall, virile, close to nature, and physically productive." Grinberg, "Neither 'Sissy' Boy Nor Patrician Man: New York Intellectuals and the Construction of American Jewish Masculinity," *American Jewish History* 98, no. 3 (2014): 133.

44 Stein, *Making Jews Modern*, 28: "Many Russian Jews, of course, read neither Hebrew nor Yiddish sources for their day's news, but turned, instead, to Russian-language sources. By the end of the nineteenth century, it was no longer uncommon for Russian Jews to have a reading knowledge of Russian. Nearly 50 percent of Russian Jewish men and 21 percent of Russian Jewish women between the ages of ten and fifty could claim literacy in Russian. This number was as high as 51 percent for urban males and 35 percent for urban females, and, in this case, too, the figures were significantly underestimated." Besides adopting Russian, at the of the nineteenth century, Jewish students also actively attended universities in Russia. See John Efron et al., *The Jews: A History* (Upper Saddle River, NJ: Pearson Education, 2009), 257.

45 Such as Ahad Ha'am's cultural Zionism and Nahman Syrkin's labor Zionism.

46 Ben-Rafael, "Di mandzhurier": "Mandzhuria un ihre ayngebarege aynvahner interesiren yetst di gantse velt tsulip di milkhome vos kumt dorten yetst far" (Manchuria and her down trodden inhabitants interest the whole world because of the war that is taking place there now).

world into countries which "are bullied by foreign countries" and strong ones. The former included the weak nations of Poland, Egypt, "Jew nation," India ... The latter includes the strong nations of Britain, France, Germany, Italy ... Until 1921, in his article "The Pacific Conference and the Weak Nations in the Pacific," he officially used the term "weak nations" to refer to colonized countries, such as India and Poland ... "Weak literature" is also understood as a counterpart of Western literature.[47]

Chen's position was followed by Chinese intellectuals and translators in subsequent decades, including the first influx of Yiddish literary works translated through other languages into Chinese during the 1920s. The relationship between Hebrew and Yiddish also drew the attention of Chinese intellectuals.[48]

At the transformative and turbulent turn of the century, both of these oppressed nations turned toward each other and expressed their hopes and fears in mirror images that transcended geographic distance and cultural isolation. Though the two nations were physically separated, the parallels between them were already there, awaiting further and deeper exploration by contemporary scholars.

References

Newspaper Articles

《俄兵骚扰电闻》，载于《大公报（天津版）》，1904年3月2日。[A telegram on Russian soldiers' atrocity. *Ta Kung Pao* (Tianjin), March 2, 1904.]
Ben-Rafael. "Di mandzhurier" [The Manchurians]. *Di yidishe velt*, July 17, 1904.

---

47 宋炳辉，《弱小民族文学的译介与20世纪中国文学的民族意识》，2003年，第17页。Song Binghui, "Translation of 'Weak Literature' and the National Consciousness of Chinese Literature in the Twentieth Century," 17: 早在1904年，陈独秀在政论《说国家》一文中论述国际大势时，就从中国的遭遇，讲到国家民族主义，并将世界分为"被外国欺负"的国家和列强国家两类，前者指波兰、埃及、犹太、印度......等弱小国家，后者指英、法、德、意......等世界列强。到1921年他在《太平洋会议与太平洋弱小民族》一文中，则正式使用"弱小民族"的概念指称印度、波兰等殖民地国家......"弱小民族文学"也是作为西方文学的对照而存在的。
48 During the New Culture movement, advocates encouraged people to write in the 'vernacular (oral) Chinese' (白话文) instead of the stubborn 'literary (written) Chinese' (文言文). Against this background, in the 1920s, Shen Yanbing (沈雁冰) discussed the "language revolution" of Yiddish literature in his article "A Survey of New Jewish Literature" (《新犹太文学概观》), but he mistakenly took Hebrew as the "stubborn" literary form of Yiddish, which was taken as the counterpart of vernacular (oral) Chinese. Thus, Chinese writers believed Yiddish literature to correspond to their goal. See 杨波，《20年代中国文学界对犹太意绪文学的介绍和借鉴》，载于《文史杂志》，1999年03期，第42页。Yang Bo, "China's Introduction and Use of Yiddish Literature in the 1920s," Journal of Literature and History 3 (1999): 42.

Forverts. "Durkh khina keyn mandzhurie" [Through China to Manchuria]. March 25, 1904.
Forverts. "Khina, di fargliverte melukhe" [China, the frozen kingdom]. April 15, 1905.
Forverts. "Khina vet zikh nit mishen" [China will not get involved]. March 16, 1904.
Di yidishe velt. "Getriben un geyogt" [Driven and driven away]. May 10, 1904.
Di yidishe velt. "Gezeyre uf korn" [Decree on rye]. May 30, 1904.

English Materials

Efron, John et al. *The Jews: A History*. Upper Saddle River, NJ: Pearson Education, 2009.
Grinberg, Ronnie A. "Neither 'Sissy' Boy Nor Patrician Man: New York Intellectuals and the Construction of American Jewish Masculinity." *American Jewish History* 98, no. 3 (2014): 127–151.
Historical Jewish Press. "The Jewish World (Die Iddishe Welt)." The National Library of Israel. http://web.nli.org.il/sites/JPress/English/Pages/AllJPressPage.aspx?p=36.
Historical Jewish Press. "The Forward (*Forverts*)." The National Library of Israel. http://web.nli.org.il/sites/JPress/English/Pages/FRW.aspx.
Nish, Ian. *The Origins of the Russo-Japanese War*. London and New York: Longman, 1985.
Rosenberg, Warren. *Legacy of Rage: Jewish Masculinity, Violence, and Culture*. Amherst: University of Massachusetts Press, 2001.
"Size of Manchuria." *Los Angeles Herald*, April 10, 1904. University of California, Riverside Center for Bibliographical Studies and Research: California Digital Newspaper Collection. Accessed October 6, 2019. https://cdnc.ucr.edu/cgi-bin/cdnc?a=d&d=LAH19040410.2.381.21&e=en201txttxIN1.
Stein, Sarah Abrevaya. *Making Jews Modern: The Yiddish and Ladino Press in the Russian and Ottoman Empire*. Bloomington: Indiana University Press, 2004.

Chinese Materials

"A Document about the Russian Army's Damage of Crops and Houses and Rapes around the Province's Capital City." In *Historical Materials of the Russo-Japanese War*, compiled by the Liaoning Archive, 355. Liaoning: Liaoning Ancient Books Publishing House, 1995. "关于俄军在省城周围蹂躏田苗，拆毁房屋，奸淫搜掠等文件"，《日俄战争档案史料》，辽宁省档案馆编，辽宁古籍出版社，1995年版，第355页。
Li Gang. "On the Losses of China in the Russo-Japanese War." Master's thesis, Hebei University, 2008. 李刚：《日俄战争给中国带来的损失问题研究》，河北大学硕士论文，2008年。
Song Binghui. "Translation of 'Weak Literature' and the National Conscious of Chinese Literature in the Twentieth Century." PhD diss., Fudan University, 2003. 宋炳辉：《弱小民族文学的译介与20世纪中国文学的民族意识》，复旦大学博士论文，2003年。
Yang Bo. "China's Introduction and Use of Yiddish Literature in the 1920s." *Journal of Literature and History* 3 (1999): 40–43. 杨波：《20年代中国文学界对犹太意第绪文学的介绍和借鉴》，载于《文史杂志》，1999年03期，第40–43页。
Yu Bian. "The Origins of the Red-bearded Bandits in *Kwantung*." *Journal of Social Studies* 1 (1980): 116. 边羽："关东'红胡子'考辨"，载于《社会科学辑刊》，1980年01期，第116页。

"Zeng Qi, Ting Jie's Announcement about Informing Farmers to Cultivate in Case They Were Discouraged by the War." In *Historical Materials of the Russo-Japanese War*, compiled by the Liaoning Archive, 313. Liaoning: Liaoning Ancient Books Publishing House, 1995. 《增祺、廷杰关于日俄开战恐民废时晓谕乡民及时播种布告》，《日俄战争档案史料》，辽宁省档案馆编，辽宁古籍出版社，1995 年，第 313 页。

Zhang Ping
16 To Speak or Not to Speak: Hanoch Levin's *Suitcase Packers* and Cao Yu's *Peking Man* in Light of Cross-Textual Dialogue

1 Hanoch Levin Meets China

The first official performance of Hanoch Levin's dramas in China was in October 2004, when Tel Aviv's Cameri Theatre was invited to perform *Requiem* at the Chekhov Forever international drama festival in Beijing.[1] The play, performed in Hebrew with subtitles in my Chinese translation, was greeted with a "tide of good reviews."[2] Two years later, the Cameri Theatre was invited to perform *Requiem* once again for the fiftieth anniversary of the Capital Theatre in Beijing. *Requiem* was the only foreign play performed during the celebration. Afterwards, the drama was performed twice more in China, in 2012 and 2019. On Douban, which can be roughly considered as China's equivalent to IMBD, the play received 1,432 reviews and an average grade of 8.8.[3] In comparison, Arthur Miller's *Death of a Salesman*, also well-known in China, had 628 reviews and was graded 8.1,[4] while *Peking Man*, one of the masterpieces of modern Chinese drama (which we will discuss further in this paper), received 1,680 reviews and was graded 8.0.[5] In addition to the original Hebrew version of the play, a Chinese version of *Requiem* was performed in several cities throughout China for six months from July to December 2019.

The success of Levin's dramas in China goes far beyond *Requiem*. Even before its arrival, his other plays, such as *Ya'acobi and Leidental* and *Ms. Ohio*, had already

---

[1] This essay is a part of the MOE (Ministry of Education in China) Project of Humanities and Social Sciences (Israel's Religion and Modernity in the Framework of Sino-Jewish Inter-traditional Dialogue, Project No. 19JJD730001).
[2] "*Requiem* (The Cameri Theatre of Tel Aviv in Israel)," Baidu Encyclopedia, accessed August 8, 2020, https://baike.baidu.com/item/安魂曲/6473967.
[3] "*Requiem* (The Israeli version)," Douban Tongcheng, accessed August 8, 2020, https://www.douban.com/location/drama/10863843/.
[4] "Death of a Salesman," Douban Tongcheng, accessed August 8, 2020, https://www.douban.com/location/drama/10574503/.
[5] "Peking Man," Douban Tongcheng, accessed August 8, 2020, https://www.douban.com/event/search?search_text=北京人&loc=israel.

been translated into Chinese (from French) and performed in academic theater institutes. In 2007, the *Theatre Arts Academic Journal* published a special issue on Israeli theater that included research papers on Hanoch Levin and the script of *Requiem*. In 2013, another play by Levin, *Suitcase Packers*, was performed by the Cameri Theatre in Beijing and "overcame the Chinese audience again."[6] In 2017, *Requiem: A Selective Anthology of Hanoch Levin's Dramas* was published by the prestigious Commercial Press in Beijing and was named one of the ten best books of the year. The success of Levin's dramas and, more broadly, of Israeli theater in China was summarized precisely by a Chinese blogger:

> *Requiem* made "Israeli drama" a tag of "high quality drama." Since then, it has been difficult to find tickets for every Israeli play that comes to China.[7]

Has Levin's work gained such popularity due to the Chinese audience's fascination with a completely alien culture? Or is it based on a deeper level of empathy that arises from shared values between the Chinese and Jewish cultures? In this essay, I will explore this question through a case study of a cross-textual dialogue between two dramas: Hanoch Levin's *Suitcase Packers* and *Peking Man* by Cao Yu, one of the leading dramatists in modern China.

2 The Encounter Between *Suitcase Packers* and *Peking Man*

The two plays in this dialogue share striking similarities. Both are considered masterpieces in the history of modern drama in their home countries. Both are living plays that are still performed decades after their initial productions. Both have drawn large audiences. Hanoch Levin and Cao Yu, who are both regarded as masters of modern drama in their own cultures, even received a similar grade from reviewers on Douban: 8.0 for *Suitcase Packers*,[8] 8.1 for *Peking Man*.

---

[6] "Israeli Drama Overcomes Chinese Audience Again," *Beijing Evening News*, March 6, 2013, accessed August 8, 2020, http://webcache.googleusercontent.com/search?q=cache:qYDHIbScsiI-J:xiju.chnart.com/index.php%3Fm%3Dcontent%26c%3Dindex%26a%3Dshow%26catid%3D15%26id%3D3235+&cd=17&hl=en&ct=clnk&gl=il&client=safari.

[7] Xiao V., December 3, 2017, "The history of Israeli drama is even longer than the state, and that's the first reason for falling in love with the state," accessed August 8, 2020, https://new.qq.com/omn/20171203/20171203A011XD.html.

[8] "Suitcase Packers," Douban Tongcheng, accessed August 8, 2020, https://www.douban.com/location/drama/21329777/.

The greatest resemblance between them, however, is the three subjects they have in common: death, the desperation of the human condition, and their respective protagonists' attempt to escape from it.

Death is the main subject in *Suitcase Packers*, as its subtitle, *A Comedy with Eight Funerals*, indicates. There are eighteen scenes in the play; starting from the fifth scene, a funeral occurs approximately once every two scenes. But the frequency of the funerals in *Suitcase Packers* is surpassed by those in *Requiem*. In fact, *Requiem* – its title referring to mourning and remembrance – is exceptional even among Levin's works, which are almost always related to death in one way or another.

The uniqueness of Levin's notion of death is its normalization. For Levin, death is not the end of life but rather an integral part of it. In his poem "Lives of the Dead: An Epic," he narrates the life of a dead person, which begins at his funeral and ends with his bones turning into dust and blowing away in the wind. During this period, the dead man feels, thinks, memorizes, and communicates with other dead people, as if he was living but confined to his grave. This sort of "life of the dead" continues even after the bones vanish:

> And at the end of many years, when even the skull is fallen away
> and become flakes of dust, the wind
> with a whistle of contempt will cast them out
> to every part, and still will be borne with them the sound
> of the cry of the dead man,
> a moan so great as to never pass:
> Hey, you up there, I was here too![9]

In a certain sense, *Suitcase Packers* is a dramatic version of the poem "Lives of the Dead: An Epic." In the former, funerals, deaths of natural causes, absurd relationships between family members, sex, and even sex with prostitutes, are all part of people's lives while they live; in the latter, these things feature regularly in the daily afterlives of the dead. The former is a death story told by the living; the latter is a life story told by the dead. In both works, there is no absolute boundary between life and death. The characters, facing the hardships of reality and the sadness embedded in the day-to-day, remain both hopeful and desperate, yearning for life elsewhere, yet confined to their limited space.

This notion of death is perhaps most clearly expressed at the end of *Suitcase Packers*. In the final scene, those who have escaped to faraway places return with

---

[9] Hanoch Levin, "Lives of the Dead: An Epic: Chapter Four," trans. Atar Hadari, *Poetry* 194, no. 2 (2009), accessed August 9, 2020, https://www.poetryfoundation.org/poetrymagazine/poems/52539/lives-of-the-dead-an-epic-chapter-four-.

their suitcases, while some of those who died are dressed like tourists joyfully starting their trip. Elkhanan, who dreamed of living in Switzerland but never made it, has decided to join his dead parents for the journey. The border between life and death disappears completely: death is just another journey in and from life. In the words of Elkhanan, "All those who stood between me and death are dead. Between me and death there is nothing."[10] Though it may be understood that Elkhanan was going to commit suicide, the way that Levin presents his death certainly obscures that intention.

Is life so terrible that death does not seem that bad? Does belief in an afterlife make a suffocating reality less insufferable? In Levin's dramas, both questions are answered positively. This leads us to the second subject of *Suitcase Packers*: the unbearably desperate human condition.

Suitcase Packers is not so fiercely violent as *Requiem*. In *Suitcase Packers*, there are no criminals around, and no murder is committed. The characters are certainly not rich, but neither are they starving. However, the torture of their trivial, boring, hopeless lives lingers at all times and is deepened by their inability to make any changes as well as by constant miscommunications between family members and loved ones. Even at their funerals, the eulogist has nothing to say. Mr. Alberto, the community orator for funerals, merely intones, "Dear so and so, today we take our leave of you."[11] Life is miserable and short, and there is nothing to say about it.

For Levin, life is changeless as the grave. The characters in *Suitcase Packers* seem to understand this very well. They do not really want to change their lives, but only desire to escape them. Many dream of starting a new life somewhere else, and some – such as Zigi, Elisha, sisters Bella and Nina, and the prostitute – succeed. At least, they make it as far as England and Switzerland. But the life they expect is in fact lived by Amatzia, who runs away to America, suffers from the same poverty, boredom, and illness there, and comes home to die. The most ironic runaway is probably the American tourist girl who travels tens of thousands of miles to Israel, only to find herself at the someone else's funeral. Some characters do not run away themselves but attempt to do away with the people around them in hopes of improving their own lives. Thus we have Munia, who tries by any means to send Bobba, his old mother, to a nursing home, and Tzippora, who tries to expel Avner, her humpbacked brother-in-law, from her house. Yet these efforts are to no avail – Bobba returns, and Avner stays. If young and

---

[10] Hanoch Levin, *Suitcase Packers*, trans. Michael Alfreds (Tel Aviv: Hanoch Levin's Heirs, 1984), 53.
[11] Hanoch Levin, *Suitcase Packers*, 14.

healthy people who run as far as America have no choice but to come back, how far can the old and helpless go?

In Levin's reality, suffering and escape from suffering become a deadly circle that no one can break. No wonder that death, against all odds, seems to be the way out.

It should be noted that *Suitcase Packers* has a certain philosophical dimension. While the scenes, the characters, the conversations, and the actions remind us of somewhere in South Tel Aviv, a neighborhood like the one where Levin himself was born, neither the location nor its historical and cultural background are ever specifically identified. Obviously, the feelings of the characters and their fate are meant to be as universal as possible. What Levin presents is the human condition in the modern era, not merely the lived realities of several specific Israelis. In contrast, Cao Yu's *Peking Man* has much clearer geographic, historical, and cultural configurations. We know that the drama takes place in Beijing City from the 1930s to the 1940s. We also know that the cultural backdrop is the conflict between deeply rooted traditions and the newly formed modern culture. Nevertheless, like Levin, Cao Yu attempts to make the narrative as universal as possible.

In "On the Modernity of Cao Yu's Early Works," Li Yang argues that presenting a universal human condition instead of a reality in a specific society "is neither an isolated phenomenon nor an improvisational action in Cao Yu's early dramas. It is an intention that lays in the deep layer of all his early writings."[12] As for *Peking Man*, Cao Yu explains that "when Zeng Ting and Ruizhen were getting divorced, a sound of the gong of the blind fortune tellers was heard, causing people to feel that there is no protection over their lives and life itself is meaningless."[13] Scholars have noted that some key facts are missing from the play: for example, it is not clear if Ruizhen and Sufang go to Yan'an at the end, if Yuan Rengan is a member of the CCP, and if the historical background of the play is the Sino-Japanese War. However, Cao Yu himself emphasized that those details were intentionally left absent, since "realism does not mean everything is real" and "if you give them specific names, the play loses its taste."[14] Although he did not say what exactly that taste was, it is clear that he was trying to distance his work from concrete reality and make it more abstract and universal.

---

[12] Quoted in Li Yang, "On the Modernity of Cao Yu's Early Works," *Social Science Front* 5 (2009): 128.
[13] Quoted in Li Yang, "On the Modernity of Cao Yu's Early Works," 128.
[14] Cao Yu, "On Peking Man," in *The Complete Works of Cao Yu*, ed. Liu Yijun (Shijiazhuang: Huashan Literature and Arts Press, 1995), 5:32.

The "desperate human condition" of Cao Yu's works, Li Yang argues, is not unique to modern Chinese literature but common throughout modern literature around the globe: "Both philosophers and writers ponder over our times and try to reach a new understanding of the human condition . . . In the world of literature, realism has changed. Writers gradually turned their eyes from the historical progress of society to the desperate human condition."[15]

Although Li Yang's assertion about world literature in general is debatable, his viewpoint holds true for the dialogue between Hanoch Levin and Cao Yu. Both *Suitcase Packers* and *Peking Man* should be understood in the context of modernization: that of the Jewish and Chinese civilizations respectively. It is within the framework of modernization that we can better comprehend the human condition as represented by Hanoch Levin and Cao Yu. But while discussing their similarities, we should also emphasize the underlying differences in their literary traditions, their lived experiences, and their cultures' respective paths toward modernization.

In both plays, poverty is crucial. Although no one starves, the characters' finances are far from satisfactory. In *Suitcase Packers*, those who desire to go abroad do not have the money to do so. Elkhanan and the prostitute try to plan for their future journeys by saving every penny in their daily lives, while Bella relies on a relative's financial assistance. Elisha, who is a medical doctor, is the only character who can afford his flights abroad; the others struggle to pay for tickets to a dance hall. Similarly, in *Peking Man*, there is also a rich family: the Dus, who never actually appear onstage, but whose existence shows how poor the Zengs really are. Once a large and wealthy family, the Zengs are now living hand to mouth, and, since they cannot pay their debts on time, their property, including the coffin of the dying family patriarch, is gradually lost to them.

Closely related to poverty are the characters' failed attempts at improvement. These failures are mainly due to their incompetence or inability to act. Shabatai, the deceased at the first funeral in *Suitcase Packers*, dies of bowel movement failure. He is not a hero who fails in a magnificent struggle but a human who lost control of one of his basic bodily functions. Elkhanan fails to go abroad because he cannot control his desires and eventually loses all his traveling money to the prostitute. Zigi cannot communicate because he does not have the ability to speak properly. The widows, besides playing bridge, cannot lead normal lives. Even the community's funeral orator, Mr. Alberto, can say only one sentence. Similarly, in *Peking Man*, the characters cannot properly perform the basic tasks of daily life, although they come from the traditional elite and were expected to

---

[15] Li Yang, "On the Modernity of Cao Yu's Early Works," 126.

accomplish great things. Zeng Hao, the head of the family, worries about only one thing: his coffin must be lavishly painted. Zeng Wenqing, the eldest son, hates his old-fashioned relatives but cannot escape due to his own cowardice and incompetence. Jiang Tai, the son-in-law who studies abroad, can express his anger only by smashing utensils and beating his wife. The three men who should support the family cannot do anything but collapse with it.

Even love is hardly meaningful. In both plays, love is pathetic and powerless. Such is the love in *Peking Man* between Sufang and Zeng Wenqing, which falls apart when Zeng Wenqing fails to keep his promise to Sufang on running away from their suffocating family. Such is also the love between Zeng Ting and Yuan Yuan: while Zeng Ting is attracted to Yuan Yuan for her liberal personality, Yuan Yuan dreams of an imaginary "Peking Man," who, for her, represents absolute freedom and independence. A similar kind of love appears in *Suitcase Packers* between Avner and Bella. While Avner loves Bella with all his heart, Bella refuses the monotony of her home town. As for Alberto, his narrative is merely that of a philanderer who never really has love in his mind. In such a reality, love cannot bring happiness, let alone change people or the world.

Although both plays portray the human condition as desperate, their respective behind-the-scenes dynamics are quite different. In *Peking Man*, society is divided into two antithetical groups: on the one hand, the evil, traditional, older generation; on the other, the good, revolutionary, younger generation, whose members are influenced by modern culture. The desperation of the human condition is caused by the older generation, which is mired in useless old customs, while it is the younger generation that is resisting and seeking a way out. In *Suitcase Packers*, all people were born into the same desperate human condition, in which everyone suffers and causes suffering at once. A brief comparison between the characters of Zeng Hao, in *Peking Man*, and Bobba, in *Suitcase Packers*, is illuminating. In a certain sense, both men can be defined as old people who are objected to by the younger generation. However, Zeng Hao is deserted due to his own personality and misbehavior: selfish and hypocritical, he uses the tenets of traditional morality to manipulate the younger generation. His only concern is the magnificence of his coffin. In contrast, Bobba is sent away to a nursing home without any apparent reason. Neither she nor her son have done anything wrong. The conflicts in *Suitcase Packers* are limited to the practical arrangements of the characters' daily lives, whereas, in *Peking Man*, the fate of the nation is at stake.

Given the unchangeable reality of suffering, the desire to escape is an obvious and natural response. In both plays, the young people try to run away, while the old people stay put. In *Peking Man*, it is the older generation that created this reality and wishes stay in it. In *Suitcase Packers*, the widows stay on to preserve the life of the community: "We are the life and strength of this neighborhood. We won't die, we will play bridge. We'll represent the neighborhood, our late husbands, our children, our whole life – we'll represent them at bridge."[16]

Failed escape attempts occur in both plays for different reasons. In *Peking Man*, Zeng Wenqing chooses to return home after a short period, as he mentally belongs to the older generation, who have created this reality. In *Suitcase Packers*, Amatzia returns from America after failing to create a new life there. Such is the fate of those who run away in Levin's world. But for the most part, this kind of failure is not found in Cao Yu's works. For Cao Yu, escape truly belongs to the younger generation. It is the way out of despair, a faraway place that symbolizes hope. In *Peking Man*, it is not necessary to ask where people will run or what they will do after they reach their destination. A successful escape is a victory for its own sake – life afterwards does not matter. For Levin, however, to run away is merely to prolong one's dilemma and desperation. Levin's characters know exactly where they want to go and what they will do there. They even understand that life 'over there' is not necessarily much better than the present one, as Bella says:

> Not that I have any illusions about London. London isn't waiting for me. I'll be lonely there, too. Maybe that's true for the whole of my life – to be alone. But in London, there are more films, good music, excellent television, nicer people. That way, the despair becomes more comfortable, you understand? If I am going to end my days like a dog, then at least let the television be television.[17]

This is also true of Elkhanan, who imagines Switzerland as a place where he will find his lover, and of the prostitute, who wants to go to Switzerland to continue her old business.

A similarity in difference can also be found in the understanding of death in the two plays. Cao Yu draws a clear borderline between good and evil, while Hanoch Levin's reality is far more obscure. *Suitcase Packers* is organized around eight funerals; *Peking Man*, around one coffin. Nonetheless, in *Peking Man*, death belongs solely to the evil older generation. For Cao Yu, dying and running away are two opposite directions: the good young people run away to find a new life, while the evil old people die in despair. In *Suitcase Packers*, as we have seen, death is part of life, and dying, like running away, is simultaneously a way out of despair and a way to drown in it. For Levin, death does not belong only to people of a certain age.

---

16 Hanoch Levin, *Suitcase Packers*, 50.
17 Hanoch Levin, *Suitcase Packers*, 47.

Perhaps more significantly, both dramatists were searching for a solution to the desperation of the human condition, a way out of the dilemma of modern life.

In *Suitcase Packers*, the solution is presented by Motke, who refuses to pack a suitcase and go away or to drive others from his side. He breaks the deadly circle of suffering, escape, and death by making a seemingly insignificant change: giving a proper eulogy at a funeral instead of sending a corpse to its grave with one simple sentence. In his words, "a man is not a worm."[18] If we give life a new and expressible meaning, life will find its true value, as he says:

> Yet the real things – we should say – we don't say. And I ask: surely, when we lie on this trolley and white sheets cover us, and when, in a short while, the earth will cover us too, when we lie here, everything suddenly becomes very clear, what is trivial and what is important. It's clear that there was something else to say and we didn't say it. We squandered, we chewed, we spat out, but we didn't speak. Lord, you gave us funerals to remind us of our lives; help us also not to forget this trolley and these sheets between funerals.[19]

In *Peking Man*, Cao Yu shows us another way out:

> Look, this is the Peking Man ages ago. Back then, people loved whenever they wanted to love, hated whenever they wanted to hate, cried whenever they wanted to cry, shouted whenever they wanted to shout. Year after year, they lived following their nature, lived in freedom without being restrained by traditional sayings and civilization values. There was no hypocrisy, no cheating, no tricks, no evilness, no traps, no conflicts, and no agony. They ate raw meats, drank fresh blood, were exposed to sunshine, to blowing wind and heavy rain, yet without the presence of cruel civilizations, they were very, very happy![20]

There are three significant differences between the two solutions. First, while Levin accepts reality regardless of how miserable it is and proposes to improve the human condition by limited reforms, Cao Yu proposes to turn the whole world upside down by categorically rejecting traditional civilization and returning to the primitive way of life of our ancestors. Second, while Levin believes that the problem lies in human conduct and advocates for its modification, Cao Yu finds that human nature is the crux of the issue and that the solution lies in the creation of an entirely new type of human. Third, while Levin encourages people to speak out rather than remain silent, Cao Yu advocates for exactly the opposite. For Cao Yu, the desperation of the human condition is caused by the restrictions

---

18 Hanoch Levin, *Suitcase Packers*, 29.
19 Hanoch Levin, *Suitcase Packers*, 52.
20 Cao Yu, *Peking Man*, in *The Selected Dramas of Cao Yu*, (Beijing: PLA Press, 2000), 376.

imposed by traditional sayings: therefore, speaking is the problem and silence is the solution.

If Hanoch Levin and Cao Yu both understand the desperation of the human condition similarly, why are their solutions so different – indeed, almost completely opposed? To explore this question, it is worth examining Jewish and Chinese traditions more closely.

3 A Dialogue Between the Traditions

Confucius once said, "I hate your glib-tongued people."[21] Throughout his life, he spoke negatively of 'specious speakers' (*ning* 佞). He believed that "specious speakers are dangerous" and that one should "keep far from specious speakers."[22] In the Confucian tradition, Heaven, which is considered the source of the ultimate truth, is silent, and it issues its teachings through action. That is perhaps the basis upon which Confucius considered words insignificant, or even dangerous, just as the following story shows:

> The Master said, "I would prefer not speaking." Zi Gong said, "If you, Master, do not speak, what shall we, your disciples, have to record?" The Master said, "Does Heaven speak? The four seasons pursue their courses, and all things are continually being produced, but does Heaven say anything?"[23]

Perhaps because the belief in a silent Heaven is shared by various schools in ancient Chinese philosophy, contempt of speech is not limited to Confucianism. One prominent example is Laozi's famous saying in the *Daodejing* 56:

> He who knows (the Dao) does not (care to) speak (about it); he who is (ever ready to) speak about it does not know it.[24]

Contrary to the silent Confucian Heaven, the God in Judaism hardly ever stops talking. He created the world by uttering words, communicates with humans by speaking, and passes down his teachings in spoken language. In Rabbinic Judaism, not only is speaking important, it is also sacred, since the carrier of the most important canon, the Oral Torah, was given and transmitted through

---

21 *Analects*, Chapter *Xianjin* 25.
22 *Analects*, Chapter *Weilinggong* 11.
23 *Analects*, Chapter *Yanghuo* 19.
24 Laozi, *Tao Te Ching, or the Tao and its Characteristics*, trans. James Legge (New York: The Floating Press, 2008), 102.

speech. Rabbinic perfection is first and foremost the perfection of the Hebrew language. Moreover, the importance of speech is also stressed in daily religious practices. One of the Halachah in the Babylonian Talmud is that words that are not spoken out loud do not count, do not have any significance:

> If a man betroths a woman, stating as a condition "that I am a priest" and he is found to be [only] a Levite or he is a Levite and he is found to be a priest ... a resident in a small town and he is found to be a resident of a large town or a large town and he is found to be of a small town ... in all these cases the betrothal is invalid even if she [subsequently] stated: "It was my intention [lit. 'in my heart'] to be betrothed unto him" [regardless of his status or condition]. The same law applies where she misled him. ... Rava said ... unspoken matters that remain in the heart are not significant matters.[25]

Did these traditional beliefs influence Hanoch Levin and Cao Yu in their search for a solution to the problems of modernity? We may never know for certain. Nevertheless, the parallel between their different traditions and their different solutions is clear. We know that Hanoch Levin was highly familiar with rabbinic literature and that Cao Yu did not attend a regular elementary school but spent his childhood reading Chinese classics instead. Although both are modern writers whose works exhibit little enthusiasm for the customs of the past, it is worth asking whether it is ever possible for thinkers to separate themselves completely from tradition.

Another parallel can be found in the understanding of human nature in the Jewish and Chinese traditions. I have argued in a recent article:

> This contrast between internal mean and external deeds can be understood on a more profound level: it reflects the radical differences in the understandings of the meaning of being human and the fundamental basis of identity between the two traditions. Both traditions talk about perfecting oneself; yet one refers to perfect personalities, while the other to perfect deeds.[26]

In Confucianism, one perfects oneself by becoming a better person; in Rabbinic Judaism, by engaging in better deeds. This leads to another important distinction: a perfect sage in Confucianism is judged by his refined and accomplished personality; in Rabbinic Judaism, by "every single deed he committed throughout his entire lifetime."[27]

---

25 *Babylonian Talmud*, Kiddushin 49b.
26 Zhang Ping, "The Middle Way Without a Middle: A Dialogue between the Confucian *Zhongyong* 中庸 and the Rabbinic *Derech Haemtza*," *Journal of Chinese Philosophy* 45, nos. 3–4 (2018): 217.
27 Zhang Ping, "The Middle Way Without a Middle," 218.

These differences between the Jewish and Chinese traditions provide a solid foundation for understanding the difference between Hanoch Levin, who prefers to modify human conduct, and Cao Yu, who believes in a radical transformation of human nature.

Conclusion

Peking Man and *Suitcase Packers* should both be understood in the context of modernization. To a certain extent, Westernization is an unavoidable step toward modernization in non-Western countries. For non-Western civilizations, the first question is almost always what to do with the local tradition, which may be radically transformed or totally discarded. Ideally, co-existence between the local and Western cultures is attained, so that the local tradition is left intact while the civilization is modernized. China, whose modern history largely consists of fierce internal conflicts and revolutions, essentially took the former route, while Israel, whose major challenge is external conflicts, chose the latter. This is probably the reason Joseph Levenson posed his famous question to China yet not to the State of Israel: "Why should Confucianism have withered into this anomaly? Why should it be Europe and not a Confucian China that has been able to sustain its self-image as a cultural history-maker coterminous with the world, regardless of political recession?"[28]

These different routes toward modernization are presented clearly in the two plays. In *Peking Man*, tradition is portrayed as an enemy of modernization, an obstacle in the way of progress. The play is full of anger and hatred toward tradition, and there is no space for compromises in the conflict between the old and the new. In *Suitcase Packers*, tradition is almost non-existent, which reflects the reality of the State of Israel, where traditional and modern societies co-exist in parallel and often separate worlds. Ironically, the suffocating world that Levin created is, to some extent, the ideal world that the youngsters in Cao Yu's drama believe in and want to run away to. Modernization may offer a way out of the difficulties imposed by tradition, but it cannot ensure happiness. While escape attempts like those in *Peking Man* are unavoidable, how to avoid falling into the trap of *Suitcase Packers* becomes a more profound question.

And this is exactly the question faced by contemporary Chinese audiences. Their traditional value system collapsed, yet no new system has been estab-

---

[28] Joseph R. Levenson, "Genesis of Confucian China and its Modern Fate," in *The Historian's Workshop*, ed. L. Perry Curtis (New York: Alfred A. Knopf, 1970), 290.

lished. As a result, even though their standard of living has materially improved, their quality of life is less meaningful and more anxious. For those who live in a world of "suitcase packers," it is no wonder that Hanoch Levin is more attractive than Cao Yu.

References

Beijing Evening News. "Israeli Drama Overcomes Chinese Audience Again." March 6, 2013. Accessed August 8, 2020. http://webcache.googleusercontent.com/search?q=cache:qYDHIbScsiIJ:xiju.chnart.com/index.php%3Fm%3Dcontent%26c%3Dindex%26a%3Dshow%26catid%3D15%26id%3D3235+&cd=17&hl=en&ct=clnk&gl=il&client=safari.
Cao Yu. "On Peking Man." In vol. 5 of *The Complete Works of Cao Yu,* edited by Tian Benxiang and Liu Yijun, 74–77. Shijiazhuang: Huashan Literature and Arts Press, 1995.
Cao Yu. *Peking Man,* in *The Selected Dramas of Cao Yu,* 293–465. Beijing: PLA Press, 2000.
Jacobs, Louis. *The Talmudic Argument: A Study in Talmudic Reasoning and Methodology.* Cambridge: Cambridge University Press, 1984.
Laozi. *The Tao Te Ching, or the Tao and its Characteristics.* Translated by James Legge. Auckland, New Zealand: The Floating Press. 2008.
Legge, James, trans. *The Chinese Classics, Vol. I: Confucian Analects, the Great Learning, and the Way of the Mean.* Taipei: SMC Publishing, 1991.
Levenson, Joseph R. "Genesis of Confucian China and its Modern Fate," in *The Historian's Workshop,* edited by L. Perry Curtis, 276–291. New York: Alfred A. Knopf, 1970.
Levin, Hanoch. *Suitcase Packers.* Translated by Michael Alfreds. Tel Aviv: Hanoch Levin's Heirs, 1984.
Levin, Hanoch. "Lives of the Dead: An Epic: Chapter Four." Translated by Atar Hadari. *Poetry* 194, no. 2 (2009). Accessed August 9, 2020. https://www.poetryfoundation.org/poetrymagazine/poems/52539/lives-of-the-dead-an-epic-chapter-four-.
Li Yang. "On the Modernity of Cao Yu's Early Works." *Social Science Front* 5 (2009): 125–137.
Xiao V. December 3, 2017. "The history of Israeli drama is even longer than the state, and that's the first reason of falling in love with the state." Accessed August 8, 2020. https://new.qq.com/omn/20171203/20171203A011XD.html.
Zhang Ping. "The Middle Way Without a Middle: A Dialogue between the Confucian *Zhongyong* 中庸 and the Rabbinic *Derech Haemtza.*" *Journal of Chinese Philosophy* 45, nos. 3–4 (2018): 207–221.

Li Dong

17 Teaching American Jewish Literature to Chinese College Students: Anzia Yezierska's "Children of Loneliness" as a Case Study

How to effectively teach a course in American Jewish literature to Chinese college students is an important subject that has attracted much attention from the academic arena. This article employs Anzia Yezierska's short story "Children of Loneliness" as an example in order to show how the instructor can organize the class, motivate students, and maximize efficiency in the classroom. Only by studying this work from religious, cultural, and historical perspectives can the instructor meet his or her students' needs and accomplish his or her teaching objectives.

Before beginning to research materials or plan a syllabus for a course in American Jewish literature, the instructor should first consider and assess his or her target students. It is critically important to get to know the students – to understand their needs and priorities – in order to teach the class effectively and efficiently.

In general, teaching Chinese college students American Jewish literature is extremely challenging. Average Chinese students tend to have fixed and shallow points of view concerning Jews, whom they believe to be smart, wealthy, and good at business. These students are certainly aware of the Jewish catastrophe during the Second World War, but they can hardly explain the workings of anti-semitism. They know that Israel is a Jewish state, but they have no idea at all why there are so many Jewish people in America. Most have only a vague, distant impression of Jews and are entirely ignorant of American Jewish literature. But they are intrigued by the Jewish people's ancient religion, rich culture, fascinating history, and unique way of life. They want to know more.

A course on literary texts by American Jewish writers will satisfy Chinese college students' curiosity about Jewish culture, religion, and history. After all, a literary text is a unique medium that perfectly intermingles all of these elements. What is needed is a multi-dimensional approach.

My class on American Jewish literature is an elective course open to all students at my university. The majority of those who enroll are law students, who tend to be pragmatic, professionally ambitious, and practical. They want to acquire skills and expertise that will be useful for their future careers. Some choose my class because they intend to improve their English proficiency, while others, who have a better command of English, hope to learn more about Jewish culture,

https://doi.org/10.1515/9783110683943-021

history, and religion in order to better equip themselves to deal with Jews in a professional context. Very few are interested in literary value, criticism, theory, or aesthetics. Consequently, I know first-hand the extent to which the instructor has to bear in mind these students' needs and aspirations in order to teach this class smoothly and effectively.

The lectures will be in English for the purpose of linguistic immersion, i.e., so that the students can learn and practice English during the lectures and seminars. The class will be organized and taught from three distinct perspectives: the religious, the historical, and the cultural.

In terms of class structure, many researchers have suggested the following method as the ideal one: the students should play a major role in their own learning, while the teacher should organize and facilitate their discussions, answer questions, and provide assistance whenever necessary. To more effectively motivate the students and allow them to better understand the content conveyed in the literary text, the whole process will be divided into three parts: before, during, and after class.

Before class, the students will be required to preview the text, to watch online videos regarding Jewish immigration from 1881 through 1924, and to ask questions concerning any themes or specific issues in "Children of Loneliness" that they have not completely understood.

During class, the instructor should check the students' questions and organize a class discussion to help them determine the answers. The instructor should also provide the following background information: 1) the definition of Ashkenazic Jews and the distinction between Ashkenazic and Sephardic Jews; 2) the characteristics of Orthodox Judaism; 3) the characteristics and causes of Ashkenazic Jewish immigration to the United States between 1881 and 1924; and 4) specific geographic locations, such as the Lower East Side in Manhattan, where those immigrants settled.

After class, the students will be required to summarize what they have learned. In addition, the instructor will organize a field trip to the Shanghai Jewish Refugees Museum, which is located in the Hongkou District of Shanghai, so that the students can learn more about Jewish refugees in Shanghai during the Second World War. More importantly, the instructor will ask the students to compare and contrast the experiences of Jewish refugees in China with those of Jewish immigrants in America.

In this essay, I will employ Anzia Yezierska's short story "Children of Loneliness" as a case study in teaching American Jewish literature to Chinese college students. Before the class embarks on its journey of intellectual exploration, the instructor should first give a detailed account of the author's biographical information, which is powerfully conveyed in *Jewish American Literature: A Norton*

Anthology and may be summarized as follows: Anzia Yezierska was born in a small town near Warsaw around 1885 and traveled with her family to New York City prior to 1898. Upon arrival in New York City, she and her family lived in a tenement apartment on the Lower East Side. Her parents faithfully adhered to traditional Jewish religious practice, while she hated it with every fiber of her body. Hence their fierce confrontation, which may well have found its full expression in the struggle between the protagonist and her parents in "Children of Loneliness."

1 Teaching from the Religious Perspective

It is almost impossible for Chinese students to comprehend Anzia Yezierska's fiction – let alone American Jewish literature in general – if they are not equipped with some basic knowledge of Judaism. Accordingly, the course should start out with an exploration of Orthodox Judaism.

The Jewish family depicted in "Children of Loneliness" practices Orthodox Judaism, since the author casually mentions that "*mincha* was the prayer just before sunset of the orthodox Jews."[1] Given Chinese students' limited knowledge of Judaism, they are often puzzled by the word "orthodox," which is the key to understanding the confrontation between the protagonist and her father and, more importantly, the main idea and essential messages conveyed in Yezierska's work.

By sheer coincidence, in the course of my doctoral research, I became captivated by this specific group of American Jews – the Orthodox Jews, a branch of Judaism with highly distinctive features and unique beliefs whose pious practitioners have immersed themselves in Judaic tradition and law and set themselves apart from other American Jewish communities. The Orthodox Jews are influential among American Jewish communities. Accordingly, a thorough investigation of this group affords students an opportunity to better understand not only the Orthodox Jews but also American Jewish communities in general. In this way, I apply the results of my scholarly research to the courses I teach so that my students can more easily and readily grasp the central theme of Yezierska's work.

The instructor should above all inform students that Orthodox Jews do whatever they can to adhere to the Judaic law and tradition by which their lives are guided. A case in point should be emphasized: angry at his daughter's betrayal

---

[1] Anzia Yezierska, "Children of Loneliness," in *Jewish American Literature: A Norton Anthology*, eds. Jules Chametzky, John Felstiner, Hilene Flanzbaum, and Kathryn Hellerstein (New York: W. W. Norton, 2001), 236.

of the Orthodox sect and her total disregard for Judaic law, the Orthodox father in this fiction fumes, "No respect for old age. No fear for God. Stepping with your feet on all the laws of the holy Torah. A fire should burn out the whole new generation."[2]

The Orthodox father's rage shows that he considers his daughter's apostasy an intolerable betrayal. Here, the instructor will employ another anecdote from the text to illustrate how observant the Orthodox Jews are and to underscore the contrast between the irreligious protagonist and her devout parents. As the story develops, the father's wrath intensifies until "the old man was on the point of striking his daughter." Rachel's mother is quick-witted enough to step in, bringing the whole thing to a halt only by uttering a simple sentence: "*Mincha*! Yankev, you forgot *Mincha*!"[3]

Rachel's mother knows that *Mincha* is "the only thing that could have ended the quarreling instantly." The narrator goes on to explain what *Mincha* is and its significance to Orthodox Jews: "*Mincha* was the prayer just before sunset of the Orthodox Jews. This religious rite was so automatic with the old man that at his wife's mention of *Mincha* everything was immediately shut out."[4] This vivid account provides a unique opportunity for Chinese students to catch a glimpse of the lives of the Orthodox Jews who settled in the United States from 1881 through 1924. In addition, the instructor should return to the historical experiences of Orthodox Jews, such as their merciless persecution in Russia and eastern Europe. Historical accounts will enrich the students' understanding of this Judaic denomination's past, present, and future. The instructor can even go one step further and introduce Conservative Judaism and Reform Judaism to his or her students in order to familiarize them with other denominations of American Judaism.

The instructor should also explain the concept of "covenant mindset," which is the signature characteristic shared by Jews all over the world. The Jewish people believe that they have a covenant with God. If they act in accordance with God's commandments, they will receive their redemption. Strikingly, the Shanghainese are also known for their covenant mindset.[5] In terms of public management, the

---

2 Yezierska, "Children of Loneliness," 235.
3 Yezierska, "Children of Loneliness," 235.
4 Yezierska, "Children of Loneliness," 236.
5 The covenant mindset is a product of grassroots culture. According to Zhong Caixiang, "The Covenant Spirit of Modern Shanghai," *Inheritance* 5 (2012), the formation of the Chinese covenant mindset took three phases. First, toward the end of the Qing dynasty (1644–1911), the covenant (or contract) spirit originated in Shanghai business when several leading entrepreneurs called for the spirit of "thrift, honesty, mildness, and so on in business dealings" (89). Second, the trade guild's supervision and management of different trades in Shanghai cemented the covenant spirit. Third, the whole society's collective efforts made the covenant spirit a widely

city of Shanghai is run and governed by covenant ideas, which, many believe, may account for the transparent environment and just atmosphere of Shanghai. In the field of social interaction, the average Shanghainese's personal activity is guided and directed by covenant ideas. Is it possible that Shanghainese "covenant mindset" could be traced to those Jewish refugees who arrived in Shanghai during the Second World War? This is an open question that will arouse the students' attention and stimulate class discussion while broadening students' worldviews and expanding their horizons.

2 Teaching from the Historical Perspective

Some of the historical context will be difficult for Chinese students to understand. For example, in response to an assertion by Frank (a Gentile friend from college) that "I found him [a senior Jew] a great scholar," the main character, Rachel, protests that the old man is "a lazy old do-nothing, a bloodsucker on his wife and children." Rachel goes on to illustrate her point of view: "How else could he have time in the middle of the afternoon to pore over his books? Did you see his wife? I will bet she was slaving for him in the kitchen. And his children slaving for him in the sweat-shop."⁶ Chinese students may often be stunned and confused by Rachel's remarks. They are likely to raise questions such as: Why on earth would the man's wife and children slave for him? Why doesn't the man work to support his family? Adult men and women are supposed to be the family breadwinners.

To answer questions such as these, the teacher should guide his or her students back through the history of Jewish communities in eastern European countries. As Irving Howe mentions in *World of Our Fathers*, "A man's prestige, authority, and position depended to a considerable extent on his learning. Those who were learned sat at the eastern wall of the synagogue, near the Holy Ark. Women

---

accepted norm among the Shanghainese. Everyone in Shanghai is brought up to live up to this mindset: if they obey the rules, they will be rewarded. Possibly the most widely known example is that of the taxi stand at Hongqiao International Airport. After a long line had formed, two burly men jumped the queue and rushed to claim a taxi. A short security guard attempted to stop them, but the two men entered the taxi nonetheless. To their great surprise, the taxi driver stopped the engine and got out of the car. Both the driver and the security guard asked the would-be passengers to exit the car and obey the rule: first come, first served.
6 Yezierska, "Children of Loneliness," 243.

often became bread-winners so that their husbands could devote themselves to study..."⁷

If provided with historical background, Chinese students will understand the aspects of the literary text that were previously unfamiliar to them. In this particular case, the old gentleman is only continuing to act as he always did in eastern Europe, while the protagonist is dissatisfied with her father's refusal to adapt to life in America. With some historical context, the students will readily grasp that this is one of major reasons for the confrontation between Rachel and her father.

The author mentions that Rachel's family lives in New York City, on the Lower East Side. Rachel's mother exclaims, "Why must the whole world know how we are tearing ourselves by the heads? In all Essex Street, in all New York, there ain't such fights like by us."⁸ Essex Street is "an impoverished street of tenements on the Lower East Side of New York City."⁹ When teaching American Jewish literature, the instructor should introduce the location of the Lower East Side, where many eastern European Jewish immigrants originally settled, and discuss it in detail in order to familiarize students with the general setting of American Jewish literature during this period.

After settling in America, first-generation Orthodox Jews, especially their offspring, began to diverge. Some, like Rachel's father, continued to adhere to traditional Judaic laws; others, like Rachel, turned their backs on those ancient religious rites and strove to assimilate into secular American life; still others strove to balance law-abiding traditions with secular realities, transitioning to what is called Modern Orthodoxy. Orthodox Jews from eastern Europe displayed strikingly different responses when they encountered the free land and democratic institutions of the United States. Collectively, they constitute a very colorful picture, from which Chinese college students can appreciate the complexity not only of the Orthodox group but also of American Jewish communities more generally, which are very far from being a monolithic organization.

Anzia Yezierska's short fiction features these conflicts prominently – especially the internal conflict experienced by the female protagonist, a daughter of immigrant Orthodox parents. On the one hand, she longs to break free from her Orthodox past; on the other, her attempts to completely Americanize are ultimately in vain. The encounters and confrontations depicted in this fiction reflect

---

7 Irving Howe, *World of Our Fathers: The Journey of the East European Jews to America and the Life they Found and Made* (New York: Bantam Books, 1980), 6.
8 Yezierska, "Children of Loneliness," 235.
9 Jules Chametzky, John Felstiner, Hilene Flanzbaum, and Kathryn Hellerstein, footnote to Yezierska, "Children of Loneliness," 235.

and to some extent record the real lives of Jewish immigrants in the United States. By reading Yezierska, Chinese students of American Jewish literature can familiarize themselves with this chapter in Jewish history.

Many Chinese students already know that America is a "melting pot" with the power to change and re-forge the young people living there. With almost no prior knowledge of American Orthodox Jews or their unique way of life, Chinese students can become tremendously interested in America and its almost unbelievable capacity to assimilate and transform. This story affords Chinese students an opening through which to measure the power of American assimilation and, more importantly, to learn about Orthodox Jews within an American context.

3 Teaching from the Cultural Perspective

Yezierska emphasizes the sharp contrast between the immigrant parents' Yiddish-inflected English dialect and the more Americanized English of the main character, Rachel. Her parents' dialect results from their traditional education and their willingness to dwell in the past, while the protagonist's standard English bespeaks her wish for complete Americanization. From the exchanges between Rachel and her parents, students can easily discern the difference that marks the parents' Yiddish-inflected English: " 'Oh, Mother, can't you use a fork?' 'Here, *Teacherin* mine, you want to learn me in my old age how to put the bite in my mouth?' "[10] The characters' speech patterns reflect their family conflicts and demonstrate their different mindsets: the parents, immersed in tradition and the past; their daughter, adapting to the new and the present.

As a general rule, Chinese students are exposed to standard and formal English in the classroom. They are also encouraged to emulate a refined and polished English, to read the classical works of English and American literature, and to imitate native speakers when speaking and writing. Many try to acquire the so-called "Oxford accent." For these students, the immigrant parents' Yiddish-inflected English will be at once interesting and somewhat challenging. Even for those who have been learning English for quite some time, the Yiddish language will be brand new. The instructor should not expect them to know any Yiddish. Many will even find the word "Yiddish" itself outlandish and bizarre.

Here, the instructor should step in and introduce the definition of "Yiddish" as well as its appearance and development. For example, Howe briefly comments

---

10 Yezierska, "Children of Loneliness," 234.

on the two languages closely associated with European Jews: Hebrew and Yiddish. Howe's comments could be directly quoted in the classroom:

> Near and beneath Hebrew flowed another language, Yiddish. Elbowed away from the place of honor, it grew freely and richly. Based originally on a mixture of Middle High German dialects, it soon acquired an international scope, borrowing freely from almost every European language. Neither set nor formalized, always in rapid process of growth and dissolution, Yiddish was a language intimately reflecting the travail of wandering, exile, dispersion; it came, in the long history of the Jews, like a late and beloved, if not fully honored, son.[11]

This general introduction to Yiddish should be followed by a brief account of the Ashkenazic Jews, their previous homelands in central and eastern European countries, and their immigration to America from 1881 through 1924.

The Yiddish-inflected English of Rachel's immigrant parents is a reflection of the language that was actually spoken by first-generation immigrant Jews. Accordingly, it brings students into direct contact with the language and its speakers. It is also an important part of the author's endeavor to develop a bond of empathy between herself and her readers and, as the editors' biographical introduction states, "to give the mark of authenticity to her impassioned fiction about the struggles of Jewish immigrant women."[12] Through the instructor's general introduction, as well as previous homework assignments that will have provided further background information on Orthodox Jews, Chinese students should become aware of the differences between first- and second-generation Jewish immigrants. They should also gradually realize that these intergenerational conflicts are reflected and symbolized in the language patterns of the characters themselves. This should remind the Chinese students of generational differences they may have encountered in their own lives. Here, the teacher should step in and raise questions: "What exactly was the difference between you and your parents? What did you do to resolve it?" Later, the teacher should direct the students to discuss any similarities and differences they perceive between Chinese and immigrant Jewish parent-child relationships.

Most students at my university major in law. They are skilled in analyzing and especially adept at critical thinking. They are also deeply concerned with equity, freedom, and the rights of ethnic minorities. For these students, I throw in questions like the following: Why are American Jews a frequent object of bias and prejudice? Does the law effectively and efficiently safeguard equity and justice for minorities who have recently immigrated to America? When religious and secular

---

11 Howe, *World of Our Fathers*, 11.
12 Jules Chametzky, John Felstiner, Hilene Flanzbaum, and Kathryn Hellerstein, introduction to Yezierska, "Children of Loneliness," 233.

laws conflict, how have Jewish communities responded? Which is more effective in regulating people's behavior, secular law or Judaic law?

The instructor can also lead students to observe Rachel's (and/or Yezierska's) spirit of rebellion. She rebels against her father and the old, traditional way of life he represents. She bravely fights for her dreams, her ambitions, and her own identity. She fights for justice and equity as a Jewish woman who has long been neglected in a male-dominated society, and for the equity every American should enjoy regardless of one's gender or ethnicity. My students, many of whom are young women, are often inspired by Yezierska's fighting spirit to pursue a feminist way of life after their graduation.

There is no better way to teach Jewish literature in China than to incorporate Chinese elements into the teaching process. One point that should catch the scholar's attention and pique the students' interest is the fact that during the Second World War, about 18,000 European Jews came to China and settled in Shanghai at a time when almost all Western countries had closed their doors to Jewish refugees. Shanghai citizens were hospitable to those European Jews, who in turn left an enduring and indelible influence on the city. However, in contrast to those American Jewish immigrants, many of whom ultimately assimilated, the Shanghai Jews kept their European way of life intact and departed as soon as the war was over. In China, there was no assimilation issue. What might have caused this difference? Questions like these prompt Chinese students to think, consider, and investigate.

Appendix

1 Why Did I Choose this Particular Author and Work?

I chose Anzia Yezierska's "Children of Loneliness" because it gives a detailed account of the relationships between immigrant Jewish parents and their children. Herman Wouk, an author affiliated with the Modern Orthodox movement, also touches on this elusive relationship. There are some minor differences between Rachel's family (as portrayed by Yezierska) and Natalie's (as portrayed by Wouk). Rachel's father remains faithful to his Orthodoxy, while Natalie's father chooses to betray it. However, both Rachel and Natalie choose to assimilate into American secularism. This similar arrangement of episodes by two authors writing several decades apart (Yezierska in 1923 and Wouk in the 1970s) attracted my attention. Why did both writers, separated by almost fifty years, commit themselves to discussing similarly delicate relationships between Orthodox parents and their children? Why did both writers choose to depict the child of immigrant Orthodox parents as an apostate? Was the Orthodox movement at a low ebb during the 20s as well as the 70s? Or could there be some other reason?

2 Why Is It Important to Teach Anzia Yezierska in China?

Yezierska can serve as a representative for American Jewish writers. Students of her work can be guided toward a fuller understanding of Orthodox writers in general: what subjects they tended to write on and where their interests generally resided during the twentieth century. Chinese students can also familiarize themselves with the Orthodox movement and, more importantly, with Orthodox Jews.

When I read Yezierska's short story for the first time, I was greatly impressed by the author's vivid account of the main character's subtle change of mind, her aspiration to become educated and Americanized, and her wish to break away from her Orthodox parents. But despite her claim that she cannot endure her parents and does not even want to live under the same roof with them, she cannot ignore the affection and love she feels for them. What interested me the most in this short story were the relationships between first-generation immigrant Orthodox Jews and their children.

References

Howe, Irving. *World of Our Fathers: The Journey of the East European Jews to America and the Life they Found and Made.* New York: Bantam Books, 1980.
Yezierska, Anzia. "Children of Loneliness." In *Jewish American Literature: A Norton Anthology*, edited by Jules Chametzky, John Felstiner, Hilene Flanzbaum, and Kathryn Hellerstein, 234–244. New York: W. W. Norton, 2001.
Zhong Caixiang. "The Covenant Spirit of Modern Shanghai." *Inheritance* 5 (2012): 88–90.

Rebecca KOBRIN

18 Chinese and Ashkenazic Encounters in the American Immigration Regime: Max J. Kohler, Immigration Legal Practice, and the Chinese Exclusion Act

In a 1901 *New York Times* opinion piece titled "Our Chinese Exclusion Laws: Should They Not Be Modified or Repealed?" Max Kohler, a former United States district attorney, argued that it was time to rethink the laws that barred Chinese migrants from entering the United States.[1] Arguing that Congress should allow the Chinese Exclusion Act (originally enacted in 1882) to expire, Kohler maintained that despite the increasingly vociferous calls to restrict immigration throughout the country, it was in the United States' best interests to repeal this law. Summoning American history to buttress his argument, he wrote: "Our civil war, it may reasonably be stated, went far to establish the fact that the statements made in our declaration of independence regarding 'all men being created free and equal' were no mere glittering generalities but an essential foundation stone of our democracy."[2] It was this ideal, he added, that attracted those "Chinese persons who came to this country from 1868 until 1882," as they "came here not merely in reliance upon abstract American principles of equality of men and equal rights of citizenship but under the pledge of the treaty of 1868," which recognized both countries' sovereignty as well as "the inherent and inalienable right of man to change his home and allegiance, and also the mutual advantage of free migration and emigration of their citizens, respectively, from one country to the other."[3] For Max Kohler, a Jewish man of Ashkenazi descent, it was belief in freedom and equality – not race – that defined who could become American.[4] For him, open

---

[1] Max Kohler, "Our Chinese Exclusion Laws: Should They Not Be Modified or Repealed?" *New York Times*, November 24, 1901, 9.
[2] Kohler, "Our Chinese Exclusion Laws," 9.
[3] Kohler, "Our Chinese Exclusion Laws," 9.
[4] My use of the analytical category of race to describe anti-Chinese immigration laws draws on the following foundational texts, which examine the legal, administrative, and sociocultural contexts in which these laws were promulgated: Erika Lee, *At America's Gates: Chinese Immigration During the Exclusion Era* (Chapel Hill: University of North Carolina Press, 2003); Mae Ngai, *Impossible Subjects: Illegal Aliens and the Making of Modern America* (Princeton, NJ: Princeton University Press, 1998); and Lucy E. Salyer, *Laws Harsh as Tigers: Chinese Immigrants and the Shaping of Modern Immigration Law* (Chapel Hill: University of North Carolina Press, 1995).

immigration and free settlement were as central to the American project as the freeing of the slaves. He fought tirelessly against Chinese exclusion, seeking to keep the doors of the United States open to all who wished to come.

Kohler's opinion piece in the *New York Times* was part of a larger war that was being waged during the early twentieth century by Jewish lawyers of central and eastern European (Ashkenazi) descent against the ever-increasing expansion of the United States' immigration regime. Among his contemporaries, Kohler is distinctive in his deployment of US trade policy with China in the legal challenges he brought to bear on restrictive immigration policies. He understood, in the words of historian Donna Gabbacia, that "immigration has never been a purely domestic matter."[5] As Gabaccia points out, "American campaigns for immigration restriction ... unfolded against a backdrop of domestic political struggles over the global role of the United States."[6] The United States expanded its international trade and influence as it developed its exclusionary immigration policies. "Immigrants," Gabbacia observes, "came to mirror the geography of an American global empire built through trade, military intervention, and international investment."[7] In other words, Kohler appreciated the ways in which US immigration policies intersected with global concerns "about the status, extension, and maintenance of the United States' power in the world."[8] His goal was to convince the federal government that open immigration, if handled properly, could be an instrument of US power.[9]

Max Kohler's advocacy for excluded Chinese migrants is not only a striking example of Ashkenazi Jewish and Chinese encounters in the critical arena of US immigration courtrooms; it also illustrates why historians should not accept the currently-prevailing chronologies concerning Jews' relationships with whiteness in Gilded Age America.[10] Although most Jews, like the Chinese, were not seen as "black" by the American legal system, lawmakers and popular writers did write

---

[5] Donna Gabaccia, *Foreign Relations: American Immigration in Perspective* (Princeton, NJ: Princeton University Press, 2012), 4.
[6] Gabaccia, *Foreign Relations*, 9.
[7] Gabaccia, *Foreign Relations*, 9–10.
[8] Paul Kramer, "The Geopolitics of Mobility: Immigration Policy and America Global Power in the Long Twentieth Century," *American History Review* 123, no. 2 (April 2018): 394.
[9] Kramer, "The Geopolitics of Mobility," 397.
[10] David Schraub, "White Jews: An Intersectional Approach," *AJS Review* 43, no. 2 (November 2019): 379–407; Libby Garland, *After They Closed the Gates: Jewish Illegal Immigration to the United States, 1921–1965* (Chicago, IL: Chicago University Press, 2014); Kirsten Fermaglich, *A Rosenberg By Any Other Name: A History of Jewish Name Changing in America* (New York: New York University Press, 2018); and Jeffrey Gurock, "The 1913 New York State Civil Rights Act," *AJS Review* 1 (1976): 93–120.

about Asians and Jews as belonging to a different racial categories, and some politicians believed that they could not assimilate into American society. While some legal scholars have recently argued that by "the 20th century, 'white ethnic hierarchies began to fade' as East European immigrants were swallowed into whiteness with all its associated privileges," men like Kohler saw the racial and ethnic landscape very differently.[11] For them, exclusion was not only a moral issue but also a pragmatic one. What Congress had done to the Chinese with a stroke of a pen, it could easily do again to the Jews.

Kohler appreciated the specific connection between racist stereotypes of Chinese migrants and antisemitic stereotypes of eastern European Jews within the context of America's broader discussion of immigration and national identity. Prior to the Civil War, this debate had been framed by the institution of chattel slavery. Now, in the post-Reconstruction era, the specter of racialized immigration loomed large in public discourse.[12] Between 1899 and 1922 alone, 321,874 people – of whom only 23,672 were Jews – were denied admission to the United States, never having seen the country beyond the confines of Ellis Island.[13] In the year after the Kishinev riot of 1903, Jewish emigration from Russia to any locale outside the empire rose by more than sixty percent.[14] Anathema to Kohler and other Ashkenazi lawyers of central European descent was the notion that race could be deployed as a legal category in evaluations of prospective immigrants.

---

[11] On the issue of Jews and "whiteness" in the American legal system, see Kideste Wilder Yusef, "Criminalizing Race, Racializing Crime: Assessing the Discipline of Criminology through a Historical Lens," in *The Handbook of the History and Philosophy of Criminology,* ed. Ruth Ann Triplett (New York: John Wiley and Sons, 2017), 278–288.

[12] Najia Aarim-Heriot, *Chinese Immigrants, African Americans, and Racial Anxiety in the United States, 1848–82* (Urbana: University of Illinois Press, 2003), and Edlie Wong, *Racial Reconstruction: Black Inclusion, Chinese Exclusion, and the Fictions of Citizenship* (New York: New York University Press, 2015).

[13] Britt Tevis, "'The Hebrews Are Appearing in Court in Great Numbers': Toward a Reassessment of Early Twentieth-Century American Jewish Immigration History," *American Jewish History* 100, no. 3 (2016): 320; Erika Lee and Judy Yung, *Angel Island: Immigrant Gateway to America* (New York: Oxford University Press, 2010); *Annual Report of the Commissioner-General of Immigration for the Fiscal Year Ended June 30, 1909* (Washington, D.C.: Government Printing Office, 1909), 5; Hebrew Sheltering and Immigrant Aid Society, *First Annual Report – 1909* (New York, 1910); and "Williams Regains Immigration Office," *New York Times,* May 19, 1909, 2. Moreover, while deportations between 1892 and 1907 numbered a few hundred per year, between 1908 and 1920, that number jumped to between two and three thousand. Geoffrey Heeren, "Illegal Aid: Legal Assistance to Immigrants in the United States," *Cardozo Law Review* 33, no. 2 (2011): 632.

[14] Liebmann Hersch, "International Migration of the Jews," in *International Migrations, Vol. 2: Interpretations* (National Bureau of Economic Research, 1931), 473–474, https://www.nber.org/system/files/chapters/c5117/c5117.pdf.

They were already familiar with similar debates in central Europe concerning Jews' "racial" differences and (in)admissibility to the nation.[15]

In its focus on Max Kohler and the special role played by Jewish lawyers of Ashkenzi descent in the fight against Chinese exclusion from the United States, this essay does not look at the dynamics shaping Chinese exclusion along America's West Coast. Kohler worked in a larger group of central European Jews on the East Coast who fought against the ever-expanding immigration restrictions from their offices near Ellis Island in New York and near the halls of the Capitol building in Washington, D.C.[16] Kohler's fight against Chinese exclusion was part of a larger fight to protect America from expanding its racist ideals. Through an analysis of Chinese exclusion in American immigration history and those Jews who fought it, the coming pages shed light on the larger and longer encounter between Ashkenaz and China during the twentieth century.

1 Jews of Ashkenazi Descent in the Fight Against Immigration Restriction

Kohler was part of a larger group of Ashkenazi Jews who fought to keep the doors of the United States open to all prospective immigrants and limit the expansion of the United States' immigration regime. Leading the racist efforts to close America's gates were groups like the Immigration Restriction League (IRL). Founded in Boston in 1894 by recent Harvard graduates Charles Warren, Prescott F. Hall, and George DeCourcy Ward, the IRL reflected, in the words of historian Barbara Miller Solomon, "the conviction that neither the economic nor the social promises of democracy seemed to work in the divided society of rich and poor, native and foreigner."[17]

Rejecting this kind of nativism, Jewish men of Ashkenzi background such as Simon Wolf (1836–1923) would regularly spar with leading IRL representatives such as Henry Cabot Lodge. Wolf, who had emigrated from Bavaria at age 12 in 1848, hailed from a small town outside Cleveland, Ohio. Other Jewish leaders

---

[15] David Sorkin, "Is American Jewry Exceptional? Comparing Jewish Emancipation in Europe and America," *American Jewish History* 96 (2010): 175–200.

[16] Louis Anthes, *Lawyers and Immigrants, 1870–1940: A Cultural History* (El Paso, TX: LFB Scholarly Publishing, 2003); Katherine Benton-Cohen, *Inventing the Immigration Problem: The Dillingham Commission and Its Legacy* (Cambridge, MA: Harvard University Press, 2018).

[17] Barbara Miller Solomon, *Ancestors and Immigrants: A Changing New England Tradition* (Cambridge, MA: Harvard University Press, 1956), 99–100.

of central European descent involved in this fight were Louis Marshall, born in upstate New York in 1856; Cyrus Adler, raised in a merchant and plantation family in Van Buren, Arkansas, to become the nation's pre-eminent Jewish intellectual and head of the Smithsonian Institution; and Oscar Solomon Straus, who was born in Germany but raised in rural Georgia and had become a wealthy New York merchant, one of the co-owners of Macy's, and, from 1906 to 1909, the nation's first Jewish cabinet member as secretary of commerce and labor under President Theodore Roosevelt.[18] In Congress, Wolf debated senators and representatives who were part of the Immigration Restriction League, while Straus, as secretary of labor, shaped and molded the department charged with controlling immigration. Straus played a pivotal role in humanizing the application of restrictive immigration laws even as Congress continued its decades-long debate over whether or not the arrival of immigrants from southern and eastern Europe threatened what they called "the American way of life."[19]

Despite the efforts of Jewish civic leaders such as Wolf, Adler, and Straus, Congress continued to pass legislation aimed at curtailing the "flood" of unwanted people. The Immigration Act of 1903 denied entry to such categories of people as "idiots, insane persons, epileptics and persons who have been insane within five years previous," "persons likely to become a public charge," "persons who have been convicted of a felony or other crime or misdemeanor involving moral turpitude," and "[those] whose ticket or passage is paid for with the money of another."[20] Congress passed these laws as its members saw such legislation as necessary to protect the nation against any threats to its physical health, racial composition, and political stability. Their effects reached far beyond the walls of the immigration stations at Angel or Ellis Island.

As executive and legislative efforts failed to halt the expansion of America's immigration regime, Max Kohler dedicated himself to challenging these new laws and regulations through the judicial system. Max James Kohler was born in Detroit, Michigan in 1871. His father, Reform Rabbi Kaufmann Kohler (1843–1926), leader of Detroit's Beth-El Congregation, had arrived in the United States in 1869 after completing his doctoral training at the University of Erlagen in 1867 and two years of postdoctoral study at the University of Leipzig. Max Kohler's maternal grandfather, David Einhorn (1809–1879), leader of New York's Reform Congregation Beth-El, had spearheaded the Reform movement in America from 1855 until his death in 1879. As legal scholar William Forbath argues, this family background

---

[18] Cyrus Adler, *Louis Marshall: A Biographical Sketch* (New York, 1931); Naomi Cohen, *A Dual Heritage: The Public Career of Oscar S. Straus* (Philadelphia, 1969).
[19] This is discussed at length in Benton-Cohen, *Inventing the Immigration Problem*, 77–103.
[20] Immigration Act of 1903, 32 Stat. 1213, at 1214 and 1222 (1903).

inculcated young Max with a deep drive for social justice based on the American Reform movement's understanding of Judaism's central mission.[21] Max Kohler graduated from the City College of New York in 1891 and received his law degree from Columbia University in 1893. After his admission to the bar, he became a district attorney for the Southern District of New York, tasked with arguing for the deportation of immigrants who entered the United States illegally. Deeply troubled by what he saw in the courtroom, Kohler left his position five years later and went into private practice, forming Lewinson, Kohler, and Schattman, a firm that became famous for its pro bono work.[22]

As a partner at this firm, he began taking on gratis cases concerning detained immigrants. For twenty-five years, starting in 1901, he never accepted payment for any immigration suit he argued. Broadly speaking, Kohler's practice was an effort to graft a sympathetic and even positive perception of immigrants – as economically beneficial, as ideal citizens, as central to "American" history – onto the American legal system. He accomplished this by challenging immigration officials' violations of the law on a case-by-case basis and by calling into question the arbitrary application of the law to people of different ethnic groups. Through individual appeals, petitions, and courtroom challenges, Kohler sought to prod the country towards more open immigration laws. He firmly believed that the constitutional due process requirement took effect as soon as one entered the United States, and thus he worked for free on Ellis Island, arguing that all migrants had the right to representation and that the United States had originally been founded as a "haven of refuge" for the oppressed of all countries.[23] Inspired by some of the most influential rabbis of American Reform Judaism, Kohler contended that the American government must pay heed to the "hallowed traditions" of Mosaic Law, which promised sanctuaries to the vulnerable and less fortunate.[24] Kohler's activism on behalf of excluded Chinese immigrants was part of a larger project: making America's immigration regime compatible with his understanding of biblical moral imperatives.[25]

---

[21] William Forbath, "Jews, Law, and Identity Politics" (Annual meeting of the Law and Society Association, Westin St. Francis Hotel, San Francisco, CA, 2014). Also see William Forbath, "The Jewish Constitutional Moment" (n.d.), 23–24.

[22] Irving Lehman, "Max J. Kohler," *The American Jewish Year Book* 37 (1935–1936): 24. William Forbath, "Jews, Law and Identity Politics" (Annual meeting of the Law and Society Association, Westin St. Francis Hotel, San Francisco, CA, 2014), 35.

[23] Memorial speech, unknown author, [1934], box 1, folder 5, Max James Kohler Papers, American Jewish Historical Society Archives, New York (hereafter cited as Max Kohler Papers, AJHS Archives).

[24] Max Kohler, "The Right of Asylum, with Particular Reference to the Alien," *American Law Review* 51, no. 3 (June 1917): 406.

[25] Forbath, "The Jewish Constitutional Moment" (n.d.), 24.

2 Chinese Exclusion and the Expansion of the US Immigration Regime

In United States history, Chinese immigrants have the rare distinction of being singled out as the only national origin group to have been completely barred from entering the United States. The Congressional Act of May 6, 1882, c. 126, had sweeping effects:

> In the opinion of the Government of the United States the coming of Chinese laborers to this country endangered the good order of certain localities within our territory. It was therefore provided that from and after the expiration of ninety days from the above date, and until the expiration of ten years from such date, the coming of Chinese laborers to the United States should be suspended, and during such suspension it was made unlawful for any Chinese laborer to come, or having come after the expiration of said ninety days, to remain within the United States. Penalties were imposed upon the master of any vessel who should knowingly bring within the United States on his vessel and land or permit to be landed any Chinese laborer from any foreign port or place.... "[N]o Chinese person shall be permitted to enter the United States by land without producing to the proper officer of customs the certificate in this act required of Chinese persons seeking to land from a vessel. And any Chinese person found unlawfully within the United States shall be caused to remove therefrom to the country from whence he came, by direction of the President of the United States, and at the cost of the United States, after being brought before some justice, judge or commissioner of a court of the United States and found to be one not lawfully entitled to be or remain in the United States."[26]

Passed with the desire to protect American laborers, this federal law marks the dramatic expansion of the American immigration regime. This was the first – and, to this day, the only – time Congress has ever acted to bar all members of a specific nationality from entering the United States, constructing them in racial terms. Because of their race, the congressional law cast Asians as "permanently alien," incapable of assimilating. To be sure, Chinese exclusion came after other immigration restriction laws, such as the 1875 Page Law, which barred sex workers (primarily targeting Chinese) and felons.[27] At the same time that Congress passed the 1882 Chinese Exclusion Act, it also enacted the Immigration Act of 1882, which barred the entry of "lunatics, Idiots, any person unable to take care of himself or herself without becoming a public charge."[28] But as scholars

---

[26] 22 Stat. 58, 61, quoted in United States v. Lee Yen Tai, 113 F. 465, pp. 215–216 (2d Cir. 1902).
[27] Kerry Abrams, "Polygamy, Prostitution, and the Federalization of Immigration Law," *Columbia Law Review* 105, no. 3 (April 2005): 641–716.
[28] Roger Daniels and Otis L. Graham, *Debating American Immigration, 1882–Present* (Lanham, MD: Rowman and Littlefield, 2001), 7–13. For the actual text of the act, see https://immigrationhistory.org/item/1882-immigration-act.

note, the Chinese Exclusion Act marks a turning point in American history, as it was the first time Congress had ever defined illegal immigration as a criminal offense. Moreover, it established race as a dominant category in immigration law for the rest of the century.

From 1882 onward, the categories of exclusion continued to expand. In 1889, the Supreme Court decisively declared in a case pertaining to Chinese exclusion that the federal government had the right to regulate immigration.[29] In 1890, Castle Garden, the New York State facility for processing immigrants, was closed; in 1892, the vast, intimidating federal processing center at Ellis Island was opened under the control of the Bureau of Immigration, with medical inspections conducted by the Marine Hospital Service (precursor to the US Public Health Service). Today, Ellis Island is preserved as a national monument – testifying to America's immigrant heritage, with tourists flocking there to see where their family members entered the United States. But it is actually a testament to the triumph of the notion that the federal government had the right to regulate immigration. In 1891, congressional legislation barred entry to "insane persons, paupers, those suffering from loathsome or a dangerous contagious disease, persons convicted of a felony or other infamous crime or misdemeanor involving moral turpitude, polygamists, or contract laborers."[30] By 1903, the immigration regime had expanded to include political beliefs and social class, barring the entry of "professional beggars, anarchists, persons who believe in or advocate the overthrow by force or violence of the Government of the United States or of all governments or of all forms of law, or the assassination of public officials."[31]

---

[29] The case was Chae Chan Ping v. United States. See Kevin R. Johnson and Bernard Trujillo, *Immigration Law and the US-Mexico Border: ¿Sí Se Puede?* (Tucson: University of Arizona Press, 2011), 48.

[30] The full text of the 1891 congressional act, from which this quote was taken, can be found on the Library of Congress's website at https://www.loc.gov/law/help/statutes-at-large/51st-congress/session-2/c51s2ch551.pdf.

[31] "Act to Regulate the Immigration of Aliens to the United States," March 3, 1903, https://www.loc.gov/law/help/statutes-at-large/57th-congress/session-2/c57s2ch1012.pdf. For a full discussion of Chinese exclusion and the expansion of American immigration law, see Lucy E. Salyer, *Laws Harsh as Tigers: Chinese Immigrants and the Shaping of Modern Immigration Law* (Chapel Hill: University of North Carolina Press, 1995).

3 Max Kohler and the Fight Against Immigration Restriction

Not only did the Chinese Exclusion Act of 1882 bar Chinese immigrants from entry, it did not allow Chinese residents already in the United States to naturalize as citizens.³² Because only citizens could stand for bar exams, there were only a handful of lawyers among the thousands of Chinese living in the United States. On the East Coast, many Chinese migrants began to turn to Jewish lawyers for representation. Contemporary observers noted that "Jews protested exclusions more frequently than people belonging to any other immigrant group."³³ Indeed, as Britt Tevis argues, "Jewish lawyers stood in the vanguard of immigration law as both practitioners who helped individual aliens secure admission into the United States and as public advocates who lobbied for less restrictive laws."³⁴

Max Kohler's approach to detained Chinese visitors – and to all the immigrants he represented – was to argue for a standardized, non-discriminatory application of the law. In 1901, Kohler's activism prompted the Chinese ambassador to write to him as follows: "In view of the fact that the American Congress is certain to enact new legislation respecting Chinese immigration in its present session, I do not deem it advisable for me at this time to take any step, even unofficially, to have those questions raised by you brought before the Supreme Court as you suggest ... I hope you will continue the good work you are doing in defending the rights of my countrymen."³⁵

In 1909, citing Hightower v. Hawthorne 12 F. Cas. 142, Kohler argued that any immigrants without proper representation (as most immigrants did not understand the language or questions of their inquisitors at the US border) had been illegally stripped of their Constitutional right to understand the proceedings against them and to participate in their own defense. The lawyers and bureaucrats working for the US Immigration Service frequently excluded evidence that might have shed favorable light on the detainees.³⁶ Stationing himself on Ellis Island under the

---

32 Mae Ngai, *Impossible Subjects: Illegal Immigration and the Making of Modern America*, 3–8.
33 Britt Tevis, "'The Hebrews Are Appearing in Court in Great Numbers,'" 322.
34 See Britt Tevis, "From Prosecutor to Protector: Max Kohler and 'The Chinese Question'" (working paper, Biennial Scholars' Conference in American Jewish History, USA, 10–12 June 2014). I thank the author for sharing this paper with me. Also see her article, "'The Hebrews are Going to Court in Great Numbers': Max J. Kohler and the Advent of Immigration Lawyering," *American Jewish History* 100 (2016): 319–347.
35 Wu Ting Fang to Max Kohler, December 3, 1901, box 10, folder 14, Max Kohler Papers, AJHS Archives.
36 Max Kohler, "Brief for the Petitioner in the Matter of Hersch Skuratowski," July 24, 1909.

aegis of the Hebrew Immigrant Aid Society (founded in 1892), an eastern European Jewish immigrant organization established to help eastern European Jews with the hardships of migration, Kohler made sure that detainees designated for deportation were provided with representation. What he saw Chinese detainees subjected to prompted him to declare that Chinese exclusion was "the most un-American, inhuman, barbarous, oppressive system of procedure that can be encountered in any civilized land today."[37] While these words echoed sentiments voiced in the Yiddish press, which opposed the Chinese Exclusion Act, Kohler's proclamation was heard around the world, even in China. Wu Tingfang, then Qing ambassador to the United States, formally recognized and thanked the attorney in a personal letter for "defending the rights of [his] countrymen."[38] In short, Kohler was known as the man who provided legal aid free of charge to dozens of Jews, Chinese, and "Hindus" (a term then used for South Asians).

A few of Kohler's cases highlight the unconstitutional administration of the Chinese Exclusion Act that was common in the early twentieth-century United States. On April 14, 1904, Toy Tong boarded a train from Hamilton, Ontario. Ticket in hand, he was supposedly traveling to another station in Ontario but changed trains, heading instead to Buffalo, New York. He entered the United States through the US-Canadian border, as did at least 17,300 other Chinese migrants between 1882 and 1920, using the United States' northern neighbor as a back door into the United States. Only six days after his departure, Toy Tong and five of his companions were arrested in Hoboken, New Jersey, by border inspector H. R. Sisson, who was performing a general round-up of all Chinese men. Unable to present any identification or certificates proving legitimate entry, Tong faced immediate deportation.[39] Kohler used this case to point out the racist assumptions involved in Tong's arrest and in Chinese exclusion writ large, as sweeping raids like the one that captured Tong were characteristic of the immigration commissioner's unconstitutional approach to the enforcement of the Chinese Exclusion Act. Kohler pointed out that "in almost every city with a large Chinese population . . . wholesale raids

---

[37] Max Kohler, "Our Chinese Exclusion Laws: Should They Not Be Modified or Repealed?" *New York Times*, November 24, 1901, 9.

[38] Wu-Ting-Fang to Max Kohler, November 27, 1901, box 10, folder 14, Max Kohler Papers, AJHS Archives.

[39] Toy Tong v. United States, 146 F. 343, accessed September 20, 2020, https://advance-lexis-com.revproxy.columbia.edu/document/?pdmfid=1516831&crid=555b70fa-ac1e-4bde-a9f0-d492a84d-c0fc&pddocfullpath=%2Fshared%2Fdocument%2Fcases%2Furn%3AcontentItem%3A3S 4W-V0P0-003B-J0FP-00000-00&pddocid=urn%3AcontentItem%3A3S4W-V0P0-003B-J0 FP-00000-00&pdcontentcomponentid=6387&pdshepid=urn%3AcontentItem%3A7XX0-5ND1-2 NSD-K030-00000-00&pdteaserkey=sr 0&pditab=allpods&ecomp=sp79k&earg=sr0&prid=8c3f-4da2-d2dc-486b-9a50-000c824 b326f.

were attempted at one time or another, in which every Chinaman without a registration or other certificate was arbitrarily arrested."[40] These raids were problematic, Kohler contended, because "an enormous percentage of Chinese residents (merchants, teachers, students, United States citizens, etc.) are here lawfully without certificates."[41] The immigration inspector's issuing of warrants with no specific persons in mind, apart from the general targeting of "Chinamen," rendered Tong's detainment unlawful, and thus, Kohler argued, he should not be deported.[42]

While Kohler failed to prevent Tong's deportation, he was more successful in defending In Ng Quong Ming in 1905.[43] Ming, the grand master of the Chinese Masonic Society of the United States, had traveled to Canada for official business related to the Masonic order. Ming had lived in the United States for forty-six years and was legally classified as a non-laborer (a group that was not excluded), but he was nonetheless detained at the border. He hired Kohler, who appealed for habeas corpus based on both his long residence and an 1894 treaty with China, thereby linking the United States' restrictive immigration policy with its foreign economic policy. The judge acknowledged the unjustified nature of Ming's exclusion and handed down an "elaborate decision" establishing Chinese non-laborers' right to return even after periods of temporary absence.[44]

In his defense of Chung Gnock, Kohler brought further attention to the unconstitutional targeting of Chinese used by immigration officials. Chung's case, like Ming's, highlights the long reach of racist American immigration laws in shaping the lives of legal residents of Chinese descent. In one of the immigration commissioner's many targeted sweeps of Chinese-run businesses around the New York area, Chung was arrested "while working in a laundry at no. 181 Broadway, Bayonne on October 22, 1908." He was not a recent arrival. Chung had come "to the United States over twelve years earlier" with his father, Chung Lum Yin, a recognized merchant and "member of the mercantile firm of Qu Sang Ham of no. 710 Dupont Street, San Francisco." Chung Lum Yin had long legally resided in the United States, like many Chinese merchants, and he had "sent for his son [in China] to learn the mercantile business." Thus, the younger Chung had legally entered the United States. He "tried to work by his father's side in his store for about six

---

40 Ibid.
41 *Immigration and Labor: Hearings Before the Committee on Immigration and Naturalization, House of Representatives, Sixty-seventh Congress*, Fourth Session on H. R. 7826 and H. R. 11730, January 3, 4, 5, 22 and 24, 1923, 458.
42 *Immigration and Labor*, 458.
43 Ex parte Ng Quong Ming, 135 F. 378 (S.D. NY 1905).
44 "CHINAMAN WINS CASE: Non-Laborers Can Return After Temporary Absence, Judge Holds," *New York Times*, 1905.

months but did not like it, and then came East, learning the laundry business at the Bayonne laundry."[45] He had worked in Bayonne for three years, then dabbled in another business before returning to the Bayonne laundry the previous year, where he was arrested.[46] Kohler argued that the defendant could not be legally detained, as the Chinese Exclusion Act protected Chinese merchants and their families.

What is unique about Kohler's approach to fighting individual detainments at the border and Chinese exclusion more broadly is his recognition of the ways in which US immigration policy and foreign trade policy were intertwined. When President Chester Arthur signed the Chinese Exclusion Act in 1882, the original law only sought to shut down the immigration of Chinese laborers for a period of ten years. In 1892, Congress debated whether or not the law should be extended; in 1902, it was made permanent. Over those two decades, the United States had been seeking to reshape itself as a global economic power by acquiring more trading partners. Ironically, by passing increasingly restrictive immigration laws against Chinese visitors, Congress was failing to implement through legislation the obligations which the United States had taken on in its treaties designed to promote international trade. It was this contradiction that Kohler sought to exploit. He drew on the language of the 1892 extension of the Chinese exclusion act to show how it contradicted obligations the United States had taken on in its subsequent trade treaties:

> The preceding article shall not apply to the return to the United States of any registered Chinese laborer who has a lawful wife, child or parent in the United States, or property therein of the value of one thousand dollars, or debts of like amount due him and pending settlement. Nevertheless, every such Chinese laborer shall, before leaving the United States, deposit, as a condition of his return, with the collector of customs of the district from which he departs, a full description in writing of his family, or property, or debts, as aforesaid, and shall be furnished by said collector with such certificate of his right to return under this treaty as the laws of the United States may now or hereafter prescribe and not inconsistent with the provisions of this treaty; and should the written description aforesaid be proved to be false, the right of return thereunder, or of continued residence after return, shall in each case be forfeited.[47]

Appreciating the power of trade treaties was central to Kohler's defense of another client, Lee Yan Tai, a Chinese American merchant who entered the United States in 1900 and was detained at Ellis Island. While border officials claimed that Lee

---

[45] United States vs. Chung Gnock, Brief for Defendant 1908, pp. 1–2, box 10, folder 15, Max Kohler Papers, AJHS Archives.
[46] Ibid.
[47] This amendment, Act II, is quoted in United States v. Lee Yen Tai, 113 F. 465, p. 217 (2d Cir. 1902).

Yan Tai "unlawfully came into the United States from China" because he was "a Chinese person and laborer, and not being a diplomatic or other officer of the Chinese or any other Government . . . who was not entitled to be or remain within the United States,"[48] in fact, as Kohler pointed out, he was a merchant. A warrant for Lee Yan Tai's arrest was issued by the United States immigration commissioner; the defendant was slated for immediate removal to China by the United States marshal of the Northern District of New York.[49] It was after all this took place that Max Kohler became involved, petitioning for a writ of habeas corpus to halt the deportation. The petition averred, among other things, that the said Lee Yen Tai was a merchant having an interest of one thousand dollars ($1,000) in the capital of the firm, and was not a laborer, but rather a wealthy merchant and member of a firm.[50]

In his arguments before the court, Kohler made it clear that deporting this merchant would jeopardize America's global standing, precisely when it sought to increase its dominance through international trade. What countries would want to trade with the United States if government officials arrested their merchants every time they tried to check on their business assets? As Kohler made clear, the detainment of any Chinese

> would seriously violate the rights under subsisting treaties of all Chinese residents of the United States. Article VI of the Treaty of 1868 between China and the United States, which is still in force . . . provided that "Chinese subjects visiting or residing in the United States shall enjoy the same privileges, immunities and exemptions in response to travel or resident as may be enjoyed by the citizens of the most favored nation"; the treaty of 1880 reaffirmed this right and provides (Article II) that all Chinese persons in the United States, including even Chinese laborers **shall be allowed to go and come of their own free will and accord and shall be accorded all the rights, privileges, immunities and exceptions which are accord to the citizens and subjects of the most favored nation.**[51]

By positioning this merchant's fate within the larger debate around the United States's standing as a world trade partner, Kohler struck at the heart of his goal: to demonstrate that restrictive immigration policies were ultimately a disservice to the United States on the international stage. A lawyer for the Chinese Consulate noted, "I have read with some care Mr. Kohler's brief in the case of Lew Yen Tai. He makes the strong argument in support of his contention that the Acts of Congress to execute the treaty of 1880 and others relating to Chinese laborers have

---

48 United States v. Lee Yen Tai, 113 F. 465, p. 217 (2d Cir. 1902).
49 Ibid.
50 Ibid.
51 Petition to His Excellency the Chinese Minister, January 29, 1910, p. 4 (emphasis in the original), box 10, folder 14, Max Kohler Papers, AJHS Archives.

been repealed by the treaty of 1894."⁵² In another petition, Kohler argued not only that the "closing of the ports [to Chinese merchants] would, as already pointed out, greatly impair the rights of your petitioners under treaty and statute and work great inconvenience, hardship and expense for them," it would simultaneously have grave implications for American trade. His client, like many Chinese merchants, had "important commercial interests in the United States and the large volume of trade between the United States and China which would be materially impaired by thus checking and restraining the right of free ingress and egress of Chinese merchants in the United States under subsisting treaties."⁵³

Targeting his attack against the Chinese Exclusion Law as well as an executive policy laid down by President Roosevelt, which, starting in 1905, had made Chinese exclusion a permanent feature of the American immigration legal code, Kohler contended that "in the effort to carry out the policy of excluding Chinese laborers, Chinese coolies, grave injustice and wrong has been done by this nation to the people of China and ultimately to this nation itself."⁵⁴ He argued:

> Chinese students, business and professional men of all kinds – not only merchants, but bankers, doctors, manufacturers, professors, travelers and the like should be encouraged to come here and treated on precisely the footing that we treat students, businessmen, travelers the like of other nations. Our laws and treaties should be framed ... to state that we will admit all Chinese except Chinese of the coolie class.⁵⁵

By concluding his petition with this argument, Kohler acknowledged the widespread fears harbored by many American workers of "Chinese coolies" taking their jobs, but made clear that these concerns did not warrant the exclusion of an entire nation of people.⁵⁶ He insisted that it would be beneficial to the United States to allow "merchants, bankers, doctors, manufacturers, professors, and travelers" to enter the country. But more importantly, he used the argument that if the United States recognized Chinese sovereignty in its trade treaties, it also had to treat its "students, businessmen, travelers the like of [those of] other nations," if America ever wanted to be seen as a desirable trade partner. By linking immi-

---

52 John Foster to Wu Ting Fang, November 27, 1901, box 10, folder 14, Max Kohler Papers, AJHS Archives.
53 Ibid.
54 Petition to His Excellency the Chinese Minister, January 29, 1910, 10.
55 Petition to His Excellency the Chinese Minister, January 29, 1910, 11.
56 For the general vision of the threat posed by Chinese "coolie" workers, see "Some Reasons for Chinese Exclusion, Meat vs. Rice, American Manhood Against Asiatic Coolieism, Which Shall Survive?" (Washington, D.C.: American Foundation of Labor, 1902), Fales Library and Special Collections, New York University.

gration with American global economic concerns, he highlighted the problems with the evolving American restrictive regime.

4 US Foreign Policy and Immigration

Kohler made it clear that although nativist fears of "coolies" were cast by Congress as a domestic issue that could be addressed by immigration restriction, they were actually part of a broader foreign policy concern. As he argued in his defense of Lee Yen Tat, the United States' power to make treaties and ensure its dominance in global trade hinged on keeping its doors open to immigrants:

> Whereas, on the 17th day of November, A. D. 1880, and of Kwanghsii the sixth year, tenth moon, fifteenth day, a treaty UNITED STATES v. LEE YEN TAT. Opinion of the Court was concluded between the United States and China, for the purpose of regulating, limiting or suspending the coming of Chinese laborers to, and their residence in, the United States;
> And whereas the Government of China, in view of the antagonism and much deprecated and serious disorders to which the presence of Chinese laborers has given rise in certain parts of the United States, desires to prohibit the emigration of such laborers from China to the United States;
> And whereas the two Governments desire to cooperate in prohibiting such emigration, and to strengthen in other ways the bonds of friendship between the two countries;
> And whereas the two Governments are desirous of adopting reciprocal measures for the better protection of the citizens or subjects of each within the jurisdiction of the other...

Emphasizing that both China and the United States were sovereign nations, Kohler pointed out that Chinese exclusion laws tarnished America's international reputation. The final paragraph of his *New York Times* 1901 opinion piece declared: "The system of [Chinese] exclusion and deportation that is a blot and disgrace upon our National fame... [forcing] our Government to hide itself shame-facedly behind other Governments while making requests for trade privileges and concessions and right of residence for American citizens in China in order to avoid the inquiry as to whether American civilization has afforded similar rights in America to Chinese merchant princes!"[57]

In the end, Kohler's litigation efforts and and public writing did little to sway Congress, which enacted more restrictions over the next several years. By 1917, the following groups were barred from entry as enumerated in the Congressional Immigration Act of 1917:

---

[57] Max Kohler, "Our Chinese Exclusion Laws: Should They Not Be Modified or Repealed?" *New York Times*, November 24, 1901, 9.

> Imbeciles, feebleminded persons, epileptics, persons afflicted with tuberculosis, mentally or physically defective persons which may affect the ability of such an alien to earn a living, persons who admit their belief in the practice of polygamy, persons coming for immoral purposes, all unaccompanied children under 16; constitutional psychopathic inferiority, chronic alcoholism, vagrants, persons who are members of or affiliated with any organization entertaining and teaching disbelief in or opposition to organized government . . . of the United States or of any other organized government, because of his or their official character, or who advocate or teach the unlawful destruction of property, persons who are supported by or receive in whole or in part the proceeds of prostitution, persons whose ticket or passage is paid for by any corporation, association, society, municipality, or foreign government, anyone from the whole Asian continent, known as the Asiatic barred zone.[58]

As historian Mae Ngai points out, the expansion of these restrictive immigration laws ultimately lay in the service of racist prejudices among white Protestant Americans from northern European backgrounds who desired to maintain their social and political pre-eminence.[59] In short, Chinese exclusion was merely the first step in the construction of a broader immigration regime, which, by the 1920s, had constructed a vision of the American nation in which Jews of eastern Europe as well as Chinese were deemed undesirable.

Conclusion

What is the legacy of Max Kohler's failed effort to repeal Chinese exclusion? In his numerous court battles challenging the exclusion of individual Chinese as well as other restrictive laws, Kohler demonstrated that using racialized national categories to expand the American immigration regime could lead the US government down a slippery slope.[60] Although Chinese are still the first and only racial group to be singled out for exclusion in American immigration law, Kohler feared that they would not be the last. He modeled for generations to come the ways in which US lawmakers' concerns over foreign policy and international trade could be deployed by advocates to combat the racial politics that were molding US immigration and national identity.

---

58 Congressional Immigration Act of 1917, 39 Stat. 874 (1916).
59 Mae Ngai, *Impossible Subjects*, 21–25.
60 For more on his opposition to the "public charge" exclusion used to prevent eastern European Jews from entering the United States, see Tevis, "'The Hebrews are Going to Court in Great Numbers': Max J. Kohler and the Advent of Immigration Lawyering," *American Jewish History* 100 (2016): 319–347.

Kohler left a significant footprint on American jurisprudence. Fellow attorneys viewed him as the leading authority on immigration matters, and congressional committees often called on him to testify. Despite his impressive résumé, few in his day – or in the annals of history, as immigration historian Maddalena Marinari recently pointed out – have paid close attention to Kohler.[61] But he is a key figure in the long history of encounters between the Ashkenazi and Chinese cultures that took on specific shapes and contours in courtrooms in the early twentieth-century United States.

The history of American immigration law is a critical arena for understanding Ashkenazi–Chinese encounters. Ashkenazi Jews' commitment to an ideology of keeping the gates of immigration open in the United States was rooted in a belief that anyone could "become American." Max Kohler's pro bono casework for detained Chinese immigrants challenged immigration officials who were, as he saw it, unjustly implementing the country's immigration laws. He campaigned to secure immigrants' rights to legal representation, demanded immigrants be accorded due process, fought the government's use of racial classifications, and challenged discriminatory admissions mechanisms. He imagined a world in the courtroom that was entirely different from the one he saw around him: a world in which one's religion or place of birth would not be obstacles to starting a new life. The campaign waged by Kohler (along with other legislators, politicians, and lawyers of Ashkenazi background) in order to secure immigrants' rights to legal representation and due process and to fight against the government's use of racial classifications and other discriminatory admissions mechanisms demands more attention from scholars of US history. Their deeper understanding of immigration's relationship to the American project was rooted in the fact that they saw things others did not.[62] Aside from promoting immigration to strengthen the nation, Max Kohler understood that the practice of the law could be harnessed in the service of legal and civic equality for all and to break down the assumptions about respective groups that were slowly being forced into the legal code.

---

[61] Maddalena Marinari, *Unwanted: Italian and Jewish Mobilization Against Restrictive Immigration Laws 1882–1965* (Chapel Hill: University of North Carolina Press, 2020).

[62] William Forbath argues that Kohler's perspicacity was linked to the fact that his father was a major Reform rabbi who saw Jews' role in the modern state as that of promoting "Judaism's universal ethics." See "Jews, Law and Identity Politics," paper given at the annual meeting of the the Law and Society Association, Westin St. Francis Hotel, San Francisco, CA, 2014.

Figure 18.1: Portrait of Max James Kohler (1871–1934). (Photograph courtesy of the American Jewish Historical Society, New York.)

References

Aarim-Heriot, Najia. *Chinese Immigrants, African Americans, and Racial Anxiety in the United States, 1848–82*. Urbana: University of Illinois Press, 2003.
Adler, Cyrus. *Louis Marshall: A Biographical Sketch*. New York, 1931.
Anthes, Louis. *Lawyers and Immigrants, 1870–1940: A Cultural History*. El Paso, TX: LFB Scholarly Publishing, 2003.
Benton-Cohen, Katherine. *Inventing the Immigration Problem: The Dillingham Commission and Its Legacy*. Cambridge, MA: Harvard University Press, 2018.
Cohen, Naomi. *A Dual Heritage: The Public Career of Oscar S. Straus*. Philadelphia, 1969.
Daniels, Roger and Otis L. Graham. *Debating American Immigration, 1882–Present*. Lanham, MD: Rowman and Littlefield, 2001.
Fermaglich, Kirsten. *A Rosenberg By Any Other Name: A History of Jewish Name Changing in America*. New York: New York University Press, 2018.
Forbath, William. "The Jewish Constitutional Moment" (n.d.), 1–72.
Forbath, William. "Jews, Law and Identity Politics." Paper given at the annual meeting of the Law and Society Association, Westin St. Francis Hotel, San Francisco, CA, 2014.
Gabaccia, Donna. *Foreign Relations: American Immigration in Perspective*. Princeton, NJ: Princeton University Press, 2012.
Garland, Libby. *After They Closed the Gates: Jewish Illegal Immigration to the United States, 1921–1965*. Chicago, IL: Chicago University Press, 2014.
Gurock, Jeffrey. "The 1913 New York State Civil Rights Act." *AJS Review* 1 (1976): 93–120.
Heeren, Geoffrey. "Illegal Aid: Legal Assistance to Immigrants in the United States." *Cardozo Law Review* 33, no. 2 (2011): 619–674.
Hersch, Liebmann. "International Migration of the Jews," in *International Migrations, Vol. 2: Interpretations* (National Bureau of Economic Research, 1931), 473–474. https://www.nber.org/system/files/chapters/c5117/c5117.pdf.

Johnson, Kevin R. and Bernard Trujillo. *Immigration Law and the U.S.-Mexico Border: ¿Sí Se Puede?* Tucson: University of Arizona Press, 2011.
Kramer, Paul. "The Geopolitics of Mobility: Immigration Policy and American Global Power in the Long Twentieth Century." *American History Review* 123, no. 2 (April 2018): 393–438.
Kohler, Max James. Papers. American Jewish Historical Society Archives. New York.
Kohler, Max James. "Brief for the Petitioner in the Matter of Hersch Skuratowski." July 24, 1909.
Kohler, Max James. "Our Chinese Exclusion Laws: Should They Not Be Modified or Repealed?" *New York Times*. November 24, 1901. 9.
Kohler, Max James. "The Right of Asylum, with Particular Reference to the Alien." *American Law Review* 51, no. 3 (June 1917): 381–406.
Lee, Erika. *At America's Gates: Chinese Immigration During the Exclusion Era*. Chapel Hill: University of North Carolina Press, 2003.
Lee, Erika and Judy Yung. *Angel Island: Immigrant Gateway to America*. New York: Oxford University Press, 2010.
Lehman, Irving. "Max J. Kohler." *The American Jewish Year Book* 37 (1935–1936): 21–25.
Marinari, Maddalena. *Unwanted: Italian and Jewish Mobilization Against Restrictive Immigration Laws 1882–1965*. Chapel Hill: University of North Carolina Press, 2020.
New York Times. "Williams Regains Immigration Office." May 19, 1909. 2.
New York Times. "CHINAMAN WINS CASE: Non-Laborers Can Return After Temporary Absence, Judge Holds." 1905.
Ngai, Mae. *Impossible Subjects: Illegal Immigration and the Making of Modern America*. Princeton, NJ: Princeton University Press, 1998.
Salyer, Lucy. *Laws Harsh as Tigers: Chinese Immigrants and the Shaping of Modern Immigration Law*. Chapel Hill: University of North Carolina Press, 1995.
Schraub, David. "White Jews: An Intersectional Approach." *AJS Review* 43, no. 2 (November 2019): 379–407.
"Some Reasons for Chinese Exclusion, Meat vs. Rice, American Manhood Against Asiatic Coolieism, Which Shall Survive?" Washington, D.C.: American Foundation of Labor, 1902. Fales Library and Special Collections, New York University.
Solomon, Barbara Miller. *Ancestors and Immigrants: A Changing New England Tradition*. Cambridge, MA: Harvard University Press, 1956.
Sorkin, David. "Is American Jewry Exceptional? Comparing Jewish Emancipation in Europe and America." *American Jewish History* 96 (2010): 175–200.
Tevis, Britt. " 'The Hebrews are Going to Court in Great Numbers': Max J. Kohler and the Advent of Immigration Lawyering." *American Jewish History* 100 (2016): 319–347.
Tevis, Britt. "From Prosecutor to Protector: Max Kohler and The Chinese Question." Biennial Scholars Conference in American Jewish History, USA, June 10–12, 2014.
Wong, Edlie. *Racial Reconstruction: Black Inclusion, Chinese Exclusion, and the Fictions of Citizenship*. New York: New York University Press, 2015.
Yusef, Kideste Wilder. "Criminalizing Race, Racializing Crime: Assessing the Discipline of Criminology through a Historical Lens," in *The Handbook of the History and Philosophy of Criminology*, edited by Ruth Ann Triplett, 278–288. New York: John Wiley and Sons, 2017.

Song Lihong
19 A Homeless Stranger Everywhere: The Shadow of the Holocaust on an Israeli Sinologist

1 Where Angels Fear to Tread

To probe the interrelation between individual experience and academic choice is a worthwhile and even scintillating project, although it is not immune from justifiable qualms. On the one hand, applying the views, perspectives, and emotions formed by personal experience to the object of study has undeniable legitimacy, and may even play a pivotal role in opening up new vistas. On the other hand, highlighting these points of connection may create the impression that subjectivity trumps objectivity, thus not only affecting the credibility of the research, but also unavoidably touching upon the initial motivation and ultimate concern in the spiritual journey of scholars. Therefore, once the personal is involved, one would rather be reproached for hesitancy than for boldness.

The above observation may be offered to answer a question: Given the disproportionately high number of Jewish scholars among Western Sinologists, or scholars of China studies, why is the research on the impact of Jewish identity on the scholarship so bewilderingly scarce? An exception to the rule is a recent study on Joseph R. Levenson (1920–1969) which argues that Levenson's understanding of Jewish tradition plays a crucial role in his analysis of the history of modern China.[1] Indeed, as early as 1972, the great Arnaldo Momigliano was convinced that had Levenson lived longer he would have reinterpreted Judaism in terms of what he had learned from the Chinese historiographical tradition.[2] In another memorial essay, the eminent Harvard intellectual historian Benjamin Schwartz (1916–1999) alluded to his and Levenson's Jewishness as a key to their deep empathy with China:

---

[1] Madeleine Yue Dong and Ping Zhang, "Joseph Levenson and the Possibility for a Dialogic History," *Journal of Modern Chinese History* 8, no. 1 (2014): 1–24.
[2] Arnaldo Momigliano, "Tradition and the Classical Historian," *History and Theory* 11, no. 3 (1972): 292–93.

> His interest in the relationship of modern Chinese to their cultural heritage was intimately tied to his undisguised concern with his own Jewish past. It is a concern which I share with him and which made me feel very close to him. Far from impairing his objectivity, it seems to me that it lent an honesty and authenticity to his thought which is not readily found in the writing of many supposedly objective scholars who vainly fancy that they are leaving themselves outside of their work.[3]

Unfortunately, due to his premature death, Levenson's own testimony to his Jewishness can be measured only tantalizingly from an unfinished draft entitled "The Choice of Jewish Identity." The cluster of tensions – between history and value, cosmopolitanism and provincialism, separation and assimilation, authenticity and artificiality, continuity and change – that characterizes all his historiography also informs this vignette. Nonetheless, not a few felt it was "incongruous" with the rest of his writings.[4]

Almost thirty years after its appearance, the specter of Levenson's "choice" manifested in the title of a truly inimitable memoir of the Holocaust, *The Choice: Poland, 1939–1945*.[5] Irene Eber (1929–2019), its author, who was also a renowned Sinologist and, in my eyes, the high priestess of China studies in Israel, obviously felt an intellectual affinity with Levenson's magnum opus *Confucian China and Its Modern Fate*, which she cited in the memoir. It seems almost certain that the paths of the two Sinologists crossed. In 1966, when Eber received her PhD from the Claremont Graduate University in California with a dissertation on Hu Shi (1889–1962), the leader of China's New Culture movement, Levenson was already Sather Professor of History at the University of California, Berkeley. And when Levenson drowned in a canoeing accident in 1969, Eber had just ensconced herself at the Hebrew University of Jerusalem, where she would eventually retire as the Louis Frieberg Professor of East Asian Studies.[6]

In any event, the memoir, which is overtly incongruous with the rest of her writings, offers an unparalleled opportunity to unravel how China is understood

---

[3] Benjamin I. Schwartz, "History and Culture in the Thought of Joseph Levenson," in *The Mozartian Historian: Essays on the Works of Joseph R. Levenson*, eds. Maurice Meisner and Rhoads Murphey (Berkeley: University of California Press, 1976), 101. See also Thomas M. Levenson, "Joseph R. Levenson: A Retrospective," *The Harvard Crimson*, April 6, 1979, https://www.thecrimson.com/article/1979/4/6/joseph-r-levenson-a-retrospective-pithis/, accessed 28 June, 2020.
[4] Joseph R. Levenson, "The Choice of Jewish Identity," in *The Mozartian Historian*, 180–193. According to his wife, he "took a deep and somewhat surreptitious delight in the writing of it" (178). See page 3 for the "incongruous" remark made by the editors.
[5] Irene Eber, *The Choice: Poland, 1939–1945* (New York: Schocken Books, 2004).
[6] For the story of the endowed chair and Eber's move to Israel, see Yitzhak Shichor, "Professor Irene Eber, 1929–2019," April 12, 2019, http://www.mei.org.in/mei-remembers-18, accessed December 10, 2020.

by a Jewish Sinologist haunted by an all-pervasive mood of subdued obsession and inner wrestling with her memories of the Holocaust, as well as an irresistible temptation to rush in where angels fear to tread – that is, to explore the nexus between her Jewish identity and her academic vocation.

2 The Choices in *The Choice*

The memoir is fraught with choices Eber made, but one of the choices is perceptible only in its Chinese rebirth. Her mother and sister survived the Holocaust because their names appeared on the famous Schindler's list.[7] In the Chinese translation, "Schindler" was idiosyncratically rendered into *xin de le er* 辛得乐尔 rather than the standard *xin de le* 辛德勒. Not only that, all the words with the sound of *de* in Jewish names are invariably rendered into 得 instead of the conventional 德, which habitually means 'German' in modern Chinese, evincing therefore an unmistakable avoidance of the association of "German" with Jews and the Righteous Gentiles. According to the translator, this is Eber's choice: the word 德 that denotes 'German' cannot appear under any circumstances in the names of Jews and the Righteous Gentiles who saved the Jews, in order to "show respect for the dead."[8] This attitude is not uncommon in some of the German-speaking Holocaust survivors, who never again spoke or wrote in German, visited Germany, or bought German goods – they are constantly struggling with the memories of the past.

In effect, Eber revealed only on the very last pages of the memoir that she was born in Halle, Germany, where she lived until age eight and was engulfed by racial discrimination from her classmates and teachers. Eventually the family was forced to depart for her father's hometown, Mielec, in Poland. In later years, realizing that her family had been unwelcome strangers in Halle all along, she never bothered to return to her birthplace.

Mielec was her home in the true sense of the word, albeit for less than four years: "After Mielec all other homes were merely places for me, the sojourner's impermanent rest."[9] In the aftermath of the German invasion of Poland, Jews were driven out of Mielec in 1942 and deported to death camps. At this point, she

---

[7] She once remarked to me, "There are nearly 1,000 men on the list and less than 200 women." Personal correspondence, on October 30, 2010.
[8] Yi Ailian, *Jueze: Bolan, 1939–1945* [Irene Eber, *The Choice: Poland, 1939–1945*], trans. Wu Jing (Beijing: Xueyuan Chubanshe, 2013), 1–2 (under "The Translator's Words").
[9] Eber, *The Choice*, 208.

made what was clearly the most critical, and traumatic, choice in her life: when an opportunity came, she escaped alone and left behind her family, as if imposing orphanhood on herself. Yet this was *the* choice against the will of her father, Yedidia Geminder. The last thing he said to her, which was etched in her memory and would haunt her forever, was "Don't go."[10] In this zero-sum game between survival and family, she chose life and, as punishment, the ordeal of self-acceptance for the rest of her life. She didn't hear of her father's death until much later, and at the time she "had not learnt how to mourn," as she confessed on the very first page of the memoir.

Gone with her father was the belief of father's generation. After the War, she was convinced that she was the last Jew left alive, even embarking on constructing a new self to become a Catholic nun and to pursue a noble cause of peace and selfless dedication. At this juncture, her sister showed up out of the blue, as though *deus ex machina*, and dragged her out of the convent. But it was no longer possible to return to her father's traditional Judaism, and Jewish festivals such as Passover would only bring back the guilty memories of her betrayal and of the irretrievable integrity of the family. Because of the Holocaust, the evil of man and the intention of God are the subjects of innumerable theological reflections. However, during the conversation in which the survivors in a displaced persons (DP) camp gathered to discuss why they were spared, she heard the name of Darwin for the first time in her life, but she did not remember that they also talked about God. "It was enough to know that the catastrophe had not been averted. Why bother speculating about theological reasons it hadn't?"[11] She told a friend that she survived out of sheer luck and for no explainable reason, and "there seemed to have been only two ways after 1945: fervent belief, despite God's design which strangely seemed to include the destruction of an entire culture together with those who cherished and nourished it, or abandoning belief."[12] She chose the latter; meanwhile, it occurred to her that "being Jewish with other Jews – all of them so different – was increasingly comfortable."[13] In other words, she chose to be a Jew without Jewish faith, or what Isaac Deutscher called a "non-Jewish Jew."[14]

---

10 Eber, *The Choice*, 47.
11 Eber, *The Choice*, 156.
12 Marián Gálik, " 'Wild Goose' Letters: A Correspondence of Three Decades as Seen from the Other Side," in *At Home in Many Worlds: Reading, Writing, and Translating from Chinese and Jewish Cultures. Essays in Honour of Irene Eber*, eds. Raoul David Findeisen, Gad C. Isay, Amira Katz-Goehr, Yuri Pines, and Lihi Yariv-Laor (Wiesbaden: Harrassowitz Verlag, 2009), 15.
13 Eber, *The Choice*, 155.
14 Isaac Deutscher, *The Non-Jewish Jew and Other Essays* (London: Oxford University Press, 1968), 25–41.

In the DP camp, whether or not to emigrate to Eretz Israel/Palestine was keenly discussed. The glib Zionist emissaries from Palestine preached the gospel of redemption through labor, depicting the kibbutz as a paradise of carefree singing and dancing. Yet in the eyes of Eber, by then age fifteen, right out of unspeakable darkness in a chicken coop where she had been hidden for almost two years, it was simply too surreal to believe in. The agricultural training in preparation for life in Palestine increasingly made Eretz Israel seem "to be made up of kibbutz kitchens, where I would be told to peel potatoes until the end of my days." Her claustrophobia persisted. Quite understandably, she did not wish to go to the Promised Land. Nor did she opt for marriage, which was so popular and powerful a means among the Jewish DPs to reestablish a normal life and to banish the despair and loneliness of being *She'arit Haplita* – the saving remnant. Instead, her mind was on books, study, learning, and a career.[15] Soon, she made another fateful choice: to depart for the United States, apparently a vast and brave new world – the polar opposite of the chicken coop – and to leave behind the newly reunited sister and mother as well as a shredded self. This choice was made not for survival, but for knowledge, to make up for lost learning opportunities. She unequivocally rejected her German roots, but paradoxically embodied the very ideal of *Bildung* – a self-cultivation or character formation, a moral imperative to grow into free, creative, and independent individuals through the continuous and enlightened pursuit of knowledge – which was enthusiastically embraced and enshrined as a sort of civil religion by many German Jews.[16]

It was in the United States that she began to navigate in the sea of knowledge, thanks to a public library in New York. She first dabbled in Western philosophy, thinking with dismay that it "is not dealing with human beings." When she started reading Chinese philosophy, she felt that "it was like coming home,"[17] thus "beginning a new journey, a journey of the mind, which took me far away from Mielec and from Poland."[18] Poland was never far away, in fact – it had simply metamorphosed into a crouching beast in the jungle. Whenever it jumped out to bite, she felt that

---

[15] Eber, *The Choice*, 166–167. For her reflections on the DP Camps, see also Irene Eber, "Holocaust Education and Displaced Persons (DP) Camps," *Contemporary Review of the Middle East* 3, no. 3 (2016): 231–236.

[16] For the centrality of *Bildung* to the German Jewry, see George L. Mosse, *German Jews beyond Judaism* (Bloomington: Indiana University Press, 1985).

[17] An interview of Irene Eber by Pei-Ying Lin dated February 1, 2015, at Eber's apartment in Jerusalem, 18, accessed July 20, 2020, http://www.china-studies.taipei/comm2/eber%20interview_locked.pdf?fbclid=IwAR1AxeFc7_u42Gyx0zvwJf3oCFY9buwjxxbWYgU_g_23kTZs7uKdE9cTLYQ.

[18] Eber, *The Choice*, 175.

> [i]t was important to conceal from others our anxieties, and the physical maladies such as various intestinal disorders, undiagnosable aches, and fatigue. More difficult to hide were skewed emotional reactions to certain situations, when we laughed instead of crying, or reacted stonily when an emotional response was called for.[19]

These abysmal symptoms of post-traumatic stress disorder (PTSD) obsessed her on her journey to learn the Chinese culture and language, which must have functioned as a sort of therapeutic balm in alleviating the wound that the beast of darkness had caused. Eventually, these two heterogeneous elements ended up being in the same cluster, like a grain of sand in an oyster turned into a pearl. At the age of eighty-six, Eber commented on a Hasidic story to describe how she felt when she saw Chinese script:

> [B]efore the souls are born as human beings, they learn Torah in Heaven. Then comes the angel, who puts his fingers on the [souls'] head, with a clink. And when they are born, they forget everything. Then, when they go to school and learn Torah it is really relearning what they learned already. Therefore, learning Torah is very easy. Now, I have a commentary to this story. Some of the souls are very mischievous. They ran away from the Heaven of Torah learning and they came to the Chinese Heaven. There they lived, learned the *Lunyu* 论语, *Mengzi* 孟子, the *Daodejing* 道德经 ... When they are born they forgot everything, and when they started to learn Chinese, it was easy and sweet.[20]

She did not forget to tell the Chinese interviewer that Hasidism "originated in the vicinity of the town where I lived" – that is, Mielec. Learning Chinese was literally a journey of homecoming indeed.

Back in 1980, at the age of fifty, Eber had already opened her heart and revisited Mielec, her father's home and her home of choice, perhaps guided by her father's lingering injunction – "Don't go." As a result, awakening memories emerged one after another, in a fragmented and elusive way, with images and implications both familiar and strange, near and far, revealed and concealed. Her journey would finally lead to the birth of this poignant and disturbing memoir more than twenty years later. The long period of gestation and recollection resulted in a variety of choices. Many Holocaust survivors permanently sealed away the past, preferring to live only in the present. The past was a shameful burden, the mark of Cain. She not only saw in it the depravity of an innocent girl next door, but also had to confront her own betrayal driven by the instinct for survival. To tell, or not to tell, or how to tell: that is the question.

A prolific scholar of academic writings notwithstanding, Eber had a passion for writing, reading, and translating poetry. She chose to intersperse her memoir

---

19 Eber, *The Choice*, 175.
20 An interview of Irene Eber by Pei-Ying Lin, 18.

with classical Chinese poems, which makes it truly one of a kind in the avalanche of Holocaust literature. Those poems, conveying grief over war-inflicted human suffering or sorrow at parting with friends, seem to have had special appeal for her. Most strikingly, she felt that the vain quest for some meaning in the wanton destruction of the European Jews could best be articulated in a couplet of Lu Ji, a poet of the third century CE: 恒遗恨以终篇 / 岂怀盈而自足? ('Always dissatisfaction remains when the end is reached / – dare we then be complacent and cherish our conceit?'), with which she ended the memoir. As the son of a great general, Lu Ji witnessed the demise of his father's country and lived in an extremely tumultuous time. His poems are imbued with laments on the lost country and friends, the vicissitudes of fate, and the hardships of life. Interestingly, Lu Ji has often been belittled by modern literary critics of China as the primary representative of formalism and 无病呻吟, 'groaning without illness' or 'namby-pamby.'[21] Eber's quotation not only exhibits her profound empathy with Lu Ji, as well as her ingenuity in figuring out how to bear witness with poetry after Auschwitz, but also may well help reevaluate the modern criticism of Lu Ji.

On setting out to translate her memory into words, she would be tempted to forge from the enigmatic past a coherent and seamless narrative, as the Auschwitz survivor Primo Levi brooded: "A memory evoked too often, and expressed in the form of a story, tends to become fixed in a stereotype, in a form tested by experience, crystallized, perfected, adorned, which installs itself in the place of the raw memory and grows at its expense."[22] Eber kept a vigilant eye on this trap while writing her own memoir. She understood that her horizons were like those of a frog looking at the sky from the bottom of a well. She knew "that even if it is a small portion of history regained, other fragments of history will in turn be lost."[23] Accordingly, her memoir does not have a coherent or single narrative thread, and the past scenes in her life are presented neither in a chronological order nor in the form of a story, but in a cascading series of discontinuous shards. The gaps between the shards are filled with her research, reflection, and introspection, so that the whole narrative moves back and forth between a past that could hardly be recalled and a present that could vaguely sense the past – a choice of literary elegance and eloquence.

---

21 I am grateful to Professor Zhang Bowei for bringing my attention to this point.
22 Primo Levi, *The Drowned and the Saved*, trans. Raymond Rosenthal (London: Abacus, 2013), 16.
23 Eber, *The Choice*, 5.

3 Repairing the Self through Academic Choices

The various choices in *The Choice*, on the other hand, bespeak a character of great fortitude, immense powers of concentration, and an unflinching determination to go her own way upon setting a goal. She herself admitted, "Because I have once saved myself from certain death, obediently dependent behavior could not be expected of me."[24] In other words, once the choice was made against her father's wish, it would be no longer possible to remain passively as one of the chosen.

Eber chose a career studying China, a sheer Other with no connections whatsoever to her previous social, spatial, and intellectual backgrounds. One's ability to connect and understand is often the result of how adept one is at creatively transforming the Other. It was Chinese culture that soothed this tormented scholar at a time when the memory of Poland remained dormant in her. To pursue knowledge of China, I would like to argue, was to repair (*tikkun*) the shredded self.

For Eber, Chinese culture held not only the promise of a road that went the long way home, but also, as many Western Sinologists in her generation must have sensed, a vast and strange new world. The understanding of this world involves what Joseph Levenson called "an appreciation of amateurism":

> In studying something about which little was known, there was the promise of no boredom. There was no attraction in becoming involved in a very developed field like American history, where one had to fit himself into an environment of nasty arguments over minor details or over issues of revisionism.[25]

By contrast, inspired by her Chinese mentor, Chen Shouyi (1899–1978), who pioneered the studies of Western receptions of Chinese culture, especially the influence of China on central thinkers in the West,[26] Eber developed an abiding interest in this intellectual and cultural history from an intercultural perspective. Her publication topics range from classical Confucianism and its Hebrew translations to Daoism and Martin Buber, from the reception of modern Chinese litterateurs such as Lu Xun (1881–1936) in Europe and America to Kafka, Yiddish, and Polish literature in Chinese translation. In an age of specialization, she was unabashedly catholic in her choice of subject matters and is eulogized as "at home in many worlds," to borrow the title of a festschrift in her honor.[27] Yet she did create a niche for herself by writing with particular authority on three aspects

---

24 Eber, *The Choice*, 153.
25 Quoted in *The Mozartian Historian*, 77.
26 See Chen Shouyi, *Zhongou Wenhua Jiaoliushi Luncong* [Essays on the history of cultural exchange between China and Europe], Taibei: Taiwan Shangwu Yinshuguan, 1970.
27 For her partial bibliography, see Findeisen et al., eds., *At Home in Many Worlds*, 312–320.

of Sino-Jewish connections: Yiddish letters and China, the Bible in China, and, above all, the Jews in China.

In the beginning, she paid attention to the translations of Yiddish literature from English or Esperanto by such prominent Chinese writers as Mao Dun (1896–1981) and Zhou Zuoren (1885–1967). Yiddish, a kind of lingua franca spoken and read by the majority of Jews in central and eastern Europe before World War II, is one of Eber's three mother tongues, the other two being German and Polish. She pointed out that the reason these Chinese writers thought Yiddish mattered was not merely that they had great empathy toward 弱小民族, 'weak and small peoples,' or 被压迫民族, 'oppressed peoples,' but also from a misunderstanding. That is, Yiddish was mistaken for the 'vernacular' (*baihua* 白话) of the Jewish people whereas Hebrew was deemed as their 'literary language' (*wenyan* 文言). Just as *baihua* was taking the place of *wenyan* in literary composition in China, which was championed relentlessly by these Chinese writers, Yiddish, they believed, was also replacing Hebrew. Thus, in Yiddish literature, the Chinese writers found affirmation and endorsement of their own goals. It never occurred to them, however, that Hebrew was also undergoing a similar literary revolution, much less that it was being revived as a modern spoken language of the Jews. A thorny issue she particularly noted was that these Chinese writers frequently translated under pseudonyms, making the identities of some of the translators elusive.[28] For Eber, transculturalism was by no means a one-way street. In her later years, she also investigated the image of China in the eyes of Yiddish writers contemporaneous with those Chinese writers.[29] Her earlier concerns with how cultures and peoples so different have found ways to communicate through translated texts, where such communication becomes problematic, and with the quest for identification of the translators and sources, went on unabated.

The same concerns are arguably most palpable in her magnum opus on S. I. J. Schereschewsky (1831–1906).[30] Born a Jew in Russian Lithuania (later an American citizen) and educated in a progressive rabbinic school (*yeshiva*), Schereschewsky eventually fashioned himself into an Episcopal bishop in Shanghai and

---

28 Irene Eber, "Yiddish Literature and the Literary Revolution in Modern China," *Judaism* 16, no. 1 (Winter 1967): 42–59; Irene Eber, *Jews in China: Cultural Conversations, Changing Perceptions*, ed. Kathryn Hellerstein (University Park: Penn State University Press, 2019), 132–156.
29 Yi Ailian [Irene Eber], "Renzhi bici: Yidixuyu zuojia he zhongguoren" [Getting to know one another: Yiddish writers and Chinese] in *Youtai Liusan zhong de biaozheng yu rentong* [Representations and identities in the Jewish Diaspora: Essays in honor of Professor Xu Xin], ed. Song Lihong (Beijing: Shehui kexue wenxian chubanshe, 2018), 3–13.
30 Irene Eber, *The Jewish Bishop and the Chinese Bible: S. I. J. Schereschewsky (1831–1906)* (Leiden: Brill, 1999). See also Eber, *Jews in China*, 87–120.

the founder of the first Christian college in China. He translated the Old Testament into northern vernacular Chinese directly from the Hebrew Masoretic Text for the first time. Later on, this translation provided the basis for the Bible translation most widely used by Chinese Protestants within and outside of China in the twentieth century. In her definitive biography, Eber explored what had been terra incognita in previous scholarship, that is, Schereschewsky's Jewish background. Among the missionaries who came to China, he benefited from his unparalleled proficiency in Hebrew and familiarity with the traditional Jewish biblical exegeses. This Jewish past was finally crystallized in his translation techniques and notes. He opted to avoid being literal by giving a more explicit rendition in the Chinese where the Hebrew text tended to be suggestive and ambiguous. Eber thus restored the hidden traditional Jewish learning to the history of Protestant missionary work in modern China.

In her view, Schereschewsky is "the Jewish bishop." From a Christian perspective, this coinage is pointless, because once baptized, "there is no such thing as Jew and Greek [Gentile], slave and freeman, male and female; for you are all one person in Christ Jesus."[31] However, as she pointed out, in terms of Jewish law (*halakha*), Schereschewsky was an apostate (*mumar*), who accordingly lost certain legal rights under Jewish law but did not cease to be a Jew by conversion, as it is technically impossible for a Jew to change his religion.[32] The apostate is a sinner, but he is a Jewish sinner, or a "non-Jewish Jew," so to speak. What strikes her most is Schereschewsky's independence and his

> uncanny ability to make the right decisions at the right time. He was in Germany when the great emigration to the New World was under way; he was in New York when missionary recruitment for China was beginning; he was in Shanghai when foreign residence in Peking became possible. Whether he made these decisions on the advice of friends is again not important – ultimately it was he who had to decide whether or not to grasp the offered opportunities. Deciding between one course of action and another also meant that choices existed.[33]

This credo is without doubt a confirmation of her own life choices. She was in Europe when rising antisemitism forced her to make the fateful choice against the will of her father; she was in New York when her intellectual fascination for China was beginning; she was in Israel when the return to Mielec became possible. She believed that the way in which Schereschewsky made his choices had much to do with his self-perception as an outsider.[34] In this central figure in the history of

---

[31] Gal. 3:28.
[32] Eber, *The Jewish Bishop and the Chinese Bible*, 243–244.
[33] Eber, *The Jewish Bishop and the Chinese Bible*, 236.
[34] Eber, *The Jewish Bishop and the Chinese Bible*, 237.

Chinese translation of the Bible, what she saw and stressed was his marginality: as an orphan, he was marginal in Jewish society; as a Christian, he was much more interested in translating than in preaching and evangelizing, which placed him in a marginalized position within the missionary community.

Isn't Eber herself defined by marginality? She was a Jew amidst Germans and Poles, a runaway from her family, a "non-Jewish Jew" among Jews, an immigrant in the United States, a Holocaust survivor pretending to live a normal life in Israeli society, and a female professor of Sinology at the male-dominated Mount Scopus. The reconstruction of Schereschewsky's life seems to blur the distinction between the author and her subject and intermingle the subjective self with the objective other, while at the same time insisting on the subject's distinct personality. The resultant tension between biographical and autobiographical writing must have been therapeutic, providing a healing not just for history but for the integrity of self as well. In her later years, an unexpected telephone call gave her an afterglow of this research. A man in Jerusalem telephoned, full of excitement, saying that his mother's maiden name was Schereschewsky and that the family was from the same town as the bishop – he was probably a descendant of the bishop's half-brother. She could not help but meditate with delight, "It is not often that we find our place in this world of imponderables."[35]

Besides the "non-Jewish Jew" Schereschewsky, Eber's quest to find a meaningful place in history for the Jews coming to China runs through her academic career. According to Bernard Lewis, a distinguished Jewish scholar of Islam and the Middle East, Jews in the Diaspora can only flourish under the aegis of Christianity and Islam, two successor religions of Judaism; Jewish communities elsewhere, such as those in India and China, "appear to have played no role of any importance in the history or culture of those countries or of the Jewish people."[36] Eber the Sinologist would certainly have disagreed.

With regard to Kaifeng Jews in traditional China, the so-called 'Sinification' (华化) issue is controversial.[37] Chinese scholars, almost without exception, regard Sinification as a process that leads to total assimilation into Chinese culture. In contrast, Eber's stance can be captured in the following key words, which are central to her life experience: "survival" and "family-centered." Sinification, she

---

[35] Personal correspondence, on January 27, 2014.
[36] Bernard Lewis, *Notes on a Century: Reflections of a Middle East Historian* (New York: Penguin Books, 2012), 240; Bernard Lewis, *The Jews of Islam* (Princeton, NJ: Princeton University Press, 1984), ix.
[37] For a full discussion, see Song Lihong, "Reflections on Chinese Jewish Studies: A Comparative Perspective," in *The Image of Jews in Contemporary China*, eds. James Ross and Song Lihong (Boston: Academic Studies Press, 2016), 217–226.

posited, meant the gradual adaptation of customs from the Chinese environment that led not to assimilation and disappearance, but to retaining a Jewish identity for 800 years. Of these customs, the adoption of patrilineal kinship organized into lineage families was, in her eyes, of paramount importance. As a result, the Jewish identity, while becoming geographically defined – since Chinese lineages are always associated with specific localities – shifted from the community (*kehillah*)-centered to the family-centered. This transformation of Jewish identity, on the one hand, made them no longer strangers and allowed them to integrate into Chinese society. On the other hand, by virtue of maintaining this new identity, they managed to preserve the Jewish memory to this day as long as they were domiciled in Kaifeng.[38] Sinification guaranteed survival. The historical experience of Kaifeng Jewry thus underscored the importance of institutional life in the preservation and perpetuation of Jewish values.

The meaning of the Jewish presence in China was also personal for Eber. She confessed in 2015:

> I came to feel very strongly that, since I survived the war, remained alive, I owe a debt. Nothing is free in this world. You have to pay for everything. And I survived. I still, sometimes, wonder how I managed writing the books, but I really have to pay my debt, so I started writing about Jews in China.[39]

In retirement, after the publication of the memoir in particular, she continued to work hard, focusing on the problem of Jewish refugees in Shanghai during World War II. Her career even entered an admirable second summer that led to the birth of a trilogy on Ashkenazi Jews in modern Shanghai.

This renewed and accelerated productivity must have something to do with a growing awareness of the shortness of time. If not now, when? She sensed at this stage, as indicated in her previous quote, the destined imperative to retrospectively locate a point of origin for herself, to lay out the path to her present being, and to wrap up her career. It was a spiritual journey of homecoming. The choice of Shanghai is a natural extension of her work on Schereschewsky, but it also betrays "a form of exile," in the parlance of what Edward Said remarked of "late style,"[40] the wisdom and sadness that come from experience. Just as Schereschewsky, who published the foundational Chinese translation of the Hebrew Bible, never went to Palestine, Eber, who did the foundational work on Jewish

---

[38] Irene Eber, "K'aifeng Jews Revisited: Sinification as Affirmation of Identity," *Monumenta Serica* 41 (1993): 231–247; Eber, *Jews in China*, 3–53.
[39] An interview of Irene Eber by Pei-Ying Lin, 25.
[40] Edward W. Said, *On Late Style: Music and Literature against the Grain* (New York: Pantheon, 2006), 3–24.

refugees in Shanghai, never set foot in mainland China. To anchor her concern with Shanghai Jewry is a form of self-imposed intellectual exile that is both heroic and intransigent, and both *in* and oddly *apart* from the present.

In *Voices from Shanghai*, she compiled and translated (mostly from Yiddish and Polish) the letters, diary entries, poems, and short stories written by the central and eastern European Jews who took refuge in Shanghai during the Nazi rule.[41] Recovered from archives, private collections, and now-defunct newspapers, this literary collection testifies to, as Kathryn Hellerstein aptly puts it, "the role that literature and culture play as modes of human survival under the direst circumstances" in general,[42] and to the variety of Jewish secular culture in the assertion of Jewish identity in particular.

Wartime Shanghai and the Jewish Refugees from Central Europe reconstructed the exile condition of the refugees, shedding an indispensable light on the context in which those literary compositions were produced. Eber upheld the necessity for truth in historical studies and maintained that the growing number of Holocaust memoirs was not a substitute for historical research. This position may serve as a corrective to some of the current scholarship motivated by contemporary agendas. For instance, she pointed out that the Jewish arrivals had little or no inkling of Shanghai's war-afflicted situation; they did not realize that the pictures of abject poverty and of Chinese indifference to the suffering and death of the needy that they saw daily in streets were those of refugees made homeless in war. In light of this reminder, the heated debate concerning how much interaction occurred between the Jewish refugees and the resident Chinese smacks of anachronism. She also discussed with candor the crimes the refugees committed.[43] On the other hand, she defined the story of Shanghai as part of the history of the Holocaust – "a story of survival, even of heroism, and of stubbornly defying fate"[44] – and warned that "neglecting or ignoring even a portion of this history puts us in danger of forgetting that, above all, this is also the history of human lives and human loss."[45] Subjectivity amalgamated with objectivity, which "lent an honesty and authenticity" to this book.

In the course of writing the book, she managed to collect over 2,000 documents. And from these she selected 184 documents in six languages (German,

---

[41] Irene Eber, ed. and trans., *Voices from Shanghai: Jewish Exiles in Wartime China* (Chicago, IL: University of Chicago Press, 2008).
[42] In Eber, *Jews in China*, ix.
[43] Irene Eber, *Wartime Shanghai and the Jewish Refugees from Central Europe: Survival, Co-Existence and Identity in a Multi-Ethnic City* (Berlin: De Gruyter, 2012), 133–137.
[44] Eber, *Wartime Shanghai*, 3.
[45] Eber, *The Choice*, 205.

English, Yiddish, Hebrew, Russian, and Chinese), classified them into eight chapters, and added long introductions and copious footnotes, thereby achieving a stupendous 700-page tome of documentary history examining the whole gamut of the story from multiple perspectives.[46] Its self-evident foremost importance for the field notwithstanding, her meticulous attention to – indeed her obsession with – the biographical information of each and every refugee mentioned in the documents, as embodied in her footnotes, is noteworthy. Knowing her days were numbered and the passing of her generation inevitable, Eber concurred with Yosef Hayim Yerushalmi's endorsement of historical research: "My terror of forgetting is greater than my terror of having too much to remember."[47] Her Sisyphean efforts to provide the forgotten refugees with identifications might be viewed as an echo to Saul Friedlander's suggestion for historians of the Holocaust, i.e., historians should heed the individual voice of the victims and introduce it into "a field dominated by political decision and administrative decrees which neutralize the concreteness of despair and death."[48] In tracing these victims' whereabouts before and after their sojourn in Shanghai, Eber was somewhat like a medieval artist, working in grottos on the Silk Road of western China, who repeatedly repainted the Buddhist frescos therein and untiringly delineated facial expressions and gestures of the tiny figures thereon. With this panorama of the Jewish refugees of Shanghai, she paid off her debt.

4 Exile in the Holy Land

Yet there is no redemptive end at the individual level, which was undeniably true at least for Eber. In China studies there were big open spaces and the promise of a road that went the long way home. That home, however, no longer exists: "Polish Jewish culture was Yiddish culture."[49] After the Holocaust, the obliterated Yiddish-speaking community is a lost home toward which the saving remnants can only look back with nostalgia, and Yiddish becomes "a language of exile, without

---

[46] Irene Eber, ed., *Jewish Refugees in Shanghai 1933–1947: A Selection of Documents* (Göttingen: Vandenhoeck & Ruprecht, 2018). In many ways, it is modelled after her friend Mendes-Flohr's widely acclaimed documentary history. See Paul Mendes-Flohr and Jehuda Reinharz, eds., *The Jew in the Modern World: A Documentary History*, 3rd ed. (New York: Oxford University Press, 2011).
[47] Cited in Eber, *The Choice*, 205.
[48] Saul Friedlander, "Trauma, Memory, and Transference," in *Holocaust Remembrance: The Shapes of Memory*, ed. Geoffrey H. Hartman (Oxford: Blackwell, 1994), 262.
[49] Personal correspondence, on October 30, 2010.

a land, without frontiers, not supported by any government."⁵⁰ Of all the marginal features defining Eber, perhaps the most nagging one is that she, no matter how prolific, could not write and publish in *mame-loshn* – the mother tongue, and had to make do with the adopted languages. This imposed state of linguistic orphanage was doomed to accompany her to the very last of her days. Even after living in Jerusalem for many years, she could not blend in:

> I am a stranger here, because when walking in these sunlit, noisy streets, I also continue to walk through fields of snow and death where Father's song of Zion is no longer heard and where my childhood picture of Jerusalem was long ago torn to shreds.⁵¹

Being a polyglot in academia established her international reputation of being "at home in many worlds," but she was a homeless stranger everywhere nonetheless, eternally wandering on the earth that the Lord has given to humankind.

At the collective level, the mushrooming of Holocaust museums and monuments seem to promise a redemption of its universal memory. Desirable as this would be, she contends that the "museumification" of a living, changing culture is lifeless.⁵² This neologism is borrowed from Joseph Levenson, who has a comment on Lu Xun which undoubtedly resonates with Eber. Lu Xun

> would not see himself as a happy antique. He could not bear to see China as a vast museum. History had to be made there again, and the museum consigned to the dead, as a place of liberation for the living, not a mausoleum for the modern dead-alive.⁵³

Likewise, Eber, as a saving remnant, could not bear to see the Yiddish culture that nurtured and nourished her as a vast museum. Being alive meant she could choose to assume the "responsibilities not only to ourselves but to the dead for whom we had to speak."⁵⁴ To view the story of Jewish refugees in Shanghai as part of the history of the Holocaust was thus to accommodate a past that is apart from her to a past that is in her. It was her personal memory of the Holocaust that bridged the past with the present, and connected her life experience to her academic choices. This memory was indeed the source of incurable trauma, but it was also the driving force moving her forward step by step. Just as the Jewish past of Schereschewsky was not an obstacle but an asset to his later translation

---

50 Isaac Bashevis Singer, "Nobel Lecture, 8 December 1978," Nobel Prize website, accessed August 5, 2020, https://www.nobelprize.org/prizes/literature/1978/singer/lecture/.
51 Eber, *The Choice*, 24.
52 Eber, *The Choice*, 210.
53 Joseph R. Levenson, *Confucian China and Its Modern Fate, Vol. 3: The Problem of Historical Significance* (Berkeley: University of California Press, 1968), 118.
54 Eber, *The Choice*, 157.

project, Eber eventually sublimated her dark early years into a lush achievement in China studies. In this self-fashioning crucible, the ingathering of the sparks of Yiddish culture that were scattered to the four corners of the world, in my opinion, is both *the* choice she made in her academic career and the most steadfast embodiment of her Jewish identity. Yet it is precisely here that we may perceive the most profound discrepancy between her life experience and her academic choice. She found herself in exile in the Holy Land on the one hand, but internalized the Zionist discourse of the ingathering of the exiles (*kibbutz galuyyot*) in her scholarly efforts on the other. This irreconcilable discrepancy not only attests to the flesh and blood of her being but casts a long shadow of the Holocaust whose darkness is visible or sensible on almost every page of her writings.

At the end of World War II, Abraham J. Heschel (1907–1972), the scion of a Polish Hasidic dynasty, delivered a speech in Yiddish in New York, which was later translated into English and published under the title *The Earth is the Lord's*. In this poetically charged little book bathed in a dreamlike glow, Heschel composed an elegy for the lost Jewish world in eastern Europe.[55] In *The Choice*, by contrast, Eber reproduced in a realistic style the guilt, despair, and agony of bereavement experienced by a survivor from a middle-class Jewish family in eastern Europe. If Heschel's book is an echo in an empty mountain to a vanishing *niggun* (Hasidic melody), then Eber's memoir is a recitative mourner's *Kaddish*, with which she finally learned how to mourn for the annihilated congregation (*Gemeinde*) in the world of her fathers.

---

55 Abraham Joshua Heschel, *The Earth is the Lord's: The Inner World of the Jew in Eastern Europe* (New York: Henry Schuman, 1950).

Figure 19.1: Irene Eber (1929–2019), Louise Frieberg Professor of East Asian Studies at the Hebrew University of Jerusalem and Senior Fellow of the Harry S. Truman Research Institute. (Photograph by Miriam Eber; Jerusalem, 2017.)

References

Chen Shouyi. *Zhongou Wenhua Jiaoliushi Luncong* [Essays on the history of cultural exchange between China and Europe]. Taibei: Taiwan Shangwu Yinshuguan, 1970.
Deutscher, Isaac. *The Non-Jewish Jew and Other Essays*. London: Oxford University Press, 1968.
Eber, Irene. "Yiddish Literature and the Literary Revolution in Modern China." *Judaism* 16, no. 1 (Winter 1967): 42–59.
Eber, Irene. "K'aifeng Jews Revisited: Sinification as Affirmation of Identity." *Monumenta Serica* 41 (1993): 231–247.
Eber, Irene. *The Jewish Bishop and the Chinese Bible: S. I. J. Schereschewsky (1831–1906)*. Leiden: Brill, 1999.
Eber, Irene. *The Choice: Poland, 1939–1945*. New York: Schocken Books, 2004. Published in Chinese as Yi Ailian, *Jueze: Bolan, 1939–1945*, translated by Wu Jing (Beijing: Xueyuan Chubanshe, 2013).
Eber, Irene, ed. and trans. *Voices from Shanghai: Jewish Exiles in Wartime China*. Chicago, IL: University of Chicago Press, 2008.
Eber, Irene. *Wartime Shanghai and the Jewish Refugees from Central Europe: Survival, Co-Existence and Identity in a Multi-Ethnic City*. Berlin: De Gruyter, 2012.
Eber, Irene. "Holocaust Education and Displaced Persons (DP) Camps." *Contemporary Review of the Middle East* 3, no. 3 (2016): 231–236.
Eber, Irene, ed. *Jewish Refugees in Shanghai 1933–1947: A Selection of Documents*. Göttingen: Vandenhoeck & Ruprecht, 2018.
Eber, Irene. *Jews in China: Cultural Conversations, Changing Perceptions*. Edited by Kathryn Hellerstein. University Park: Penn State University Press, 2019.
Yi Ailian [Irene Eber]. "Renzhi bici: Yidixuyu zuojia he zhongguoren" [Getting to know one another: Yiddish writers and Chinese]. In *Youtai Liusan zhong de biaozheng yu rentong* [Representations and identities in the Jewish Diaspora: Essays in honor of Professor Xu Xin], edited by Song Lihong, 3–13. Beijing: Shehui kexue wenxian chubanshe, 2018.
Friedlander, Saul. "Trauma, Memory, and Transference." In *Holocaust Remembrance: The Shapes of Memory*, edited by Geoffrey H. Hartman, 252–263. Oxford: Blackwell, 1994.
Gálik, Marián. " 'Wild Goose' Letters: A Correspondence of Three Decades as Seen from the Other Side." In *At Home in Many Worlds: Reading, Writing, and Translating from Chinese and Jewish Cultures. Essays in Honour of Irene Eber*, edited by Raoul David Findeisen, Gad C. Isay, Amira Katz-Goehr, Yuri Pines, and Lihi Yariv-Laor, 9–18. Wiesbaden: Harrassowitz Verlag, 2009.
Heschel, Abraham Joshua. *The Earth is the Lord's: the Inner World of the Jew in Eastern Europe*. New York: Henry Schuman, 1950.
Levenson, Joseph R. *The Problem of Historical Significance*. Vol. 3 of *Confucian China and Its Modern Fate*. Berkeley: University of California Press, 1968.
Levenson, Joseph R. "The Choice of Jewish Identity." In *The Mozartian Historian: Essays on the Works of Joseph R. Levenson*, edited by Maurice Meisner and Rhoads Murphey, 180–193. Berkeley: University of California Press, 1976.
Levenson, Thomas M. "Joseph R. Levenson: A Retrospective." *The Harvard Crimson*, April 6, 1979. Accessed 28 June, 2020. https://www.thecrimson.com/article/1979/4/6/joseph-r-levenson-a-retrospective-pithis/.

Levi, Primo. *The Drowned and the Saved*. Translated by Raymond Rosenthal. London: Abacus, 2013.
Lewis, Bernard. *The Jews of Islam*. Princeton, NJ: Princeton University Press, 1984.
Lewis, Bernard. *Notes on a Century: Reflections of a Middle East Historian*. New York: Penguin Books, 2012.
Lin Pei-Ying. An interview of Irene Eber dated February 1, 2015, at Eber's apartment in Jerusalem. Accessed 20 July, 2020. http://www.china-studies.taipei/comm2/eber%20interview_locked.pdf?fbclid=IwAR1AxeFc7_u42Gyx0zvwJf3oCFY9buwjxxbWYgU_g_23kTZs7uKdE9cTLYQ.
Mendes-Flohr, Paul and Jehuda Reinharz, eds. *The Jew in the Modern World: A Documentary History*, 3rd ed. New York: Oxford University Press, 2011.
Momigliano, Arnaldo. "Tradition and the Classical Historian." *History and Theory* 11, no. 3 (1972): 279–293.
Mosse, George L. *German Jews beyond Judaism*. Bloomington: Indiana University Press, 1985.
Said, Edward W. *On Late Style: Music and Literature against the Grain*. New York: Pantheon, 2006.
Schwartz, Benjamin I. "History and Culture in the Thought of Joseph Levenson." In *The Mozartian Historian: Essays on the Works of Joseph R. Levenson*, edited by Maurice Meisner and Rhoads Murphey, 100–112. Berkeley: University of California Press, 1976.
Shichor, Yitzhak. "Professor Irene Eber, 1929–2019." April 12, 2019. Accessed December 10, 2020. http://www.mei.org.in/mei-remembers-18.
Singer, Isaac Bashevis. "Nobel Lecture, 8 December 1978." Accessed 5 August, 2020. https://www.nobelprize.org/prizes/literature/1978/singer/lecture/.
Song Lihong. "Reflections on Chinese Jewish Studies: A Comparative Perspective." In *The Image of Jews in Contemporary China*, edited by James Ross and Song Lihong, 206–233. Boston: Academic Studies Press, 2016.
Yue Dong, Madeleine, and Zhang Ping. "Joseph Levenson and the Possibility for a Dialogic History." *Journal of Modern Chinese History* 8, no. 1 (2014): 1–24.

Contributors

Ai Rengui 艾仁贵 is the deputy director of the Israel Studies Center at Henan University. His research interests include Zionism and the transformation of modern Jewish identity, Jewish body images, and Jewish memory in the modern world. He is the author of *An Introduction to Jewish History* (Beijing, 2017) and "The Construction of National Memory in the Contemporary Israeli State," in Zhang Qianhong et al., *The New Dimensions of Jewish History Studies* (Beijing, 2015).

Bao Anruo 包安若 is a PhD candidate in Yiddish studies and comparative literature at Columbia University. Her academic interests include comparative studies of Chinese and Jewish culture, modern Jewish literature and culture, pre-modern and modern Jewish history, and modern Chinese literature. She is the author of a series of articles introducing Yiddish literature to a Chinese audience and presenting the current situation of Yiddish studies in China to American readers. She is now working on her dissertation and hopes to continue to bridge the two cultures in the future.

Nancy Berliner is the Wu Tung Senior Curator of Chinese Art at the Museum of Fine Arts in Boston. Her research, writing, and curatorial work often consider fields beyond the traditional canon of Chinese art, including Chinese architecture, gardens, and furniture, as well as popular and vernacular visual culture. In 2017, she curated a first-ever exhibition on *bapo*, a previously un-explored genre of Chinese painting, and authored the book *The 8 Brokens: Chinese Bapo Painting* (Boston, 2018). Until 2012, she was the curator of Chinese art at the Peabody Essex Museum, spearheading the Yin Yu Tang project, the relocation of a 250-year-old Chinese home to the museum. Berliner completed her undergraduate and graduate studies at Harvard University. She has also studied at the Central Academy of Art in Beijing.

Cao Jian 曹坚 is a professor of philosophy at Sun Yat-sen University in Guangzhou, China. He completed his PhD in biblical studies at the Hebrew University of Jerusalem in 2009. His research focuses on the Hebrew Bible, with particular attention to its reception among modern Chinese and Jewish intellectuals. He is the author of *Chinese Biblical Anthropology* (Eugene, 2019) and serves on the editorial committee of *Logos & Pneuma: Chinese Journal of Theology* (A&HCI) and *Journal for the Study of Biblical Literature* (CSSCI).

Irene Eber (1929–2019) was the Louis Frieberg Professor of East Asian Studies at the Hebrew University of Jerusalem. Born in Halle, Germany, she was living in the small town of Mielec, Poland, when the German armies invaded Poland in September 1939. She survived World War II in hiding, when a merciful Polish family saved her life, and was reunited with her mother and sister, who survived on Schindler's list, in 1945. She emigrated to the United States in 1947. A scholarship enabled her to study Chinese languages and history at Pomona College, California. Continuing her studies at the Claremont Graduate University, she earned her PhD in Chinese intellectual history in 1966. She taught Chinese history at Whittier College, California, and then accepted a position in 1969 at the Hebrew University of Jerusalem when the Department of Asian Studies was established.

Eber published 12 books and over 66 articles, as well as reviews and short fiction. Her books include *Jews in China: Cultural Conversations, Changing Perceptions* (University Park, 2020), *Jewish Refugees in Shanghai, 1933–1947: A Selection of Documents* (Göttingen, 2018), *Voices from Shanghai: Jewish Exiles in Wartime China* (Chicago, 2008), *Wartime Shanghai and Jewish Refugees from Central Europe: Survival, Co-Existence, and Identity in a Multi-Ethnic City* (Berlin, 2012), and *Chinese and Jews: Encounters Between Cultures*, which was published in Hebrew (Jerusalem, 2002) and in English (Chicago, 2008). She edited *Confucianism: The Dynamics of Tradition* (New York, 1986). Eber's volume in German on Martin Buber's writings on Chinese philosophy and literature (Gütersiohe, 2014) was ground-breaking. Her searing account of her life as a young girl in Poland during World War II, *The Choice* (New York, 2004), was translated into German (Munich, 2007) and Chinese (Beijing, 2013). Eber's essay in this volume develops a topic from her definitive biography of the translator into Chinese of the Hebrew Bible, *The Jewish Bishop and the Chinese Bible, S. I. J. Schereschewsky, 1831–1906* (Leiden, 1999) (published in Chinese translation in Taiwan in 2003), and her co-edited collection, *Bible in Modern China: The Literary and Intellectual Impact* (Sankt Agustin, 1999) (published in Chinese translation in Hong Kong in 2003).

Fu Xiaowei 傅晓微 is a professor of comparative literature and culture and the director of the Center of Judaic and Chinese Studies at Sichuan International Studies University in China. Her recent English publications include "Confucius on the Relationship of Beauty and Goodness," *Journal of Aesthetic Education* (Spring 2015); "The Name Survives Death: The View of Immortality in Hebrew and Confucian Traditions," *Confucius Studies* 3 (2016); and "Confusing Judaism and Christianity in Contemporary Chinese Letters," *Judaism* 55, nos. 1–2 (Spring 2006).

Samuel Heilman is a distinguished professor emeritus of sociology at Queens College and the Harold Proshansky Chair in Jewish Studies at the Graduate Center CUNY. He is the author of 15 books, some of which have been translated into Spanish and Hebrew, and the winner of three National Jewish Book Awards. He was awarded the Marshall Sklare Lifetime Achievement Award from the Association for the Social Scientific Study of Jewry and has received four Distinguished Faculty Awards at the City University of New York. He has been a Fulbright Fellow and Senior Specialist in Australia, China, and Poland.

Kathryn Hellerstein is a professor of Yiddish and the director of the Jewish Studies Program at the University of Pennsylvania. Her books of translations are *In New York: A Selection (Moyshe Leyb Halpern)* (Philadelphia, 1982) and *Paper Bridges: Selected Poems of Kadya Molodowsky* (Detroit, 1999). Her monograph, *A Question of Tradition: Women Poets in Yiddish, 1586–1987* (Stanford, 2014), won the 2014 National Jewish Book Award in Women's Studies and the 2015 Modern Language Association Fenia and Yaacov Leviant Memorial Prize in Yiddish Studies. She co-edited *Jewish American Literature: A Norton Anthology* (New York, 2001) and edited the selected essays of Irene Eber, *Jews in China: Cultural Conversations, Changing Perceptions* (University Park, 2021). Hellerstein's current projects include *China through Yiddish Eyes: Cultural Translation in the Twentieth Century*; *The Rosewaters and the Colmans: Jewish Identity in Two Cleveland Jewish Families (1840–1915)*; and *Jewish Women Poets as Translators: Changing Liturgy and Canon.*

Rebecca Kobrin is the Russell and Bettina Knapp Associate Professor of American Jewish History at Columbia University, where she is also the co-director of the Institute for Israel and Jewish Studies. She works in the fields of immigration history, urban studies, and Jewish history, specializing in modern Jewish migration. Her book *Jewish Bialystok and Its Diaspora* (Bloomington, 2010) was awarded the Jordan Schnitzer Prize. She edited *Chosen Capital: The Jewish Encounter with American Capitalism* (New Brunswick, 2012) and co-edited *Purchasing Power: The Economics of Jewish History* (Philadelphia, 2015). Her writing regularly appears in *The Washington Post*, *CNN*, *The Guardian*, and *Bloomberg News*.

Li Dong 李栋 received his PhD from Shanghai International Studies University. He is a lecturer in the Foreign Languages Department at the East China University of Political Science and Law. He specializes in American Jewish literature, Jewish culture, and legal literature. He lives with his wife and two children in Shanghai.

Liu Yan 刘燕 obtained her doctoral degree in literature at Beijing Normal University and is now a professor in the School of Culture and Communication at Beijing International Studies University. Her research interests include world literature, comparative literature, and cross-cultural communication. She has been a visiting scholar at the University College Dublin (2011–2012) and the University of Michigan (2018–2019). She is the author of *T. S. Eliot* (Chengdu, 2001), *The Beginning of Modern Criticism: On T. S. Eliot's Poetics* (Guilin, 2005), and *The Space-Time Narrative: On James Joyce's 'Ulysses'* (Beijing, 2010). She has also edited *From Goethe and Nietzsche to Rilke: Studies in Sino-German Cross-Cultural Communication* (Fuzhou, 2017), *Translation and Influence: Bible in China* (Beijing, 2018), and *James Joyce and the Orient: Critical Collections* (Fuzhou, 2018).

Maisie Meyer broke new ground with her research into the Baghdadi Jewish community of Shanghai. She has lectured widely on Baghdadi Jews in the eastern Diaspora, presented papers on the subject worldwide, and published numerous articles. Her book *From the Rivers of Babylon to the Whangpoo: A Century of Sephardi Jewish Life in Shanghai* (Lanham, 2003) is widely considered the definitive history of the Baghdadi Jewish merchants who settled in Shanghai in the mid-nineteenth century. Her determination to preserve the memory of this community and the unrivalled access that she has enjoyed to key characters and previously unseen source material have resulted in another volume, *Shanghai's Baghdadi Jews: A Collection of Biographical Reflections* (Hong Kong, 2015). Meyer received her PhD in international history from the London School of Economics with funding from the British Academy.

Marc B. Shapiro holds the Harry and Jeanette Weinberg Chair in Judaic Studies at the University of Scranton. His most recent book is *Changing the Immutable: How Orthodox Judaism Rewrites Its History* (Liverpool, 2015).

Song Lihong 宋立宏 is a professor in the Department of Religious Studies and the Glazer Institute of Jewish and Israel Studies at Nanjing University, China. He has served as a postdoctoral fellow, fellow, or visiting scholar at Tel Aviv University, the Reconstructionist Rabbinical College, the University of Pennsylvania, the Albright Institute of Archaeological Research in Jerusalem, and the Harvard-Yenching Institute. His recent publications include two edited volumes: *Representations and Identities in the Jewish Diaspora* (Beijing, 2018; in Chinese) and *The Image of Jews in Contemporary China* (Boston, 2016; in English, with James Ross). He is currently on the editorial board of the *Journal of Modern Jewish Studies*.

Wang Jian 王健 is the director of the Institute of International Relations in the Shanghai Academy of Social Sciences (SASS), a visiting professor of history at Shanghai University, the vice president of the Shanghai Association for International Studies, a member of the executive board of the Chinese Association of the Middle East, the director of the Center for West Asia and North Africa Studies (CWANAS) of SASS, and the executive dean of the Center of Jewish Studies in Shanghai. He received his MA in modern world history from the East China Normal University and his PhD in world economics from the graduate school of SASS. He has been a visiting scholar at the Truman Institute of the Hebrew University of Jerusalem and at the Center for Security and Cooperation at Stanford University; a member of the US Department of State's International Visitor Leadership Program; and the delegate of the Asia 21 Young Leadership Summit initiated by the Asia Society of the United States. His research has mainly focused on international political economy, Middle East studies, Jewish studies, and international relations. He is the author of several monographs, including *Escape and Rescue: Jewish Refugees and Shanghai in World War II* (Shanghai, 2016; in Chinese), *History of Jewish Social Life in Shanghai* (Shanghai, 2008; in Chinese), and *Jewish Cultural Map of Shanghai* (Shanghai, 2010; in Chinese).

Wang Yi 王毅 is a professor of aesthetics and aesthetic education and director of the Institute of Tourism and Aesthetics at Sichuan International Studies University in China. His recent English publications include "An Exegesis to the So-called Proposition of Confucian Aesthetics," *Journal of Aesthetic Education* (2008), and "The Aesthetic Standard of Wen: A Comparative Study of Chinese and Western Early Artworks," *Asian and African Studies* (2011).

Xu Xin 徐新, professor and director of the Diane and Guilford Glazer Institute for Jewish and Israel Studies at Nanjing University, is the president of the Chinese National Institute of Jewish Studies. He is the author of *Anti-Semitism: Past and Present* (Beijing, 2015), *The Jews of Kaifeng, China: History, Culture, and Religion* (Jersey City, 2005), and *Aliens in a Strange Land: Jews and Modern China* (Taipei, 2017), plus numerous essays. His activities in promoting the study of Jewish subjects among the Chinese have been supported by a number of foundations. In 1995, he was honored with the James Friend Memorial Award. In 2003, Bar-Ilan University awarded him the degree of Doctor of Philosophy, *honoris causa*.

Yang Meng 杨梦, an assistant professor at Peking University, is the singer of and a co-contributor to the first Chinese-Yiddish song, published by *The Forward* (http://forward.com/culture/music/323094/the-first-chinese-yiddish-song), and the first Chinese-Yiddish duet, published by *J-Wire* (http://www.jwire.com.au/yiddish-2-with-a-chinese-twist). She has been teaching the first course and organizing the first lecture series on Jewish civilization at Peking University. Her public lectures in North America, Europe, and China and publications have covered Jewish civilization, Holocaust education in China, Jewish exile in Shanghai, Sino-Israeli cooperation and innovation, antisemitism, and German studies.

Zhang Ping 张平 is a professor of Chinese and East Asian studies at Tel Aviv University. One of his current projects is the critical analysis, annotation, and translation of the Mishnah into Chinese. His publications include *Pirkei Avoth: The Wisdom of Our Forefathers* (Beijing, 1996; co-authored with Rabbi Adin Steinzaltz), *Derech Eretz Zuta: The Jewish Way of the World* (Beijing, 2003), *The Mishnah: A Study and Translation of Seder Zeraim* (Jinan, 2011), and *The Mishnah: A Study and Translation of Seder Moed* (Jinan, 2018).

Zhong Zhiqing 钟志清 received her PhD in Hebrew literature at Ben-Gurion University. She is a research professor and the director of the Department of Oriental Literary Studies at the Institute of Foreign Literature of the Chinese Academy of Social Sciences. She has been a visiting scholar at Tel Aviv University, the British Academy, and the Harvard-Yenching Institute. She is the author of *Twentieth-Century Hebrew Literature in Transition* (Beijing, 2013), which was selected for the National Achievements Library of Philosophy and Social Sciences in 2012, and *A Study of the History of Biblical Interpretation* (Nanjing, 2019) and the editor for *Hebrew Classics: A Collection of Biblical Criticism* (Nanjing, 2019). She is also the translator of *Modern Hebrew Fiction*, by Gershon Shaked, and of *My Michael*, *Black Box*, *A Tale of Love and Darkness*, *Rhyming Life and Death*, *A Panther in the Basement*, *Scenes from Village Life*, and *Between Friends*, by Amos Oz.

Illustrations

Figure 7.1	A sports class at the Jewish Youth Association School; Shanghai, China. (Photograph courtesy of the Yad Vashem Photo Archive.) —— **114**
Figure 7.2	Members of the Maccabi Sports Association; Harbin, 1922. (Photograph from Pan Guang, ed., *The Jews in China* [Beijing: China Intercontinental Press, 2005], 75.) —— **117**
Figure 7.3	The Shanghai Betar exercising in 1935. (Photograph courtesy of Leo Hanin.) —— **119**
Figure 7.4	Members of Betar Harbin at an athletics display at the Harbin sports stadium, China, 1934. (Photograph reproduced from the Beth Hatefutsoth Photo Archive, courtesy of Vera Shtopman, Israel.) —— **120**
Figure 7.5	A Jewish team participated in the International Football Championship of the Far East. (Photograph from *Shun Pao* [Shanghai News].) —— **124**
Figure 9.1	Sir Elly Kadoorie with his sons Lawrence (left) and Horace (right). (Photograph courtesy of the Hong Kong Heritage Project.) —— **148**
Figure 9.2	Silas Aaron Hardoon with his wife, Eliza Roos; Shanghai, ca. 1925. (Photograph courtesy of Leo Hardoon.) —— **150**
Figure 9.3	Silas Aaron Hardoon's adopted children; Shanghai, 1930s. (Photograph courtesy of Leo Hardoon.) —— **150**
Figure 9.4	Nissim Ezra Benjamin; Shanghai, ca. 1925. (Photograph courtesy of Rose Jacob Horowitz.) —— **152**
Figure 9.5	Sir Ellice Victor Elias Sassoon, Third Baronet, GBE; Shanghai, ca. 1935. (Photograph courtesy of Evelyn, Lady Barnes.) —— **154**
Figure 9.6	Caricature: "Sir Victor Sassoon, the new president of the Royal Air Force Association of Shanghai." (Photograph from the *North China Herald*, October 20, 1927.) —— **155**
Figure 9.7	A party in D. E. J. Abraham's garden; Shanghai, ca. 1938. (Photograph courtesy of David Dangoor.) —— **159**
Figure 9.8	Baghdadi Jews on a boating excursion on the Huangpu River; Shanghai, ca. 1938. (Photograph courtesy of Rebecca Toueg.) —— **160**
Figure 10.1	*Mr. Nobody, Shanghai*, by David Ludwig Bloch, 1947. (Photograph courtesy of the Leo Baeck Institute at the Center for Jewish History.) —— **169**
Figure 12.1	Title page of *Or Torah mi-Mizrah*. (Image from HebrewBooks.org.) —— **202**
Figure 12.2	Title page from one of the volumes of the Shanghai Talmud. (Image from Wikipedia Commons, https://commons.wikimedia.org/wiki/File:Shanghai_behorot.jpg.) —— **206**
Figure 14.1	"Scenes from 'The Chalk Circle,'" Yiddish *Forverts*, New York, January 10, 1926, 21. (Image courtesy of the Museum of the City of New York.) —— **245**
Figure 18.1	Portrait of Max James Kohler (1871–1934). (Photograph courtesy of the American Jewish Historical Society, New York.) —— **314**
Figure 19.1	Irene Eber (1929–2019), Louise Frieberg Professor of East Asian Studies at the Hebrew University of Jerusalem and Senior Fellow of the Harry S. Truman Research Institute. (Photograph by Miriam Eber; Jerusalem, 2017.) —— **333**

Table

Table 7.1 Winners of the Jewish League Championship, 1940–1945 —— **122**

Personal Names

Abraham (biblical character) 47, 48
Abraham, Isaac 161
Adler, Cyrus 301
Agnon, Shai 68
Ai Rengui 6, 8, 9, 97
Akiva ben Yosef, Rabbi 4, 66
Aleichem, Shalom 103
Alekseev, Evgenii 258
Almi, A. (pen name of Elihu-Khayim Sheps) 232
Alter, Robert 29, 66
Amos, prophet 3, 54, 58, 60
Avshalomov, Aaron 106

Bao Anruo 16, 18, 229
Barnes, Maude Evelyn 158
Barron, Reyzele 242
Bassnett, Susan 90
Behrend, R. C. W. 129
Ben Uri 68
Benjamin, Benjamin David 146
Ben-Rafael (journalist) 262, 263, 265
Bension, Ariel 151
Berenbaum, Shmuel, Rabbi 205
Berliner, Nancy 7, 11, 12, 97
Bin Xin 81
Birnbaum, Nathan 243
Bitker, R. B. 120
Bloch, Ariel 66
Bloch, David Ludwig
– archives of 174, 178
– artistic style of 174
– Chinese name of 12, 173
– depiction of beggars 175
– exhibitions of 172
– life and career of 8, 106, 170, 171, 181
– media attention to 170, 173
– paintings of 11, 12, 105, 165, 177
– poster of 176
– streetscapes of 171, 176
– Venice watercolors of 12, 171
– visit to Shanghai Art Gallery 172
– woodblock prints of 168, 169, 171, 172, 173, 175, 177

Bloch, Louis 171
Bloch, Simon 170
Boaz (biblical character) 42, 43
Bodan, Karl 188
Brandt-Bukofzer, Max 185
Brecht, Bertolt 246, 247
Bregel, David 123
Brenner, Athalya 64, 66
Breuer, Adolf 185
Buber, Martin 24, 232
Byron, George Gordon, baron 57

Cao Jian 3, 27
Cao Yu
– comparison to Hanoch Levin 278, 282
– education of 20
– influence of rabbinic literature on 281
– *Peking Man* 19, 229, 272, 275, 276, 282
– rejection of tradition 279
– view of human nature 279
– works of 276, 278
Carlyle, Thomas 55
Chaplin, Charlie 166
Chen Duxiu 267
Chen Mengjia 69, 73, 81
Chen Shouyi 324
Chung Gnock 307
Chung Lum Yin 307
Churchill, Winston 156
Cohen, Gerson 67
Cohen, Israel 151
Confucius 47, 60, 280
Coogan, Michael 64
Coward, Noel 166

Dangoor, David 159
Dangoor, Niam 163
Dangoor, Renée 163
David, King (biblical character) 264
Davis, Bette 157
Deutscher, Isaac 320
Di Vito, Robert 42
Dietrich, Marlene 157
Dinah (biblical character) 68

Doron, Melville 163
Dou Lixun 106
Drachman, Bernard 152
Dreifuss, Alfred 177, 179

Eber, Irene
- background and education of 319, 321
- birthplace of 319, 322
- Chinese studies of 17, 23, 24, 79, 91, 318, 322, 324, 328, 329, 330, 332
- displaced person110 320
- essay in memory of 51
- essays of 2, 3, 27
- identity of 325, 327
- international reputation of 331
- interview with 23, 24
- life and career of 23, 24, 229
- memoir of 23, 319, 324, 333
- mother tongues 325, 331
- passion for writing 322
- photograph of 332
- study of Scherescheswky 2, 5, 23, 91, 325
Einhorn, David 301
Elizabeth II, Queen of Great Britain 156
Engel, Erwin 185
Epstein, Israel 101, 110
Er (Judah's son) 40
Esklund, Paula 180
Even-Zohar, Itamar 6, 89
Ezekiel, prophet 68
Ezra family 11
Ezra, Nissim Ezra Benjamin
- career of 115, 152
- petition to the League of Nations 153
- photograph of 152
- political affairs 152
- reputation of 147
- Shanghai Zionist Association and 115
- studies of 11

Faisal, King of Iraq 148
Favorsky, Vladimir A. 178
Feng Sanmei 74
Findeisen, Raoul David 83, 85
Finkel, Eliezer Judah, Rabbi 110, 196, 198
Fischer, Paul
- life in Shanghai 165

- portrait of Jewish refugees 179
- post-Shanghai period 181
- refugee artist 12
- reputation of 11, 179
- Shanghai Sketches 178
Fishbane, Michael 65
Flegg, William 161
Flohr, Lily 189
Foa, Arrigo 106
Franklin, C. S. 136
Freer, Osi 122
Freidele (literary character) 68
Freundlich, Rabbi 219
Friedlander, Saul 330
Fu Xiaowei 3, 27

Gabbacia, Donna 298
Gálik, Márian 69, 91
Germant, Nathan 118
Gilrod, Louis 233
Goering, Hermann 157
Goldman, Shalom 29
Golitberg, H. 116
Gottlieb, Claire 46
Grain, Peter 151
Graves, Frederick R. 81
Greenberg, Dina 16, 220, 221, 222
Greenberg, Shalom 16, 220, 221, 222
Grodzinski, Hayyim Ozer, Rabbi 195, 196
Grossman, Edith 30
Grün, Desiderius 185
Gulevsky, Chaim Dovber 200
Guo Moruo 81

Hai, Isaac 161
Haile Selassie, Emperor of Ethiopia 148
Hakohen, Israel Meir, Rabbi 205
Hakuson, Kuriyagawa 55
Hall, Prescott F. 300
Halpern, Isaac (Ying) 242
Halpern, Moyshe Leyb
- journalistic career of 243
- play of 231
- reputation of 243
- translations of 18, 231, 241, 242, 243, 247, 251
Handel, Ernst 177, 180

Hardoon family 11
Hardoon, Catherine Levy 145
Hardoon, George 163
Hardoon, Leo 163
Hardoon, Reuben 163
Hardoon, Silah Charlie 163
Hardoon, Silas Aaaron
– Beth Aharon synagogue 14, 203
– business of 104
– career of 149
– children of 150
– photograph of 150
– reputation of 11, 110
– wealth of 104, 147, 151
Hayeem, Dick 146
Hayeem, George 146
Hayim, Ellis 136
Hearn, Lafcadio 232
Heilman, Samuel 7, 14, 15, 16
Heine, Heinrich 243
Hellerstein, Kathryn 16, 17, 229, 329
Henschke, Alfred. see Klabund (pseud. for Alfred Henschke)
Heschel, Abraham J. 332
Hitler, Adolf 113, 130
Horowitz, Maximillian 241, 242
Howe, Irwing 289, 291
Hu Shi 54, 59, 318
Huang Zhulun 74
Hudson, W. H. 58
Hume, Frances 239
Huo Yuanjia 112

Ignatov, David 232
Inuzuka, Captain 136
Isaacs, Harold 129
Isaiah, prophet 58
Israel ben Eliezer (a.k.a. Ba'al Shem Tov) 220

Jacob (biblical character) 29, 32, 33, 47, 48
Jacob, Abraham 161
Jacob, Cissy 161
Jacob, Ezekiel Sion110 147
Jacob, Isaac 161
Jacob, Joe (Yaacob) 160
Jacob, Leah 147, 162
Jacob, Ritchie 162

Jacob, Silas Isaiah 145
Jacoby, Sasson 161
Jakubowski, Hugo 130
Janovic, Y. Z. 117
Jeremiah, prophet
– Chinese intellectuals on 55, 60
– comparison to Chinese poets 3, 57
– moral perfectionism of 3, 58, 59, 60
– preacher of ethical monotheism 58
– prophecies of 60
– resemblance of Jesus 59
– universalism of 58
– works written by 57
Jerome, William 236
Jian Youwen 57
Jin Shihe 89
Joachim, Walter 106
Job (biblical character) 47
Jolson, Al 236
Jonah, prophet 58
Joseph (biblical character) 29, 31, 32, 34, 47
Judah (biblical character) 40, 41, 42, 47, 48
Julien, Stanislas 231, 240

Kadoorie family 8, 11, 149
Kadoorie, Eleazar (Elly) Silas
– background of 11, 147
– charity work 115, 149
– photograph of 148
– reputation of 147
– sons of 148
Kadoorie, Horace 177
Kadoorie, Laura 115
Kafka, Franz 24
Kahana, Zvi 204
Kahaneman, Joseph, Rabbi 196
Kalmanovitsh, Harry 234
Kalmanovitz, Abraham, Rabbi 205
Karelitz, Abraham Isaiah, Rabbi 196, 199
Kaspé, Joseph 105
Katz, Ben Zion 244
Katz, J. B. 112
Katz, Mickey 236, 237
Kaufman, Teddy 117
Kipling, Rudyard 145
Klabund (pseud. for Alfred Henschke) 240
– background of 242

– *Der Kreidekreis* 231, 240, 241, 242, 243, 246
– translation of Li Qianfu 240, 246, 247, 251
Kobrin, Rebecca 17, 22, 229
Kohler, Kaufmann, Rabbi 301
Kohler, Max J.
– advocacy for Chinese migrants 22, 298, 300, 302, 305, 306, 308, 309, 310, 311, 312
– background of 297, 301
– criticism of US immigration policies 22, 229, 298, 309
– education of 302
– father of 313
– impact on American jurisprudence 313
– legal practice of 17, 302, 306, 307, 308, 311, 313
– *New York Times* opinion piece 297, 298
– portrait of 314
Kohn, David 179
Kollwitz, Kathe 178
Kotler, Aharon, Rabbi 197
Kotovich, Lela 116, 118, 119

Lankin, Eliyalhu 118
Lao She 175
Laozi 280
Lasair, Simon 31
Laski, Neville 153
Lasky, Steven 234, 241
Lee Yan Tai 308, 309, 311
Lee, Archie 74
Legge, James 79
Levenson, Jon D. 46, 75
Levenson, Joseph 24, 46, 282, 317, 318, 331
Levenstein, Yehezkel, Rabbi 196, 197, 199, 204, 208, 210
Levi, Primo 323
Levin, Hanoch
– characters of 278
– comparison to Cao Yu 282
– education of 20
– influence of rabbinic literature on 281
– perception of reality 278
– performance of dramas of 271
– praise of human courage 279
– *Requiem* 271, 272, 273
– *Suitcase Packers* 17, 19, 20, 229, 272, 273, 276, 282
– view of death 273
Levina, R. 118
Levine, Harry 225
Levine, Peter 125
Levy, Clive Jackie 162
Levy, Hannah 161
Lewis, Bernard 327
Leymanshteyn, Lev I. 116
Li Bai 18, 231, 232, 247, 248
– translations of poems of 248, 252
Li Chenyang 44, 46
Li Dong 17, 20, 21, 229
Li Qianfu
– *The Story of the Circle of Chalk* 17, 18, 244, 246, 247, 251
– translations of plays of 239, 240, 242, 247, 251
Li Rongfang 52, 58, 59
Li Yang 275, 276
Lian Yinghuang 34, 89
Liberman, Yaacov 123
Lifshitz, R. 118
Lin Pei-Ying 23
Lin Yüsheng 56
Lin Yu-tang 73, 129
Liu Songyun 53
Liu Yan 5, 6, 27
Lo Shun 129
Loewenberg, Richard 130
Lu Hsuen 174
Lu Ji 323
Lu Xun
– European revolutionary art and 13
– exhibitions organized by 178
– idea of heaven 56
– inspiration for 81
– on Jeremiah 3, 55
– reputation of 54, 178
– studies of 324, 331
Lü Zhenzhong 81
Lublin, Yeshivat Hakhmei 203, 210
Lunačarskij, Anatolij V. 55, 56

Lung Chu 72
Lyon, James K. 247

Ma Sihong 106
Madigan, Kevin 46
Malin, Leib, Rabbi 197, 205
Mamoru, Shigemitsu 153
Mao Chuen 106
Mao Dun 81, 325
Mao Wenlong 258
Marinari, Maddalena 313
Marshall, Louis 301
Marshman, John 79
Marshman, Joshua 81
Marx, Karl 55
Masereel, Frans 178
Mateer, Calvin Wilson 79
Matelin, Jacob S. 121
McIndoe, Archibald 157
Mencius
 – idea of benevolence 53
 – idea of heaven 53
 – influence of 37
 – on permission from parents
    38
 – on posterity 37, 38
 – on Shuns marriage 39, 47
 – studies of 27, 37, 47
 – teaching of 48
Meyer, Maisie 7, 10, 11, 16, 97
Micah, prophet 58
Miller, Arthur 271
Moalem family 162
Moalem, S. J. 113
Momigliano, Arnaldo 317
Mordokhovich, G. 119, 121
Morgenstern, Hans
 – background of 186
 – career of 186
 – escape to China 186
 – plays of 13, 14, 186, 188, 190
Morrison, Robert 79, 81, 102

Naomi (biblical character) 42
Ngai, Mae 312
Nida, Eugene 86
Niditch, Susan 42

Nissim, Matook Rahamim 162
Nordau, Max 8, 111

Obata, Shigeyoshi 248, 251
Olmert, Ehud 118
Onan (biblical character) 40

Pan Guang 131
Peretz, Isaac 103
Philipp, Michael 185, 192
Phillips, G. Godfrey 136
Pope, Alexander 224
Porter, Lucius C. 53
Pound, Ezra 231
Pyastunovich, L. I. 118

Qu Yuan 4, 73

Rachel (biblical character) 48
Rainer, Luisa 246
Rakov, N. 233
Rankin, Eliyalhu 118
Rappoport, I. L. 116
Raskov, David 116
Reiger, Simcha Zelig, Rabbi 196
Reinhartz, Adele 43
Reuben, Sassoon 146
Ricci, Matteo 37, 43, 47, 79
Roos, Eliza 149, 150
Roosevelt, Theodore 301, 310
Rosenfeld, Hersh 232
Rosenfeld, Jacob 110
Rousseau, Jean-Jacques 55
Russell, Bertdand 37
Ruth (biblical character) 42, 43

Safdie, Joe 162
Said, Edward 328
Salmon, Jacob E. 153
Sandrow, Nahma 235
Sanneh, Lamin 85
Sassoon family 11
Sassoon, David 145, 154
Sassoon, Elias 145, 154
Sassoon, Ellice Victor Elias
 – background of 154
 – business ventures of 155, 158, 166

- caricature of 155
- charity work of 157
- contribution to the British war effort 157
- death of 159
- hobbies of 157, 158
- influence of 147, 156
- life in Hollywood 11, 157
- marriage of 158
- media attention to 156
- military service of 154
- photograph of 154
- reputation of 11
- retirement of 147
- travels of 156, 158
- wealth of 158

Sassoon, Jacob 155
Sassoon, Victor 136
Saul, King (biblical character) 264
Schereschewsky, S. I. J.
- annotations to the Song of Songs 27, 81, 82, 90
- approach to translation 33, 85, 86, 88
- background and education of 2, 79, 325
- ecclesiastical career of 326
- emigration of 2
- influence of 91
- legacy of 91, 92
- linguistic skills of110 6, 32, 80, 82, 83, 84, 85
- missionary work of 89
- personality of 326
- reputation of 89
- respect for Chinese culture 87
- translation of the Chinese Bible 2, 5, 6, 27, 29, 31, 79, 80, 92, 326, 327

Schiff, Friedrich
- artistic style of 166
- background of 166
- book illustrations of 167, 180
- drawings of 180
- exhibitions of 181
- ink sketches of 180
- life and career of 8, 166, 180, 181
- paintings of 11, 12, 105, 165, 166, 168
- rickshaw illustrations of 175

Schneersohn, Joseph Isaac, Rabbi 201

Schneersohn, Shalom Dovber 217
Schneerson, Menachem Mendel 217, 220
Schwartz, Benjamin 317
Schwartz, Jean 236
Schwartz, Maurice 240, 242, 243
Schwartzman, Solomon, Rabbi 212
Shahmoon, Ezra 153
Shaked, Gershon 69
Shandler, Jeffrey 251
Shapiro, Abraham Dov Ber Kahana, Rabbi 196
Shapiro, Marc B. 7, 10, 14, 97
Shapiro, Sydney 101
Shelah (biblical character) 40
Shen Congwen 71, 72
Shepherd, Catherine 187
Shinpei, Kusano 173
Shiro, Ishiguro 136
Shlomovits, Avraham, Rabbi 199
Shmulevitz, Chaim, Rabbi 203, 210, 212
Shtiker, Meyer 18, 231, 232, 247, 248
- translations of Li Bai's poems 248, 250, 251, 252

Shun, King (legendary Chinese character) 38, 39, 43
Siegelberg, Mark
- autobiography of 187
- background of 186
- internment in the Dachau and Buchenwald 110 187
- plays of 13, 14, 186, 188, 190
- work for the British Legation in Shanghai 187

Silas, Hardoon 8
Sisson, H. R. 306
Situ Xingcheng 106
Slavkov, David 117
Smedley, Agnes 129
Smith, Gerald B. 57
Solomon, Barbara Miller 300
Solomon, King (biblical character) 64, 74, 242, 244
Soloveitchik, Isaac Zev, Rabbi 196, 197
Somekh, David Silman 153
Sommadossi, Thomas 187
Song Jinlan 44

Song Lihong 17, 23, 24, 229
Sopher, Stephen 162
Sorkin, S. 8
Soroviyi, I. 118
Soskin, S. 105
Spearman, Michael 136
Speelman, Moritz 188
Stein, Sarah Abrevaya 257
Steiner, George 86
Stern, David 65
Straus, Oscar Solomon 301
Sugihara, Chiune 14
Sun Ke 129
Sun Yat-sen 8, 102, 115, 153
Sun Yat-sen, Madam 129

Takehiko, Ohashi 174
Talan, M. 120
Taler, Liva 123
Tamar (biblical character)
– death of 42, 43
– interpretation of actions of 41, 42, 44
– Onan and 40
– righteousness of 47
– seduction of father-in-law 40, 43
Tan Jizhen 106
Tevis, Britt 305
Thorbecke, Ellen 167
Tobias, Sigmund 210
Tolstoy, Leo 55
Tong, Toy 306
Tonn, Willy 174
Toueg, Rebecca 146, 160
Triguboff, Boris 122
Trudeau, Pierre 162
Tsai Yuan-pei 129
Tuchman, Gaye 225
Tuczynski, E. S. 114
Turnheim, Rabbi 219

Venuti, Lawrence 244

Wainhaus, Abraham 204
Waley, Arthur 44
Wan Zhang 39
Wang Benchao 72

Wang Jian 7, 9, 10, 97
Wang Qingxin 46
Wang Yi 3, 27
Warhaftig, Zorach 142
Warren, Charles 300
Wasserman, Elhanan, Rabbi 196
Weiss-Cyla, Robert 189
Westermann, Claus 41
Wiener, Hans 186
Williams, Gwyn 239
Witt, Bernard 232
Wittenberg, Alfred 106
Wolf, Simon 300, 301
Wouk, Herman 294
Wu Leichuan 57
Wu Shutian 69, 73
Wu Tingfang 306

Xia Yu 81
Xu Dishan 69, 73, 81
Xu Xin 6, 7, 8, 97

Yang Bingjun 106
Yang Ching 129
Yang Meng 7, 13, 14, 97
Yao, King (legendary Chinese character) 38, 45
Yasue, Colonel 136
Yasuya, Uchida 153
Ye Shandang 89
Yehoash (pseud. of S. Bloomgarden) 232
Yerushalmi, Yosef Hayim 330
Yezierska, Anzia 17, 291
– Children of Loneliness 20, 21, 229, 285, 286, 287, 294
– background of 287
– fiction of 290, 293, 294
Yitzchak, Yosef 217
You Bin 74
Yu Baisheng 89
Yu Songhua 8, 103
Yuan Dingan 53, 59

Zakheim, Zvi, Rabbi 212
Zeitin, Joseph 203

Zengzi (desciple of Confucius) 45
Zhang Dongsun 3, 54, 55
Zhang Guoling 106
Zhang Longxi 74
Zhang Ping 17, 19, 229
Zhang Zhijie 110, 89
Zhao Qi 44
Zhao Zichen 52, 58

Zhong Caixiang 288
Zhong Zhiqing 4, 27
Zhou Zuoren 5, 70, 71, 73, 325
Zhu Tianlun 75
Zhu Weizhi 3, 5, 52, 53, 56, 73
Zhu Xi 40
Zhu Ziqing 73

Place Names

Anchorage, AK 221
Argentina 11, 163
Australia
– Jewish Diaspora in 11, 101, 124, 129, 162, 163
– White Australia Policy 162
Austria
– cultural life 14
– foreign relations 106
– German annexation of 131, 187
– Jewish exodus from 7, 100, 110, 113, 118, 132, 141, 198
– theatrical portrayal of events in 190

Baghdad
– antisemitism 145, 153
– Jewish community 7, 11, 100, 110, 145, 152
– Laura Kadoorie School 149
Bahamas 101, 158
Baltimore, MD 234
Basrah 145
Batavia 145, 152, 162
Bavaria 300
Beijing
– Jewish community 2, 15, 110, 219, 223
– Penn Wharton China Center 1
– publishing 272
– theater 229, 271
– theatrical portrayal of events in 19, 275
Belgium 141
Berlin 141
Bolesław (Wrocław), Poland 141
Bombay 7, 100, 110, 145, 155
Brazil 157
British Indies 152
Brooklyn 234
Buenos Aires 162

Calcutta 145
Canada
– Jewish Diaspora 11, 101, 124, 129, 200
– theater 234
Canton 162
Cape Town 162

Cardiff 152
Chengdu 15, 219, 222, 223
China
– biblical studies 2, 3, 5, 30, 51, 59, 63, 68, 73, 80, 81, 92
– Boxer Rebellion 255
– Chabad mission 15, 112, 219, 224, 225
– Christianity in 90, 102
– Civil War 111
– commonalities with modern Judaism 20
– Communists rise to power 7
– cultural life 8, 13, 102, 105, 271
– education 20, 149
– filial piety 43, 44, 45, 47
– foreign relations 106, 110, 129, 152
– industrialization of 156
– Jewish Diaspora in 1, 7, 8, 15, 97, 99, 100, 101, 107, 110, 116, 125, 218, 219, 220
– literary tradition 6
– Manchu rule of 256, 262
– marriage laws 47, 48
– May Fourth movement 3, 4, 27
– modern history of 100
– New Culture movement 3, 267
– news reports about 112, 257, 260, 262, 264
– Opium Wars 100, 102, 110, 256
– paper manufacture 99
– positive image of 14, 265
– religions 265
– Russo-Japanese War and 17, 18, 256, 261, 266
– Second World War 111
– sports 9, 109, 110, 111, 116, 121, 122
– studies of 23, 324
– traditional culture 20
– woodcut movement 178
– Zionist organizations 114, 117, 125, 139, 151
Cleveland, OH 300
Cracow 200
Curaçao 112, 142, 198
Czechoslovakia 131, 141

Dairen 135
Dalian 9, 110, 112
Danzig 141
Durban 162
Dutch Indies 152

Edinburgh 152
Europe
– antisemitism 107, 111, 125, 135, 170, 288
– cuisine 222
– Jewish exodus from 21, 97, 100, 111, 129, 134, 139, 140, 192, 195, 202, 218, 231, 329
– Zionism in 114

France
– foreign relations 255
– Jewish refugees 143
– Nazi occupation of 141
– Second World War, 112, 140, 141
French Indies 152

Geneva 141
Germany
– antisemitism 131, 135, 141
– foreign relations 112, 140, 255
– invasion of Poland 195, 319
– Jewish exodus from 7, 10, 100, 113, 118, 130, 131, 132, 139, 141, 198
– Nazi rule 113, 130, 188
– status of housewives 192
Great Britain 11, 140, 141
Greece 141
Guangzhou 15, 99, 110, 219

Halle 23, 319
Hangzhou 99, 209
Harbin
– businesses 105
– cultural life 106
– Jewish community in 7, 8, 9, 15, 110, 112, 135, 218
– Jewish studies 107
– Russian press 118
– sporting events 8, 9, 110, 112, 116, 117, 120, 121, 122, 123, 125
– wartime daily life 107

– youth organizations 118
– Zionist organizations 115
Hengdaohezi 15, 218
Hollywood 11, 157, 246
Hong Kong
– banks 162
– British control of 100
– businesses 101
– cultural life 106
– education 149
– Jewish community in 7, 11, 15, 100, 110, 133, 140, 145, 163, 219
– post-war economic restoration of 149
Hungary 141

India 129, 149, 152
Iran 149
Iraq 11, 115, 149
Israel, ancient
– ethical monotheism 58
– family relations 42, 44, 46
– individual identity 46
– lifestyle 55
– marriage laws 41, 47
Israel, modern
– creation of the State of 9, 11, 124, 160, 162, 266
– Jewish relocation to 11, 218
– modernization of 20, 282
Italy 139, 140

Japan
– foreign relations 152, 153, 255, 256
– Jewish refugees in 14, 100, 137, 198
– occupation of China 9, 12, 11, 120, 138, 168
– Second World War 101, 124
– theater 233
– treatment of Jews 137
– Treaty of Shimonoseki 255
Java 152
Jerusalem 222
Johannesburg 152

Kaifeng 15, 109, 218, 328
Kobe 14, 100, 142, 198, 199, 205
Korea 256

Kowloon 15, 219
Kuling 152

Liaotung Gulf 258, 261
Liaotung Peninsula 255
Lithuania 79, 142, 195, 197
London 10, 152, 161
Luoyang 99
Luxembourg 141

Macau 162
Manchuria
– Jewish community in 15, 110, 218
– news reports about 262
– ports 255
– provinces 255
– Russian control of 255, 259, 263
– sports 122
– Trans-Siberian Railroad112 7
Manila 133, 162, 163
Mauritius 162
Melbourne 189
Mielec 23, 319, 321, 322
Mir (Belarusian city) 195
Montevideo 162
Montreal, QC 161, 234
Mukden 15, 135, 218, 255, 258
Munich 141

Nanjing 99
Nassau 158, 159
Netherlands 141
New York City
– Chinatown 235
– Chinese culture 16, 17
– cuisine 222, 238
– Jewish community 225, 229, 290
– literary journals 233
– newspapers 260
– theaters 17, 233, 234, 238, 240, 242, 243, 251
– Yiddish culture 231, 232, 235
New Zealand 112, 129
Ningbo 15, 99, 223
Ningxia 99
Niuchuang 258

Palestine
– Arab-Israeli relations 120
– Jewish immigration to 112, 115, 118, 124, 143, 153, 321
– Maccabiah Games 123
– promotion of culture 149, 151
– tourism 153
Paraguay 200
Pearl Harbor 10, 15, 142, 204, 213
Peking 99
Persia 152
Philadelphia, PA 241, 246
Philippines 152
Pittsburgh, PA 234
Poland
– German invasion of 319
– Jewish refugees 7, 23, 118, 141, 142, 143, 195
– Nazi and Soviet occupation of 195
Port Arthur 255, 256, 258

Qingdao 9, 110
Quanzhou 112 99
Quiqhar 15, 218

Rangoon 145
Rio de Janeiro 162
Russia
Russia. *see also* Soviet Union
– antisemitism 7, 288
– control of Manchuria 255
– Far East ports 255
– Jewish emigration from 100, 299
– pogroms 218
– war with Japan 18, 255, 256, 259

Saigon 143
San Francisco 162
São Paulo 162
Shanghai
– architecture 104, 176
– art galleries and exhibitions 172, 176, 179
– Ashkenazi Jews in 10, 110, 111, 135, 201
– atmosphere of 171
– Baghdadi Jews in 10, 97, 146, 151, 152, 154, 160

- brothels 191
- businesses 7, 103, 222
- Chabad Jews in 15, 16, 219, 220, 223, 224
- Communist conquest of 160
- covenant mindset 112, 289
- cultural life 11, 14, 105, 106, 166, 168, 176, 178, 185
- German immigrants 130, 185
- governance of 289
- Hasidic Jews in 219
- Hongkou District of 14, 120, 136, 141, 180, 286
- hotels and clubs 168
- infrastructure 104
- international settlement 165
- Japanese citizens in 136
- Japanese occupation of 9, 11, 14, 120, 168
- Jewish communities in 7, 8, 9, 10, 13, 15, 24, 100, 110, 113, 118, 129, 130, 132, 133, 134, 135, 136, 138, 139, 140, 141, 142, 143, 145, 170, 188, 192, 207, 213, 218, 293, 331
- Jewish Recreation Club (JRC) 9
- Jewish Refugees Memorial Museum 8
- Mir Yeshiva in 7, 14, 100, 199, 203, 209, 210
- Nanjing Road 203
- newspapers 170
- population 165, 221
- poverty 175
- publishing industry 206, 209
- religious life 14
- rickshaws 172, 174, 175, 204
- Sephardic Jews in 10, 14, 110, 135, 202, 203
- sports culture 8, 9, 110, 111, 112, 113, 121, 122, 123, 125
- St. John's University 2
- Temple Road 172
- theater 8, 13, 185, 186, 189, 193
- trading port 112
- Treaty of Nanking and112 145
- wartime daily life 107
- Western radio stations 156
- women in 192
- working people 174
- yeshiva students in 112, 210, 212
- youth organizations 118
- Zhu Baosan Road 171
- Zionist organizations 115

Shenzhen 15, 110, 219
Siam 152
Singapore 140, 145, 152, 162
Solon, OH 223
South Africa 129
Soviet Union
- German invasion of 10, 141
- occupation of Lithuania 195, 197
- occupation of Poland 195
Sydney, Australia 162, 163
Syria 149

Tianjin 107
Tientsin
- Jewish Club KUNST 9
- Jewish community 9, 110, 112, 207
- sporting events 110, 113, 121, 122, 123, 125
Tokyo 81, 156
Toronto, ON 234
Tripoli 162
Tshifu 258
Turkey 115, 145, 149

United States 14
- art exhibitions 181
- Chinese exclusion laws 17, 22, 229, 297, 303, 305, 306, 308, 310, 311
- Chinese immigrants 17, 22, 297, 303, 305
- foreign policy 312
- immigration policy 112, 301, 306, 308, 313
- Jewish immigration to 11, 21, 101, 124, 163, 200, 217, 290, 300, 306
- Jewish literature 291
- Orthodox Judaism in 21
- racism 300, 312
- Torah education in 210
- trade policy 308

Venice 171
Vienna 180, 181
Vilna (Vilnius) 14, 195, 196, 200

Vladivostok 142, 255
Warsaw 200
Washington, D.C. 234

Xi'an 99

Yangzhou 99

Yiwu 15, 110, 219
Yokohama 142
Yugoslavia 141
Yunnan province 129

Zhitomir 2, 80
Zlochev 242

www.ingramcontent.com/pod-product-compliance
Lightning Source LLC
Chambersburg PA
CBHW020218170426
43201CB00007B/250